# Commodore 64
# Getting the Most From It

Executive Editor: Terrell Anderson
Production Editor/Text Designer: Paula Huber
Art Director: Don Sellers
Assistant Art Director: Bernard Vervin
Photographer: George Dodson

Indexer: Cindy Shore
Typesetter: Harper Graphics, Waldorf, MD
Printer: R.R. Donnelley and Sons Company, Harrisonburg, VA
Typefaces: Aster (text and display), Monospace (programs)

# Commodore 64

## Getting the Most From It

**Tim Onosko**

Robert J. Brady Co.
*A Prentice-Hall Publishing and Communications Company*
Bowie, MD 20715

**Commodore 64: Getting the Most From It**



**Library of Congress Cataloging in Publication Data**

Onosko, Tim.
Commodore 64, getting the most from it.

Includes index.
1. Commodore 64 (Computer)—Programming. I. Title.
QA76.8.064056 1983 001.64'2 83-14127
ISBN 0-89303-380-4

Prentice-Hall International, Inc., London
Prentice-Hall Canada, Inc., Scarborough, Ontario
Prentice-Hall of Australia, Pty., Ltd., Sydney
Prentice-Hall of India Private Limited, New Delhi
Prentice-Hall of Japan, Inc., Tokyo
Prentice-Hall of Southeast Asia Pte. Ltd., Singapore
Whitehall Books, Limited, Petone, New Zealand
Editora Prentice-Hall Do Brasil LTDA., Rio de Janeiro

Printed in the United States of America

83 84 85 86 87 88 89 90 91 92 93 10 9 8 7 6 5 4 3 2 1

# Contents

# Introduction

If you are reading this book, you have either bought a computer, will buy one, or are at least considering the idea. Its purpose is to provide you with enough information about the Commodore 64 computer to use it well. You will learn what it is, where it came from, and what it can and cannot do for you.

First, and to the point, this book is only about the Commodore 64 and other computers in the same family (a portable and a classroom version). Aside from certain basic ideas common to most computers and references to other computers manufactured by Commodore—the VIC-20 in particular—you'll learn little or nothing about how to use an Apple, or TRS-80, or Atari, or any other personal computer.

Are you trying to decide which computer to buy? This book (and books about other computers, too) may help you make that decision. Getting information this way is better than being bombarded by the propaganda that computer salesmen might heap on you. This book contains both information and a little opinion as well.

Are you still deciding whether or not to buy a computer at all? This book, too, might help you realize just how a computer can help you at home, in school, or in your profession.

If you're an "old pro" and have been in personal computing from the "beginning"—How long ago was that? Five or six years?—there's something here for you, too. The Commodore 64 is a computer designed with many interesting, powerful and *unique* features.

Most likely, though, you've either just purchased a Commodore 64 or have access to one at work or at school. You may be ill at ease about just what a computer is. You may feel that you are not good enough at mathematics to use it, or that you lack the skills necessary to program it. It seems complicated and, perhaps, intimidating.

Despite the advances of the last decade, computers often appear to be "cold" machines (no matter how much manufacturers call them "user-friendly"). You may think that the computer doesn't like you or anyone else that comes near it.

Forget it. Computers are amazing, intriguing machines, but are no more complex, really, than an automobile. And you need about as much skill—perhaps less—to begin to use one. Programming doesn't necessarily rely on complex mathematics. It only requests that you think a problem through and learn how to break it down into a number of smaller problems. And as for math, many personal computer users who were terrible at math while in school soon learn that they are quite good at it when it comes to doing practical things. In a classroom, mathematical exercises for their own sake aren't always the most rewarding of challenges. When you program a computer, however, it is possible to see the numbers go to work for you.

Even though programming has its own rewards, some computer users program very seldom, if at all. They choose, instead, to use any number of good, commercially available programs. Learning to use a program usually requires much less skill than writing one. You simply load it into the computer, then follow directions. Be forewarned, though. Many very powerful programs also require that you learn how to take full advantage of their capabilities, a process that can demand almost as much attention and concentration as learning to program.

If you don't need a computer to solve any pressing problems or aid you in your day-to-day life, don't worry about it. It also happens to be the best toy you can buy. It can make music and pictures and will keep you amused for hours on end. It will play with you when no one else wants to. Computers are just as much for play as they are for work, and don't let anybody tell you otherwise.

One good reason to own and use a computer is just to learn about them. You could go to a special school or take a class to learn about computers. Or maybe you are learning about them in school or on the job right now. Those are good ways to learn, too. But buying and using a personal computer might be the best tuition you will every pay.

Sometimes, people are confused or afraid of computers because an entire language of its own has developed around these "thinking" machines. Most often, computer lingo is just "techno-babble." But some computer words aren't just jargon. Computers do require a few particular words to describe what they're made of and how they operate. You'll find those words in this book (and, at the end, there's a glossary for you to consult, just in case you forget what a word means). What you won't find, though, is jargon for the sake of jargon. This book can't teach you how to talk like a computer "hacker," but maybe it might help you decipher what these people are talking about.

Are you a professional? Do you bring your work home with you? Do you want to get ahead at the office? Are you one of many who have a difficult time keeping yourself organized? Then you are probably asking one question: What, exactly, will a computer do for me? The answer to that question may or may not be here. It can come only from you, once you know the computer's capabilities and limitations. You must remember that computers aren't magical solutions to unknown problems. (Any sales pitch that tells you otherwise is just plain hype.)

In this book, you'll get some information about the most common professional computer applications. From it, you might decide that a computer can ease your work load.

The book is organized into two main sections. The first is about the computer and how to use it. It includes lessons in BASIC programming as well as information about applications, particularly word processing. At the end of the book is a section prepared by and for more experienced Commodore users. It will help you better understand how the machine works, and about computer graphics, music, and sound.

You should remember, though, that neither this book nor any other will teach you *everything* there is to know about computers. If such a book existed, there would be no need for others. Instead, much like a smorgasbord, this book is intended for many different tastes.

As you read this book and begin to use your computer, keep a few important things in mind.

- Be patient. Don't get frustrated. *Everyone* can learn to use the computer. Don't be tempted to give up too soon.

- Don't expect the computer to start *giving* immediately. You must first learn how to ask it to help you.

- NEVER assume your own level of intelligence. A computer demands that you only be smart enough to *follow instructions* carefully.

- The computer doesn't always know what you are talking about or trying to do, so follow directions to the letter. You will be talking (via the keyboard, naturally) to a machine—nothing more. The computer is literal and logical, sometimes (it seems) to a fault.

- If possible, make learning about the computer easy for yourself by approaching it with someone else—a friend, a son or daughter, mother or father, a wife or husband, boyfriend or girlfriend, a next door neighbor, etc. By doing so, you will help each other and understand the ideas more quickly.

- Finally, remember that you will only get out of the computer what you put into it in time and effort.

Above all, try to keep your interest in the computer balanced with the rest of your daily life. Maybe the most "magical" thing about any personal computer is how it can absorb your time. It is all too easy to become preoccupied with the machine, or try to stay with a problem until you can walk away with the answer. Learning does not come easy, though, when you have spent hours on a problem or are fatigued. If you don't seem to be making progress, turn the machine off and come back to it another time. A fresh approach is all that may be necessary.

Ideally, the computer should *save* you, not *cost* you, time. It is intended to make your life easier, not more difficult.

## TRADEMARKS

# 1

# Where Did It Come From?

In 1953, it was the "electronic brain." Thirty years later, it had become "Machine of the Year," and had displaced a human being on the cover of *Time* magazine's prestigious year-end issue. Today, there is probably one in front of you. What is this thing called computer?

A computer bears little resemblance to your brain. Whether it "thinks" or not is a question of how you use the word. Left to itself, it does little or nothing and is completely dependent on you, the human. Computers, simply put, are complex collections of simple devices. They take instructions, move numbers into and out of their memory, and make elementary decisions. That's all they do.

The first electronic computer was ENIAC, a now legendary machine built in the late 1940s by two scientists named Eckert and Mauchly. It followed centuries of mechanical machines, from the abacus of the ancient Chinese to the "analytic engine" of British mathematician Charles Babbage. There has even been speculation that Britain's mysterious Stonehenge was the "computer" of early astronomers. None of these, however, were computers as we know them today.

The ideas behind ENIAC became UNIVAC, the first commercial computer built by Remington Rand in the 1950s. The company whose name was to become synonymous with computers, International Business Machines (IBM), made its entry into computers soon after. IBM's major business at the time was office equipment, including adding and tabulating (counting) machines. The hallmark of the tabulating era was the rectangular punched card, nick-named the "IBM card" but actually named the Hollerith after its originator

**The ENIAC Computer.** *Smithsonian Institution Photo No. 617989*

Herman Hollerith, IBM's chief engineer. The Hollerith became the first standard for humans to communicate with computing machines.

The early electronic computers used vacuum tubes, like those still to be seen in old radios, and mechanical relay switches. By the middle 1950s, the semiconductor transistor had been developed. It had the ability to switch streams of electrons passing through it and led to computer-like logical designs. Transistors had replaced tubes in computers by the next decade, and opened the way for larger, more powerful machines. Still, even the smallest and most reliable computers of the 1960s were as big as several refrigerators and often as temperamental as antique wristwatches.

The breakthrough in computer design came late in that decade, as scientists discovered ways to put tens, then hundreds of transistors on a single "chip" of silicon metal. These were the first integrated circuits. One problem, though, was still to be solved.

Inside the computers of old, numbers were stored in "core memory." Each little bit of memory was a tiny ring or donut which could be magnetized in one direction or another. There could be thousands, or even tens of thousands, of such memory devices in a computer. The steady development of electronic integrated circuits paved the way for electronic memories on microchips, which became popular during the 1970s and have all but replaced core memory. The difference between core and the kind of modern electronic memory widely used today is that core memory was permanent, its contents remained after the computer's power was turned off. Today's random access memory chips lose what is stored in them when power is shut off.

Shortly after memory chips made their appearance, the first microprocessor integrated circuit was developed. Like a computer, the microprocessor could be given a sequence of instructions to carry out. It wasn't long before engineers and basement tinkerers began imagining real computers constructed from microprocessors and RAM memory chips.

"Personal" computers were born of these early, sometimes halting attempts. Computers with strange-sounding names came and went. There were the MITS Altairs, IMSAIs and SOLs. (SOL deserves a footnote in modern computing for being named after a magazine editor, Leslie Solomon, who extolled its virtues.) Most of these tiny computers were sold as kits for hobbyists, but once assembled, they did little other than flash their front panel of lights. The potential was unmistakable, though.

By 1976, two companies saw their promise and began to design personal computers that could be used by almost anyone. At a new company called Apple, two young men, Steve Jobs and Steve Wozniak, built a computer on a single circuit board and took it around to meetings of computer and electronics enthusiasts in northern California. It was the Apple I. (The Apple II would follow when Jobs' and Wozniak's business was established.)

Commodore Business Machines grew from a typewriter repair business started after World War II by Jack Tramiel, a Polish-born immigrant and survivor of the Nazi concentration camps. Commodore had become a major seller of electronic calculators, a business near death due to fierce competition, when a team of young engineers led by Chuck Peddle, a microprocessor pioneer, started work on Commodore's own computer, the PET. Both the PET and Apple were based on the same microprocessor chip, the 6502. It came from MOS Technology, a company now owned by Commodore. A version of the same 6502 further popularized the chip by being at the heart of Atari's incredibly successful video game system as well as their personal computers.

(The name PET started as something of a joke based on the "pet rock" novelty craze of the time. When it came time to make the name "legitimate," PET became short for **P**ersonal **E**lectronic **T**ransactor. Some in the industry joked that PET stood for **P**eddle's **E**go **T**rip, recalling the days when the steamboat was "Fulton's Folly.")

The Pet was designed for another company to sell. That company was Radio Shack, which, after evaluating the Commodore computer, decided to design and sell its own, eventually named the TRS-80. By late 1977, all three computers were on the market, vying for the few brave souls who were interested in owning their own machines and willing to answer others who wondered why anybody would buy one. The age of personal computing had begun.

# Inside the Commodore 64

The Commodore 64 computers owe much to the design of the original PET computer and to the VIC-20. An early forerunner of the 64 was designed but never built. It used the same microprocessor as the PET, originated the concept of keys for controlling color, and presaged its advanced sound capabilities. Like the PET, it too had an odd name—the TOI computer. (TOI supposedly stood for the high-minded **T**he **O**ther **I**ntellect, but the joke around the office soon said it stood for **T**ool **O**f **I**diots.) The TOI was put on hold, though, when designers were told to come up with an inexpensive color computer, the VIC-20. Many of the TOI's features eventually became part of the Commodore 64.

Inside the 64 computers is a new version of the 6502 microprocessor which performs a neat trick. It can control the "shape" of the machine's internal design. Most microcomputers were originally designed with one portion—the master program called the "operating system," and the BASIC programming language—stored permanently in ROM, or **R**ead **O**nly **M**emory chips. The 64 breaks from this design in that there is the maximum allowable memory (for the 6502 and other so-called "eight-bit" microprocessors) inside the computer. The BASIC programming language can be "dropped" from the computer by the microprocessor, or replaced by a cartridge program, or switched between ROM and random access memory. This chameleon-like structure, or "architecture" in computer jargon, is extremely clever and is now being imitated by other manufacturers.

In addition to being distinguished by its memory and design structure, the 64 also delivers exceptional graphic and sound capabilities because of two new chips, its video controller and sound generator. Other powerful integrated circuits connect the computer with the outside.

There is a world inside this computer, one that deserves exploration. Throughout this book, you will learn how to travel its highways and byways via the BASIC programming language and programs designed for special purposes. Learning what is here, you can begin to make the computer's power work for *you*. Ready? Let's go . . .

# 2

# Setting Up

This section is about the most down-to-earth aspects of computing: Setting up your computer system and checking the machine out. This is the practical side of personal computing, one that isn't always considered.

## Unpacking

If you are like most people, you have probably already taken the computer out of the box and have plugged it in. Even though instruction books always say to "read these instructions thoroughly first," it is difficult to follow directions when your excitement is running high. And, since a computer is one of the most exciting purchases you've ever made, this enthusiasm is understandable.

Your eagerness shouldn't get in the way of inspecting what you've bought. Make sure you've gotten your money's worth. For instance, is everything in the box? The Commodore 64 should come with its own power supply—that is the heavy black box with two electrical cords connected to it. There should also be a video cable, a small metal switch box that allows you to choose between the computer and normal television reception, and a book entitled the *Commodore 64 User's Guide.* Is it all there?

Look at the power supply and, in particular, the plastic case housing the computer and keyboard. Does the plastic appear cracked or chipped? If it does, it means the computer could have been dropped or otherwise damaged

in shipment. These could be symptoms of hidden internal damage. If anything looks suspicious, take it back to where you made your purchase and insist on a new one. Don't let a dealer tell you the damage is only cosmetic without having it thoroughly checked.

## Finding a Home

You should decide where you're going to use your computer. Your first thought may be to put it in the living room, near the television set. The computer isn't a video game, though. A video game doesn't have a keyboard, and you wouldn't think of using a typewriter on the floor or on a living room coffee table, would you?

If at all possible, choose another place, one more conducive to thinking and work. Where do you do homework, tend to your personal records, pay bills or write letters? Wherever that is, it is probably the best place for the computer.

Like a typewriter, the correct placement of a computer is ideally lower than a standard desk or table top. This is so you can type on the keyboard without straining your hands and arms. Some desks have little shelves that slide out to accommodate a typewriter. Others are designed with computers

in mind. Of course you don't need a new desk. A dining room table will do in a pinch.

Since a complete computer system is more than just the computer itself, consider space. If you have a Commodore 64, you will need a television set or a video monitor, to start. (The portable and classroom versions of the 64 have their own video screens.) You may choose to use either a tape recorder or a floppy disk drive for data storage. If you want to use a *modem*—a telephone link to talk to other computers—it, too, takes up space. So does the power supply. All of these pieces of equipment should be layed out so that they are not cramped. There should be enough space between the computer and screen, for example, so that you can get to the computer to plug and unplug cables and game or program cartridges.

One space-saving accessory is a small shelf stand for a monitor or TV set. These come from various manufacturers and usually provide room for extensions and accessories attached to the back of the computer, as well as a shelf for a cassette tape recorder and/or a floppy disk unit.

The table top or desk that you choose should also have enough room for books and other working materials that you'll use with your computer. To make things easier while copying data into the machine, you might consider using a typist's page stand, available at most office supply or stationery stores. If you are going to copy programs from books or magazines, take a look also at some of the cookbook stands that are available. They work very well, keeping your hands free.

Lighting is an important consideration. Overhead lighting is probably the best. A desk lamp is good for illuminating the keyboard and printed materials. In either case, make sure that the light is neither too bright nor too dim, and above all, that it does not reflect off the video screen. Don't put the screen opposite a window in the room. Window glare and reflections are distracting and can cause eyestrain.

Consider your access to electric power and to wall sockets. For the Commodore 64 system, you will need one outlet for the computer (actually the power supply), another for the video screen, another for a floppy disk drive, and possibly one more for a printer, if you have one. If you choose not to use Commodore's modem (which requires no external power connection) but another brand, you'll need still another outlet.

The solution to this minor energy crisis is to use an electrical accessory called a "power strip" or junction box. Hardware stores sell them and most models are useful. Make certain, however, that the box or power strip is *fused* or has its own "circuit breaker." This will prevent a socket from becoming overloaded. Overloading is dangerous, but there is one more consideration. If you are programming or entering data and blow a fuse, you will lose the program or data you have entered.

Junction boxes can be mounted at the back or underneath a table or desk. One switch usually controls all the outlets, eliminating the need to turn individual pieces of equipment on or off. One flip of the switch will power up your entire computer system.

## Television Sets vs. Video Monitors

You have two choices in selecting a video display for the Commodore 64. You can choose to use either a TV set or a video monitor. Here are the differences between them.

A television set is a receiver. Like a radio, it is meant to tune in broadcast (or cable) TV stations. These stations put out RF, or *radio frequency* signals. The 64 puts out a similar television signal on channel 3 or 4 that looks, to a TV set, like any other station. Inside the television, circuitry separates out the video signal and feeds it to the picture tube.

A video signal is different from an RF signal and is usually considered to be visually "cleaner." A video monitor is designed to accept video signals—most TV sets can't. Since a monitor does not need to process the signal and separate it from its radio frequency components, it usually displays clearer, sharper images. Furthermore, since most monitors don't contain TV channel selectors (tuners), they are not sensitive to strong signals from nearby TV stations or other types of radio frequency interference.

Some of the very newest consumer television systems are called "component" TVs. These sets consist of a separate monitor and tuner and are usually ideal for computer use.

One very common kind of interference is produced by the computer itself. The microchips inside, as well as wires attached to it, can and often do interfere because of the speed at which the chips operate. For example, some early computers put out interference that disturbs reception on a standard TV set. The video monitor is also insensitive to this.

Not all television sets work well with personal computers. Many older sets were not designed with computers (or even video games) in mind. Pictures on these sets tend to lack stability—they look "squeamish." Other older sets (and a few new ones) are just not sharp enough to read the characters a personal computer sends to the screen.

Color can also be a problem. If the picture tube of an old set is bad, it may not display colors correctly, or a condition known as "blooming" can occur. When this happens, one color on the screen lights up brighter than others and blurs the words on the screen. It can cause fringing and smearing and make a line printed by the computer difficult or impossible to read.

Another condition common to television sets (and found on monitors, too) is "overscanning." Basically, this means that a portion of the picture on the top and bottom or sides of the screen is chopped off. All TV sets and most monitors overscan slightly (otherwise you'd always see a black border around a TV picture), but the degree to which the cropping occurs varies wildly. Occasionally an old TV set will overscan so badly that it will crop valuable screen information. This kind of set is totally useless with any computer. (One advantage of the Commodore 64 family computers is that the screen is surrounded by a border, so overscanning is somewhat less of a problem.)

If you are going to use a television set—and because of cost considerations, many people do—a good rule of thumb says that a new, but inexpensive TV is almost always better than an old one. Bargain hunting for a used set is the least preferable of the alternatives.

There's a difference, too, between the quality of black-and-white and color monitors. All video screens (except those found on some of the new, high-tech pocket portables) are comprised of phosphors, chemical coatings which light up when struck by a beam of energy inside the picture tube.

Color video screens use an arrangement of green, blue and red colored phosphors. Screens that aren't designed for color—monochrome screens that display white, green, blue or amber images against a dark background—use only one kind of phosphor. Green is the most popular color for a monochrome monitor since most people believe it is easiest on your eyes.

The color monitor, on the other hand, makes its black-and-white picture by a combination of its colored phosphors, so the characters on its screen are generally not as sharp. Most monochrome monitors can easily display as many as 80 computer-generated characters on a single line. Color monitors that can be used with the Commodore 64 family are usually limited by their resolution to about half that many screen characters.

One type of color monitor is known as "RGB" (for **R**ed, **G**reen and **B**lue), and its picture is especially sharp, with almost the clarity of some monochrome monitors. RGB monitors require a special video output other than the one found on the Commodore 64 family. (Don't worry, most other computers in their price range don't have RGB outputs either.) So you're restricted to using most other monitors which accept so-called "composite" video, the most common type.

The Amdek Color-I is an example of an industry standard color monitor and is well suited for use with the Commodore 64. It is rugged and displays a very high-quality picture. In addition, the 64's sound can be piped through its internal amplifier and speaker. Commodore also sells its own line of color monitors specially designed for use with its computers.

If you have purchased your computer primarily for recordkeeping tasks or to use as a word processor, color and graphic capabilities are of much less importance to you. You should consider using a monochrome monitor as it will be much easier to read and could minimize eyestrain.

A standard, black-and-white television set will not always work as well as a monochrome monitor. When using a monochrome monitor, you can use a special video signal the computer puts out. This signal does not contain color information and is easier to read on a monochrome monitor. There is no such black-and-white signal that can be readily used with a standard television set, however.

# Hooking Up

Connecting a Commodore 64 is about as simple as attaching the pieces of a stereo hi-fi system. You shouldn't need any help, even if you consider yourself technically inept.

To get going, here is a list of the most important connections on the computer itself.

***Power*** The electric power connector is located on the right side of the Commodore 64, near the rear. It is a round, 7-pin socket that is used to attach the power supply. If the cords at either end of the power supply are bent or broken, do not plug it in. It could have a disastrous effect on the computer. Never attach any other kind of power supply to the computer, either, even if the plugs fit correctly.

***Cassette Port*** Looking at the back of the Commodore 64, this is the second opening from the right. Actually, it is the edge of the printed circuit board on which the computer is built. Attach the Commodore cassette recorder to this flat connector, making sure the "key" (a piece of plastic inside the plug on the cassette cable) is in the same position as the slot on the connector.

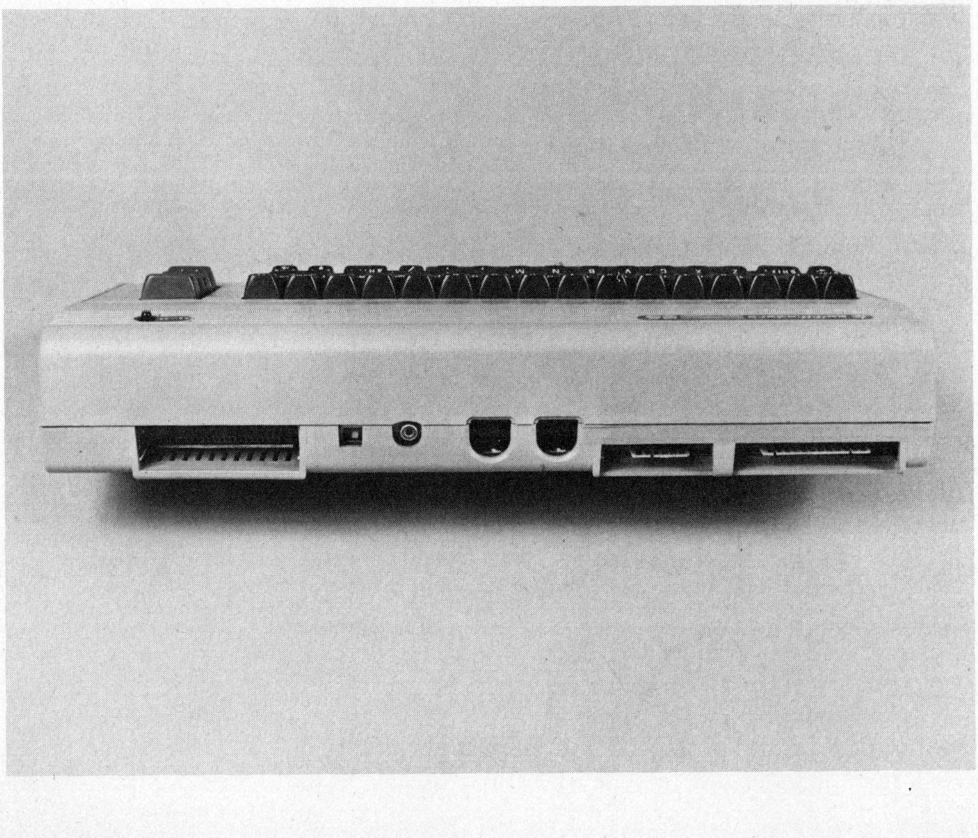

***RF Modulator*** "RF" stands for *radio frequency* modulator. (It is also called the "TV Connector" by Commodore.) This is the connection that feeds a TV signal from the computer to a standard television set. Plug the thin cable that comes with the 64 between this round connector (fifth hole from the right, looking at the back) and the switch box that connects to the TV set. Connect the switch box to the antenna terminals of the television set.

***Serial Port*** This is an all-important connection between the computer and floppy disk storage units, printers, etc. Located third from the right at the rear, it uses a 5-pin round plug. The cable furnished with Commodore's floppy disk drive or printer fits it. Plug one end into the computer, the other into either similar socket at the rear of the disk unit or printer. To distinguish the serial port from the connector that accommodates the modem, or telephone link, it is often called the "VIC serial bus."

***Cartridge Port*** Located at the far left of the machine, when looking at it from the back, this connection has a myriad of uses. This is where games or other programs packaged as cartridges will be plugged in. Some adapters that allow you to use disk drives other than Commodore's also use this port, as do cartridges containing optional microprocessor chips.

***User Port*** Located in back on the far right side, this is an all-purpose connector. Primarily, it is used to connect Commodore's telephone link, or modem, but is also sometimes used to connect printers and other accessories as well. Experimenters like this port for homemade gadgets. It is often referred to as the "parallel port" because it has eight *parallel* data connections.

***Control Ports*** Located on the right side of the computer, the two control ports are used mainly for connecting game controllers, joysticks, and paddles. Some programs, however, are being sold with tiny "black boxes" called "keys" that are required to be connected to one of the control ports to work. (This is a security measure that protects that program against unauthorized circulation.)

***A-V Port*** This is also called the audio-video connector. It is the socket used to connect the 64 to monochrome and color monitors, to connect the output of its sound generator to an external amplifier (like a stereo system), and to feed sound from an outside source (such as a tape recorder, microphone, or musical instrument) to the computer.

If you are handy with a soldering iron, you can make your own connecting cables based on the description of the plug in the manual that came with your computer. If not, you can have your dealer (or someone else) make them for you, or you can buy commercially available ones.

When using a standard television set, don't worry about this audio-video plug. Both sound and picture will come out of your TV.

If you plan to use a monochrome video monitor (not a black-and-white television set), ask your dealer or a technician to make a special cable for you. Pin #1 on the audio-video connector is identified as "luminance." This allows you to use only the black-and-white portion of the computer's video signal and offers the best screen sharpness.

## Checking It Out

If you already have connected the components of your computer system and know that it is working correctly, you can skip this section and read on. However, if you've just purchased your machine and want to know if everything is working as it should, here's a simple check-out you can perform.

To make sure that your computer system is working, connect all the pieces. If you are using a color television set, connect the round video cable to the RF modulator output and the antenna switch box. Attach the switch box to your television's antenna connector. If you are using a video monitor, connect the appropriate cables to it. Connect the Commodore cassette recorder and/or the floppy disk drive to the computer. If you have a printer, connect it not to the computer, but to the empty socket at the rear of the disk drive.

If you have the portable or classroom version of the Commodore 64, most of these connections are already made for you inside the case.

To get everything going, turn on each piece of equipment. Adjust the color on the monitor or television set so that the screen is blue, with light blue characters and border. On the Commodore 64 the screen should read:

```
  **** COMMODORE 64 BASIC V2 ****
64K RAM SYSTEM 38911 BASIC BYTES FREE
READY.
```

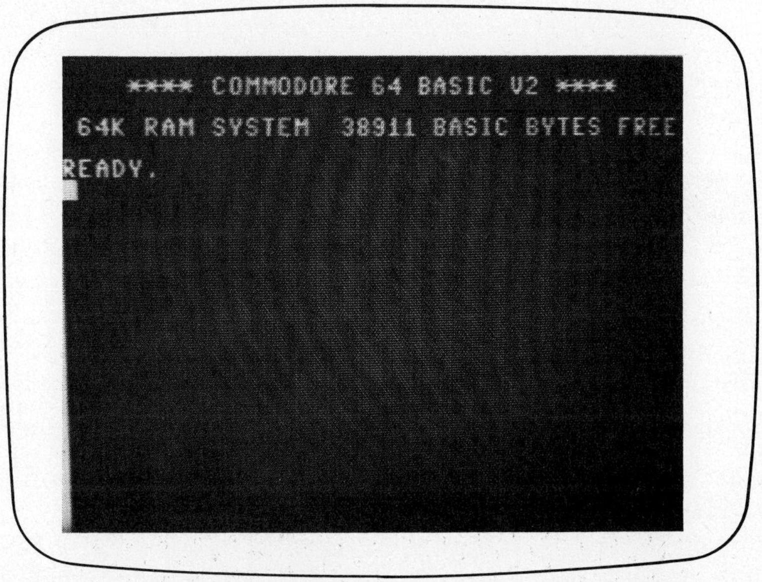

(The message that comes up on the portable and classroom computers should be similar, if not exactly the same.)

There should be a small, light blue square flashing on and off beneath the word READY. This square is called the "cursor." It is a French word that means "runner." The cursor "runs" across the screen, always indicating your current position.

What does this message mean?

The top line tells you that this is BASIC V2, or version #2 of the computer's programming language, called BASIC. Sixty-four "K" (for "kilo" or thousand) RAM means that there are over 64,000 characters of RAM, or **r**andom **a**ccess **m**emory, also called read-and-write memory, available in the system. Finally, 38911 BASIC BYTES FREE means that, of the total memory, 38,911 *bytes* (each byte is the equivalent of a character) are available for writing BASIC programs. If there is 64K of memory in the computer, why can't you use more of it? The computer itself uses the remainder of the memory for the BASIC language and for its own operation.

If your Commodore 64 doesn't come up with that magic number—38911 BASIC BYTES FREE—put it back in the box and return it to where it was purchased. Something is wrong and the computer needs to be repaired or replaced.

If the cursor is not on the screen near the word READY, or if it is not blinking on and off, this is also a sign that the computer isn't working properly.

Assuming your machine has passed inspection so far, you can now make a quick check of the system by entering a short program. Don't worry if you don't know a thing about programming. For this little test you needn't know the details of what you will be doing.

The keyboards of the Commodore 64 family work slightly differently than an ordinary typewriter keyboard. For one thing, there are more keys, and, when the machine is turned on, all of the letters typed will be in upper case (capital letters) on the screen. If you press the SHIFT key and try to type a letter, you will see an unusual symbol. For now, don't worry about those.

Type in this short program *exactly* as it appears below. At the end of each numbered line press the RETURN key. It is used to enter information into the computer.

```
10 PRINT "THIS IS MY COMMODORE COMPUTER"
20 GOTO 10
```

Briefly, line number 10 of this little program tells the computer to type the sentence THIS IS MY COMMODORE COMPUTER on the video screen. Line number 20 tells the machine to do it again and again and again. This, by the way, is probably the kind of BASIC computer program anyone who has used a personal computer has written first.

Now type the word RUN and press the key marked RETURN to enter this command.

The screen should quickly fill with the sentence THIS IS MY COMMODORE COMPUTER. Although the bottom line should be flickering on and off (indicating that several new lines per second are being displayed on the screen), the sentence should be clear and easy to read. If the screen is filled with "snow" or other interference, it has flunked the test. Take it back to where you bought it and ask them for a new computer.

Some of Commodore's computers come off the assembly line in less than perfect condition. One of the more common problems (at least with early models) is that the Commodore 64's screen becomes "snowy" when a program is running. This is Commodore's problem, not yours, and you are entitled to a computer that works properly.

If this test program RUNs and the computer works well, stop the program by pressing the key marked RUN/STOP at the left of the keyboard. The screen should now read:

```
BREAK IN LINE 10
READY.
```

or

```
BREAK IN LINE 20
READY.
```

The cursor should again be visible and blinking.

Now, try to SAVE and LOAD this program to and from a cassette tape. Put one in the recorder and make sure it is rewound. To SAVE the program to tape, type the words:

```
SAVE "PROGRAM ONE"
```

Press the RETURN key.

The computer should come back with:

```
PRESS RECORD & PLAY ON TAPE
```

Do what the computer tells you. Press the keys marked RECORD and PLAY on the Commodore cassette recorder. The screen should go blank and turn the same color of light blue as the border for about 20 seconds. When the screen comes back, it should again say READY. Now, rewind the tape.

By the way, if you are attempting to use any cassette recorder other than Commodore's, it won't work unless you have the proper adapter. The Commodore Datasette cassette recorder has special circuitry which senses when its keys are pressed down. Several commercially available adapters allow you to use standard cassette recorders and mimic the functions of Commodore's recorder.

With the tape rewound, turn the computer off and on again. This completely clears whatever was in its memory. (This is just one way to reset the machine. You'll learn about other, better ways.) Type the word LOAD and press the RETURN key. The computer should say:

```
PRESS PLAY ON TAPE
```

Press the key marked PLAY on the cassette recorder. The screen will again go blank for a few seconds. When the tape recorder stops, the screen will return with the words:

```
FOUND PROGRAM ONE
```

The machine is waiting for you to tell it to go ahead and LOAD the program. To do so, press the key in the lower left-hand corner of the keyboard with the Commodore logo on it. The screen will again go blank for a few seconds. When it comes back it should say:

```
LOADING
READY.
```

Type RUN and press the RETURN key. The program should operate as it did before. Since the computer's memory was cleared when you flipped the power switch off and on again (no matter how briefly it was off), this proves that it can SAVE and LOAD a program to and from cassette tape. If it passed this test, it's in good shape.

If you have a disk drive, try to SAVE and LOAD to and from a floppy disk. Turn the disk drive on, making sure that there is no disk inside of it.

NOTE: Unlike many other computers, Commodore's disk drive is likely to damage the data on the disk if it is turned on or off with a floppy disk locked inside.

Insert a new, blank floppy disk with the label up and the oblong disk opening to the rear. Push it in until the disk stops in place inside the drive. Close the disk drive door by pulling the metal tab down and toward you until it latches.

You will first need to prepare the disk before you use it. This preparation writes invisible tracks onto the magnetic disk surface. This procedure is required *only* for disks that are either new or are being erased and reused. Each time you prepare a disk this way you destroy the data or programs that were previously stored on it.

To prepare a disk, type:

`OPEN 1,8,15` [then press RETURN]
`PRINT #1, "N:PROGRAM DISK,PD"` [then press RETURN]

The red light on the front of the disk drive should go on for a minute or two and you should be able to hear the disk spinning inside.

There are two small lights on the front of the Commodore disk drive. The green light shows that the machine is turned on. The second light, a red one, has two functions. First, it shows you that information is being taken from or given to the floppy disk. But if this red light flashes, it is an indication that an error has occurred. Such an error might be yours, or it might be the machine's.

If the red light is flashing, try again and make certain you type the above sequence exactly as shown. If it is not flashing on and off, you have successfully prepared the disk. Now type:

```
SAVE "PROGRAM ONE",8
```

Press the RETURN key. The disk drive should activate for a few seconds, showing you that it is storing the program on the disk.

When the disk drive stops (you'll hear it and the red light will go out), turn the computer off and on again. Then type this:

```
LOAD "$",8
```
[then press RETURN]

When the machine comes back with READY, type LIST and press RETURN. You should see something like this:

```
0  "PROGRAM DISK    " PD 2A
1      "PROGRAM ONE"     PRG
663 BLOCKS FREE.
READY.
```

This is the disk directory—it tells you the name of the disk ("PROGRAM DISK"), the programs stored on it (just one, called "PROGRAM ONE"), and how much room is left (663 blocks, or approximately 168,000 bytes of memory). For now, just be assured it's all there.

Finally, type:

```
LOAD "PROGRAM ONE",8
```
[then press RETURN]

This should LOAD our little program back into the machine so you can RUN it.

Putting the Commodore disk drive through this test is very important. As with the computers themselves, Commodore occasionally ships untested disk drives to its dealers. A number of these will fail a test like this one. You will know that it has failed if the disk unit does not correctly prepare the disk, or LOAD and SAVE programs to and from it.

Most often, the problem with a new disk drive is the speed at which it rotates the disk inside. If you have purchased your disk drive from an electronics store or a computer specialty shop, you can probably return it for a simple adjustment. If you have purchased it from a department or discount store which does not have its own computer repair service, ask the store for a new one instead of leaving it for repair. Or, you may choose to locate a "factory authorized" Commodore service department at a computer store and ask if they will check the drive for you.

(Be forewarned, though, some computer stores will not be completely cooperative if you did not purchase the machine from them.)

So far, you may be confused about what you have just done. If you don't understand, don't worry. You'll learn the "whys" as well as the "hows" in a few pages from now. You have seen, though, the basic way to LOAD and SAVE programs to and from cassettes and disks.

Our main job here was to perform a quick system check. Needless to say, this isn't a complete test run. If your computer system passes the test, you'll only know if it appears to be working and LOADs and SAVEs programs.

Everything working as it should? Good. On to the keyboard.

# Lots of Keys

The Commodore 64 family keyboards are somewhat unusual in their design. Generally, each key produces three different results. This can be mind-boggling, since not all of these are always clearly labeled. Taking a tour of the keyboard should familiarize you with what it can do. Don't be discouraged if you don't pick all this up the first time around. The keyboard has so many functions that it does take time to get used to.

***The RETURN Key*** This key takes a word or line that is typed on the video screen and enters it into the computer's main memory. It is probably the single most important key on the keyboard. On some other makes and models of computers it is marked ENTER, to more accurately describe its function. Its name comes from the old days of typewriters and teletype machines, when it was originally called a "carriage return," which was its real purpose.

***SHIFT Key*** On a typewriter, the SHIFT key selects upper case (capital) or lower case (small) letters. On the computer's keyboard, it works in about the same way. The difference, though, is that there are more than just capital and small letters to consider. The general rule still applies. If you press the SHIFT LOCK key once (you'll hear it click), the keyboard will act as though you always have the SHIFT key pressed. This can cause problems. So avoid using SHIFT LOCK, and occasionally check it if you think that a key isn't doing what it should. Unlock the SHIFT LOCK by pressing it again.

***The RUN/STOP Key*** This key is used to STOP a program while it is RUNning. On other computers it is sometimes labeled "Break." RUN/STOP can also be used with the SHIFT key (both pressed together) to LOAD and RUN programs from the cassette recorder.

***Graphics Mode and Typewriter Mode*** The first thing to recognize is that the Commodore keyboard acts differently than a typewriter when the computer "comes alive." The keys that would normally result in lower case (small) letters produce upper case (or capitals). This is because 64 family computers come up in what is called the "graphics mode." This means that pressing most keys along with the SHIFT key will produce special graphic symbols which are used to make simple pictures, boxes, borders, game pieces, etc. There is another mode—a "typewriter mode"—that makes the computer behave like a typewriter.

***The COMMODORE Key*** To enter the typewriter mode, depress either SHIFT key, and, while doing so, press the COMMODORE (logo) key in the lower left-hand corner. You should notice the results on the screen instantly—what were upper case (capital) letters now become lower case (small) letters. Try typing on the keyboard in this mode. Familiar, isn't it?

An important thing to remember about going from the graphics mode to this typewriter mode is that the computer isn't making the same distinction between capital and small letters that you are. When in the graphics mode, the computer expects lines of BASIC programming and other commands to the machine to be written in capital letters. But while in the typewriter mode, the computer expects to see these same words in lower case (small) letters. In other words, BASIC programming and commands to the machine are always written without using the SHIFT key, regardless of the mode you are in. If you use capital letters in the typewriter mode, the computer won't know what you're talking about.

For the time being, go back to the graphics mode, so we can look at some of the other keyboard functions. Use the COMMODORE key and SHIFT to make the change.

The COMMODORE key, you may remember, is also used to tell the computer to help LOAD a program from a cassette tape. There are still a few more uses for it, too.

***Graphic Symbols*** You may have noticed that there are two small boxes on the front of almost every key. Each of these contains a special graphic symbol.

While in the graphics mode, press the W key. It prints a W, right? Now press the SHIFT key and the W at the same time. You should see something that looks like the letter O. It is not, though. This is a graphic symbol. Now depress the COMMODORE key and press the W again. This time you should see a symbol that looks like a T tipped on its right side. You've just produced three different characters from one key.

If you press SHIFT and the COMMODORE key together, you'll see what you get by pressing this same W key in the typewriter mode. You should see a small letter w, a capital, and the same graphic symbol you got last time, the T on its side. This is usually what happens—the cases reverse (small letters become capitals and vice versa) and the left graphic symbol stays the same, from the graphics to the typewriter mode. *Usually*, that is, with a few

exceptions. Try this same experiment with the key that is marked with an "up arrow" and with the "British Pound Sterling" key. Type these the three different ways (unSHIFTed, SHIFTed and with the COMMODORE key depressed). Then go from the graphics to the typewriter mode. You should see different graphic symbols appear. This is one of the exceptions to the rule, but it probably won't get in your way too often.

***The CTRL Key*** We've learned that the COMMODORE key can be thought of as a second SHIFT key. There is another key that performs a similar function. It is the CTRL key; the abbreviation stands for "control."

***Reverse Mode*** To see one way the control key is used, press CTRL, and while holding it down, press the number 9 key on the top row. Now type anything on the screen. Everything you type now should be reversed. That is, each character you type should be the color of the screen against its own light background. They should appear dark blue, each in its own light blue box. (This is only the case with the colors the screen and characters appear in when the computer is turned on. The background color of a reverse character is always the color that the character originally was.) This reverse mode is useful for highlighting certain words or phrases in text printed on the screen.

To return to the standard (not reverse) screen mode, depress CTRL and number key 0. Notice that these two keys have their functions printed clearly on the front. RVS ON means "reverse on," and RVS OFF, of course, means "reverse off."

***Colors*** Now try pressing CTRL and any of the number keys 1 to 8 and look at the cursor. You've just found the way to change the colors of characters you type on the screen. Here is a list of the colors you get by pressing CTRL and a number key together:

| *Press* | *Color* | *Key Legend* |
|---|---|---|
| CTRL-1 | Black | BLK |
| CTRL-2 | White | WHT |
| CTRL-3 | Red | RED |
| CTRL-4 | Cyan (powder blue) | CYN |
| CTRL-5 | Purple | PUR |
| CTRL-6 | Green | GRN |
| CTRL-7 | Blue | BLU |
| CTRL-8 | Yellow | YEL |

Even though the keyboard does not indicate it, eight more colors are directly available by pressing another combination of keys. Use the COMMODORE key in the lower left-hand corner to get these new colors:

| *Press* | *Color* | *Key Legend* |
|---|---|---|
| COMM-1 | Orange | BLK |
| COMM-2 | Brown | WHT |
| COMM-3 | Light Red (hot pink) | RED |
| COMM-4 | Gray 1 (dark gray) | CYN |
| COMM-5 | Gray 2 (medium gray) | PUR |
| COMM-6 | Light Green | GRN |
| COMM-7 | Light Blue | BLU |
| COMM-8 | Gray 3 (light gray) | YEL |

Don't be alarmed if you can't read what you type in certain colors against the blue background. Many Commodore 64 computers (especially very early models) are limited in the number of background and foreground color combinations that can be used. There is no set rule about which colors "read" well against various backgrounds. You'll need to determine this on your own by trial and error.

Background and border colors, unfortunately, cannot be changed with a single keystroke, as character colors can.

***The Function Keys*** Look at the four large keys to the right of the keyboard. The tops of the keys are marked f1, f3, f5, f7. The fronts are marked f2, f4, f6, f8 and should be thought of as the SHIFTed versions of the keys. Ironically, though they are called "function keys," they have no function at all without programs that take advantage of them. These keys will be utilized in different ways in many programs, however.

***The RESTORE Key*** The key marked RESTORE, on the right side of the keyboard, is an important one. Pressing the RUN/STOP and RESTORE keys together interrupts a program (as does pressing RUN/STOP alone) and brings the computer back to its original condition. This means that the screen will revert to its original colors (light blue on a dark blue background) and

that any sounds the computer was making will stop, too. Other internal conditions are reset to what they were when the machine was turned on.

The best thing about using the RESTORE key, however, is that any program in memory will remain there, even though the computer has been reset. Turning the machine off and on to reset it is often referred to as a "cold start," and destroys the program in memory. RESTORE can be thought of as a "warm start," since memory is not cleared.

***The Editing Keys*** Among the most powerful keys on the Commodore 64 family keyboards are the four editing keys. Commodore computers have always had excellent editing capabilities that make program writing as easy as possible. In addition to editing programming lines and other screen text, the editing keys can be used in a special way in programming. To get you acquainted with these keys, here is a quick explanation of what they do.

***The CRSR Keys*** At the bottom right corner of the keyboard are two keys that control the cursor. They are marked CRSR up and down and CRSR left and right, and function just as they appear. Press the CRSR up and down key. It should move down. Now press the SHIFT key and the same CRSR key. The cursor moves up. Press the CRSR left and right key and it will move right. Pressing SHIFT and this key moves the cursor back to the left. (If it doesn't appear to be working properly, check the SHIFT LOCK key to make certain it isn't depressed.)

***The CLR/HOME Key*** The editing keys at the top right corner of the keyboard are marked CLR/HOME and INST/DEL. HOME stands for the cursor's "home," which is at the top left corner of the video screen. Pressing CLR/HOME will return the cursor to this position each time. CLR means "clear the screen." Pressing SHIFT and CLR/HOM brings the cursor back to its home, but also erases whatever is on the screen. If you press SHIFT and CLR/HOME before you've pressed RETURN, you'll lose any new line you may have been typing or working on.

***The INST/DEL Key*** DEL stands for "delete," and INST means "insert." Try typing a line into the computer. Now press the INST/DEL key. Each time it is tapped, the cursor will move back one space and delete whichever character it is passing over. Pressing SHIFT and the INST/DEL key together inserts blank spaces in a line.

Type something on the screen. Now put the cursor anywhere in the middle of the line by using the CRSR left and right key. Press SHIFT and tap the INST/DEL key a few times. Everything to the right of the cursor will move farther right on the screen, leaving empty spaces where the letters once were. These spaces can be filled by pressing any character key or even the SPACE bar.

Together, the eight functions on these four keys comprise a unique and extremely convenient way of entering data into the computer. Nothing comes easy, though, and using the editing system can be difficult at first. After you get accustomed to what these keys do and where they are, you'll be zipping all over the screen with total control.

It is also important to learn these editing keys if you are going to use your computer to do word processing (electronic writing and editing), since they are used heavily by most such programs.

***Repeating Keys*** Four keys on the Commodore keyboard automatically repeat if they are held down for even the shortest length of time. These are the two CRSR keys (left and right, up and down), the INST/DEL key, and the SPACE bar at the bottom of the keyboard. This was designed into the machine because these keys are used heavily during editing.

The very best way to make yourself comfortable with this, or any keyboard, is to spend some time with it. Type on it as you would a typewriter, using the editing keys to change what you've written.

(Don't bother pressing the RETURN key as you would when typing on a typewriter. The computer might not understand what you're trying to say and signal that you've made a mistake.)

## Typing on QWERTY

Many people have trouble with any kind of typewriter-like keyboard. Your Commodore computer (as well as almost every other personal computer) has what is called a QWERTY keyboard, after the arrangement of the top row of letter keys. The actual top row is QWERTYUIOP. Legend has it that it was designed so that salesmen who sold typewriters when they began to appear in 1873 could type the word "typewriter" on the top row of keys alone. (Look closely, it can be done.)

The real logic behind the clumsy QWERTY keyboard, however, is that it was designed to actually slow down typing speed. By widely separating the most often used keys, its designers meant to insure that typists would stay confused and type slowly enough so that early, delicate printing mechanisms wouldn't jam up. Over 100 years later, we're still using the ancient and inconvenient QWERTY keyboard, and, now, with the advent of personal computers, the inventors of QWERTY have even further reason to chuckle at us from their graves. There are more QWERTYs than ever before.

Why hasn't someone done something about it? A few have tried. QWERTY was replaced by keyboards in alphabetical order on some of the tiny pocket computers sold in the last few years. It turned out they were even more difficult to use than QWERTY. Another alternative was the DSK (for Dvorak Simplified Keyboard), which originated in 1932 after two decades of research. The DSK brought the most often used letters to the "home row" of keys (ASDF . . . on the QWERTY). It was claimed that the 3,000 most often used words in the English language could be typed on just this one row of keys. In the last decade, an attempt was made to introduce a one-handed keyboard, where combinations of fingers were used to enter a single character. (A miniature, hand-held word processor sold in Great Britain also uses this keyboard.)

The dominance of QWERTY, however, remains virtually unchallenged, and other keyboard styles have been all but forgotten. Few typewriters are equipped with alternatives and, for all intents and purposes, no personal computers.

In order to communicate with your personal computer you will need to struggle with the poor design of the traditional keyboard. One side benefit of personal computing is that you will learn to type almost without effort—you will grow more and more comfortable at the keyboard. Of course, after reading the section in this book on word processing, you may wonder why anyone would want to use a typewriter anyway.

# 3

# Some Essential Skills

Whether you intend to program your computer or use it with commercial programs, you must acquire a few essential skills. These will allow you to LOAD and SAVE programs to and from cassette or disk and to RUN them. You should also know about some peculiarities of editing BASIC programs, how to use the computer as a calculator, and its built-in timekeeping functions.

## The RETURN Key

Throughout this book you will be asked to type in programming examples and demonstrations of how keyboard commands work. In order to send this information to the computer, you must always press the large key at the right of the keyboard marked RETURN. If you do not, the computer will wait, thinking that more instructions are coming. In some places, you will be reminded to press this key. In others, however, it will be assumed that you've learned this all-important step. The RETURN key should always be pressed when you've finished entering a BASIC program line, after you've changed something on a line, or when you want to send a command directly from the keyboard.

# LOADing Up

Computer programs originate by typing them into the machine's memory from the keyboard. It would be incredibly time-consuming, though, to type every program each time you want to use it. Instead, the computer can SAVE programs to a cassette tape or a magnetic disk, also called a "floppy disk." (Computer lore has named it "floppy" to distinguish it from a different kind of disk storage system, a rigid or "hard" disk which holds enormous amounts of memory.)

After a program is SAVEd to either disk or tape, it can later be recalled to the computer's memory with the LOAD command. Both SAVE and LOAD function similarly in that they *copy* the program into or out of memory or other outside storage device. When you SAVE a program, a copy is made on the tape or disk, but it is still inside the computer. Likewise, when you LOAD a program into memory, it still exists on the tape or disk.

The computer's main read-and-write memory called RAM (for **R**andom **A**ccess **M**emory), is temporary. Anything put here—a program, data, or a picture—will be lost as soon as the power is turned off, even for a fraction of a second. LOAD takes digital signals from a disk or audio signals from a tape and stores them in RAM memory. SAVE converts the contents of memory into these same kinds of signals and sends them to the tape or disk.

LOAD always clears the computer's memory and then fills it with the new program. (You cannot use LOAD twice to add one program to another.)

## LOAD From Tape

To begin LOADing, you can use the tape you created if you followed the testing directions in the section of this book entitled "Setting Up." Or, you may use another tape that contains a prerecorded program.

LOAD can be used with or without a program name. Type:

LOAD [and press the RETURN key]

or

LOAD "PROGRAM ONE" [and RETURN]

Typing LOAD and pressing the RETURN key will always cause the computer to respond with this message on the video screen:

PRESS PLAY ON TAPE

Pressing PLAY on the tape recorder "blanks" the screen. Actually, it turns the entire screen the same color as the border and anything written on it will temporarily vanish. When the screen returns to normal, you'll see another message.

FOUND

This means the tape recorder has located a program. If the program has a name, you will see it, too. The next move is yours. You must press the COMMODORE (logo) key in the lower left-hand corner of the keyboard. If you did not use a name when you typed LOAD, the first program on the tape will be LOADed.

If you used a name, the computer will ignore any program unless it is the program you named. It will stop and display each name, and you must press the COMMODORE key to continue your search for the proper program.

Once the program has been LOADed, the screen returns to normal and says:

READY.

Now, you can type RUN (and press the RETURN key) and the program begins operating.

On earlier Commodore computers, including the PET, CBM (an upgraded PET model), and the VIC, you did not need to press a key to LOAD the program. But the video microchip inside the Commodore 64 family makes new demands on the system, and it became necessary to blank the screen when a program was being LOADed or SAVEd. If you have used those earlier Commodore machines, be sure to remember this extra step; otherwise, the computer will not LOAD your program.

Another way to LOAD the first program from a tape is to hold down either SHIFT key and then press the RUN/STOP key. When you do this, the words LOAD and PRESS PLAY ON TAPE will instantly appear. You still must press the COMMODORE key when FOUND appears. This time, though, the program RUNs automatically—a handy shortcut.

When you use LOAD with a program name, it insures that only the program with that name will be LOADed. The name must always be preceded by a quotation mark; however you need not always type the entire name.

Let's say that three programs, named PROGRAM ONE, PROGRAM TWO, and PROGRAM THREE, are all stored on the same side of a cassette tape. The command LOAD "PROGRAM THREE" will LOAD only that program.

The Commodore computers use a technique called "pattern matching" to identify the programs they should LOAD. IF you use only the first letter of the name—LOAD "P—the computer will LOAD any program that begins with the letter P—"PROGRAM ONE," "PROGRAM TWO," or even "PING PONG" (if it were on the tape). If you use the first word—LOAD "PROGRAM—the computer will LOAD every program that begins with that word, and so on.

For pattern matching to work, the last quotation mark must not be used. If it is, the computer thinks of the name in quotes as unique, and will only LOAD programs that match it *exactly*.

```
LOAD "PRO
LOAD "PROGRAM"
```

The first command will LOAD any program with PRO as the first three letters of its name. The second will LOAD *only* the program named PROGRAM.

From time to time, you will encounter a program that needs to be LOADed in a particular manner. Instructions for LOADing will look something like this:

```
LOAD "PROGRAM NAME",1,1
```

What does this mean? The two numbers, 1 and 1, give the computer unique instructions. The first number 1 stands for the *device number* of the cassette recorder, which is always 1. (You'll learn more about device numbers as you go along and in the section entitled "How the Computer Stores Information.") This is how the computer knows you are using a cassette recorder. But, if LOAD is used without *any* numbers following it, the computer *assumes* you are using the recorder.

The second number 1 tells the computer to LOAD the program in a special place. Beginning with the VIC, Commodore computers incorporated something called a "relocating LOADer." This is a program in the machine's operating system that allows many BASIC programs written for the Commodore PET and CBM computers to be used with the VIC and 64 family. It is necessary because of differences in the way that the various computers store programs.

Unless this second number 1 is used, the computer will always begin LOADing programs in the place where BASIC programs are stored. Some programs, however, are not written in BASIC but in a code referred to as "machine language," which operates much, much faster. Often, you will be asked to LOAD using ",1,1" to insure that they LOAD properly.

## My Program Won't LOAD

There are dozens of reasons why programs won't LOAD correctly. Here are the four most common.

Reason One: There's something wrong with your cassette recorder. It can range from a faulty plug to damaged electronic circuitry inside. If anything is obvious, see the dealer you purchased it from. Unfortunately, coming to this conclusion can sometimes be frustrating.

Reason Two: Your recorder is in working condition except for one thing—it is out of alignment. This is most often the case if you can LOAD program cassettes that *you* have recorded, but have trouble with tapes recorded by others. The solution is to align the recording/playback head. It is not, however, a simple chore, since you cannot hear what is coming from the tape. You can make a minor adjustment and see if the problem is corrected.

There is a small hole located on top of Commodore's cassette recorder. When you press the PLAY key, you can put a tiny jeweler's screwdriver through this hole to turn an adjustment screw. Once you fit the screwdriver in, you should memorize its position. Turn it a quarter turn or so, and try LOADing the cassette. If that doesn't work, try turning it in the opposite direction.

Caution: Try this *only* if you feel confident that you know what you're doing. If you do not remember the screw's original position, or turn it too far, you could misalign the recorder further so that even your own tapes will not LOAD.

If you have had good luck LOADing other cassettes from a variety of sources and should happen upon one or two that don't LOAD correctly, your recorder is probably in good shape. The problem may be with the recorder that those tapes were made on, not yours.

If you continue to have problems you think are due to misalignment, take the recorder to your dealer or to a Commodore service shop so that it can be aligned properly.

Reason Three: If you have trouble LOADing when another program is in the machine and has been running, the fault may be neither the computer's nor the tape recorder's. Some programs can change the way the computer works to prevent you from making copies of it. Other programs might use special features that could affect the way programs LOAD, too.

One situation likely to occur when using tape happens when a program, most likely a game, uses "sprite" graphics. (Sprites are colored objects that are moved around the screen, and are one of the many graphic features of the Commodore 64 family.) Sometimes programmers will use an area of memory called the "cassette buffer" to store these pictures. If these sprites are visible on the screen, programs may not LOAD properly. The easiest way to get rid of the sprites is to press the RUN/STOP and RESTORE keys together.

A good rule to follow if you are having trouble LOADing and suspect these problems is to turn the computer off then on again.

Reason Four: If the program will not LOAD from your cassette recorder or any other you've tried, it is probably because it was recorded on bad or damaged tape. Tape quality is a difficult thing to judge. Generally, you should use a good grade of cassette tape, at least suitable for quality voice reproduction. Too much, however, has been made of the necessity to buy expensive cassettes. Some discount store and "off" brand cassettes will work perfectly well for storing programs, and you should experiment to find a good tape at a low cost. When you find a good brand, stay with it.

Damaging the tape inside a cassette can destroy a program, too. Since the program is stored as audio information, the slightest interruption in the sound will cause a bad LOAD. If you do damage a cassette, throw it away or don't use it again with the computer. Don't even try to fix it or smooth out a wrinkled portion.

## SAVE to Tape

SAVE is almost always used with a program name.

```
SAVE "PROGRAM NAME"
```

This command will store a BASIC program on cassette tape. If you do not use a name, the program will still be SAVEd, but you will not be able to identify it when LOADing. SAVE, like LOAD, will not work with certain programs—those which have been protected to avoid unauthorized copies, and certain programs that are not written in BASIC.

When you type SAVE and a program name (remember to press the RETURN key), the computer will respond with:

```
PRESS RECORD AND PLAY ON TAPE
```

When you press these two keys on the cassette recorder, the screen will go blank until the program has been SAVEd on tape.

You must remember to press both the PLAY and RECORD keys when you SAVE to tape. The computer cannot actually tell if both have been pressed, and will act the same even if you only press PLAY. (If you do, of course, the program will not be SAVEd.)

If you want to protect this copy from accidental erasure, remove the leftmost small plastic tab on the back edge of the cassette. This will prevent you from pressing RECORD and PLAY together on the recorder. If you change your mind, a piece of tape (masking tape or transparent tape) will fix the cassette so you can record on it again.

## Checking Your Work

It would be nice to know if you have successfully SAVEd your program, wouldn't it? This would insure that the program you wrote is safely stored on tape. The VERIFY command does just this. It compares what is on the tape to what is stored in the computer's memory.

If you use VERIFY with a program name, the cassette recorder will go through all programs on the tape, looking for the program with that name to compare. If you use VERIFY alone, the first program on the tape will be compared.

When a program is successfully checked, you will see the message "OK" appear on the video screen. If the program does not match, you will see this line instead:

```
? VERIFYING ERROR
```

This indicates that the tape copy of the program is not the same as what is in memory. The tape may be bad, or you may have changed something on a program line by mistake.

VERIFY can also be used to find your position on a tape. Say that you have two programs, named "PROGRAM ONE" and "PROGRAM TWO," stored on the same side of the tape. You have made some changes in "PROGRAM TWO," which is in the computer's memory, and want to SAVE it again on the tape. If you LOADed "PROGRAM ONE," the program in memory would be destroyed. You can VERIFY "PROGRAM ONE," though, and the tape will advance to the beginning of "PROGRAM TWO" without disturbing the program in memory. You will still see the above ERROR message, but you can ignore it. After this, you can SAVE "PROGRAM TWO" again and record over the previous version, as long as the changes haven't dramatically affected the length of the program. (If the program is too long, the new version will begin to record over the next program on the tape.)

## RUNning the Program

The RUN command starts a program operating. Most programs will be interrupted when the RUN/STOP key is pressed.

RUN always resets all the information in the program. (Read about variables in Chapter Four.) This means that numbers, names, and other data that a program is using will be gone the next time you RUN it. There are two ways to interrupt a program and keep the information it uses.

After using the RUN/STOP key—whether you've pressed it by mistake or on purpose—you can type the command CONT, which stands for CONTinue. (Type it directly from the keyboard and press RETURN.) The program will resume at the place where it left off.

The other way to get back into the program is with the word GOTO, which must be followed by the number of the BASIC line you want the program to begin operating from. (Again, you can use the GOTO command directly from the keyboard but remember to press RETURN.) To use GOTO, you should have a firm understanding of how the program works, either by reading REM (REMark) statements in the program or by being able to read BASIC. Don't ever try to use GOTO with a random line number if you don't know the correct number to use.

You can also use RUN with a number. This will start the program operating from that particular line number, but it will also erase all the variable information, just as using RUN by itself will.

## About Commodore's Disk Drives

The Commodore 1541 disk drive plays back and stores information to and from the computer, just like the cassette recorder does. Information is stored on the magnetic surface of a flexible ("floppy") round disk enclosed in a square black plastic envelope. Unlike the recorder, the disk drive can randomly access many different programs, much faster than from cassette. (Programs LOAD about seven times faster from disk than cassette.) Moreover, the disk allows you to select programs and files out of sequence, and eliminates the need to ever have these stored in any particular order.

In the upper right-hand corner of the black plastic envelope is a notch. This notch is used to tell the disk drive whether or not it should try to record information on the disk. If the notch is open and visible, you can LOAD and SAVE programs and data on it. When the notch is covered (usually by one of the small adhesive tabs that come with floppy disks), it is "write protected." That is, you can LOAD from the disk, but not SAVE to it.

Blank disks must first be prepared for use with the disk drive. Almost any blank disk can be used, but make sure that the disks you buy are labeled "single-sided double density." This means that only one side of the disk can be used. (Some disk drives record on both sides—your 1541 doesn't.) Double density is a holdover term from the days when the amount of information that could be stored on a disk was growing. Your 1541 disk drive isn't a "double density" drive (strictly speaking), but you should use this type of disk to avoid problems.

Other terms used to identify types of blank disks are "soft sector" or "hard sector." You needn't worry about these. Either kind will work equally well in the 1541. Any manufacturer's brand of disk can be used. As with cassettes, shop around and find one that offers good performance at a reasonable price and stick with it.

Preparing a disk is called *formatting* it. When the disk is formatted, several things are done. It is given a name and a two-character identification number. A portion of the disk is made into a directory, where the names of programs and other files will be stored. Finally, 35 *tracks* are constructed on the disk's surface. Each of these tracks is used for storing information; one particular track, number 18, is used for the directory. Each track, in turn, is divided into *sectors*, each containing 256 bytes, or characters, of information. These sectors are also called *blocks*. The total usable storage space on a disk is 664 blocks, or almost 170,000 bytes or characters.

You should understand, right from the start, that you cannot use a disk prepared on another type of computer—an Apple or Atari, for instance—on your Commodore 64, even if it contains a BASIC program that will operate on your machine. Not only does every computer have a different way of using and storing BASIC programs within it, but each also has a different way of storing information on the disk itself. (The same thing goes for cassettes. Don't even bother trying to LOAD a cassette prepared on another computer.)

Floppy disks should be treated very gently. Even though the fragile nature of floppy disks is usually exaggerated (they do stand up to everyday handling quite well), it is easy to damage the information on the disk itself. Handling and storage tips are packed with most commercial brands of blank disks, but a few are always worth repeating.

- Never touch the surface of the disk visible in either of the cut-out holes in the outside plastic envelope. Be particularly careful of the hole on the bottom side of the disk; that's the side the 1541 records on. Don't ever bend the disk, either.
- When not using it, always keep the disk inside its protective paper envelope. Keep your disks in a box or other storage container and away from tobacco smoke, dust, and dirt which could ruin the information stored on them. Make sure that disks are stored in a cool, dry place. (Not, for example, in a car with the windows rolled up on a summer day.)
- Keep the disks away from magnets or any strong magnetic fields like those given off by electrical transformers in stereo amplifiers or television sets.

# Using the Disk Drive

On the front of the disk drive are two colored lights. (They're actually LEDs, or **L**ight **E**mitting **D**iodes.) The green light indicates that the disk drive is turned on. The red light tells you two things: It will stay on or flash on and off occasionally when the disk drive is LOADing or SAVEing. When the red light flashes on and off regularly and the motor has stopped running (you won't hear its familiar whirr), it indicates an ERROR. Always watch this light when using the disk drive.

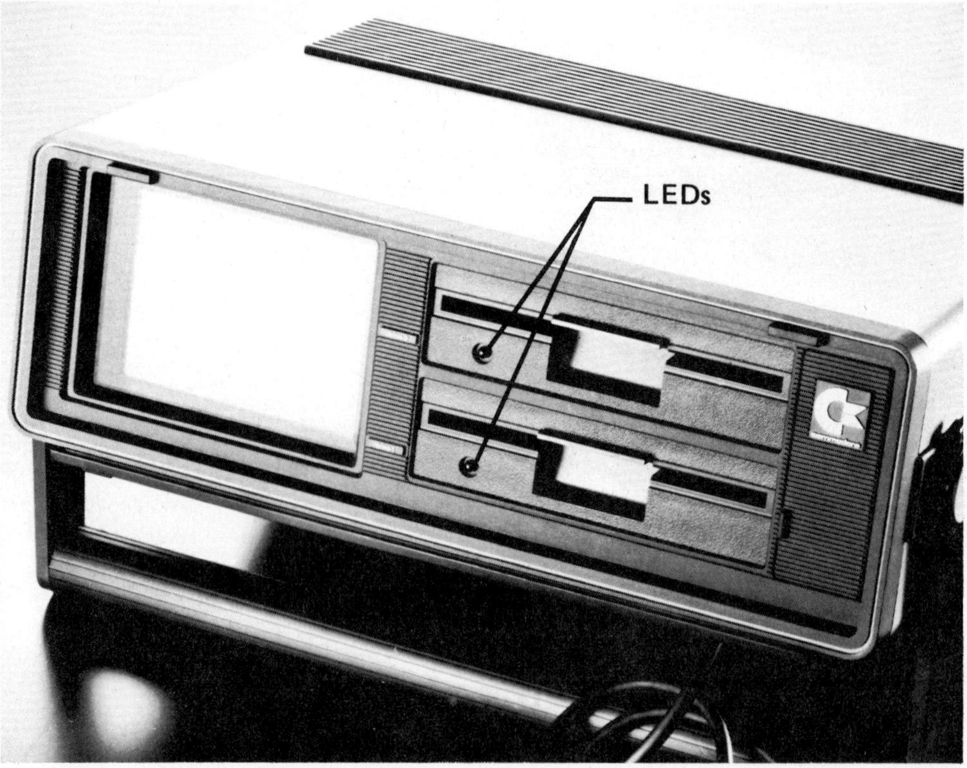


You should have the disk that comes packed with each 1541 disk drive. It is called VIC-1541 TEST/DEMO. In addition to some test programs, it contains a program called "Wedge" or DOS Manager. This program is so useful that you will not want to be without it. (The test programs on this disk are an absolute necessity, too. RUN them to evaluate your disk drive and return it to your dealer if the drive does not pass these tests.)

Wedge lets you easily LOAD programs, see the disk directory, erase (scratch) programs and files, format the disk, and read disk ERRORs. It is called Wedge for two reasons: Its commands are "shoehorned," or wedged into the computer's operating system. It also uses a special character— ">"—the "greater than" sign before each disk command. The name DOS Manager comes from the fact that this little program manages the machine's **D**isk **O**perating **S**ystem, a program that runs the whole disk show.

You can do things with Wedge that are difficult to do using conventional disk commands. As we go along, you'll see the proper BASIC form for these commands.

To LOAD Wedge, open the door on the disk drive, insert the disk with the label up and the open windows to the rear, then carefully close the door by gently pulling the tab-like latch down and toward you. Then type

LOAD "C-64 WEDGE",8 [and press the RETURN key]

The computer should respond with:

```
SEARCHING FOR C-64 WEDGE
LOADING
READY.
```

You will hear the disk drive spinning and the RED light will come on. If you notice, LOADing from disk is almost exactly the same as LOADing from tape. The exception is the addition of a comma and the number 8.

All devices like cassette recorders, disk drives, printers and modems, or telephone links are given identifying numbers in a Commodore system. These numbers are set inside each device. The cassette recorder is always number 1. The printer is almost always device number 4. The disk drive comes from Commodore's factory as device number 8. So, when you tell the computer to LOAD "C-64 WEDGE",8 you're telling it to LOAD from device number 8, the disk drive.

When the computer comes back with READY, type RUN. The red light on the disk drive should come on again, letting you know that another program is being LOADed. (The purpose of the first part of the Wedge program is to LOAD the next one.) You won't need to type RUN again. Instead, you'll see a message that confirms Wedge has been LOADed. It will say:

DOS MANAGER (then a version number)
BY BOB FAIRBAIRN

Until the machine is turned off, you'll have Wedge in the machine, sitting in a part of memory where it will not be disturbed by most BASIC programs. It will continue to be in the computer even after you reset it using the RUN/STOP and RESTORE keys.

## The Disk Directory

If you walk into a building and want to know where a certain office is located, you look at the building directory. You can see what is on a disk by looking at its directory, too. It tells you the name of the disk, its two-character ID number, the program names, and the number of empty blocks, or sectors, left on it. Here is a sample of what a disk directory looks like. (It will differ, of course, from disk to disk.)

```
0 "1541TEST/DEMO      " ZX 2A
13     "HOW TO USE"        PRG
5      "HOW PART TWO"      PRG
4      "VIC-20 WEDGE"      PRG
1      "C-64 WEDGE"        PRG
4      "DOS 5.1"           PRG
11     "MAIL"              SEQ
47     "DATA BASE"         PRG
579 BLOCKS FREE
```

The first number on the top line is the *drive number*. This is a carryover from a previous Commodore disk drive system which had two drives which were numbered Drive 0 and Drive 1. Since the Commodore 64 so closely resembles its predecessors, it still thinks of your 1541 disk drive as Drive 0. Remember this because you'll find this drive number useful with other disk commands.

Next on that line is the name of the disk, in this case "1541TEST/DEMO." The next two letters, ZX, are the disk's ID. This is part of the directory required by the disk drive. Each disk must have its own *unique* two-character ID. The 2A refers to the version of Commodore's disk operating system—the program that runs the disk drive—that wrote the disk. For now, it's unimportant.

The numbers in the left-hand column show how many blocks or sectors on the disk are used for each program. In the middle is the program name, followed by a three-letter abbreviation. This abbreviation indicates whether it is a program or another kind of file. Only programs with the abbreviation PRG can be LOADed directly from disk. If the abbreviation after the name is SEQ or REL (for "sequential" or "relative" files), it is an information file, not a program file, and must be recalled by another program specifically designed to use this data. (See "How the Computer Stores Information.")

Finally, at the bottom of the directory is the number of blocks or disk sectors left for storage.

You can see the disk directory using either Wedge or a BASIC command. You have already seen how to LOAD a program from disk when you LOADed Wedge. You use LOAD with a program name, followed by a comma and the number 8 (",8"). If you remember, you use the "greater than" sign (">") with a Wedge command. (For your convenience, you can also use another character, the commercial "at" symbol—"@"—with Wedge.) Type either of these disk directory commands:

```
LOAD "$",8
```

or

```
>$ (or @$)
```

Both of these do the same thing—they allow you to see the disk directory. When you use the BASIC form—LOAD "$",8—the directory will be LOADed into the computer's memory. To see it, you must type LIST (and press RETURN). LOADing a directory this way always destroys whatever is in the computer's memory, including any BASIC program that may be there.

It is better, then, to use the Wedge version—>$ or @$—because Wedge transfers the directory directly from the disk to the video screen without destroying the program in memory.

If the disk is blank and not formatted, you will not see any directory. Instead, the disk will spin and you might even hear a grinding noise or two from it. Then, the red ERROR light will begin flashing.

## Preparing a Disk

You can prepare a new disk using either BASIC or Wedge. Since the 1541 disk drive is "smart" (it has its own microprocessor chip, memory, and a program inside that runs it), it can look at a group of commands and perform the correct disk operation. The commands are letters, punctuation marks, and numbers inside the quote marks that contain the program or disk name. For example, this is the way you prepare a disk using BASIC commands typed from the keyboard:

```
OPEN 1,8,15
PRINT#1,"N0:DISK NAME,ID"
```

The first command that you typed—OPEN 1,8,15—is the way that you tell the disk drive to get ready for a special disk operation, like formatting and naming the disk. The first of the three numbers after OPEN—1—is called a *file number*. Though it can be any number between 0 and 255, there's no real reason to use a number other than 1 if you're just preparing disks. The second number —8—is the device number. It means that we're talking to the disk drive. The last number is called a *secondary address*. You'll read more about secondary addresses in another part of this book called "How the Computer Stores Information." For the time being, however, you should understand that the number 15 is always used by the system to tell the disk to prepare for a special command.

It is a good idea to CLOSE the file you have OPENed after you are done with it, especially if you will be using information files in your programs. Just type:

```
CLOSE 1
```

Again, you will learn more about the how's and why's of OPEN and CLOSE in "How the Computer Stores Information."

Inside the quotes, the numbers and letters form a code for the disk drive to understand. "N" tells the disk that the special operation will be to prepare or format a *N*ew disk. The next character is the number 0 (zero), which tells the disk drive you'll be using drive 0. (If you recall, your drive is always drive 0 since the 1541 is a single disk drive unit.) The colon—":"—is a necessary punctuation mark that separates that command from the disk name. (Here called DISK NAME.)

Following another punctuation mark, a comma, is the disk's ID mark, a two-character identification mark that Commodore disks require. You should try to make each ID mark unique. In the example, the ID is of course ID.

You can begin to see the advantage of using Wedge for your disk commands by its simple way of preparing a new disk.

```
>N0:DISK NAME,ID
```

With Wedge, you don't need either the OPEN, PRINT#, or CLOSE command to format a new disk. Notice, too, that you no longer need the quotation marks around the command letters, numbers, and name.

Preparing a disk takes a few minutes. So if your disk drive seems to be going forever and the red light stays on, don't worry. Everything is going as it should. When the disk drive has finished its preparations, the red light will go out and the video screen will say READY. Check your disk by looking at the directory. It should look like this:

```
0 "DISK NAME       " ID 2A
664 BLOCKS FREE
```

Of course, the disk name and ID mark you choose will be there instead of the ones used in this example.

## LOAD from Disk

LOADing a program from disk is about as simple as LOADing from cassette, with a few exceptions. Remember that you can only LOAD a program off the disk if it really is a program, indicated by the PRG abbreviation. You can always look at the disk directory, then use this command:

```
LOAD "DISK NAME",8
```

If you choose to type in the entire program name, you must type it exactly as it is shown on the directory. If you do not, the computer will respond with a FILE NOT FOUND ERROR and the red light on the front of the disk drive will flash on and off regularly. If you're lazy—or, in fairness, just want to save time and effort, like everyone else—you can use a shortcut.

Just as you can LOAD a cassette program with only the first few letters of the name, you can do the same with disk programs. Instead of omitting the last quotation mark, you'll use an asterisk—"*"—and close the quotes.

Commodore's designers were very clever in the way they have used the asterisk to make using the disk drive easier. Here are the rules for its use:

- When you begin using the disk drive, LOAD "*",8 will LOAD the first program listed on the disk directory. (This can be especially handy if the first program is always Wedge, for example.)
- After LOADing any program, LOAD "*",8 will always LOAD that program again, even if it was not the first program.
- Using the asterisk in any program name will have the effect of LOADing the first program on the directory whose name matches the letters that come before it. Example: LOAD "PRO*",8 will LOAD programs

named PROGRAM, PROGRAM ONE, PROGRAM TWO, PROFESSIONAL, etc.

Wedge lets you LOAD programs two different ways. (You can always use the asterisk with Wedge commands, too.)

To LOAD a program, you can use:

```
/PROGRAM NAME
```

The character is a "slash," found on the same key as the question mark. It LOADs a program and waits for you to type RUN to start it operating.

You can automatically LOAD and RUN the program with another Wedge command:

[Up Arrow] `PROGRAM NAME`

You don't type the words "Up Arrow," of course. Instead, you press the "up arrow" key on the keyboard, which is located in the second row from the top between the asterisk and RESTORE keys. When a BASIC program is LOADed, the computer will then immediately start the program.

Some programs will require a LOADing procedure to LOAD them in a specific place in the computer's memory. Usually, these are programs that are not written in BASIC. This LOAD command looks like this:

```
LOAD "PROGRAM NAME",8,1
```

The last number 1 tells the computer to LOAD the program, not in the place where BASIC programs are usually stored, but in the place in memory where they must reside to operate properly. If you have used a Commodore PET or CBM computer, you will recognize that this is a different procedure from what you're used to. (With those machines, no special LOAD command is needed. Programs always LOAD in their proper place.)

The equivalent command in Wedge looks like this:

```
% "PROGRAM NAME"
```

In almost every case, you will be specifically told to use this LOAD command with the programs that require it. If you aren't told to LOAD this way, use the conventional form or Wedge commands above.

## SAVE and VERIFY

You SAVE a program to disk just like you SAVE a program to cassette tape. The only difference is the addition of the comma and the device number 8.

```
SAVE "PROGRAM NAME",8
```

If you are using Wedge, SAVE a program using the "left arrow" key found at the top left corner of the keyboard.

[Press the left arrow key] `"PROGRAM NAME"`

You can also use the drive number (0) when you SAVE a program.

```
SAVE "0:PROGRAM NAME",8
```

With cassette tape, you can always rewind the tape and record a new version of the program over the last one. Since you cannot rewind a disk, a particular character is used to record over a program with the same name. This character is the commercial "at" symbol, "@." It is used before the program name and is separated from it by a colon.

```
SAVE "@:PROGRAM NAME",8
```

or

```
SAVE "@0:PROGRAM NAME",8
```

You must be careful to type the name exactly as it appears on the disk directory, or you will not SAVE over the original program.

You can check your work to make sure the disk has SAVEd any program correctly. Use VERIFY with the program name and the device number 8.

```
VERIFY "PROGRAM NAME",8
```

Since the asterisk can be used instead of the last name recognized by the disk drive, you can SAVE the program with the proper name, then immediately VERIFY it with the asterisk.

```
VERIFY "*",8
```

If the program has not been SAVEd correctly, you will see a VERIFY ERROR message on the video screen.

## Erasing Disk Files

Even though a single disk can hold almost 170,000 bytes, you'll find that disks fill up quickly with early versions of programs, miscellaneous information files and programs that you just don't want anymore. You can erase—or "scratch"—these programs and files to make room on the disk for others.

Like formatting or preparing a disk, scratching programs and files can be done either from BASIC or with Wedge.

```
OPEN 1,8,15
PRINT#1,"S0:PROGRAM NAME",8
```

or

```
>S0:PROGRAM NAME
```

# Validate the Disk

Unlike a cassette tape, the disk is a complicated organization of information with pieces of programs scattered about tracks and sectors, and something called the Block Availability Map (BAM) which maintains the overall order. Occasionally, the total number of blocks used for programs and information files and the number of free blocks won't add up to the magic number of 664 blocks or sectors.

Essentially, the disk is messy, even though it may continue to work properly. You run the risk, however, of further disorganizing it and losing a valuable program or file. To clean up the disk and restore order, you can "validate" it, using either BASIC or Wedge. It is a good idea to validate your disks from time to time, or whenever you spot a potential problem.

```
OPEN 1,8,15
PRINT#1,"V"
```

or

```
PRINT#1,"V0"
```

With Wedge, use this command:

```
>V
```

or

```
>V0
```

# Disk ERRORs

You know there is a problem with the disk drive whenever the red light flashes on and off regularly. A disk ERROR has occurred, although you can't tell what kind of ERROR it is since a message doesn't appear on the video screen. And, the light will continue flashing until you find out what the ERROR is. So how do you find out?

The solution to this problem isn't an easy one if you are not using Wedge.

First, try intentionally causing a disk ERROR by asking for a program that doesn't exist.

```
LOAD "MMFPLTSK",8
```

Unless you actually have a program with this name (which is unlikely), the red disk light will regularly flash on and off. Now type in this little program exactly as it appears and RUN it.

```
10 OPEN 1,8,15
20 INPUT#1,A$,B$,C$,D$
30 PRINT A$,B$,C$,D$
40 CLOSE 1
```

The video screen should look like this:

```
62 FILE NOT FOUND 00 00
```

The first number is the ERROR number which is spelled out to the right, FILE NOT FOUND. The next two numbers are the track and sector numbers where the ERROR occurred. (These aren't used for the FILE NOT FOUND ERROR.)

Typing in this program, however, is inconvenient, and sometimes you can't use it because a program is already in memory. The best way to see disk ERRORs, then, is to use Wedge. Just type the "greater than" (">") symbol anytime you see the red disk light flashing on and off. You will see the same information, the ERROR number, ERROR message, and track and sector numbers where the ERROR occurred.

## Some Disk Cautions

Using Commodore's disk drive is much more convenient than using the cassette recorder. And since it offers advantages in addition to speed, it makes your computer system much more powerful.

No system, however, is perfect, and the 1541 disk drive is no exception to this rule. A few cautions when using the disk drive are in order.

- If you forget to close the door on the disk drive, you will see a FILE NOT FOUND ERROR message on the video screen. Even after closing the door, trying to LOAD the same program may not work, and you'll see the same ERROR. Open the door on the disk drive, take the disk out, and reinsert it. This usually solves the problem.
- If you want to use two disk drives, one must be assigned a device number other than 8. Unless you have electronic experience, ask your dealer to change the device number for you, since it requires cutting a piece of the printed circuitry inside. Once you have both drives connected to your computer, always remember to turn on the power to the computer *last*. This way, it will properly recognize both drives. If you forget, press the RUN/STOP and RESTORE keys together to "wake up" the system.
- Be careful when using the same floppy disk in both your 1541 and the original Commodore 4040 dual disk drive units. Although they are supposed to be, the two machines are not always compatible. The problem lies with the disk operating system inside some 1541 drives. This can be identified by any good computer dealer. Until you know if you have a 1541 in which the problem has been corrected, never mix disk drives. In other words, if a disk has been created on a 1541 drive, don't record on the same disk in a 4040 drive unit. It could spell disaster.
- Some 1541 disk drives come from the Commodore factory slightly out of adjustment. The problem is usually speed. Always check your drive

with the "Performance Test" program on the disk furnished with your 1541. Then try your disk on another 1541. If it LOADs smoothly, everything is probably all right. If it doesn't, you may have an adjustment problem. Usually this has to do with the speed at which the disk rotates. Though it is possible to do the job yourself (there is a "strobe" pattern and a tiny adjustment on the bottom of the drive itself), you should take the disk drive back to your dealer for this adjustment.

- If you need, for any reason, to bring the 1541 into a dealer for repair or adjustment, have him check the metal pulley that connects the spindle to the motor with a belt. On some disk drives, this pulley will work itself loose and fall off. If you happen to be recording a program or file to the disk when this happens, it could ruin your disk and destroy valuable information. Ask your dealer to make certain this pulley fits tightly or have him make the necessary repairs.
- Never block the ventilation holes on the plastic case of the 1541 drive. This means don't pile papers and books on top, covering the vent slots, and don't put the drive on carpeting or any other surface that will block the vents underneath. It is quite easy for the drive to overheat and ruin sensitive electronic parts inside.

## Commodore LOAD Compatibility

One of the nicest features of the Commodore 64 family is its ability to use programs written for other Commodore computers, the PET, CBM, and VIC. Unfortunately, the computers are not 100% compatible. Programs that will *not* RUN on the Commodore 64 include:

- Most programs written in a language other than BASIC.
- BASIC programs with machine references, usually PEEK and POKE commands.
- Programs that were written for the VIC's 22 character-wide screen.
- Programs written with commands from Commodore 4.0 BASIC.

This probably looks like there aren't many programs that are interchangeable among machines. That's not exactly so, although you'll need to experiment to find out which transfer successfully.

Among the programs written on a Commodore 64 computer that will not work correctly on a PET, VIC, or CBM are:

- Most programs written in a language other than BASIC.
- Many programs that use color commands, and almost all programs that use 64 sound techniques.

In addition:

- Programs that use the function keys will not transfer to the PET and CBM, but may work on the VIC.

- Programs with screen widths wider than 40 characters will not transfer to the VIC.
- Programs that take up more than 32K of memory won't work on the VIC (even when its memory is expanded), CBM, or PET.

For LOADing some programs from the PET and CBM into a Commodore 64 computer, you'll need a little program called a "PET Emulator." One, written by Bob Fairbairn, is available through Commodore. (At press time, price and method of distribution were uncertain.) Fairbairn has designed the program so that it RUNs PET software written for Commodore 2.0 BASIC (which is closest to the version inside the 64 computer family). The Emulator will even allow the 64 to use PET-style sound effects, includes the Wedge DOS Manager program, and LOADs from disk.

The PET Emulator does not allow you to RUN all existing PET software, though. (Two of the most popular PET/CBM programs, "VisiCalc" and "WordPro" will *not* run.) You'll have to experiment to see which programs will work.

Three quick commands are all that are necessary to LOAD programs written on a Commodore 64 into a PET or CBM computer. On the PET or CBM, type these:

```
POKE 41,8
POKE 2048,0
NEW
```

Then LOAD your 64 program. Again, not every 64 program will RUN correctly on the PET and CBM.

## Using Your Computer as a Calculator

It is possible to use the very powerful mathematical features of the Commodore 64 as a calculator without the need to write a program. On a conventional pocket calculator, you start an equation from the beginning and end with an equal sign ("="), like this:

$$12+484.25=$$

The only difference when using the computer is that you skip the equal sign and, instead, ask for the answer with the PRINT command.

`PRINT 12+484.25` [and press RETURN]

The answer will appear on the next line on the video screen.

You can also use *variables* directly from the keyboard. If you don't know what variables are, you'll learn about them in the first chapter on BASIC programming. Type this:

```
A=484.25
PRINT 12+A
```

Use the standard plus (+) and minus (−) signs for addition and subtraction. Use the asterisk (*) for multiplication and the slash mark (/) for division. Negative numbers are preceded by a minus sign; exponential numbers by the "up arrow" symbol. Square root is available with the word SQR. The computer also supports "less than" and "greater than" symbols (< >), and so-called logical operators AND, OR, NOT. There are also the trigonometric functions SIN (sine), COS (cosine), TAN (tangent), ATN (arctangent) and LOG (logarithm). You use these words with object numbers that are enclosed in parentheses. For instance, you can get the square root of 2 by typing:

```
PRINT SQR (2)
```

Parentheses can also be used, as in paper mathematics, to enclose a complete thought within an equation.

```
PRINT (12+484.25)*53
```

This equation first adds 12 and 484.25 then multiplies it by 53.

Two quick cautions: Never use commas in numbers more than three digits (1000 instead of 1,000); and, don't try to use equations longer than 80 characters, or two screen lines, directly from the keyboard.

If you do not plan to use the machine as a calculator or program it for "number crunching," don't be frightened by these functions. Just remember they are there if you need them.

A shorthand form of the word PRINT is available. The question mark (?) can be used instead of typing out the entire word PRINT every time. Try it. You'll hear about it again in the first chapter on BASIC programming and see a caution about it in the chapter about data handling.

## How Much Memory Is Left?

You know that the Commodore 64 has over 64,000 bytes, or characters, of memory inside it. From the message you see when you turn the machine on, you also probably know that 38,911 of these are available for programming in BASIC. (The programming techniques and not BASIC.)

While programming, or after LOADing a program into memory from tape or disk, you can ask the computer how much of its memory is still available. You ask it to PRINT the number of free bytes.

```
PRINT FRE(0)
```

The word FRE means FREe bytes. Any number or letter can be inside the parentheses. (Since it makes no difference, this is called a "dummy.") The number that appears on the screen is the number of FREe bytes minus 3. The command PRINT FRE(0), you see, takes 3 bytes by itself.

If the number you see on the screen is a negative number (it is preceded by a minus sign), you must do a little arithmetic and subtract it from 65536. This number is actually the 64K you hear about all the time, since 1K of memory (computer jargon for a thousand bytes) is actually 1,024 bytes.

(This is apparently a tiny mistake in the design of the Commodore 64. The routine that returns the number of FREe bytes is the same as in the PET, but the 64 has twice the memory.)

## Beware the Quote Marks

A good way to familiarize yourself with the Commodore 64 editing functions—the CRSR right and left keys and INST/DEL key—is to practice typing on the keyboard. An even better way is to type in all the BASIC programming examples and programs in this book. Practice is the only way to grow accustomed to the excellent screen editing system built into the computer. (If you get a chance to use other personal computers, you'll soon realize just how good the 64 is.)

It's easy to get yourself into a situation where it looks like you're stuck or you've broken the computer. (You're not and you haven't.) This will happen after you type one set of quote marks (") or an odd number of quote marks. Here's what happens.

When typing a line, you type the quote mark, intentionally or unintentionally. You change your mind and use a CRSR key to make a correction. Instead, you see a funny-looking symbol. What's going on?

You're in something called the "quote mode." This means that seven of the eight editing functions work differently. CLR (clear the screen), HOME ("home" the cursor), CRSR right, left, up, down, and INST (insert) all leave these odd symbols instead of working as they should. Only DEL (delete) works the same and allows you to erase the quote mark or anything else you've typed. The reason for this is discussed in Chapter 4 on BASIC programming about the word PRINT. In brief, when these editing functions are used within quotes and with the word PRINT in a BASIC program, they work at the time the program is RUN.

Even though the DEL key will erase what you've typed by mistake, you'll still be in the quote mode. You will remain that way until you either type another quote mark or press the RETURN key. Or, if you don't want to enter what you've written into the computer's memory, you can press the SHIFT and RETURN keys together. (The computer won't recognize SHIFT and RETURN as the signal to enter the line.)

Another problem could seem to appear, though, if you go back to the line and *want* to get into the quote mode when a program demands it. The solution is to position the cursor over the place where the first quote mark should be, then type a new first quote.

With a little experience, the quote mode won't seem as awkward as it does reading about it. The key to this dilemma is to remember that you are always in the quote mode after typing *odd numbers* of quotes in a single program line.

## What Time Is It?

There's a clock inside each Commodore 64 computer. It starts when you turn the machine on, and stops when you turn it off.

This clock is represented by the initials TI and TI$. These are known as "reserved variables"—variables because they stand for other information, reserved because you cannot use TI or TI$ in any other way. The computer thinks of TI as a number and TI$ as a string of characters. (You'll learn about variables and strings in the pages ahead.)

To see the numbers in the computer's clock, type this:

```
PRINT TI$
```

You should see a number six digits long, something like 012236, for example. What do they mean?

Think of these six digits as three groups of two numbers each—01 22 36. The first two numbers, 01, represent the number of hours since the computer was turned on. The second set, 22, represents the minutes, and the third set, 36, the seconds. So the computer has been on 1 hour 22 minutes and 36 seconds.

Since turning the computer off and on again is not a very good way to reset the clock, you can do it from the keyboard. Type this:

```
TI$="000000"
```

Now ask the computer to PRINT TI$ again. The numbers you see should be close to 000000. Try this:

```
TI$="020510"
```

When you type PRINT TI$ now, the time will begin advancing from 2 hours 5 minutes and 10 seconds because that's what you've set it to.

You can use TI$ this way, or in a BASIC program, reading the clock and resetting it under program control. You must remember to use the quote marks surrounding the time you are setting the clock to, otherwise an ERROR message will appear.

This clock is often referred to as the "real time" clock, because it keeps *real time*. That's logical, isn't it? It is a 24-hour clock, meaning that if you set it to 00 00 00 at midnight, it would read 13 00 00 at 1 o'clock pm, and 23 00 00 at 11 o'clock at night.

A major caution about the real time clock is that it *stops* while the cassette recorder is LOADing or SAVEing programs or other information. Actually, the clock stops each time the screen is blanked, for whatever reason. This means that you should only use it between cassette operations.

There's another clock inside the computer, though it is less useful for timekeeping. It is called the "jiffy" clock, a so-called jiffy being 1/60th of a second. It starts from 0 (zero) and keeps going until it reaches 51,839,999 jiffies, then resets to 0. If you use the jiffy clock, don't be too concerned that it will reset in the middle of something you're keeping track of. Fifty-one million jiffies is over 230 hours.

You can see the time in jiffies by typing this:

```
PRINT TI
```

The number that appears on the screen is the number of jiffies since the machine was turned on. If you divide it by 60, you'll get the total number of seconds the machine has been on. If you divide it by 3600 (60 times 60), you'll get the total number of minutes, and so on.

The jiffy clock cannot be reset by making TI equal to 0 (zero). Instead, it is reset by setting TI$ to "000000."

# 4

# Programming—An Introduction

In the not too distant past, anyone who could program a computer was considered to be a "genius," or worse, in possession of magical powers. In reality, these people only knew the computer's capabilities and how to break a large problem down into smaller parts. They also knew the language of the computer, just as they knew their own language.

Today, people who can program a computer are no longer considered special, only skilled. Many more people can program computers than those who choose to make their living at it. This is a skill that can enhance your life and can be used personally, as well as professionally. Taken solely as an intellectual exercise, there are few challenges as rewarding as learning to program.

Learning how to use only a few simple words, you will begin to acquire this skill and discover how to make the computer do some very impressive things.

After reading this section, you will know something about what a computer program is, how the computer stores words and numbers, and how the word PRINT works.

A word of encouragement: If you are new to programming, you will be surprised at how much you can do after learning to use only a few words.

Lines of BASIC programming are offered as examples throughout this book. Each time you want to see how one of these examples works, you will need to clear the computer's memory and make it ready for a new program. Unless you are told otherwise in the text, type NEW and press the RETURN key for each new example you want to try for yourself.

While you are learning BASIC you are almost certain to make mistakes. This is a normal part of the process and you shouldn't get frustrated by the problems you encounter. For every mistake just retype the example and try again.

Scattered throughout the next few sections on programming (as well as other parts of this book) you'll find information on ERROR messages. ERROR messages are the computer's way of telling you that you've made a mistake. Each ERROR and its possible causes are described, as well as hints for correcting it. The reasons behind ERRORs are sometimes very subtle and your best clue to them, overall, is that the computer is literal and exacting in its demands.

## Basically BASIC

The computer language that the Commodore computers use most commonly is called BASIC. It was developed by John Kemeny and Thomas Kurtz in the 1960s and introduced at Dartmouth College to offer people an alternative to computer languages that were considered less than "human." With few exceptions, its words are English words or clear derivations of them.

The name BASIC is an acronym for **B**eginners' **A**ll-purpose **S**ymbolic **I**nstruction **C**ode. It is not the "basic" computer language on which others are built, but rather a collection of simple, useful commands. Nor is BASIC the most powerful computer language. There are others better suited to certain particular uses. One computer language, FORTRAN, is especially good for recordkeeping and mathematics. Another, called COBOL, is said to be good for compiling statistical information. The language known as LISP is well suited for keeping and updating lists and for artificial intelligence experiments.

Like any language, BASIC has its own *vocabulary* (the BASIC words) and *syntax*, which is the proper way to use them.

BASIC is good for introducing people to computers and for general programming. Although almost any program can be written in BASIC, other languages may require less effort, use less memory, or may run more quickly.

A word about speed: The version of BASIC in Commodore computers is called an *interpreted* BASIC. This means that the computer looks at each step in the program, item by item, and does what it is told. Another kind of BASIC is called *compiled* BASIC. The program is converted to another set of numbers that the machine can execute much more quickly. Programs converted with a BASIC compiler run much faster than with the version built into your Commodore computer.

To find out more about a compiled BASIC for the Commodore 64 family, look at the section of this book entitled "Beyond BASIC." It includes information on a BASIC compiler available for your computer.

Commodore BASIC is a version of the language originally written for the company by Microsoft, a Bellevue, Washington programming group. It was first written for the MITS Altair, an early personal computer that is no longer manufactured. Since its introduction, Microsoft BASIC has gone on to become closest to a "standard" version of BASIC for tiny computers.

Still, there are differences in the versions of BASIC that Microsoft has designed for the TRS-80, the Apple II, and other machines. Most BASIC words function the same in all these computers, but there are still many significant variations from machine to machine. So a program written in the Commodore version of Microsoft BASIC won't necessarily run correctly on an Apple, and vice versa. This isn't your computer's fault; it is just a fact of life.

**All BASICs are not equal.**

Commodore has also modified its first Microsoft BASIC over the years, and each generation of its computers used slight variations of the original. For example, early Commodore PET computers had a BASIC with certain annoying mistakes, or "bugs" in it. When Commodore introduced an upgraded version of the PET, it also upgraded the BASIC to fix some of these bugs. The version of Commodore BASIC used in the 64 family is closest to this upgraded revision, called V2, or version #2.

## A Program Defined

A computer program is a list of things that the computer should do. Remember that the program takes a large task and breaks it down into smaller ones.

Take, as an example, the list of things to do—the "program"—for making a TV dinner.

1. Pre-heat the oven to 400 degrees.
2. Take the frozen dinner out of the box.
3. Put it in the oven.
4. Wait 45 minutes.
5. Unwrap and eat.

Or at least that's what it says to do on the box. In reality, you may choose to do things a bit differently. You might check first to see if the oven is heating up properly, and if it isn't, then determine the cause of the problem. This TV dinner "program," then, could be rewritten to ask questions like "is the stove in working condition?"

So, too, can a computer program perform these kinds of tests, ask questions, and make decisions.

## Numbering and Listing

Just like the TV dinner example, a BASIC program is a numbered list of instructions. Since BASIC is a language, you can think of each line of instructions as a kind of sentence. Each line in Commodore BASIC is given a number from 0 to 63999. (The computer won't accept program lines numbered any higher.)

You can see the complete list of program lines inside the computer by typing the word LIST and pressing the RETURN key. The lines will appear one after another on the screen, so quickly that you can't usually read them. To slow down the LIST, press the CTRL (control) key. The LIST will continue, but it will slow down considerably.

(While you have the CTRL key depressed, you can press the SPACE bar to speed up the LISTing again. Pressing CTRL also slows the speed at which most BASIC programs RUN.)

Pressing the RUN/STOP key while a program is LISTing to the screen will freeze the action altogether and READY will appear. (You'll need to type LIST to get going again.) LIST can also be used to see only the lines or portions of the program you want to see. Some examples:

| *Type* | *The Computer Lists* |
|---|---|
| LIST | All program lines in computer memory |
| LIST 100 | Only program line 100 |
| LIST 100 - 150 | All program lines numbered between 100 and 150 |
| LIST - 150 | All program lines up to and including line 150 |
| LIST 150 - | All program lines beginning with line 150 |

If you can't remember the exact numbers of the program lines you're looking for, don't worry. The third, fourth, and fifth examples use the numbers only as a range. So if there is no line 100 or 150, LIST will still print out lines numbered between 100 and 150, like 101 or 149.

Usually, when writing a program, you begin with a line number higher than 0 so that, if you wish, you can later add new lines before the first one you wrote. Likewise, good BASIC programmers tend to leave gaps between numbers so that other lines can always be inserted between existing lines later on. It is a good idea to number program lines in increments of ten, so that you have enough room for these kinds of insertions.

Each line of Commodore BASIC can be longer than a single line on the video screen. Including the line number, each can be up to 80 characters long. (Since the video screen is 40 characters wide, this is the equivalent of two lines on the screen.)

When you begin programming, make sure the computer's memory is clear. Either type the word NEW and press the RETURN key, or turn the machine off then on again to enter the command. (Try to avoid turning the computer on and off too often. This can be hard on its electronic components.) This readies the computer for a new program and voids any previous program that may have been in the machine. Start a program line with a number, followed by the appropriate BASIC instructions. Pressing the RETURN key will enter that line into memory. Pressing RETURN is essential. Until you do so, the program line is only on the video screen.

While typing, you can go anywhere in the program line (up to two screen lines long) and edit it with the INST/DEL and CRSR (cursor) keys. The screen editor built into the computer is designed to always keep track of what you are doing.

Once RETURN is pressed and the line is entered into memory, the cursor will automatically move to the next available line on the screen. If you have made a mistake or have changed your mind about entering the line you're working on, either move the cursor to the next line on the screen or hold down the SHIFT and press RETURN. (If you press SHIFT and RETURN, the cursor will jump to the next line, but you'll "fool" the computer and the line will not be entered.)

Remember that 80 characters is the longest BASIC line you can enter. If you go over this limit, the computer will not accept what you've typed.

To eliminate unwanted program lines, type the line number all by itself, then press RETURN. To get rid of line 100, for example, just type `100` on a blank line and press RETURN. When you try to LIST that line, it will no longer appear.

Using the very powerful editing features of the Commodore computers, you can also duplicate lines or portions of lines. Type the BASIC line:

```
10 PRINT "LINE 10"
```

Press RETURN to enter it. Now move the cursor back up to the line and change the line number to 20, then change the number 10 (in quotes) to 20, as well. Pressing RETURN will enter the line as if it were a brand new one.

LIST the program and you will see both lines. This handy feature allows you to enter several similar lines easily, and takes much of the drudgery out of programming in BASIC.

## The END

Many computers that use BASIC insist that the word END be used at the end of a program. The purpose of this word is obvious: END simply makes the program quit running. While it is probably good programming form to use END, Commodore BASIC doesn't require this word.

However, there are logical reasons to use END other than on the last line of the program. These will be explained as you begin to understand how programs are written and how BASIC works.

## Variables: How the Computer Keeps Its Facts Straight

How does a computer know what we mean when we ask it for the total of a grocery bill, or when we ask it for the answer to a question? How does it know which facts are which?

A BASIC program must give names to every piece of information that the computer will deal with, whether they are numbers, words, sentences, or even pictures. These names are called *variable* names, because the information they stand for can always be changed. Variables come in two varieties: Names that stand for numbers (and numbers only) and names that stand for letters and other symbols. Here are some examples of variable names:

```
A=10.20
A$="THIS IS MY COMMODORE COMPUTER"
AB=4096
AB$="THIS IS ANOTHER COMPUTER"
A2=45.50
A2$="45.50"
```

The computer knows the information on the right side of the equal sign (=) by the name given to it on the left side. Ask for what A is, and the computer will answer 10.20. Ask what AB$ stands for, and it will give you the sentence "THIS IS ANOTHER COMPUTER," etc.

Names for letters and numbers are recognized by Commodore BASIC as being one or two characters long. The first character must always be a letter. The second can be a number or a letter. So, a variable name can be a single letter (A=10.20), two letters (AB=4096), or a letter and a number (A2=45.50). For obvious reasons—it would confuse the computer—a variable name cannot be two numbers (like 22=25).

Names that stand for numbers are called *numeric* variables. (A=10.20, AB=4096 and A2=45.50 from the above list.)

Names that stand for words, sentences, or other symbols are called *string* variables. They are always followed by a dollar sign ($). (A$="THIS IS MY...," AB$="THIS IS ANOTHER..." and A2$="45.50" from the list.)

It should be obvious by looking at them that strings—called that because the computer sees them simply as characters strung together—are always enclosed in quotation marks ("). Numbers can be part of a string, but the computer recognizes them only as any other character, letter, or symbol.

Quote marks are used by journalists to separate the word-for-word comments of a noted person in a longer sentence or paragraph in a news story. The quote marks perform roughly the same function in a BASIC line. They are the only way the computer knows where any string begins and ends. And the computer will always remember that string word-for-word when quotes are put around it.

One possible point of confusion is the last example of a string variable above—A2$ equals "45.50." Why, if this is a number, is it a string? The clue to the answer is the quote marks. By putting quotes around it, we are telling the computer to regard "45.50" as a group of characters, just like a word or sentence, without caring about its value.

Remember, though, that A2$="45.50" *is not the same* as A2=45.50. The first is a string, the second is a number.

Numeric variables allow numbers to be manipulated—added, subtracted, multiplied and divided. If AB stands for 10 and CD stands for 250, then AB plus CD would equal 260. In the same way, CD minus AB would equal 240.

Likewise (and perhaps to your amazement and amusement), strings can be added something like numbers. If AB$ stands for "THIS IS MY " and CD$ stands for "COMMODORE COMPUTER," then AB$ plus CD$ would equal the sentence "THIS IS MY COMMODORE COMPUTER." This adding or combining of two different strings is sometimes referred to as *concatenation*, a word that means to link together to form a chain. In BASIC, this is written like this:

```
10 AB$="THIS IS MY "
20 CD$="COMMODORE COMPUTER"
30 EF$=AB$+CD$
```

The new string, EF$, equals AB$ and CD$, or the entire sentence.

Even though you can add strings together to combine words and phrases, you *cannot* subtract them or do any other kind of arithmetic with them. Nor can you add a numeric variable to a string variable. So, if A2 equals 45.50 and A2$ equals "45.50," they cannot be added to arrive at "91.00." Why? Because numbers and strings don't mix. The computer sees A2 as a number and A2$ as a string of characters.

(There is a way to get a number out of a string, but we'll save that for later.)

*****************************************************************

ERROR ERROR ERROR ERROR ERROR ERROR ERROR ERROR ERROR

**TYPE MISMATCH ERROR**

This kind of ERROR is always caused by trying to put a character into a numeric variable or an actual number into a string variable. Strings and numbers don't mix. Trouble statements look like this:

```
10 A$=9 (or) A$=A
```

or

```
10 A="EXAMPLE" (or) A=A$
```

*****************************************************************

Just like the dollar sign, a percent sign (%) gives special meaning to a variable name. The letter A, all by itself, can be virtually any number, including numbers with decimal points. The number 10.5 is the number 10 plus five tenths (or a half). Numeric variables followed by a percent sign, such as A%, can be used by the computer to name only whole numbers, also called integers, between −32768 and 32767. If you need to use numbers larger or smaller, you can always store them as plain old numeric variables, like A=365000.

Why would you use such integer variables? For one thing, programs operate slightly faster. (Only *very* slightly faster. Don't expect any dramatic increase in speed.) For another, storing whole numbers as integer variables takes up less of the computer's memory. Integer variables can also be used to turn numbers with decimals into whole numbers. Try this:

```
10 A%=103.987
20 PRINT A%
```

When you RUN this example, A% will be PRINTed as 103. You'll notice that this isn't true "rounding." Normally, 103.987 would round off to 104, not 103. Some programmers insist that it is good form to always use integer variables for whole numbers. Others seldom use them.

*****************************************************************

ERROR ERROR ERROR ERROR ERROR ERROR ERROR ERROR ERROR

**ILLEGAL QUANTITY ERROR**

Integer variables are recognized by the percent sign (%). If this ERROR occurs in a line with an integer variable, check to see that the variable does not stand for a number greater than 32767 or less than −32768. If the ERROR is not in a line with an integer variable, check for problems with POKE.

*****************************************************************

What if you want to use variable names longer than two characters for numbers or strings? Fine, go ahead and use them. The Commodore computers will remember the entire name, but will only recognize the *first two letters*. So be cautious of confusing the computer. If, in a program, you use GAS=25.87 and GAMES=35.55, the computer won't know the difference between how much you paid for GAS and how much you spent on GAMES. The version of BASIC in some personal computers (particularly the Atari computers) will allow these kinds of long variable names. Commodore BASIC will not.

Finally, you should know that Commodore computers cannot use a few particular variable names. These "forbidden" names include IF, TO, OR, and GO because they are in BASIC. Neither TI nor TI$ can be used because they are reserved for use with the internal clocks built into all Commodore computers. The name ST$ can be used for strings, but ST cannot be used to stand for a number.

To help you remember how the computer uses variable names, here is a quick chart you can refer to:

| *Variable Name* | *Okay?* | *Why?* |
|---|---|---|
| A$, A or A% | Yes | Any single letter (A-Z) can be used. |
| AA$, AA or AA% | Yes | Most two-letter combinations are okay. |
| 22$, 2B or 22% | No | The first character must be a letter. |
| A1$, A1 or A1% | Yes | Combinations of numbers and letters are acceptable. |
| TI$, TI or TI% | No | Used by computer's internal clock. |
| TO$, TO or TO% | No | TO is a BASIC word. |
| ST | No | Reserved by BASIC. |
| ST$ | Yes | Just another two-letter name. |
| HOTEL$ or HOTEL | Yes | Names longer than two characters can be used, but only the first two letters will be recognized. |
| HOME$ or HOME | No | Confusion with above examples. |

There are limits to the size of numeric and string information that can be stored by the computer. Each number stored as a numeric variable has a limit of nine digits. This means, for example, that the variable name AB can equal the number 999999999, or the number .999999999, which is a decimal fraction.

(Unlike humans, the computer does not want to see numbers of more than three digits written the way we do. That is, never use commas in numbers over 999. The computer expects to see them written, for instance, as 1000 or 12520.)

Numbers larger than 999,999,999 and smaller than .000000001 can also be stored, but the computer thinks of them in a way other than as conventional digits. Making AB equal the number 200,000,000,000 (two hundred billion), then asking the computer for the value of AB brings the response: 2E+11.

This is the computer's way of referring to the number exponentially in scientific notation.

If you're interested, this is briefly the way exponential numbers work. The number 10 times itself, or 10 *squared* ($10^2$ or 10 to the 2nd power), is 100. Ten *cubed* ($10^3$ or 10 to the 3rd power) is 10 times 10 times 10, or 1000.

In each case, the number of zeros behind the number 1 is the same number of the exponent of ten ($10^n$). Two hundred billion (200,000,000,000) is 2 followed by 11 zeros and is *2 times $10^{11}$* (10 to the 11th power). Exponents can be negative as well. The decimal number .000000000002 is 2 times $10^{-11}$ (10 to the minus 11th power).

Since the Commodore computers can't display numbers that look like $2^{11}$, they PRINT the root number (2 in the above example, followed by the letter E for exponent, then the exponent itself from −35 to +35. The final exponential number is spoken 2 times 10 to the 11th.

(Confused? Need more information? A full explanation of exponential numbers and scientific notation can be found in most any high school math book.)

If you are not going to be using numbers so great or small that they need to be written exponentially, you shouldn't worry about not understanding the concept of scientific notation. Thousands of useful programs have been written without regard for these kinds of numbers.

******************************************************************

**ERROR ERROR ERROR ERROR ERROR ERROR ERROR ERROR ERROR**

**OVERFLOW ERROR**

> This ERROR occurs when you attempt to work with the largest number that the computer can use, 1.70141884E+38, or the number multiplied by 1 followed by 38 zeros. The solution (not always possible) is to break up your calculations so that this number is never achieved.

******************************************************************

The rule governing the length of string variables is far simpler. No string can be more than 255 characters long. That includes strings that are added together or concatenated.

******************************************************************

**ERROR ERROR ERROR ERROR ERROR ERROR ERROR ERROR ERROR**

**STRING TOO LONG ERROR**

> Strings can only be 255 characters long. String ERRORs are likely to occur when you concatenate, or add, one string to another. Check the length of each string when looking for the source of this ERROR.

******************************************************************

Very rarely, you'll see the word LET used in a BASIC program. It is used to define a variable. LET, however, is used optionally in Commodore BASIC, but it does add to the readability of a program. It is just as valid to use either line:

```
10 LET AB=4096
```

or

```
10 AB=4096
```

## BASIC Punctuation

Since BASIC is a language made up of words and rules about how they are used, wouldn't you expect rules of punctuation, too? There are such rules, just as in English or any other language. The rules of punctuation in BASIC, however, are much simpler than in English.

Just as several short English language statements can share a single line, several BASIC statements can share a program line. In English, the statements—let's say two-word sentences—are separated by periods. For example, the line:

Go home. Eat lunch.

The punctuation mark to separate statements in a BASIC line is not a period, but a colon (:). A BASIC line with more than one statement looks like this:

```
10 PRINT "THIS IS MY COMPUTER":GOTO 10
```

The important thing to notice about this line is how the colon is used, in this case to separate two distinct BASIC statements. A BASIC program line, including its number and spaces, can only be up to 80 characters, or two screen lines long.

Colons can also be used to make lines of BASIC more readable. For this purpose, one or more colons can be the first character or characters after the line number to set it apart from the rest of a program LISTing. For example:

```
10 PRINT "THIS IS MY COMPUTER"
20 ::GOTO 10
```

If you notice, the use of the two colons provides for a kind of indentation that is often visually helpful in keeping a program line recognizable.

************************************************************************

**ERROR ERROR ERROR ERROR ERROR ERROR ERROR ERROR ERROR**

**SYNTAX ERROR**

Syntax ERRORs can be caused by dozens of problems, but all are associated with BASIC "grammar." The most common problems are misspellings and missing punctuation marks, particularly colons (:) and commas (,). Also look for use of semicolons (;) in place of colons, and make certain parentheses are closed. Check rules for use of problem words.

************************************************************************

Other punctuation marks are used in BASIC programming, including the comma (,), the semicolon (;) and the quote mark, which you have already been introduced to. These are used mainly with the BASIC word PRINT.

## Programming PRINT

PRINT is one of the most often used words in the BASIC language. By itself, it is one of the easiest words to understand. With the addition of punctuation marks, though, it can be made to work in many different ways. Don't be discouraged if you find PRINT confusing at first. Since there are so many more variations to PRINT than there are to other BASIC words, it may take you longer to learn about its possibilities.

PRINT tells the computer to put something on the video screen. It can PRINT words and sentences, the results of a calculation, and even pictures.

You were shown a simple program in the section of this book about setting up and checking out your system. Its first line said:

```
10 PRINT "THIS IS MY COMMODORE COMPUTER"
```

This line does exactly what it looks like it would do.

PRINT is usually followed by telling the computer what it is you want it to PRINT. In this case, it is the sentence THIS IS MY COMMODORE COMPUTER. As you can see, the sentence is in quotation marks in the program, but the quotes vanish when it appears on the screen. The quote marks only indicate to the computer that it should PRINT whatever is *between* them.

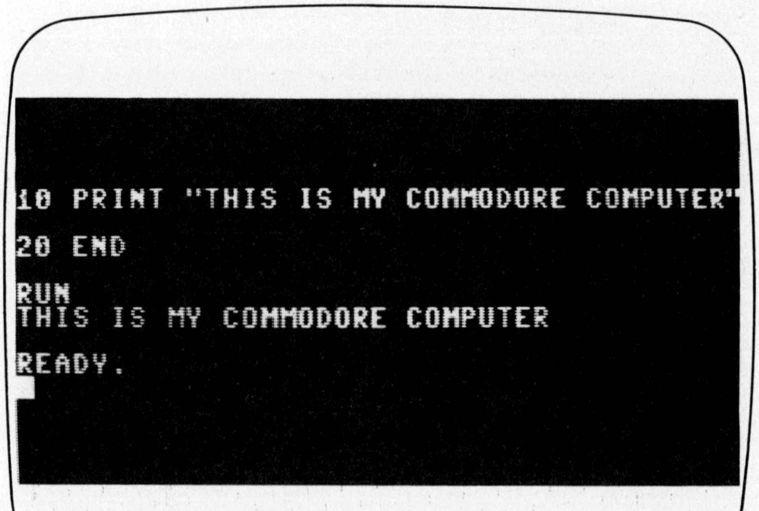


Try retyping the above BASIC line with other words in between the quotes. Then RUN. You should see whatever you put inside the quotes.

PRINT can also be used to PRINT the numbers and characters that numeric and string variables stand for:

```
10 A=4096
20 B$="THIS IS MY COMMODORE COMPUTER"
30 PRINT A
40 PRINT B$
```

***A Shortcut*** Let's try a shortcut that you can use from now on. Retype the program line like this:

```
10 ? "THIS IS MY COMMODORE COMPUTER"
```

After typing the line this way (with a question mark instead of the word PRINT), LIST the line. Even though you did not type the word PRINT, the computer understood what you meant. It knows that the shorthand version of the PRINT command is a question mark. Don't assume that it will understand anything else, though. It will not. It only knows that the question mark is a substitute for PRINT. Most of the time, unless you are told otherwise in the instructions in this book, you can use this shorthand method instead of typing the entire word PRINT.

***PRINTing a Blank Line*** Try telling the machine to PRINT without anything following the command.

```
10 PRINT "THIS IS MY COMPUTER"
20 PRINT
30 PRINT "THIS IS MY COMPUTER"
```

You should see the two identical sentences PRINTed on the video screen, separated by a blank line. Using the word PRINT, by itself, is one way to skip a line when PRINTing to the video screen.

Now, try another way of saying the same thing, but on just one program line, separated by the BASIC punctuation mark, the colon.

```
10  PRINT "THIS IS MY COMPUTER":PRINT:PRINT "THIS IS
    MY COMPUTER"
```

Two other BASIC punctuation marks, the comma (,) and the semicolon (;), are often used with PRINT statements. Using either one affects the way PRINT works.

***PRINT with Semicolon*** Type in these program lines *exactly* as shown, including spaces. (You can substitute the shorthand ? for the word PRINT.)

```
10 PRINT "THIS IS ";
20 PRINT "MY COMPUTER"
```

RUN the program and see what happens. If you typed it in correctly, paying close attention to the space between the word "is" and the last quote mark in line 10 and the semicolon at the end of that line, it should type our sentence "THIS IS MY COMPUTER."

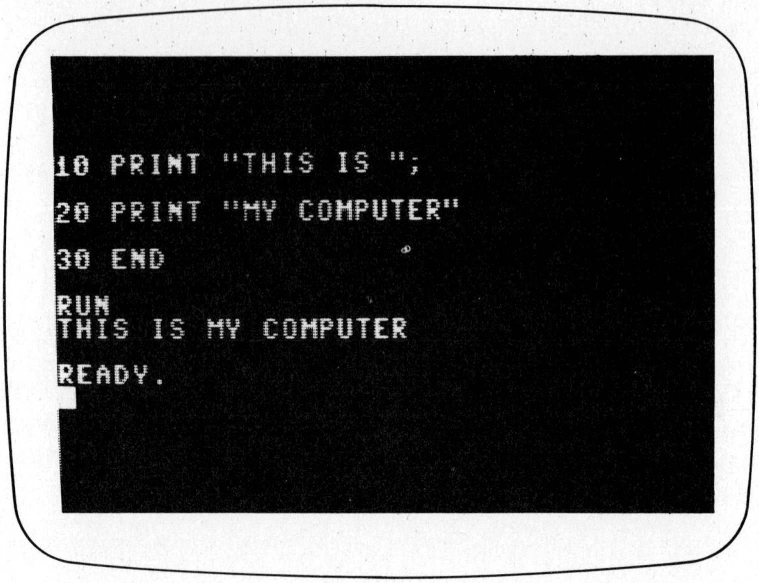


The semicolon is a way of telling the computer where it should begin PRINTing. Ordinarily, every time a PRINT command is used in a program the computer will begin PRINTing on the next line of the video screen. The semicolon tells the computer *not* to go to the next line, but to keep its place on the screen and begin PRINTing in the very next space. This way, two parts of a single sentence or a group of characters can be linked. It is a quick way of linking sentences and text together on the screen. (This occurs *only* on the screen. Strings stored separately as variables remain separate in memory.)

The space between the word "is" in line 10 and the last quote mark in the same line is important. Without it, the sentence would read "THIS ISMY COMPUTER."

Numbers as well as words can be written on the video screen using the PRINT command and the semicolon.

```
10 A=100
20 B=1
30 C=A+B
40 PRINT C
```

In line 10 you are plugging in the number 100 for the variable name A, and in line 20, the number 1 for B. RUNning this program will first assign the names to the numbers, then print out the sum of A (100) plus B (1), or 101.

Without looking at the program, the PRINTed result of A plus B may appear meaningless. To identify it on the video screen, we can instruct the program to tell us what this number is each time it is PRINTed. Change line 40 to this: (Don't type NEW!)

```
40 PRINT "A + B =";C
```

This might look like you are repeating yourself, but you are not. Line 40 first tells the computer to PRINT A + B =. Then the semicolon tells it to continue PRINTing on the same line. Finally, the computer PRINTs the *value* of C, the sum of A + B, or 101. If this line PRINTs two things on the screen, the statement (A+B=) and the result, why is the BASIC word PRINT used only once? The computer makes an important assumption when it sees a semicolon in a line. Unless a colon is encountered, the computer assumes that it should continue PRINTing whatever follows.

You may notice that the number 101 isn't PRINTed exactly next to the equal sign =. This is because the semicolon treats numbers slightly differently than it does strings. It PRINTs two spaces away from the last thing PRINTed. This is not a mistake in BASIC. It is designed to keep numbers separate from each other at all times to avoid confusion. Here is a variation on the same program:

```
10 A=100
20 B=1
30 C=A+B
40 PRINT A;B;C
```

It PRINTs the number values of all the variables in the program, separated by two spaces each. This kind of logical separation also happens when you PRINT a string after a number using the semicolon. Try this:

```
10 A=100
20 B=1
30 C=A+B
40 PRINT A;B;C; "THESE ARE THE VALUES of A, B and C"
```

***PRINT with Comma*** Another punctuation mark that is used with PRINT is the comma. It is used in the Commodore 64 family to organize the video screen in columns. Here is a program that will graphically illustrate how commas work:

```
10 A$="COLUMN 1"
20 B$="COLUMN 2"
30 C$="COLUMN 3"
40 D$="COLUMN 4"
50 A=1
60 B=2
70 C=3
80 D=4
90 PRINT A$,B$,C$,D$
100 PRINT A,B,C,D
```

When you RUN this program, you will see that the 40-character video screen is divided into four columns, each 10 spaces wide. You should also see the difference between PRINTing strings and PRINTing numbers in these columns. Strings will begin PRINTING in the very first position in a column. (The string columns start on the video screen at positions 1, 11, 21, and 31, when you count the first position as number 1.) Numbers skip a space and begin PRINTing in the second space. (Starting locations of columns containing numbers are screen line positions 2, 12, 22, and 32.)

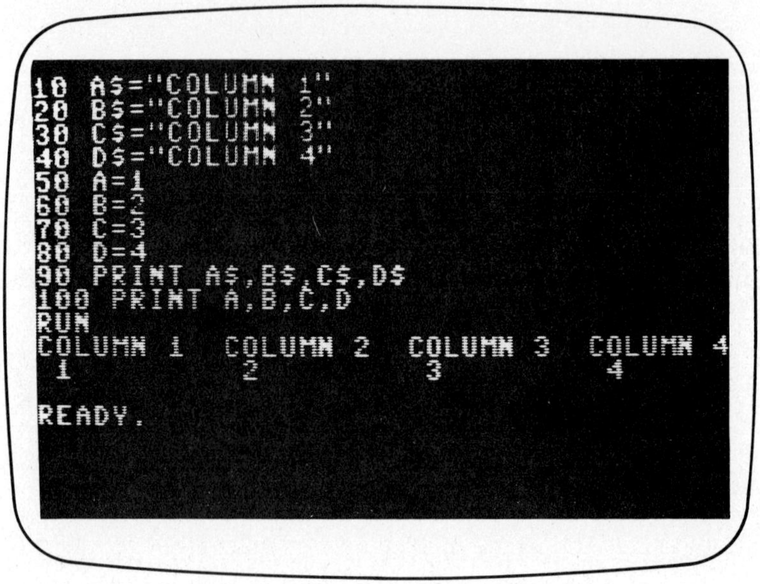


Change line 40 in the program above to this:

```
40 D$="THIS IS COLUMN NUMBER FOUR"
```

RUN the program again. You will see what happens when the information in a column takes up more than ten spaces (nine spaces when numbers alone are used) on the screen. The computer will PRINT into the next column, then advance to the next. These long columns can disturb a carefully organized screen, so to avoid this trap, it is wise to know what will be PRINTed first.

You should keep track of what you are doing each time you use the semicolon or the comma. Using either one at the end of a line will mean that the next PRINT statement will begin PRINTing in the appropriate position—in the next space or two if you use a semicolon, in the next column if you use a comma. So, if the last character in a PRINT statement is not a comma or a semicolon, the cursor will automatically move to the next line when it PRINTs again.

| *PRINT Example* | *Result* |
|---|---|
| 10 PRINT A | PRINTs the number named A on the screen—cursor moves to the next line. |
| 10 PRINT A;B;C;D | PRINTs the numbers named A, B, C and D next to each other on the same line, each separated by 2 spaces. |
| 10 PRINT A,B,C,D | PRINTs the numbers named A, B, C and D in four columns of nine spaces each. |
| 10 PRINT A;B<br>20 PRINT C;D | PRINTs the numbers named A and B on one line, separated by two spaces, then PRINTs the numbers named C and D on the next line in the same way. |
| 10 PRINT A,B<br>20 PRINT C,D | PRINTs the numbers named A, B, C and D on two lines in the first two screen columns. |
| 10 PRINT A$ | PRINTs the string named A$—cursor moves to the next line. |
| 10 PRINT A$;B$;C$;D$ | PRINTs the strings named A$, B$, C$ and D$ next to each other on the same line without spaces between them. |
| 10 PRINT A$,B$,C$,D$ | PRINTs the strings named A$, B$, C$ and D$ in four columns on the screen, length permitting. |
| 10 PRINT A$;B$<br>20 PRINT C$;D$ | PRINTs the strings named A$ and B$ on one line, next to each other without spaces, then PRINTs the strings named C$ and D$ on the next line in the same way. |
| 10 PRINT A$,B$<br>20 PRINT C$,D$ | PRINTs the strings named A$, B$, C$ and D$ on two lines in the first two screen columns, length permitting. |

***PRINTing Directly From the Keyboard*** In the event that you want an immediate answer to what the numbers or strings are that are stored by variable names, it is unnecessary to write a program line. PRINT (or the shorthand question mark) can be used directly from the keyboard.

`PRINT [or ?] AB` [then press RETURN]

The above line will print the number that AB stands for.

`PRINT [or ?] AB$` [then press RETURN]

The above line will print the string of characters that AB$ stands for, as well.

***PRINTing Screen Functions*** The PRINT command is also used for several screen functions, including moving the cursor around the screen, moving the cursor back to "home" (the top left corner of the screen), and for erasing everything on the screen.

In addition to moving the cursor around the screen from the keyboard (with the cursor up and down, left and right keys), a BASIC program can also position the cursor in a similar way. This is accomplished by PRINTing cursor commands. To see how this works, type these lines:

```
10 PRINT "LINE #1"
20 PRINT "[press the CRSR DOWN key five times]"
```

After you type the first quotation mark, don't type the above sentence, but press the CRSR DOWN key five times. Instead of seeing the cursor moving down five lines, you will see five symbols on the screen. (They look like the letter Q, reversed against the background.)

Type another set of quote marks to close the statement. Now type another line:

```
30 PRINT "LINE #2"
```

RUN the program. It will PRINT the words LINE #1, then five blank lines, then LINE #2.

Any cursor commands (up, down, left, or right) will work this way. You may have some difficulty since the movement of the cursor is often difficult to visualize. One tip is to make notes with a pencil and paper to keep track of where the cursor is moving. Once the program is RUNning, the cursor is invisible and things happen too quickly to analyze.

Using the same program (don't type NEW), add this line:

```
5 PRINT "[hold down the SHIFT key, then press CLR/HOME]"
```

You should see another symbol, a heart reversed against the background. RUN the program again. This line tells the computer to clear the video screen before RUNning the program as originally written. It also relocates the cursor to the top of the screen.

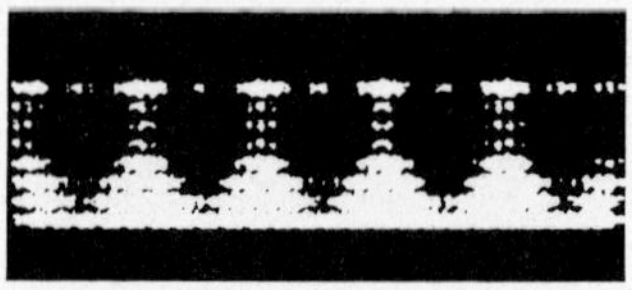

If you had pressed the CLR/HOME key *without* the SHIFT, you would have seen a different symbol inside the quotes, the letter "S" reversed against the background. It would have relocated the cursor to the top, but would not have cleared the screen. It is handy to use this "home" symbol when you are doing complicated cursor moves. It assures that you are always starting from the same place, the top left corner.

You may have noticed that this program begins PRINTing, not on the very top line of the screen, but on the second line. Without a semicolon after a PRINT "clear the screen" or "home the cursor" statement, the cursor will always go to that second line. (This is logical, and follows the rules about using the semicolon and comma.)

PRINTing to the video screen is enhanced when used with similar special keys, the RVS ON and RVS OFF keys. Typing a quote mark, then pressing CTRL (control) and RVS ON together, tells the computer to PRINT what follows as reversed characters against the background color. In the graphic mode, you will see a special character, a reversed letter "R," when you press the RVS ON key after a quote mark.

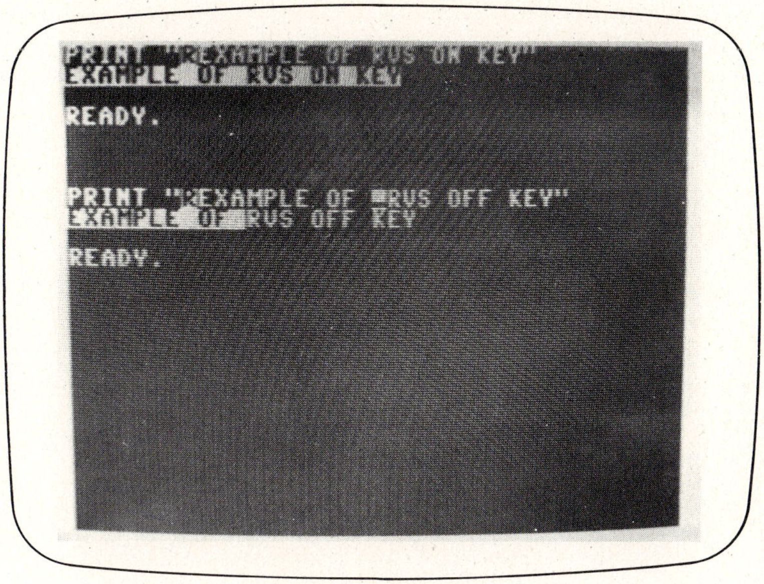


PRINTing will automatically return to normal at the end of a line with a RVS ON in it. Or, you can turn off the reverse PRINTing inside the line by typing another special character, RVS OFF. To turn off RVS, hold down the CTRL key and press RVS OFF. In the graphic mode, you will see a square with a line near the bottom, reversed against the background. When this RVS OFF character appears mid-line, between quotation marks and after a RVS ON character, anything before it will be PRINTed in reverse, and everything after it will be PRINTed normally.

```
10 PRINT "NOT IN REVERSE [press CTRL and RVS ON] IN
   REVERSE [press CTRL and RVS OFF] NOT IN REVERSE"
```

Color keys are treated in the same way, each yielding a different color of PRINTing on screen when used in quote marks. To obtain a color, press CTRL and the desired key numbered 1 through 8, or the COMMODORE key and any of the same keys. See the charts in the section entitled "Setting Up" for a description of which keys produce which colors.

A major difference when using the color keys and the reverse keys is that the machine will continue to PRINT in the color you have told it to until you indicate otherwise. So, if you begin PRINTing in blue and change to red to highlight a word, you will need to press the appropriate keys to return to the original blue color.

```
10 PRINT "[press CTRL and WHT] THIS WILL CONTINUE TO PRINT
   IN WHITE"
20 PRINT "UNTIL YOU INDICATE [press COMMODORE key and
   BLU] OTHERWISE"
```

If you are thinking that using PRINT is complicated, you are correct. Since it offers so many possibilities, there are a large number of rules that accompany its use. Most BASIC words, however, don't have as many options available to them and are considerably easier to describe and understand.

# 5

# Programming—The Big Ten

As in any spoken language, certain BASIC words form its core. These are words that are among the most useful. The ten words you'll learn about in this chapter—INPUT, GOTO, IF and THEN, GET, FOR and NEXT, GOSUB and RETURN, and REM—offer a great many possibilities. With these (and PRINT from the previous chapter) you can really begin to program. These ten words also introduce you to new concepts. GOTO, GOSUB and RETURN, for example, have to do with the order in which a program does things. INPUT and GET involve giving the computer information. With IF and THEN, the computer can test information and make simple decisions. REM lets you add comments to BASIC programs, to make them more understandable. If you learn nothing more than these few words, you will have unlocked much of your machine's power.

## Using INPUT to Ask for Information

The BASIC word INPUT is, in many ways, the direct opposite of the word PRINT. Yet, this word follows some of the same rules that PRINT does.

INPUT is used to take information from the keyboard and put it into a named variable. When INPUT is used, the program will PRINT a question mark on the screen, pause and wait for someone to type in an answer (a string or a number) and press the RETURN key. Then, if there are program lines following it, INPUT will go back to RUNning the program.

In its simplest form, INPUT is used with only a variable.

```
10 INPUT A
```

The above line PRINTs a question mark, then pauses and waits for someone to type in a number to be stored as the variable named A.

```
10 INPUT A$
```

Likewise, this line above does exactly the same thing, except that it wants a string of characters to store as "A$." One peculiarity of INPUT is that it will not accept string answers with commas in them. If an INPUT statement asks you for your city and state, for example, you cannot answer "Flint, Michigan" or "Atlanta, Georgia." INPUT will accept what is written before the comma and ignore everything after it. (You'll see why.)

*****************************************************************

**ERROR ERROR ERROR ERROR ERROR ERROR ERROR ERROR ERROR**

**EXTRA IGNORED**

> This is really an ERROR that you cannot correct, and happens when your answer to an INPUT statement contains a comma where one does not belong. Commas are used by the Commodore computers as special characters. The only time that they are allowed within an answer to INPUT is when the program is looking for several answers at once. Like this:
>
> ```
> 10 INPUT A$,B$,C$
> ```
>
> Commas in strings will also cause problems when they are stored and recalled to and from disk information files.

*****************************************************************

Using INPUT this way, simply asking for information without first PRINTing a question, is awkward. To make the program's requests clearer, you may ask it to PRINT something just before the question mark it will always put on the screen. Type your question in quotation marks, just as you would if you were PRINTing it on the video screen. For example:

```
10 INPUT "WHAT IS THE VALUE OF A";A
```

This line PRINTs WHAT IS THE VALUE OF A? (The question mark was PRINTed by INPUT.) You must use the semicolon, as above, to separate the variable name from the question you are asking.

You can also ask for more than one number at a time, by separating the numeric variables with commas.

```
10 INPUT "WHAT ARE THE VALUES OF A, B, C";A,B,C
```

This line will PRINT the question WHAT ARE THE VALUES OF A, B, C? Then it will wait for the proper responses. When INPUT asks for more than one response, all of the responses must be typed before pressing the RETURN key. For the computer to understand that each number typed is separate, you must type the numbers with commas in between, like this:

`100,10,25` [then press RETURN]

Since it is often unclear to the program user that the computer demands these commas, it is usually safer to use separate INPUT lines this way:

```
10 INPUT "WHAT IS THE VALUE OF A";A
20 INPUT "WHAT IS THE VALUE OF B";B
30 INPUT "WHAT IS THE VALUE OF C";C
```

If a program like the example above asks for numbers, nothing else will be accepted. If, for the question WHAT IS THE VALUE OF A?, you type the answer TWO, the computer will signal that you have made a mistake and will ask you to re-enter the answer as the number, rather than the word.

*****************************************************************

**ERROR ERROR ERROR ERROR ERROR ERROR ERROR ERROR ERROR**

**REDO FROM START**

This message appears whenever you answer an INPUT statement with a string, when it expects a number. Correct the situation by answering with a number.

*****************************************************************

If any question posed by INPUT is not answered—no number or string is typed—and only the RETURN key is pressed, INPUT will assume that the answer is either 0 (for a number) or *nothing at all* for a string. This empty string is often called a "null" string. Such a string, for instance, can be written A$ = "" (with no space between the quotes). Null strings can be useful, as you will learn.

(Those who have used and programmed the original Commodore PET computer should be happy to know that INPUT now accepts 0 and null strings as answers. With the PET, the response of just pressing the RETURN key would suddenly end the program.)

To better learn how INPUT is used, type in the following short program:

```
10 INPUT "WHAT IS YOUR NAME";NA$
20 INPUT "HOW OLD ARE YOU";AG
30 PRINT "YOUR NAME IS ";NA$
40 PRINT "YOU ARE";AG;"YEARS OLD"
```

This program will first PRINT the question WHAT IS YOUR NAME? Then it will pause and wait for your response. After typing in your name, it will PRINT the second question, HOW OLD ARE YOU? It will wait, again, for your response, then immediately PRINT two sentences: YOUR NAME IS (the name you typed), and YOU ARE (the number you typed for your age) YEARS OLD.

INPUT, as you may have guessed, is a relatively simple and uncomplicated word to use. Except for using it outside of a program (directly from the keyboard), there are few ways to use it incorrectly.

*************************************************************

**ERROR ERROR ERROR ERROR ERROR ERROR ERROR ERROR ERROR**

**ILLEGAL DIRECT**

While many BASIC words can be typed directly from the keyboard and used outside a program, INPUT cannot. This is logical, considering its use.

*************************************************************

# GOTO

An important idea central to computer programming is that a program needn't necessarily run in the order that it is written. The word GOTO, or GO TO, is used for "branching," or telling the program which line—out of sequence—to execute next. It is also used to put a program in a "loop," so that it runs continuously.

The first program seen in this book is an example of a loop.

```
10 PRINT "THIS IS MY COMMODORE COMPUTER"
20 GOTO 10
```

The statement GOTO 10, of course, means GOTO *line* 10. This is a perfect example of an endless loop—once set in motion, this program will continue, literally, forever.

GOTO isn't always used to create loops.

```
10 PRINT "THIS IS MY COMPUTER"
20 GOTO 40
30 PRINT "THIS LINE DOESN'T WORK"
40 PRINT "THIS IS MY COMPUTER"
```

Even though there are three lines that will PRINT to the video screen, line 20 (GOTO 40) tells the program to skip the line that should PRINT the sentence THIS LINE DOESN'T WORK. (And it doesn't, either.)

Of course, writing a program with unnecessary lines is pointless. But if we could tell the computer to make a decision based on other information it gets from the program, this kind of branching becomes practical.

*************************************************************

**ERROR ERROR ERROR ERROR ERROR ERROR ERROR ERROR ERROR**

**UNDEFINED STATEMENT ERROR**

You must use GOSUB and GOTO with line numbers that are actually used in the program. This ERROR often happens when you edit programs or change line numbers and forget to change the

GOTO and GOSUB statements that refer to them. Check line numbers in which the ERROR occurs, then try to LIST that line. Since RUN can also be used with line numbers, UNDEFINED STATEMENT ERRORs can occur this way, too.

****************************************************************

# IF, THEN, and OR

Much of the computer's power comes from its ability to make simple decisions based on the answers to simple questions or tests. The word IF checks for conditions and allows these decisions to be made. THEN is always used with IF to tell the computer what to do next. Using the words you already know, you can write this program.

```
10 INPUT "ANSWER YES OR NO. DO YOU LIKE COMPUTERS";A$
20 IF A$="YES" THEN PRINT "GOOD. KEEP LEARNING ABOUT
   THEM."
30 IF A$="NO" THEN PRINT "GOODBYE"
```

This program is the first example in this book that makes a decision. It asks the question DO YOU LIKE COMPUTERS?, using INPUT in line 10. The answer to the question—YES or NO—is stored as the variable named A$.

Then the program makes its decision, which is actually one of three possibilities. In line 20, it asks if the answer (A$) is YES. If this is true, it PRINTs the response, GOOD. KEEP LEARNING ABOUT THEM. If the answer is not true, the computer goes to the next line and asks if the answer is NO. If this is true, it responds with a curt GOODBYE. If the answer is neither YES nor NO—a third possibility, since you could have answered the question with *any* other word—it PRINTs no response at all.

You can (and often will) use IF with numbers as well as strings. In addition to matching number answers with questions, you can also test for a *range* of numbers by using signs other than the equal sign (=). The less-than sign (<) and greater-than sign (>) are used for this purpose. If you have trouble remembering which is which, think of the old trick of looking at them like you would a funnel. More always goes in the open end. Less always comes out the smaller end.

```
10 INPUT "HOW OLD ARE YOU";A
20 IF A<18 THEN PRINT "YOU ARE UNDER 18 YEARS OLD."
30 IF A>18 THEN PRINT "YOU ARE OVER 18 YEARS OLD."
```

Like the other program, these responses are based on the answer to a question. Unlike the YES/NO example, however, it asks to see if the answer falls into one of two broad age groups, under 18 years old and over 18 years old. Line 20 says that IF A (the answer in numbers) is *less than* 18, it PRINTs one response; if A is *greater than* 18, another.

The problem with this program is that it ignores the possibility that the person who is answering is exactly 18 years old. Typing 18 would produce no response at all, since the test is for numbers greater than 18 (19 and over) and less than 18 (17 and under).

One solution is to add another line.

```
40 IF A=18 THEN PRINT "YOU ARE EXACTLY 18 YEARS OLD."
```

This way, no number could be typed without getting a response from the computer.

There is another alternative. The "<" and ">" signs can be used alongside the equal sign with yet another meaning.

```
20 IF A<=18 THEN PRINT "YOU ARE 18 YEARS OLD OR
   UNDER."
30 IF A>=18 THEN PRINT "YOU ARE 18 YEARS OLD OR OVER."
```

Line 20 is read IF A *is less than or equal to* 18. Line 30 reads IF A *is greater than or equal to* 18.

Finally, you can use two IFs in a single statement to test the range.

```
10 INPUT "HOW OLD ARE YOU";A
20 IF A>=13 AND IF A<=19 THEN PRINT "YOU ARE A
   TEENAGER."
30 IF A<13 THEN PRINT "TOO YOUNG."
40 IF A>19 THEN PRINT "TOO OLD."
```

Lines 30 and 40 should be obvious. They simply test to see whether the answer (A) is less than 13 or greater than 19, the definition of a teenager. Line 20 is read IF A *is greater than or equal to* 13 *AND* IF A *is less than or equal to* 19 THEN PRINT. The response YOU ARE A TEENAGER will not appear unless both of these conditions are met. AND always checks to see that all IFs are true. Any number of ANDs can be used on the same IF line.

OR checks to see IF either (or any) of two or more tests are true.

```
10  INPUT "HOW OLD ARE YOU";A
20  IF A<=12 OR A>=20 THEN PRINT "YOU ARE NOT A
    TEENAGER."
```

The last way that "<" and ">" can be used is together, as "< >." This is the opposite of the equal sign and means "not equal." A little guessing "game":

```
10 PRINT "I'M THINKING OF A NUMBER BETWEEN 1 AND 100."
20 INPUT "WHAT IS IT";A
30 IF A<>56 THEN PRINT "WRONG":GOTO 10
40 IF A=56 THEN PRINT "YOU'RE RIGHT!"
```

In case you hadn't noticed, the "game" is rigged. (The answer is always 56.) It first tells you I'M THINKING OF A NUMBER BETWEEN 1 AND 100. The INPUT statement asks WHAT IS IT? then waits for the answer to be typed. But line 30 tells the computer that it should say you are WRONG if the number you picked (A) is *not equal* to 56, and go back to the beginning of the program. (If the number is exactly 56, you are congratulated.)

IF works in a completely logical way. It can be used not only with the PRINT and GOTO examples here, but to redefine variables and with virtually any other BASIC commands. One thing that befuddles some first-time programmers, however, is that IF the condition is *not true*, everything on the same program line is ignored. It is very important, then, to remember *not* to include anything on a line that begins with IF that doesn't depend on the correct response to a test or question.

```
10 INPUT "YES OR NO";A$
20 IF A$="YES" THEN PRINT "YOU ANSWERED YES":A=100
```

When the answer is NO, the value of A will remain zero. When the answer is YES, A becomes 100. Sometimes, programmers forget about the IF on a line and include important statements. These will always be ignored unless the line passes whatever test IF creates. Be especially careful of this as these problems are sometimes very difficult to find in a program and there is no ERROR message to warn you of your mistake.

## GETting More Information

Another word, in addition to INPUT, can be used to store information taken from the computer's keyboard. That word is GET.

Like INPUT, it temporarily stops the program until it has the information it needs. However, INPUT will accept multiple characters or numbers, and GET accepts only one at a time. And while INPUT waits for the RETURN key to be pressed to signal that the information is complete, GET automatically goes back to the program after a single key is pressed.

GET is always followed by a variable name and is almost always used with the word IF.

```
10 PRINT "PRESS ANY KEY TO END THIS PROGRAM"
20 GET C$:IF C$="" THEN GOTO 20
30 PRINT "PROGRAM ENDED"
```

The above example is used very often in BASIC programs written for the Commodore computers. Its function is to pause the program until the user wants it to continue. This is handy, for instance, for keeping PRINTed instructions on the screen until they are read, or to give players time before starting a game.

In the example, the program first PRINTs the message PRESS ANY KEY TO END THIS PROGRAM. Then, GET pauses the program, and looks for a key—any key—to be pressed. The IF statement does the actual checking. It asks IF the value of C$ is " ". These two quote marks without anything between them (not even a space) are called a *null* string, or a string of nothing, if you remember. IF C$ contains nothing, it THEN goes back to the beginning of the same line and tries to GET a key character again. When a key is pressed, making C$ anything other than "", the program leaves the GET line and continues.

Pressing certain keys, though, will have no effect on this use of GET. Those keys include both SHIFT keys, SHIFT LOCK, RESTORE, CTRL, and the COMMODORE (logo) key. For the reason that it would stop the program altogether, the RUN/STOP key can't be pressed either.

The main purpose of GET, of course, isn't just this little pause routine. It is to obtain a value—a number or a string—for the variable name that it is used with.

```
10 PRINT "TYPE Y FOR YES, N FOR NO"
20 GET A$:IF A$="" THEN GOTO 20
30 IF A$="Y" THEN PRINT "YOUR ANSWER WAS YES"
40 IF A$="N" THEN PRINT "YOUR ANSWER WAS NO"
50 IF A$< >"Y" OR IF A$< >"N" THEN GOTO 10
```

In this case, the string variable named A$ stores a letter. Either "Y" or "N" is what the program is looking for, and it makes its decisions based on either of those possibilities. Line 50 rejects *any* other choice. It is read IF A$ is *not equal* to "Y" OR IF A$ is *not equal* to "N" THEN GOTO line 10. (It is the line that asks for "Y" or "N.")

You can use GET to choose an item from a list on the video screen. Such a list is nicknamed a "menu" in computer jargon. Let's try a menu of four different choices. Instead of number keys, however, we will use those somewhat puzzling, unused "function" keys at the right of the machine. The keytops say "f1," "f3," "f5," and "f7." To the computer, they look just like any other key, even though they don't PRINT anything when pressed. When entering this example, do what you are told inside the square brackets "[ ]". *Do not* type the words as you read them.

```
10 PRINT "[Hold down the SHIFT key and press CLR/HOME]"
20 PRINT "CHOOSE AN ITEM FROM THIS LIST"
30 PRINT "PRESS THE FUNCTION KEYS NEXT TO THE
   KEYBOARD"
40 PRINT "F1--THE YEAR OF THE FIRST MOON LANDING"
50 PRINT "F3--THE HEIGHT OF THE EIFFEL TOWER"
60 PRINT "F5--THE SPEED OF LIGHT"
70 PRINT "F7--THE TEMPERATURE AT WHICH WATER BOILS"
80 GET C$:IF C$="" THEN 80
90 IF C$="[Press f1 key]" THEN PRINT "1969"
100 IF C$="[f3]" THEN PRINT "984 FEET"
110 IF C$="[f5]" THEN PRINT "186,282 MILES PER
    SECOND"
120 IF C$="[f7]" THEN PRINT "212 DEGREES FAHRENHEIT"
130 PRINT "PRESS ANY KEY TO CONTINUE"
140 GET C$: IF C$="" THEN 140
150 GOTO 10
```

In this example, line 10 first clears everything off the video screen. Lines 20 and 30 give the instructions to choose an item from the list and press the appropriate function key. Lines 40 through 70 PRINT the menu. In line 80, a pause is set up with GET, as in the previous example.

(If you noticed, there is something missing from lines 80 and 140. Instead of saying GOTO 80, line 80 only says IF C$ = "" THEN 80. The computer is smart enough to know that any number after THEN is always the line number it should GOTO.)

In line 90, you can see how the function keys work. Normally, no characters appear on the screen when a function key is pressed. But when you type a quote mark first, you will see a unique character for each one you type. For keys f1 and f3 you'll see a reversed box with a horizontal line through it. If you press f5 and f7 you'll see a similar box divided with a vertical line. When the computer sees these characters in statements like lines 90 to 120, it treats the functions keys just like any other key.

When a function key is pressed, the program PRINTs the appropriate information—the year of the moon landing, the height of the Eiffel tower, etc.—then it pauses again and waits. Then the instruction to PRESS ANY KEY TO CONTINUE is PRINTed. Pressing any key will start the program over again with the GOTO in the last line.

You can GET numbers as well as other characters by using a numeric variable name, but it is slightly more difficult. Since the way we tell the computer to wait until a key is pressed is to look for a *null* string (""), we cannot use this method for *numbers*. Strings and numbers don't mix, remember? So, you must use IF to test for the results of each possible number that you are looking for.

```
10 PRINT "CHOOSE A NUMBER BETWEEN 5 AND 8"
20 GET A:IF A<5 OR A>8 THEN 20
```

In line 20, the test is made to see whether the number pressed is less than 5 OR greater than 8. If no number is pressed, the program assumes that the value of A is 0. Since 0 is less than 5, it returns to the beginning of the line and tries to GET again until a proper number key is pressed.

## FOR the NEXT Words. . .

You've seen how you can use GOTO to make a computer program loop around inside itself, going from the end of the program back to the beginning, and so forth. You've also seen that, unless otherwise told, the computer will continue in its loop indefinitely.

There are ways to control the number of times a program goes through a loop. The simplest is by using a loop with the words FOR and NEXT.

```
10 FOR I=1 TO 20
20 PRINT "THIS IS MY COMMODORE COMPUTER"
30 NEXT I
```

This short program is almost like the first program in this book. Where the original program told the computer to PRINT the sentence THIS IS MY COMMODORE COMPUTER until you pressed the RUN/STOP key, this new version PRINTs it only twenty times.

How does it work?

In a way, FOR is like LET (but much more important). It defines a numeric variable, in this case named I. It then tells the computer to first plug in the number 1 for I. When the computer sees the word NEXT, it goes back to the line with FOR in it and advances the value of I to the NEXT number, in this case 2; then 3, and so on. This looping continues until the variable in the FOR statement reaches the number on the other side of TO.

To prove that the variable named I is advancing, substitute a new line for line 20 in the example.

```
20 PRINT I; "THIS IS MY COMMODORE COMPUTER"
```

It will number each line every time it is PRINTed on the screen, using the value of I.

Using the same idea, you can use the variable's value for something meaningful. The following program PRINTs a multiplication table.

```
10 PRINT "[press SHIFT and CLR/HOME key]
   MULTIPLICATION TABLE FOR 18"
20 FOR I=1 TO 20
30 PRINT I;"TIMES 18 EQUALS";I*18
40 NEXT I
```

You can see by this example that the variable I is used both as the number that 18 is multiplied by, as well as to calculate the necessary results, I*18.

These kinds of FOR/NEXT loops can be written inside each other. This is called "nesting" the loops. (Think of asking someone to count to ten, ten times. That's a nested loop.) They are usually used when one variable must advance independently of another. We can modify the above program to PRINT all the multiplication tables between 1 and 100 just by adding another FOR/NEXT loop.

```
10 FOR I=2 TO 100
20 PRINT "[press SHIFT and CLR/HOME key]
   MULTIPLICATION TABLE FOR";I
30 FOR J=1 TO 20
40 PRINT J;"TIMES";I;"EQUALS";J*I
50 NEXT J
60 PRINT "PRESS ANY KEY TO CONTINUE"
70 GET C$:IF C$="" THEN 70
80 NEXT I
```

These nested loops may look a bit confusing, but they really aren't. In line 10, you are selecting the number of multiplication tables you want the computer to PRINT—you want 99 of them. It sets up the first (or outside) loop, FOR I=2 TO 100. Line 20 PRINTs a "headline" for each one. When I is 2, the computer will PRINT the line MULTIPLICATION TABLE FOR, and then the number 2.

Line 30 sets up the second (or outside) loop, FOR J=1 TO 20. This will be the range of each table. Line 40 PRINTs each line, a number (J) TIMES the number of the table (I) "EQUALS," and finally the result, J times I. Line 50 is the end of the second loop.

In lines 60 and 70, we use the little trick using GET to pause the program. This keeps the tables on the screen so that they can be read. If this GET line wasn't here, the tables would PRINT so quickly you'd barely be able to tell them apart.

The last line, line 80, is the end of the first loop. NEXT I tells the computer to PRINT another table, this time for the next number.

A third loop can be added to the "multiplication table" program to replace the pause section. Remove lines 60 and 70 from the program. (Type each line number and press RETURN.) Now add this new line:

```
60 FOR K=1 TO 1000:NEXT K
```

Now there are three separate loops working inside one another. As you can see, this is an empty loop that simply increases the value of K each time it comes to NEXT K. Its purpose (a common one using FOR/NEXT loops) is simply to add a delay to the program. Now you have about two seconds between each multiplication table that is PRINTed. It is hardly enough time to read each one, but it keeps the program advancing slowly without the need to press a key.

The smaller the range of K (1 TO whatever), the less time it will take to complete this loop. Try a different number and watch the results.

By the way, you will notice that the variables I, J, and K are used quite often in other BASIC programs with FOR/NEXT loops in them. These letters have no particular meaning by themselves. (Indeed, any legitimate variable name can be used.) These are, however, part of programming lore that has separated them from other variable names. Variables in loops are "incremented," or moved up by one, hence the letter I. It is thought that J and K were used for this purpose only because they followed I in the alphabet.

It is important to remember a few things when using FOR/NEXT loops. First, keep track of what you are doing. You can become confused quickly, especially when using more than two loops inside each other. Second, try to keep GOTO and other statements that jump around inside the program out of the loops. Using these is an easy way to get completely tangled in your work.

A word that is used solely with FOR/NEXT is STEP. It tells the loop how big of a STEP to take each time a new number is used for the variable.

```
10 FOR I=1 TO 20 STEP 2
20 PRINT I;"THIS IS MY COMMODORE COMPUTER"
30 NEXT I
```

Here, STEP 2 means that the computer should advance I by 2 numbers instead of 1 each time. When you RUN this example you'll see that it numbers the lines 1, 3, 5, 7, 9 and so on. Try the same example substituting different numbers after STEP.

You can also STEP backward through a loop. Change line 10 above to this:

```
10 FOR I=20 TO 1 STEP -1
```

This negative number (-1) will number each line in descending order, from 20 to 1.

**************************************************************

**ERROR ERROR ERROR ERROR ERROR ERROR ERROR ERROR ERROR**

**NEXT WITHOUT FOR ERROR**

Using the word NEXT without opening a loop with FOR produces this message. This will happen if NEXT is used with the wrong variable.

```
10 FOR I=1 TO 10
20 NEXT K
```

No ERROR message will be given if the reverse happens—FOR is used without NEXT. Instead, the loop will simply not continue as it should.

**************************************************************

## GOSUB and RETURN

GOTO is a straightforward BASIC word. It means that the program should GO TO another line. GOSUB is almost as simple to understand. Like GOTO, it is used with a line number and directs the program to that line. Unlike GOTO, GOSUB also keeps track of where it was in the program and can RETURN to that spot after it is finished doing whatever it should. The word GOSUB, itself, is a contraction, or shortening, of the words GO to the SUBroutine.

Subroutines are an essential part of computer programming. As the name implies, subroutines are routines, or short programs, within programs. Each subroutine usually accomplishes a small task that must be done over and over. To avoid writing BASIC lines many different times in different places throughout a program, they are written as a subroutine only once. Or, a subroutine may be a major portion of a program written this way for the sake of organization.

Whenever the computer encounters a GOSUB in a program, it moves to the first line of the subroutine and does its job. When it sees the word RETURN, it does just that, hopping back to where it was even if that was in the middle of a previous line. (The BASIC word RETURN has absolutely nothing to do with the RETURN key on the keyboard—another case for calling the key ENTER.)

You can probably see that GOSUB is a potentially powerful command, useful in a way that GOTO could never be.

Using most of what you've read about (and learned, we hope!), let's take the "menu" program from the section on using the word GET and write it using subroutines.

First, here is the subroutine to clear the video screen and PRINT the menu:

```
100 PRINT "[Hold down the SHIFT key and press CLR/HOME]"
110 PRINT "CHOOSE AN ITEM FROM THIS LIST"
120 PRINT "PRESS THE FUNCTION KEYS NEXT TO THE
    KEYBOARD"
130 PRINT "F1--THE YEAR OF THE FIRST MOON LANDING"
140 PRINT "F3--THE HEIGHT OF THE EIFFEL TOWER"
150 PRINT "F5--THE SPEED OF LIGHT"
160 PRINT "F7--THE TEMPERATURE AT WHICH WATER BOILS"
170 RETURN
```

These lines, by themselves, clear the screen and PRINT the menu. They would run by themselves as a program if they did not end with the word RETURN. (If you try to run the subroutine with RETURN at the end you will get an ERROR message.)

***************************************************************

**ERROR ERROR ERROR ERROR ERROR ERROR ERROR ERROR ERROR**

**RETURN WITHOUT GOSUB**

GOSUB and RETURN work together. This message will appear if a program encounters RETURN without being told to GOSUB. It is most often seen when a program line is called with a GOTO instead.

***************************************************************

If you notice, the above subroutine example begins with line number 100, not line 10. Here, we are trying to separate it from the main body of the program.

As explained, a more useful subroutine is one that simplifies a program by reducing the number of times a program line must be written. The original "menu" program used the GET command twice. This can be reduced to the single subroutine:

```
200 GET C$:IF C$="" THEN 200
210 RETURN
```

Now we have two subroutines: Subroutine 100 to PRINT the menu and subroutine 200 to GET a character or key. Knowing the locations of these two, we can write the main body of the program. Together they should look like this:

```
10 GOSUB 100
20 GOSUB 200
30 IF C$="[Press f1 key]" THEN  PRINT "1969"
40 IF C$="[f3]" THEN PRINT "984 FEET"
50 IF C$="[f5]" THEN PRINT "186,282 MILES PER SECOND"
```

```
60 IF C$="[f7]" THEN PRINT "212 DEGREES FAHRENHEIT"
70 PRINT "PRESS ANY KEY TO CONTINUE"
80 GOSUB 200
90 GOTO 10

100 PRINT "[Hold down the SHIFT key and press CLR/HOME]"
110 PRINT "CHOOSE AN ITEM FROM THIS LIST"
120 PRINT "PRESS THE FUNCTION KEYS NEXT TO THE
    KEYBOARD"
130 PRINT "F1--THE YEAR OF THE FIRST MOON LANDING"
140 PRINT "F3--THE HEIGHT OF THE EIFFEL TOWER"
150 PRINT "F5--THE SPEED OF LIGHT"
160 PRINT "F7--THE TEMPERATURE AT WHICH WATER BOILS"
170 RETURN
200 GET C$:IF C$="" THEN 200
210 RETURN
```

This program RUNs exactly the same as the previous version of "menu," but it is organized differently. The most helpful change is that the program GOSUBs to line 200 every time the GET pause is used.

There is one potential danger in including subroutines in programs. The subroutines must be clearly separated from the main body of the program itself. Try RUNning the "menu" program after taking out line 90. (Type the line number and press RETURN.) You will see an ERROR message and the program will not RUN correctly.

This is because the computer doesn't know where to stop. Instead of understanding that the subroutines begin at line 100, it just goes on and tries to treat them as if they were more of the program.

The best way to separate the main body of a program from its subroutines is to use the word END. Think of it as setting up a fence between the program and subroutines.

```
90 END
```

Now, the "menu" program will run logically, although it will not work continously as it did before. END, if you recall, is not usually necessary in Commodore BASIC. This is the exception, but a real practical use of the word.

Do subroutines just give us another way to organize our programs? No. In addition to helping keep the number of lines in a program to a minimum, GOSUB can also be thought of as a way to make them more readable. Each subroutine is easily identifiable; it starts with the line number following GOSUB and ends with RETURN.

BASIC programs, in fact, are often criticized for being difficult to read by anyone other than the programmers who wrote them. Once in a while, it's even possible to write a program yourself, then not be able to read it six months or a year later. Using subroutines can help solve this problem. Writing subroutines wherever possible and practical is sometimes called *structured programming* (because it supposedly gives structure to a program) and many programmers believe this is good BASIC *style*.

## A Closing REMark

Making programs readable is a good goal for programmers, especially first-timers. Getting into good writing habits is as important in BASIC as it is in English. One word in BASIC, in fact, allows you to include English (or any other language that can be typed from the keyboard) in your programs. The word is REM and stands for REMark. Some people think of it as the word REMember, a way of REMinding themselves that this is a note. Almost any comment can be written into a program, as long as it is separated by REM.

```
10 REM THIS ENTIRE LINE IS A REMARK
```

The word REM can also be used at the end of a program line when it is separated with the BASIC punctuation mark, the colon (:). Everything before the colon will work normally, and when the computer sees REM, it will ignore any comment which follows.

```
10 PRINT "REMS ARE ALWAYS SEPARATED BY COLONS":REM -
   - JUST LIKE ANY OTHER WORD
```

One peculiarity of Commodore BASIC is its limitation of using only unSHIFTed letters and numbers after REM. You can demonstrate the problems caused by shifted letters by typing this line:

`10 REM` [press SHIFT and ABCDEFGHI]

Type LIST and look at the line.

```
10 REM ATNPEEKLENSTR$VALASCCHR$LEFT$RIGHT$
```

It doesn't look anything like the way you originally wrote the REMark, does it? (The computer misinterprets the SHIFTed letters after REM as BASIC words.) This won't be a problem as long as you remember to just stick to using the keyboard without SHIFTing. This means upper case only in the graphics mode, and lower case only in the typewriter mode.

Just a few short years ago, computer memory chips were very expensive and of limited capacity. Personal computers came equipped with relatively small amounts of memory, and programmers were often forced to use each byte carefully. Since the comments behind REM statements can eat up lots of memory (one byte for each character, letter or number) they weren't used as frequently as they probably should have been.

Although this conservation of memory is still important for very long programs, it is less of an issue today. The Commodore 64 family of computers allows you to use almost five times the BASIC memory of the original Commodore PET. With this increase in capacity comes the opportunity to use

REMarks more often. In doing so, you may make your program easier to understand for others and possibly even yourself.

Remember, computers are meant to make our lives less complicated, not more. What would we be like if valuable textbooks, reference manuals, and encyclopedic works were impossible to read and understand? Keep this in mind each time you write a computer program.

# 6

# Programming—How the Computer Stores Information

It's easy to store information in the computer. (You already know about variables.) It's another matter to organize that information, change it, or be able to get it out of the machine. That is what this section is all about.

Data storage is one of the practical uses for your computer. At home, an electronic filing system simplifies domestic recordkeeping. Both teachers and students can use the same kind of system in the classroom to keep track of test grades or prepare book lists. At work, accurate recordkeeping is a necessity, and a computer can help solve the problem of constantly changing facts and figures.

The computers of the Commodore 64 family are well suited to these tasks. Their ample memory is usually enough for most personal information needs. But, for serious, professional uses, most information systems use the floppy disk as an extension of that memory. (The capacity of the disk is more than triple that of the computer's.)

In this section, we'll look at how the computer, the floppy disk drive, and the cassette recorder organize and store information as files. You'll be introduced to new kinds of variables, too. Several words of BASIC are used especially for information handling. They are DATA and READ, DIM, PRINT#, INPUT#, GET#, OPEN, CLOSE, RESTORE, and CLR. How are these information-handling programs, or data bases as they're known, written? You'll understand the functions of such programs and see how they are designed from a simple demonstration program that you can enter into your own computer and use.

Finally, you'll learn about a few of the advantages that commercially available data base programs offer, and what to look for when considering these.

## Another Kind of Variable

If you remember, variables are names that identify information stored inside the computer. Look at this list:

A$="AUTOMOBILES"
B$="BIRDS"
C$="CITIES"
D$="DOGS"

We know that it is a list of string variables because each is a letter followed by a dollar sign. Each variable stands for a group of things—A$ is for autos, B$ for birds, etc. Under each of these variable names we might want to store additional information: Types of cars, birds and dogs, or the names of cities. But there is no way to store more data behind these because we've already used the names A$, B$, C$ and D$.

The solution to this problem is to use another kind of variable, called a *subscripted* variable. Now, before you turn the page and go away, rest assured. This is a relatively simple concept.

A *subscript* is a number that identifies one of a number of things in a group. In mathematics, subscripted variables look like:

$$A_6 \; B_{25} \; C_{1000}$$

These examples mean "the sixth thing named A," "the twenty-fifth thing named B," and "the one-thousandth thing named C." (The opposite of a subscript is a *superscript*, which usually indicates numbers multiplied by themselves, like $3^2$, or the number 3 squared.) The computer can organize information with these subscripts; but it can't recognize subscripts written with a number underneath the variable name, so they must be written like this:

```
A(6) B(25) C(1000)
```

The parentheses—( )—indicate which variables are subscripted or identified by number. When programmers speak about variables like these they usually use the word "sub" for subscript. So A(6) becomes "A sub 6" and B(25) is spoken as "B sub 25."

1 Triumph Herald
2 Morris Minor
3 Sunbeam Alpine
4 Citroen 2 CV
5 Honda Civic
6 Buick Century
7 Nash Rambler
8 Nissan Sentra
9 Jeep
10 Chevette

Above is a list of automobiles, numbered from 1 to 10. We can call each of these individual names A$ if we use subscripts. The position on the list will represent its subscript number. We could make A$(7) equal "Nash Rambler" and A$(2) mean "Morris Minor."

Subscripted variables can be strings, like above, or numbers, and they follow the rules governing variables stated earlier (See Chapter 5).

Type in this example to demonstrate subscripted variables to yourself:

```
10 A$="AUTOMOBILES"
20 A$(1)="TRIUMPH HERALD"
30 A$(2)="MORRIS MINOR"
40 A$(3)="SUNBEAM ALPINE"
50 A$(4)="CITROEN 2 CV"
60 A$(5)="HONDA CIVIC"
70 A$(6)="BUICK CENTURY"
80 A$(7)="NASH RAMBLER"
90 A$(8)="NISSAN SENTRA"
100 A$(9)="JEEP"
110 A$(10)="CHEVETTE"
120 PRINT "[CLR]"
130 PRINT A$
140 FOR I=1 TO 10
150 PRINT A$(I)
160 NEXTI
```

This program plugs in the word "AUTOMOBILES" for the variable named A$; then, from A$(1) to A$(10), puts our list in each of the numbered A$( ) variables. Notice that *A$* is *not the same* as *A$(1)*. Without a subscript number, A$ stands all by itself and is related to A$(1) or any other A$( ) variable in name only.

The subscript numbers inside the parentheses can be *any positive number* between *0* (zero) and *32767*. The parentheses can also hold a *numeric variable*.

Line 140 sets up a simple loop, FOR I=1 TO 10, then PRINTS each of the auto names according to their subscript number.

To prove that numbers can be stored the same way as strings, enter this three line example:

```
10 FOR I=0 TO 10
20 A(I)=I+25
30 NEXT I
```

The loop FOR I=0 TO 10 puts the numbers 0 through 10 into the subscripted variable A( ). To test this, ask for the numbers directly from the keyboard.

```
PRINT (or ?) A(5)
```

The answer should be 30, or whatever number is in the parentheses plus 25.

## A DIM View

That's DIM as in DIMension. To use subscripted variables, Commodore BASIC demands that you first determine how many of them you want to use.

But wait. Didn't we just successfully use subscripted variables without telling the computer how many?

Add this line to the earlier program example with the auto names:

```
115 A$(11)="TOYOTA TERCEL"
```

And change line 140 to this:

```
140 FOR I=1 to 11
```

Now RUN the program. What happens? You should see this ERROR message.

```
?BAD SUBSCRIPT ERROR IN LINE 115
```

The program is reminding us that we must tell it how many subscripted variables we will be using. Why now? Why not before? The answer is that Commodore BASIC will let us use up to *11* subscripted variables numbered from *0 to 10* before we must tell it how many will be used.

*****************************************************************

**ERROR ERROR ERROR ERROR ERROR ERROR ERROR ERROR ERROR**

**BAD SUBSCRIPT ERROR**

A bad subscript is just what its name implies—a subscript number too big for the size of the array DIMensioned. If a DIMension line reads DIM A$(100), for instance, there can be no variable named A$(101). This ERROR also happens when no DIM statement is used at all and variables with subscript numbers larger than 11 are used. Check variables used as subscripts for the problem.

*****************************************************************

We tell the computer about the use of subscripted variables with the DIM statement. It stands for DIMension, meaning the *extent* to which we will need the variables. When we use DIM, it sets up an *array*, that is, a definition of how many variables there will be.

```
10 DIM A$(100)
```

We are asking BASIC to reserve 101 numbered places for the subscripted variable named A$( ). (Remember, zero can be used as a subscript, too.) We can use as few of these as we want, but none can be numbered over 100. This is called setting up a *one-DIMensional array*. It has only one DIMension because it is a list of single variables like this:

```
A$(1), A$(2), A$(3). . . . .A$(100)
```

An array can be set up with more than one DIMension, too.

```
10 DIM A$(100,5)
```

Each variable A$( ) now carries two independent numbers to identify it. There can still be 101 different variables named A$( ) and numbered up to A$(100), but for each one, there can also be up to *6 more*. Think of the progression this way. The variables are now named A$(1,0), A$(1,1), A$(1,2), A$(1,3), A$(1,4) and A$(1,5). This array has become two DIMensional, with height and width, if you wish. You can visualize the list like this:

```
A$(1,5), A$(2,5), A$(3,5). . . . .A$(100,5)
A$(1,4), A$(2,4), A$(3,4). . . . .A$(100,4)
A$(1,3), A$(2,3), A$(3,3). . . . .A$(100,3)
A$(1,2), A$(2,2), A$(3,2). . . . .A$(100,2)
A$(1,1), A$(2,1), A$(3,1). . . . .A$(100,1)
A$(1,0), A$(2,0), A$(3,0). . . . .A$(100,0)
```

If this seems confusing at first, don't be worried. The concept of multi-DIMensioned arrays has eluded many first-time programmers. This kind of array is usually used to get information from a table of numbers by calculating two or more variables. For instance, if X is calculated to be 3, and Y comes up as 2, then A$(X,Y) means A$(3,2) in the example above.

Let's put a two-DIMensional array to work by making a table. The information on the table will consist of months, from January to April, each numbered 1 to 4, and weeks of each month, also numbered 1 to 4. For each week of each month, we will note how many times we've used our personal computer.

| Week / January (1) | February (2) | March (3) | April (4) |
|---|---|---|---|
| 1 / 25 | 15 | 30 | 17 |
| 2 / 19 | 6 | 11 | 22 |
| 3 / 13 | 17 | 5 | 3 |
| 4 / 15 | 9 | 8 | 21 |

Week numbers are read down, months across. We can store these numbers as a two-DIMensional array.

```
10 DIM A(4,4)
20 A(1,1)=25
30 A(1,2)=15
40 A(1,3)=30
50 A(1,4)=17
60 A(2,1)=19
70 A(2,2)=6
80 A(2,3)=11
90 A(2,4)=22
100 A(3,1)=13
110 A(3,2)=17
120 A(3,3)=5
130 A(3,4)=3
140 A(4,1)=15
150 A(4,2)=9
160 A(4,3)=8
170 A(4,4)=21
```

RUN this example. Now ask for the numbers from the table we've constructed in memory.

PRINT (or ?) A(Week number, Month number)

If you are asking for the number in the first week in February, you'd type PRINT A(1,2). The answer you receive should be the same as from the printed table.

You might never use arrays with more than one DIMension in programs that you write. Still, the general idea behind multi-DIMensioned arrays is illustrated above for you to consider.

Several different variables can be DIMensioned on a single line, like this:

```
10 DIM A$(100),B$(100),C$(100),D$(100)
```

Each of the variables above—A$( ), B$( ), C$( ), and D$( )—can now store pieces of information numbered from 0 to 100. When setting up these arrays, make sure you know how many places you will ask BASIC to reserve. You cannot change your mind and use DIM again to change the number in an array.

*********************************************************************

**ERROR ERROR ERROR ERROR ERROR ERROR ERROR ERROR ERROR**

**REDIM'D ARRAY ERROR**

DIM can be used only once to create an array of a variable. Once that array is created, it cannot be DIMensioned again, or re-DIMensioned. This will occur primarily when editing programs or trying to link two programs with DIM statements in them together.

*********************************************************************

You can, however, use a variable to establish an array.

```
10 INPUT "HOW MANY AUTO NAMES?";A
20 DIM A$(A)
```

In this example, the program asks the user for the number of automobile names it will be using and stores it as the numeric variable A. When it DIMensions the variable A$( ) in line 20, it uses that number for the size of the array.

## READing DATA

A previous programming example demonstrated how a list of automobile names was stored as subscripted string variables. The way they were stored—A$(1)="TRIUMPH HERALD," A$(9)="JEEP," etc.—is the simplest way to define these variables. It is not, however, the most convenient way. If we were to change the names on the list, we would need to change many, many program lines. You can imagine how impractical this would be if we had much more information.

The designers of BASIC had a solution to this problem. What if all the information we needed in a program could be grouped in one or more places? Then all the variables could be filled from this list.

The BASIC words DATA and READ do this. Lines that begin with DATA are set aside to contain the information. READ takes one piece of it from the list and assigns it to any variable, string or numeric, subscripted or not.

Each item, string or number on the list following the word DATA is separated by commas. (This means, of course, that strings cannot contain commas as characters.) Two entire screen lines, or up to 80 characters including the line number and the word DATA, can be used for each BASIC line of information. DATA lines look like this:

```
10 DATA 1,2,3,4,5,6,7,8,9,10,11,12,13
```

or

```
10 DATA UP, DOWN, RIGHT, LEFT, SIDEWAYS
```

The word READ is always used with a variable, either string or numeric, depending on the type of information in the DATA statements. This can be the intended variable name, or it can be another temporary variable used to transfer the information to the intended name.

```
10 FOR I=1 TO 5
20 READ A$(I)
30 NEXT I
```

or

```
10 FOR I=1 TO 5
20 READ N$
30 A$(I)=N$
40 NEXT I
```

Using this, we can rewrite our program example with the list of automobiles.

```
10 DIM A$(11)
20 FOR I=1 TO 11
30 READ N$
40 A$(I)=N$
50 NEXT I
60 FOR I=1 TO 11
70 PRINT A$(I)
80 NEXT I
100 DATA TRIUMPH HERALD, MORRIS MINOR, SUNBEAM
   ALPINE
110 DATA CITROEN 2 CV, HONDA CIVIC, BUICK CENTURY
120 DATA NASH RAMBLER, NISSAN SENTRA, JEEP, CHEVETTE
130 DATA TOYOTA TERCEL
```

While it is possible for the DATA list to have more information than necessary, it cannot have *less* than the program needs. In the above example, the DATA list could have contained several more auto names, but the program will only use the first 11. If the DATA list contained only 10 names, though, the program would be interrupted by an ERROR message.

*******************************************************************

**ERROR ERROR ERROR ERROR ERROR ERROR ERROR ERROR ERROR**

**OUT OF DATA**

Count the number of pieces of information in DATA statements, then check to see how many times the program uses READ. (One way is to look for FOR/NEXT loops with READ in them.) Check the DATA statements in the program LISTing you are entering from, or compare the information used to prepare the DATA statements.

*******************************************************************

Numbers and strings can also be mixed on the DATA list, although you must keep track of the kind of information the program wants. (Remember that a string can't be plugged into a variable that expects a number.) Here's another version of the example with auto names. In it, we will make an array of both the names as well as the price that each car might have on a used car lot. To do so, we'll alternate string and numeric information.

```
10 DIM A$(11),A(11)
20 FOR I=1 TO 11
30 READ A$(I),A(11)
40 NEXT I
50 PRINT "[CLR] CAR     PRICE"
60 FOR I=1 TO 11
70 PRINT A$(I),"$";A(I)
```

```
80 NEXT I
100 DATA TRIUMPH HERALD, 750, MORRIS MINOR, 2000
110 DATA SUNBEAM ALPINE, 2500, CITROEN 2 CV, 2000
120 DATA HONDA CIVIC, 3000, BUICK CENTURY, 4500
130 DATA NASH RAMBLER, 750, NISSAN SENTRA, 4000
140 DATA JEEP, 500, CHEVETTE, 2700, TOYOTA TERCEL,
    4000
```

Line 10 sets up two arrays, A$(11), which will hold 11 auto names as strings, and A(11), a numeric variable array to take up to 11 numbers, the corresponding prices of the cars. Lines 20 to 40 READ in the car names and numbers off the DATA list. Line 50 clears the screen, then PRINTs the words CAR and PRICE. Lines 60 to 80 PRINT the name of the car—A$( )—then a dollar sign and the price next to it for each.

You also should know that the computer always takes care of keeping its place on the DATA list, and it will recognize information even if the lines of the DATA list are widely separated by other program lines. Two other BASIC words, RESTORE and CLR, will affect how READ works, and the information contained as variables.

RESTORE has nothing at all to do with the key on your Commodore keyboard marked RESTORE. Instead, it resets the DATA process so that READ will begin READing from the beginning of the DATA list again.

CLR is used to erase all information stored as variables, either string or numeric. You must use CLR cautiously, though, because it is not selective. It will empty out every variable, including those that might be important to the way your program RUNs. If you only want to erase a particular variable, you can always do something like this:

```
10 A$=""
```

or

```
10 A=0
```

or

```
10 FOR I=1 TO 10
20 A$(I)=""
30 NEXT I
```

By the way, be sure not to confuse the word CLR in some of the program examples in this book for the CLR/HOME key. If CLR has square brackets around it—like this, [CLR], it still means to press the CLR/HOME key, *not* to type the BASIC word CLR.

## Disk and Tape Files from Arrays

Before getting into this topic, be sure that you've read everything about using the Commodore disk drive and cassette tape recorder in Chapter 3.

Once information is entered into the computer, there must be some way of storing it on floppy disk or on a tape cassette. Otherwise, it would all be lost the instant that the computer is turned off. One way of storing information on tape or disk is to SAVE it with the BASIC program. You've seen how to do this using DATA statements. But, just as DATA simplified the process of entering information for variables, another method further simplifies information handling.

The 64 family of computers, like previous Commodore machines, are called *file-oriented* machines. That is, the computer sends and receives all outside information to and from these files. Disk or tape files can be OPENed, CLOSEd, written to and read from, just like paper file folders. BASIC also thinks of the printer in a 64 system as using these files, and many file-handling commands also apply to it. New words used with files are really variations on words you already know: PRINT#, INPUT# and GET#.

There are several different types of files that the Commodore 64 can construct on tape or disk. Information is most commonly stored as *sequential files*. They are called sequential because pieces of information are stored in them, one after another. These kinds of files on tape or disk are different from programs in that they cannot be LOADed into the computer by themselves.

The BASIC word that starts the file process is OPEN. It is a word that can be used several ways; but, in this section we'll stick to a discussion of how it is used to create sequential files.

OPEN is used with a *file number*, a *device number* and a *secondary address number*.

```
10 OPEN 1,8,3
```

In this example, 1 is the file number, 8 is the device number, and 3 is the secondary address number.

File numbers are numbers that *you give* to them, and up to five sequential files can be OPEN at once. The device number is the number that the cassette recorder, disk drive, and printer are each given. (The computer doesn't understand words like recorder, disk and printer, so it "sees" them as numbers.) These device numbers are set for you. The cassette recorder is always *device number 1*. Printers are almost always called *device number 4*. If you are using two printers (one dot matrix and one letter quality, for example), a *second printer* is usually *device number 5*. Disk drives come from the Commodore factory set as *device number 8*. This number can be changed, however, and a second disk drive is usually *device number 9*.

When making tape files, there are three important secondary address numbers. If you don't use a secondary address, the computer assumes the number is 0 (zero), meaning that the file is OPEN for *recalling* information from tape. Secondary address number 1 means that the file is OPEN to *send information* to the cassette recorder. Secondary address number 2, when used with tape, writes a special mark that indicates the *end of the tape*. This is done so that you needn't go all the way to the end of a cassette searching for information that's not there. "End of Tape" files can be made to contain no information, just this mark.

****************************************************************

ERROR ERROR ERROR ERROR ERROR ERROR ERROR ERROR ERROR

**NOT INPUT FILE ERROR**
**NOT OUTPUT FILE ERROR**

Cassette tape files are OPENed as either INPUT or OUTPUT files, depending on their secondary address. An address of 1 means that the tape file is OPENed for recording information to it. You cannot use INPUT# or GET#, or the first ERROR will be seen. If no secondary address number is used with the cassette recorder, the computer assumes that information will be recalled from it. Using PRINT# will produce the second ERROR message.

****************************************************************

When making disk files, secondary address numbers are numbers you choose. Each numbered disk file should have its own secondary address. You can record information to, or recall information from, these disk files without the special secondary address you need for tape files.

Using Commodore's 1541 disk drive, it is recommended that you use only the numbers 2 or 3 as secondary addresses and try not to OPEN more than two disk files at a time. This isn't really a limitation, and you should be able to do most information handling with only one OPEN disk file.

Secondary address number 15 is used for a special purpose, to send commands to the Commodore disk drive and to read the meaning of the disk drive's flashing red ERROR light.

Following the file number, device number and secondary address, we can give the OPEN file a *name* that we can identify it by when recalling it from tape or disk.

****************************************************************

ERROR ERROR ERROR ERROR ERROR ERROR ERROR ERROR ERROR

**FILE NOT OPEN ERROR**
**FILE OPEN ERROR**

When using data-handling words PRINT#, INPUT#, and GET#, you must first OPEN a file, otherwise a FILE NOT OPEN ERROR will occur. This also happens when CMD, a word used to transfer information meant to be PRINTed on the video screen to a printer or disk drive, is used without OPENing the correct file, and with the word CLOSE, as well. FILE OPEN ERRORs will be seen when you try to OPEN a file that has been OPENed but not CLOSEd. Always check the file sequence to make sure the file is CLOSEd after use.

****************************************************************

Here is a summary of how OPEN is used to help you understand how this BASIC word works. Remember that these are just examples and that file numbers and some secondary addresses are your own choice.

**OPEN 2,1,1,"TEST"**
OPENs file number 2 on cassette (device 1) for recording sequential file called TEST. File number is chosen by the user.

**OPEN 3,1,0,"TEST"**
OPENs file number 3 on cassette (device 1) for recalling sequential file called TEST. File number is chosen by the user.

**OPEN 1,1**
OPENs file number 1 on cassette (device 1) for recalling any next sequential file on tape. File number is chosen by the user.

**OPEN 2,1,2,"END OF TAPE"**
OPENs file number 2 on cassette (device 1) for recording file called END OF TAPE with special End of Tape mark. File number is chosen by the user.

**OPEN 1,8,2,"TEST,SEQ,WRITE"**
OPENs file number 1 on disk (device 8) for recording sequential file called TEST. File number and secondary address are chosen by the user.

**OPEN 3,8,3,"TEST"**
OPENs file number 3 on disk (device 8) for recalling sequential file called TEST. File number and secondary address are chosen by the user.

**OPEN 2,8,2,A$+"SEQ,WRITE"**
OPENs file number 2 on disk (device 8) for recording sequential file with any name stored as string variable A$. File number and secondary address are chosen by the user.

**OPEN 1,9,2,"TEST,SEQ,WRITE"**
OPENs file number 1 on second disk drive (device 9) for recording sequential file called TEST. File number and secondary address are chosen by the user.

**OPEN 4,8,1,"0:"+A+"SEQ,WRITE"**
OPENs file number 4 on disk (device 8) for recording sequential file with any name stored as string variable A$ on disk #0 on dual drive system. Requires IEEE-488 interface adapter with Commodore 64 computer family. File number and secondary address are chosen by the user.

**OPEN 1,8,1,"TEST"**
OPENs file number 1 on disk (device 8) for recalling sequential file called TEST. Secondary address is chosen by the user.

**OPEN 1,8,15**
OPENs file number 1 on disk (device 8) for sending message to, or reading ERROR from Commodore disk command channel. File number is chosen by the user, but secondary address is special for accessing this command channel.

**OPEN 1,4,3**
OPENs file number 1 on printer (device 4) for printing text. File number and secondary address are chosen by the user.

**OPEN 4,4,7**

OPENs file number 4 on printer (device 4) to send special command (secondary address) to Commodore printer or smart printer interface. File number is chosen by the user.

The BASIC word that sends information to the cassette recorder, disk drive, or printer is PRINT#. The words PRINT and PRINT# are *not the same*, although they act almost exactly alike and follow the same rules of use. PRINT puts information on the video screen. PRINT# sends the information—strings or numbers—to a file with the number that follows it.

If you are accustomed to using the shorthand ? instead of typing the entire word PRINT, be careful that you use it *only* for PRINT, *not PRINT#*. You *cannot* use ?# as an abbreviation for PRINT#. If you make the mistake of typing ?#, the program will be interrupted by a SYNTAX ERROR. When you LIST the line with the ERROR, PRINT# will look correct on the screen. To the computer, however, you've still made a mistake. Sometimes, SYNTAX ERRORs caused this way are extremely difficult to find and correct.

Just as INPUT is the opposite of PRINT, INPUT# is the opposite of PRINT#. INPUT# receives information from a file on the cassette recorder or disk drive stored as a sequential file. It receives strings or numbers that are stored as variables, and, again, is used with a file number.

As with INPUT, you should take care not to use commas in strings taken from tape or disk files with INPUT#. The computer and disk drive use commas for special purposes, and any information after a comma will be ignored.

GET#, too, is related to GET. GET accepts a single key pressed down on the keyboard. GET# takes one piece of information, a single character from a string or a number stored on tape or disk as a sequential file, and stores it as a variable. If you must use commas in sequential disk or tape files, use GET#. Be forewarned that using it slows down the file-handling process.

We start using sequential files with the BASIC word OPEN. It is only logical, then, that we CLOSE the file after we are done recalling all the information we need from it. CLOSE is used with the same file number we used with OPEN.

***Cassette Files*** Sequential information files are recorded on cassette tape like program files, but, as stated earlier, they can't be LOADed by themselves. Information is recorded on the tape, then recalled by the computer *in exactly the same sequence*. So the lines of BASIC programming to recall information from the tape almost always look similar to the lines that record the information.

Let's say that we have a category, followed by information grouped under that name. We can use the previous examples of A$, which stood for automobiles, and A$( ), which contained the actual list of names. To make such a sequential tape file, we will first OPEN the file and give it a name. Then we will record the category name, A$, which stands for "AUTOMOBILES." Subscripted string variables that stand for the 11 car names are recorded next.

Let's try it. The following example will record the information on cassette tape as a sequential file.

```
10 DIM A$(11):A$="AUTOMOBILES"
20 FOR I=1 TO 11
30 READ N$
40 A$(I)=N$
50 NEXT I
60 OPEN 2,1,1,"LIST"
70 PRINT#2,A$
80 FOR I=1 TO 11
90 PRINT#2,A$(I)
100 NEXT I
110 CLOSE 2
200 DATA TRIUMPH HERALD, MORRIS MINOR, SUNBEAM
    ALPINE
210 DATA CITROEN 2 CV, HONDA CIVIC, BUICK CENTURY
220 DATA NASH RAMBLER, NISSAN SENTRA, JEEP, CHEVETTE
230 DATA TOYOTA TERCEL
```

The first thing that happens in this program is that an array for A$( ) is DIMensioned to hold 11 pieces of information. Then A$ is defined as being "AUTOMOBILES." Lines 20 to 60 READ in the list of names on DATA lines 200 to 230.

Now the process of storing the information begins. On line 60, file number 2 is OPENed on the cassette recorder (device 1), with the secondary address number 1. (The number 1 says that the file is being OPENed to send information, remember?) The file is named LIST. At this point, the computer puts an instruction up on the video screen:

```
PRESS RECORD & PLAY ON TAPE
```

When you begin recording, lines 70 to 100 PRINT# the information from A$(1) to A$(11) on the tape. Finally, file number 2 is CLOSEd in line 110.

We've made a sequential file on tape. But we can't LOAD the tape, and there's no way to look at it to prove that the information is there. The only way to tell whether our experiment was successful is to write another little program to put the information back into the computer. We'll mimic what we did above. (Be sure to type NEW before entering the program and *rewind* the cassette tape that you've recorded.)

```
10 DIM J$(11)
20 OPEN 1,1
30 INPUT#1,J$
40 FOR I=1 TO 11
50 INPUT#1,J$(I)
60 NEXT I
70 CLOSE 1
80 PRINT "[CLR]"
90 PRINT J$
```

```
100 FOR I=1 TO 11
110 PRINT J$(I)
120 NEXT I
```

This program gets right to work. It DIMensions an array of 11 places for J$( ), then OPENs file number 1 on the cassette recorder. There is no secondary address necessary because the file is being OPENed to recall information. (The secondary address number is actually 0.) Line 50 takes the first piece of information that we recorded on the tape, the word AUTOMOBILES, and calls it J$. Then, lines 40 to 60 put the appropriate information into J$(1) to J$(11). The file is CLOSEd. Finally, the program clears the screen, PRINTs J$, followed by the list of names, to prove that everything was received correctly.

As you can see, the file OPENed was a different number than the one we OPENed when we created the tape in the other program. File numbers don't need to be the same as they were when we made the sequential file since they aren't recorded as part of it. The number only needs to be the same *as itself* inside the program we're using. In the last example, the file is numbered 1 throughout. You can also see that we are using different variable names. In the first program, we called the variables A$ and A$( ). In the second program, the variables are named J$ and J$( ). We could have called them anything, as long as one was a string variable and the other a subscripted string variable DIMensioned for at least 11 spaces. Variable names are not stored in a sequential file, either.

An "End of Tape" mark was mentioned earlier. Making one is simple and you needn't even write a program. Just type this directly from the keyboard:

```
OPEN 1,1,2:CLOSE1
```

Rewind the recording made by this command, then type LOAD and press return. When the computer finds it, the word FOUND will appear. Press the COMMODORE key. A DEVICE NOT PRESENT ERROR message will appear. The cassette recorder is obviously in place and turned on, though. This is the Commodore 64's rather strange way of telling you that you've encountered an "End of Tape" mark.

The most important thing to remember about making sequential tape files is always to keep straight the order in which information is recorded, then duplicate this order when you write program lines that will recall the information. Also remember to CLOSE the file after you are through with it. Finally, don't include commas in strings written in sequential files.

As you can see, there's really nothing mysterious about sequential tape files. You'll soon see that disk files are only slightly more complicated.

***Disk Files*** If you've been successful in understanding sequential tape files, you shouldn't have any problem with disk files of the same type.

If you've looked at a disk directory, you've probably seen different three-letter abbreviations in the right-hand column on the screen. Programs that can be LOADed and RUN are labeled PRG. When you add a sequential file to the disk, it will be identified with the letters SEQ.

Like the cassette recorder, the Commodore disk drive needs to be told when it should make a sequential file. Instead of using a particular secondary address, though, this is done at the time the file is OPENed with a special naming sequence. OPEN is followed by a file number (you choose it), a device number (almost always 8, for disk) and a secondary address (choose either 2 or 3). The entire naming sequence sent to the disk looks like this:

```
10 OPEN 1,8,3,"TEST,SEQ,WRITE"
```

This command tells the computer and disk to OPEN file number 1 on device 8. The name of the file is TEST and it will be a sequential file. The word WRITE tells the disk to open the file for recording information. From time to time, you'll also see this kind of line written like this:

```
10 OPEN 1,8,3,"0:TEST,SEQ,WRITE"
```

The 0 (zero) inside the quotes means that the file should be written to the disk drive identified as drive 0. This is a carry-over from the original Commodore disk systems, which had two drives, instead of one, like the 1541. Although there were two drives, the computer recognized *both of them* as device 8. To differentiate, one drive was named drive 0, the other drive 1. Any disk commands like this, with the disk drive number 0, will still work with the 1541. Commands with the number 1, however, will not, unless you are using a Commodore dual disk drive. (This also requires an IEEE-488 interface.)

If you have two 1541 disk drives, the first one will be device 8, and the second must be assigned a different device number. (Usually this one will become device 9.) You will *not*, however, be able to treat these two as drive 0 and drive 1.

As a matter of form, and to prevent unanticipated problems with the 1541 disk drive, it is a good idea to always use the optional prefix "0:" when OPENing disk files.

To convert our "auto names" program to a sequential disk file we need to change only one line. Substitute this line for line 60 in the earlier program:

```
60 OPEN 2,8,2,"0:LIST,SEQ,WRITE"
```

To modify the program that recalled information from the tape file, you also need to change a line. This line replaces line 20 in the example:

```
20 OPEN 1,8,3,"0:LIST,SEQ"
```

What if the name of the file is not always the same? You can first use INPUT to accept a string as the name, then use the variable instead. To do so, you must *concatenate* or add the variable to the naming sequence.

```
10 INPUT "WHAT IS THE FILE NAME";N$
20 OPEN 2,8,2,N$+",SEQ,WRITE"
```

You'll notice that the disk version of the program *needs* the name of the file it is looking for, even though a name is optional when using the cassette recorder. The first file from the cassette will be recalled if no name is specified. Since a disk can contain many, many files, the disk drive always needs this name information.

You'll need to *be particularly careful* about CLOSEing sequential disk files. You can tell if a disk file is left OPEN by looking at the disk directory. If an asterisk ("*") is next to SEQ, the file has been left OPEN. Such a file is useless (you cannot add information to it) and erasing this file (see "Some Essential Skills") may damage the data on the disk. No problems should occur, though, if you always CLOSE the file after OPENing it to store information.

*************************************************************

**ERROR ERROR ERROR ERROR ERROR ERROR ERROR ERROR ERROR**

**FILE NOT FOUND**

This message will appear if you try to LOAD a program or file from disk that does not exist. If you are sure that you have the program, check the disk directory to see if it is on that particular disk, or check your spelling. This disk drive expects absolute accuracy when asking for a program by name. Avoid this ERROR by using an asterisk for pattern matching purposes.

*************************************************************

One last caution about sequential files on both tape and disk. You already know about string variables that contain no information. These are called "null strings." Even though Commodore BASIC allows you to use such empty strings, you can confuse sequential files if you try to record them.

```
10 A$="YES":B$="":C$="NO"
20 OPEN 1,8,2,"0:TEST,SEQ,WRITE"
30 PRINT#1,A$,B$,C$
40 CLOSE 1
```

When this example records the sequential file it will *skip* B$ because it is a null string. When you go back to recall the file, the second piece of information, B$, will become "NO," instead. One method of eliminating the problem is to test to see whether a string is empty or not. If it is, another string that will record properly can be substituted.

```
10 A$="YES":B$="":C$="NO"
20 OPEN 1,8,2,"0:TEST,SEQ,WRITE"
30 PRINT#1,A$
40 IF B$=""THEN B$="***"
50 PRINT#1,B$
60 PRINT#1,C$
70 CLOSE 1
```

In the example, line 40 first tests to see if B$ is empty. If it is, it substitutes 3 asterisks—"***"—for the empty string. The 3 asterisks were chosen because they will probably not interfere with any legitimate information and record properly. We could have chosen another substitute—"FFFF" or "???"—as easily and logically.

When the file is recalled, we test for the substitute.

```
10 OPEN 1,8,2,"TEST,SEQ"
20 INPUT#1,A$
30 INPUT#1,B$
40 IF B$="***" THEN B$=""
50 INPUT#1,C$
60 CLOSE 1
```

Line 40 asks if the string is "***" and, if it is, makes B$ a null string once again.

When substituting for null strings, always be certain that the substitute is unique enough so that it can't be confused with real information, which would be lost.

***Printer files*** In the Commodore 64 family, any information can be printed on paper by OPENing a file and sending it to the printer. Secondary addresses can play an important part in OPENing these files, but these numbers sometimes mean different things to different printers. The Commodore printers, in particular, use secondary addresses to go from the graphics to the text mode, and to set up other operating conditions. "Smart" printer interfaces also interpret secondary address numbers as operational commands. If you are using a printer or smart interface, make sure that you read the manual supplied with it and learn about how these secondary addresses are used. Also study the section of the manual that covers special "control" characters and number sequences.

Most printers are controlled by microprocessors that enable a variety of special features. No two printers are exactly alike, however, so it would be impossible to summarize these codes.

A printer file can be OPENed with only the file number and device number. Printing on paper is almost exactly like PRINTing on the video screen. You use PRINT# instead, but punctuation marks like commas and semicolons behave the same way on screen or paper.

```
10 OPEN 1,4
20 PRINT#1, "HEY! MY PRINTER WORKS!"
30 CLOSE 1
```

One potential problem is that extra, blank lines may creep in between the lines you are printing. This double spacing is the result of both the computer *and* the printer sending a "line feed" command. The easiest way of turning off the extra line feed is to eliminate it at the printer. (See your manual.) Some smart interfaces also remove this extra line feed before it gets to the printer.

Mastering your printer requires attention and an understanding of how it works and how special characters change its operation. Making good use of some extensive features can get confusing. For the time being, though, be satisfied with this simple way of printing using the computer's file system.

## Creating a Mailing List Program

A data base program is one used to store and read information. Such programs range from simple to complicated, depending on their features. Though the programs are often called "data bases," they are not, strictly speaking. Data bases are actually the information that these programs accumulate. A list of baseball batting averages is a data base. So are the closing stock prices that are published in a daily newspaper. Even a cookbook could be considered a data base of recipes. A data base can be thought of as any organized group of information.

At the end of this chapter you'll find a simple data base program written in BASIC that you can enter and begin using. It can act as a personal mailing list. Though you can make practical use of it, it is intended to show you how a simple data base is created. Many commercially available data base programs will be more flexible, have many more features, and store data differently. This mailing list program is limited to storing information in the computer's memory and recording it as a sequential file.

If you are new to programming, it is a good idea to finish reading how the program is written before entering it into the machine. This way, you'll begin to understand how it works and get keyboard practice at the same time.

When you are typing the program into the computer, do it a little at a time and be careful to copy each line *exactly* as it is printed in the book. As with the earlier BASIC examples, press the *keys* specified by the words inside the square brackets [like these], *not the words*. Also, be aware that the program uses both upper and lower case text, so put the computer in the typewriter mode by pressing the COMMODORE and SHIFT keys together, before you begin to program.

When entering this or any program, be sure to SAVE it to tape or disk *frequently*. You'll protect yourself against losing all of your work if the computer should be accidentally turned off. (You can rewind the cassette and record over the previously stored portion, or SAVE over your previous work on disk with SAVE "@:".) See the section on Essential Skills if you're not sure about how to do this.

Finally, you'll probably make some mistakes while typing the program. If you get an ERROR messsage, it will most likely be a SYNTAX ERROR, due to hitting the wrong key, or leaving out a colon or other BASIC punctuation mark. Some typing mistakes, however, will produce other ERRORs as well. Try to figure out what the ERROR is on your own, before coming back to the book. If you can't find the problem, look at the ERROR messages scattered throughout the text, then look at the line in the printed program LISTing to make sure you've typed everything correctly.

## Designing the Program

What do we want a mailing list program to do? We should have a plan before we start programming. We wouldn't build a house or write a book without a plan, would we? Our plan will come from thinking about the features we want to build into the program.

The mailing program should be able to store names, addresses, and telephone numbers. We should be able to read these, change them if we want to, and record them on tape or disk. We should have the option of printing out the mailing list on paper. Finally, we should be able to erase any individual piece of information, or all of it. Here is a more detailed description of the parts of the program:

***Enter*** This portion of the program will take information and store it in the proper place inside the computer in the correct format. It should be easy to use, and will ask for the information by name, giving us a little "nudge" each time it wants something. The "Enter" portion will also keep track of how many name/address entries the computer can hold and how many have been used.

***Read*** The purpose of this program is to be able to see the names and addresses in the file. Sometimes, we will want to read all of the information. At other times, we might only want to read a particular name, or maybe just the records that match with a ZIP code or phone number.

***Change*** Our information won't always remain correct or current. (People may move or change their phone number.) So this portion of the program will let us change what we want.

***Erase*** Since we are limited to the amount of memory in the computer, we may want to keep only the most important names and addresses in our file. From time to time, then, we might want to erase an entry. In this section, we can either scan the mailing list, or ask that a particular entry be erased.

***Print*** We may want a paper copy of the mailing list. It is a relatively easy task to transfer the information from our file to the printer.

***Load and Save*** Even though we'll call these sections Load and Save, we won't use the BASIC words LOAD or SAVE. Instead, we will be creating sequential files on tape or disk, then recalling them.

***Menu*** The entire program will be operated from menus. This will simplify its use and allow us to use the function keys on the keyboard. Each of the major portions of the program will be reached through a "main menu."

## Programming Considerations

Creating a mailing list is a fairly simple project, since the program is designed to store a specific kind of information—names, addresses, and telephone numbers. We will use simple arrays, one for each particular piece of information, names, street numbers, cities, states, ZIP codes and phone numbers. We will also reserve a numeric variable to keep track of how many entries there are on the list. Here's how this information will be organized:

N$( )—Names
A$( )—Addresses (Street Numbers)
C$( )—Citics
S$( )—States
Z$( )—ZIP codes
P$( )—Phone numbers

(These variables will actually appear in lower case, not capital, letters in the program printed in the book and on your video screen. Why? We put the computer in the typewriter mode and always use unSHIFTed keys to enter BASIC words and variables. For this discussion, though, you'll continue to see these in capital letters.)

Setting the above categories limits the flexibility of any data base program, but a more generalized program would have been many times larger and more complicated than the demonstration that will be offered here.

We will make room for 100 total entries by DIMensioning each array to 100. The numeric variable "N" will count the total number of entries. We set this up with this line:

```
15 X=101:DIM N$(X),A$(X),C$(X),S$(X),Z$(X),P$(X)
   :N=0
```

The variable named "X" stands for the total number of item entries that will be stored, so DIM N$(X) is the same as DIM N$(101). Why use the variable instead of 101? By changing X we can always change the total number of possible entries by just changing one line (line 120), instead of looking for other places where the number is used. (Even though we will only store 100 complete entries, X is 101 to accommodate the routine that erases an entry in the file.)

## Starting To Program

The screen colors chosen by Commodore make text on the screen somewhat difficult to read. We can choose other colors that will make reading easier.

```
20 POKE 53280,12:REM BORDER GRAY 2
30 POKE 53281,15:REM SCREEN GRAY 3
```

These numbers are POKEd into the appropriate memory locations inside the computer's video chip to change the colors. You can change these to any other colors that you prefer by POKEing in the other numbers from 0 to 15. (You'll find a list in the section about color graphics.)

Everything in the program will be PRINTed on the screen in black. (See line 60.)

Lines 40 and 50 perform two nice little tricks.

```
40 PRINT CHR$(8)
50 PRINT CHR$(14)
```

In BASIC, CHR$( ) is a special way of PRINTing characters on the screen. Each character has its own number, the number in the parentheses of CHR$(). CHR$(8) and CHR$(14), though, are special characters that don't appear on the screen.

PRINTing CHR$(8) will switch the computer from the graphics mode to the typewriter mode, the same as pressing the SHIFT and COMMODORE keys together. It is done here in the program, so that the user needn't press the keys. But what if someone presses those two keys together during the program? That's what CHR$(14) is for. It disables the SHIFT and COMMODORE key so that you can't switch between the graphics and typewriter modes without resetting the computer using the RESTORE key.

Since this is a menu-style program, all of its activities branch off a main loop. This loop does only two things: It PRINTs the main menu, then waits for a function key to be pressed, indicating what you want to do. Everything that happens in the program can always be traced back to this loop, which starts at line 60 and ends with a GOTO 60 in line 220. When a key is pressed, the appropriate subroutine is selected.

Here's what the main menu looks like:

```
f1--Enter
f3--Read
f5--Print
f7--Erase

f2--Load
f4--Save
f6--Change
```

Here is a list of the important subroutines in the program:

| *Line #* | *Purpose of Subroutine* |
|---|---|
| 10000 | ENTER—Routine for entering data |
| 11000 | READ—Reads names/addresses |
| 12000 | PRINT—Prints list to a printer |
| 13000 | ERASE—Deletes names/addresses from list |
| 14000 | LOAD—Recalls file from disk or tape |
| 15000 | SAVE—Stores file on disk or tape |
| 16000 | CHANGE—Changes information in an entry |

## Using the Program

The choices of what the mailing list program offers are quite obvious from the main menu. Pressing the proper keys will take you from place to place within the program. Two words, scan and match, are used to describe other options. Scan lets you look through all of the information in the name/address file, making decisions as you go along. Match lets you match a name with one in the file.

In the "enter" mode, the program will always prompt you, letting you know what kind of information it wants next. When you want to change something, you will be asked which category of information you'd like.

The most important thing to remember about using this program is that it is written in BASIC and subject to its limitations. The major one is that BASIC does not allow you to use commas when entering information in response to an INPUT statement. For example, this information:

Jefferson Smith, Attorney
145 Iota Court
Chicago, Illinois 60601
312-555-1212

must be given to the program without the commas, something like this:

Jefferson Smith—Attorney
145 Iota Court
Chicago
Illinois
60601
312-555-1212

You can also skip information, and enter a blank (a null string) by just pressing RETURN.

Be careful going from activity to activity within the program. In some cases you are given an opportunity to return to the main menu before continuing. In other cases, you may produce an error. If you try recalling the name/address file from disk or tape without first creating one, you will produce an error or wait interminably while the cassette player looks for a file that isn't there. If you try using the print section without having a printer attached, the program will stop. In either case, if you have entered valuable information, all of it will be lost when you type RUN to get the program going again.

The most obvious thing missing from this program is a way to sort the list by one of the categories. Sorting routines, though, can be complicated and, in BASIC, very slow.

Another limitation is the use of sequential files. The entire file is swapped between the computer's memory and the disk or tape. The program is set up to use 600 string variables in DIMensioned arrays. Since a string can be as large as 255 characters, this means that long strings would swell the computer beyond its limits if all 600 were actually used. The Commodore computers can build another kind of disk file, however, called a *relative* file.

If relative files were used, the entire capacity of a disk could be devoted to a single filing system.

(Relative files are very complicated and difficult to program. They are beyond the scope of a book like this one, but are discussed in some advanced BASIC texts.)

## Choosing a Data Base Program

All commercially available data base programs are not alike, and you should shop carefully before choosing one. As with word processing programs, people tend to stay with the program they are using since information files are not generally compatible from one data base program to another. The alternative, of course, is to use two or three such programs for applications that vary in complexity.

The first consideration in selecting a data base program should be the language that it is written in. BASIC is seldom suitable for a data base, and all-BASIC programs should probably be avoided because they will be slow and inflexible. Most good data base programs are written in machine code.

Flexibility is an all-important consideration. Some data base programs restrict you to the type, amount, and length of individual entries. A good program, however, will even allow you to go beyond a single screen of information. One point of reference to keep in mind is that you should be able to do almost anything you can with a paper filing system.

Any good data base program will also offer fast sorting capabilities. In addition to being able to sort information in one category, you should also be able to select information that matches more than one condition. Say you have a long mailing list, and the list also contains names of certain club members or professional associates. You may not only want to select those people on your mailing list who live in Florida, but also those who both live in that state and are members of your club. A flexible, well-written data base program will let you do this.

Most good programs of this type also let you print out "reports." Simply stated, a report is a list of the information you want selected from the total data base. A powerful report "generator" will offer more, too. It will let you design the way the information will be printed on the page, fill in preprinted forms, or may even offer mathematical features that let you manipulate numbers from the data base.

A data base designed for use with Commodore computers should always use relative files. Though it is possible that some data base programs will appear that use their own unique type of disk file, any program that only uses sequential files is likely to be of limited use, except for the simplest of applications.

Finally, you'll know a good data base program when you see one. Because these programs can be among the most complex, they can also be the most confusing. You should be able to use the program you select without the need for an open manual next to you at all times. The program should be logical, and its commands should be easy to remember. It is understandable that some of its more powerful functions could require some study and practice, but you should be able to use the program on a simple level without devoting much time to it.

Storing and recalling information is a valuable and practical use for any computer, and you shouldn't be without a program that performs this general task. You might be surprised to discover, though, that with a little thought and effort, you might be able to write your own filing and recordkeeping programs tailored to your own individual needs.

```
10 rem ** mailing list program **
15 x=101:dim n$(x),a$(x),c$(x),s$(x),z$(x),p$(x):n=0
20 poke 53280,12: rem border gray 2
30 poke 53281,15: rem screen gray 3
40 print chr$(14): rem switch lower case
50 print chr$(8): rem disable comm key
60 print"[clr][blk][rvs on]Mailing List"
70 print:print"[rvs on]f1[rvs off] Enter"
80 print"[rvs on]f3[rvs off] Read"
90 print"[rvs on]f5[rvs off] Print"
100 print"[rvs on]f7[rvs off] Erase"
110 print:print"[rvs on]f2[rvs off] Load"
120 print"[rvs on]f4[rvs off] Save"
130 print"[rvs on]f6[rvs off] Change"
140 getc$:if c$="" then 140
150 ifc$="[f1]"then gosub 10000
160 ifc$="[f3]"then gosub 11000
170 ifc$="[f5]"then gosub 12000
180 ifc$="[f7]"then gosub 13000
190 ifc$="[f2]"then gosub 14000
200 ifc$="[f4]"then gosub 15000
210 ifc$="[f6]"then gosub 16000
220 goto 60
10000 rem ** enter **
10002 if n>=x-1 then return
10004 print"[clr][rvs on]f1[rvs off] Continue"
```

```
10005 print"[rvs on]f8[rvs off] Return to Menu"
10006 get c$: if c$="" then 10006
10007 if c$="[f1]"then 10010
10008 if c$="[f8]"then return
10009 goto 10000
10010 n=n+1
10020 print"[clr][rvs on]Enter Names/Addresses"
10030 print"Entry #";n;"of";x-1
10040 input"Name";n$(n)
10050 input"Address";a$(n)
10060 input"City";c$(n)
10070 input"State";s$(n)
10080 input"ZIP";z$(n)
10090 input"Phone";p$(n)
10100 print:print"[rvs on]Another Entry? (Y/N)"
10110 get c$:if c$="" then 10110
10115 if n>=x-1 then return
10120 if c$="y" then goto 10010
10130 if c$="n" then return
10140 goto 10110
11000 rem ** read **
11005 if n=0 then return
11010 print"[clr][rvs on]Read  Names/Addresses"
11020 print
11030 print "[rvs on]f1[rvs off] Read All"
11040 print "[rvs on]f3[rvs off] Match Name"
11050 get c$:if c$="" then 11050
11060 if c$="[f1]"then 11090
11070 if c$="[f3]"then 11220
11080 goto 11000
11090 for i=1 to n
11100 print"[clr]Entry #";i;"of";n
```

```
11110 print "Name:      ";n$(i)
11120 print "Address: ";a$(i)
11130 print "City:      ";c$(i)
11140 print "State:     ";s$(i)
11150 print "ZIP:       ";z$(i)
11160 print "Phone:     ";p$(i)
11170 print:print"[rvs on]Press Any Key to Continue"
11180 get c$:if c$=""then 11180
11200 next i
11210 return
11220 input"[clr]Match Which Name";t$
11230 for i=1 to n
11240 if n$(i)=t$ then goto 11290
11250 next i
11260 print:print"[rvs on]No Such Name in File"
11270 print:print"Press Any Key To Return to Main Menu"
11280 get c$:if c$="" then 11280
11285 return
11290 print"[clr]Entry #";i;"of";i
11300 print "Name:      ";n$(i)
11310 print "Address: ";a$(i)
11320 print "City:      ";c$(i)
11330 print "State:     ";s$(i)
11340 print "ZIP:       ";z$(i)
11350 print "Phone:     ";p$(i)
11360 print:print"[rvs on]Press Any Key to Return to Main Menu"
11370 get c$: if c$="" then 11370
11380 return
12000 rem ** print **
12004 print"[clr][rvs on]f1[rvs off] Continue"
12005 print"[rvs on]f8[rvs off] Return to Menu"
12006 get c$: if c$="" then 12006
```

```
12007 if c$="[f1]"then 12010
12008 if c$="[f8]"then return
12009 goto 12000
12010 print"[clr][rvs on]Print"
12020 open 1,4,4
12030 fori=1 to n
12040 print#1,n$(i)
12050 print#1,a$(i)
12060 print#1,c$(i)
12070 print#1,s$(i)
12080 print#1,z$(i)
12090 print#1,p$(i)
12100 print#1,chr$(13)
12110 next i
12120 close 1
12130 return
13000 rem ** erase **
13002 ifn=0 then return
13004 print"[clr][rvs on]f1[rvs off] Continue"
13005 print"[rvs on]f8[rvs off] Return to Menu"
13006 get c$: if c$="" then 13006
13007 if c$="[f1]"then 13010
13008 if c$="[f8]"then return
13009 goto 13000
13010 print"[clr][rvs on]Erase Names/Addresses"
13030 print "[rvs on]f1[rvs off] Scan All"
13040 print "[rvs on]f3[rvs off] Match Name"
13050 get c$:if c$="" then 13050
13060 if c$="[f1]"then 13090
13070 if c$="[f3]"then 13230
13080 goto 13000
13090 for i=1 to n
```

```
13100 print"[clr]Entry #";i;"of";n
13110 print "Name:     ";n$(i)
13120 print "Address: ";a$(i)
13130 print "City:     ";c$(i)
13140 print "State:    ";s$(i)
13150 print "ZIP:      ";z$(i)
13160 print "Phone:    ";p$(i)
13170 print:print"[rvs on]f1[rvs off] Continue"
13180 print:print"[rvs on]f8[rvs off] Erase"
13190 get c$:if c$=""then 13190
13200 if c$="[f1]" then goto 13225
13210 if c$="[f8]" then gosub 13800:goto 13224
13220 goto 13190
13224 n=n-1:i=i-1
13225 next i
13226 return
13230 input"[clr]Match Which Name";t$
13240 for i=1 to n
13250 if n$(i)=t$ then gosub 13800:n=n-1:i=i-1
13260 next i
13265 return
13270 print:print"[rvs on]No Such Name in File"
13280 print:print"Press Any Key To Return to Main Menu"
13290 get c$:if c$="" then 11280
13800 fork=i to n
13810 n$(k)=n$(k+1)
13820 a$(k)=a$(k+1)
13830 c$(k)=c$(k+1)
13840 s$(k)=s$(k+1)
13850 z$(k)=z$(k+1)
13860 p$(k)=p$(k+1)
```

```
13870 next k
13880 return
14000 rem ** load **
14004 print"[clr][rvs on]f1[rvs off] Continue"
14005 print"[rvs on]f8[rvs off] Return to Menu"
14006 get c$: if c$="" then 14006
14007 if c$="[f1]"then 14010
14008 if c$="[f8]"then return
14009 goto 14000
14010 print"[clr][rvs on]Load File"
14020 print:print"[rvs on]f1[rvs off] Load from disk"
14030 print"[rvs on]f4[rvs off] Load from Tape"
14040 get c$:if c$="" then 14040
14050 if c$="[f1]"then 14100
14060 if c$="[f4]"then 14250
14070 goto 14040
14100 open1,8,3,"0:mail list,seq"
14140 input#1,n
14150 fori=1 to n
14160 input#1,n$(i)
14170 input#1,a$(i)
14180 input#1,c$(i)
14190 input#1,s$(i)
14200 input#1,z$(i)
14210 input#1,p$(i)
14220 next i
14230 close 1
14240 return
14250 open 1,1,1,"mail list"
14260 goto 14140
15000 rem ** save **
```

```
15002 if n=0 then return
15004 print"[clr][rvs on]f1[rvs off] Continue"
15005 print"[rvs on]f8[rvs off] Return to Menu"
15006 get c$: if c$="" then 15006
15007 if c$="[f1]"then 15010
15008 if c$="[f8]"then return
15009 goto 15000
15010 print"[clr][rvs on]Save File"
15020 print:print"[rvs on]f1[rvs off] Save to Disk"
15030 print"[rvs on]f4[rvs off] Save to Tape"
15040 get c$:if c$="" then 15040
15050 if c$="[f1]"then 15100
15060 if c$="[f4]"then 15250
15070 goto 15040
15100 open 1,8,15
15110 print#1,"s0:mail list"
15120 close 1
15130 open1,8,3,"0:mail list,seq,write"
15140 print#1,n
15150 fori=1 to n
15160 print#1,n$(i)
15170 print#1,a$(i)
15180 print#1,c$(i)
15190 print#1,s$(i)
15200 print#1,z$(i)
15210 print#1,p$(i)
15220 next i
15230 close 1
15240 return
15250 open 1,1,1,"mail list"
15260 goto 15140
16000 rem ** change **
```

```
16002 if n=0 then return
16004 print"[clr][rvs on]f1[rvs off] Continue"
16005 print"[rvs on]f8[rvs off] Return to Menu"
16006 get c$: if c$="" then 16006
16007 if c$="[f1]"then 16010
16008 if c$="[f8]"then return
16009 goto 16000
16010 print"[clr][rvs on]Change Entry"
16020 print:print"[rvs on]f1[rvs off] Scan & Change"
16030 print"[rvs on]f3[rvs off] Match"
16040 get c$:if c$="" then 16040
16050 if c$="[f1]"then 16100
16060 if c$="[f3]"then 16300
16070 goto 16040
16100 fori=1 to n
16110 print"[clr]";n$(i)
16120 printa$(i)
16130 printc$(i)
16140 prints$(i)
16150 printz$(i)
16160 printp$(i)
16170 print:print"[rvs on]f1[rvs off] Continue"
16180 print"[rvs on]f3[rvs off] Change"
16190 get c$:if c$="" then 16190
16200 if c$="[f1]" then goto 16230
16210 if c$="[f3]" then gosub 16800:goto 16230
16220 goto 16190
16230 next i
16240 return
16300 print"[clr]"
16310 input"Match with what name";m$
16320 fori=1ton
```

```
16330 ifn$(i)=m$ then gosub 16500:return
16340 next i
16350 print"[rvs on]No such name in file"
16360 print"[rvs on]Press Any Key to Return to Main Menu"
16370 get c$:ifc$="" then 16370
16380 return
16500 print"[clr]";n$(i)
16510 printa$(i)
16520 printc$(i)
16530 prints$(i)
16540 printz$(i)
16550 printp$(i)
16800 print"1 -- Name"
16810 print"2 -- Address"
16820 print"3 -- City"
16830 print"4 -- State"
16840 print"5 -- ZIP"
16850 print"6 -- Phone"
16860 print:input "Change Which";c
16870 on c gosub 16910, 16920, 16930, 16940, 16950, 16960
16880 return
16910 print:input"To What";d$:n$(i)=d$:i=i-1:return
16920 print:input"To What";d$:a$(i)=d$:i=i-1:return
16930 print:input"To What";d$:c$(i)=d$:i=i-1:return
16940 print:input"To What";d$:s$(i)=d$:i=i-1:return
16950 print:input"To What";d$:z$(i)=d$:i=i-1:return
16960 print:input"To What";d$:p$(i)=d$:i=i-1:return
```

# 7

# Programming—The Rest of BASIC

You'll be surprised at the number of programs that you can write with the BASIC words you've already learned. They are not all the words in the computer's vocabulary, however.

In this chapter, you'll learn a little about how the rest of BASIC works. You'll know what PEEK and POKE, SYS and USR, CMD, SPC and TAB, STOP and WAIT, and ON mean.

If you are interested in using the computer for math, you'll want to know about the mathematical functions of INT, ABS, SGN, SQR, SIN, COS, TAN, ATN, DEF and FN.

You'll see how strings can be taken apart and put back together again with LEN, VAL, STR$, ASC, CHR$, LEFT$, MID$, RIGHT$.

These, along with explanations of BASIC words in other chapters in this book, complete the BASIC story.

## PEEK and POKE

The two most straightforward words in BASIC are PEEK and POKE. Though their names sometimes evoke chuckles, the two words are completely descriptive of their functions. PEEK lets you look at the contents of a location in the computer's memory. POKE puts a number into any location in memory. The two words are often called "machine level" commands, since they deal directly with the computer's memory.

PEEK and POKE will let you play with the machine—kind of like playing with the insides of an auto engine or other mechanical device. POKE is also essential for making color graphics and sound on the Commodore 64. Putting certain numbers in specific memory locations can even affect the way the computer works. (You can also "crash" the computer so that it will no longer respond to you by POKEing the *wrong* number into the *wrong* memory location, but don't worry, you can't damage it. Just turn the computer off then on again, and everything will be back to normal. And PEEK never affects the computer at all.)

POKE is always followed by a memory location, a comma, then a number or numeric variable that will be put into that place in memory. The only numbers that can be POKEd *into* memory locations are those between 0 (zero) and 255. (Want to know why? Check the "Exploring" chapters at the back of this book.) The Commodore 64 has 64K, or 65,536 different memory locations that you can POKE numbers into. The number immediately following POKE must be a whole number between 0 and 65535, or a numeric variable that stands for one of those numbers.

POKE can be used in a program line, or directly from the keyboard.

```
POKE 53272,23
```

or

```
10 POKE 53272,23
```

In the example above, POKEing the number 23 into memory location 53272 switches the computer from the graphic character set (capital letters and graphic symbols) to the typewriter character set (capital and lower case letters). POKEing 21 into 53272 will switch the computer back again. This memory location is in the computer's VIC video controller chip.

Different numbers in different locations do different things. To use POKE, study the memory map located near the end of the book. Meanwhile, try POKEing numbers 0 (zero) to 15 into memory locations 52380 and 53281 and see what happens to the video screen.

Always use PEEK with the number of a location in memory (0 to 65535). This number should be enclosed in parentheses—( ). You can use it either in a program, or directly from the keyboard. Usually, you PRINT the results of a PEEK if you are typing directly on the keyboard.

```
PRINT PEEK(53272)
```

In a program, you can also store the number you get with PEEK as a numeric variable

```
10 A=PEEK(53272)
```

******************************************************************

**ERROR ERROR ERROR ERROR ERROR ERROR ERROR ERROR ERROR**

**ILLEGAL QUANTITY ERROR**

When this ERROR occurs in a program line with a POKE statement, check to see that no number greater than 255 or less than 0 (zero) is being put into a location in memory. If variables are used, check the numbers they stand for to see if they were calculated to greater than 255 or less than 0.

******************************************************************

Using PEEK and POKE can make a program confusing, since what you are doing is not obvious. Also, relying on too many PEEKs and POKEs can make your program incompatible with other Commodore computer models, since both words make use of specific features on each computer model. Sometimes, though, for instance, in programming graphics and sound, you just can't get away from using the two words.

# SYS and USR

SYS stands for the word SYStem and is used to switch out of BASIC and into a "machine code" program or subroutine. Machine code is a more rudimentary—though more difficult—means of programming the computer. Its advantage is speed. Machine code programs often run hundreds of times faster than their BASIC counterparts.

SYS is followed by the memory location that begins the machine code program or subroutine. It can be used in a program or directly from the keyboard. For example:

```
SYS(2061)
```

or

```
10 SYS(2061)
```

After a machine code subroutine has been executed, the computer returns to its BASIC program.

USR stands for USeR, and does just about the same thing as SYS, but works differently. It is more complicated, and is used in programs less often than SYS.

```
10 USR(10)
```

This command sends the program to a machine code subroutine that begins at the address stored in memory locations 785 and 786 and transfers the number (or value of the numeric variable) in parentheses to a part of the computer known as the "floating point accumulator."

Since both SYS and USR relate to the use of machine code programs, they aren't intended for novice programmers. However, you will occasionally use SYS, instead of RUN, to start a machine code program operating.

## CMD

It's not quite clear what CMD stands for, but it is probably short for CoMmanD. CMD performs a simple function—switching information that would ordinarily be PRINTed on the video screen to another device like the cassette recorder or disk drive. Usually, CMD is used to send information to a printer. It is followed by a device number, works with the OPEN and CLOSE statements (see "How the Computer Stores Information"), and is followed by a file number. It can be used in a program or directly from the keyboard.

Here is the most common example of how CMD is used. This procedure LISTs a BASIC program on the printer. You can enter it directly from the keyboard, or use it in a program.

```
OPEN 1,4,4
CMD 1
LIST
CLOSE 1
```

The sequence OPENs file number 1 on device number 4 (the printer), with the secondary address of 4. CMD 1 refers to the file number. LIST would ordinarily PRINT the program LISTing onto the video screen, but since CMD switched it to the printer, it will appear there instead. CLOSE 1 shuts file number 1.

## SPC and TAB

Both of these words are used with PRINT. SPC stands for SPaCe, and TAB means tabulation (similar to a typewriter function).

```
10 PRINT SPC(17) "TEST"
```

or

```
10 PRINT TAB(17) "TEST"
```

Each of these commands will move the cursor 17 spaces from its present location and then PRINT the word TEST. TAB and SPC differ from each other in that TAB cannot be used with PRINT# (a file-handling word), but SPC can. TAB always uses measures from the leftmost screen position (column 1). When either word is used with PRINT, the spaces they put on the screen are nondestructive. That is, they do not erase what was there before. In that respect, SPC and TAB don't PRINT spaces at all.

## STOP and WAIT

STOP is a handy word for testing programs. You can bury it anywhere in a program to help determine how it is working. An example: A certain portion of your program is not performing correctly. You can insert STOP in the area of the lines you are having trouble with. When STOP is encountered, it has the same effect as pressing the RUN/STOP key. You'll see a message on the video screen something like this:

`BREAK IN LINE 100` (or in whichever line the program found STOP)

This way, you'll know if the program ever got to that line, and, if it did, that it is working correctly up to that point. Restart the program by typing CONT. (If you use RUN, the program will start from the beginning with all empty variables.)

**************************************************************

**ERROR ERROR ERROR ERROR ERROR ERROR ERROR ERROR ERROR**

**CAN'T CONTINUE ERROR**

CONT can be used to continue a program after the RUN/STOP key was pressed or the word STOP was used. If you change any line in the program during a break, however, the above ERROR will appear. It will also be seen when the program has not been RUN at all. In either case, RUN the program (again).

**************************************************************

WAIT is completely different. It is used with patterns of individual *bits* in memory locations. When the computer sees WAIT, it will pause until the number stored in a particular location matches the condition set up by WAIT. Many (if not most) programmers find WAIT mystifying and even Commodore suggests that you don't use it. If you are up to the challenge, however, take a look at any reference work on Commodore BASIC.

## ON

This is one of the most intelligent and intriguing words in BASIC, yet many programmers never use it. Maybe this is because ON looks unusual in use and programmers don't take time to learn about it. It is extremely simple to use.

ON is used with a numeric variable and one or more GOTO or GOSUB statements. A typical ON line looks like this:

```
20 ON A GOSUB 100, 150, 180, 220
```

When the number that A stands for is 1, the program will GOSUB to line 100. When it is 2, it will GOSUB to 150. The number 3 for A makes the program GOSUB to line 180, and so on.

Try this example:

```
10 INPUT "TYPE A NUMBER FROM 1 TO 5";A
20 ON A GOSUB 100, 150, 180, 220
30 GOTO 10
100 PRINT "ONE"
110 RETURN
150 PRINT "TWO"
160 RETURN
```

```
180 PRINT "THREE"
190 RETURN
220 PRINT "FOUR"
230 RETURN
```

The program first PRINTs TYPE A NUMBER FROM 1 TO 5, then waits for you to INPUT a number and press RETURN. That number becomes the numeric variable A. If in line 20, A=1, then the program GOSUBs to line 100, PRINTs the word ONE, and RETURNs. The whole thing starts over again and it asks for another number. If you type a number from 1 to 4, the correct spelling of the number is PRINTed. If you type the number 5, or answer with 0 (zero), the ON statement is ignored.

In some cases, ON can be used to replace several IF/THEN statements. Look for places in programs where IF looks for specific numbers. Here's what the above example would look like if IF and THEN were used instead of ON:

```
10 INPUT "TYPE A NUMBER FROM 1 TO 5";A
20 IF A=1 THEN GOSUB 100
30 IF A=2 THEN GOSUB 150
40 IF A=3 THEN GOSUB 180
50 IF A=4 THEN GOSUB 220
60 GOTO 10
100 PRINT "ONE"
110 RETURN
150 PRINT "TWO"
160 RETURN
180 PRINT "THREE"
190 RETURN
220 PRINT "FOUR"
230 RETURN
```

Using ON is one way to help make your programs more "elegant," or more cleanly and efficiently written. It saves programming time, and though you may never run up against the computer's limits, saves memory, too.

## Mathematical Functions

One of the obvious uses for a computer is to have it perform repetitive, complicated math. Computer veterans call this "number crunching."

Since this is a computer book and not a math text, only short descriptions of the math function words in Commodore BASIC are included here. For more information on what these mean and how to use them in equations, look at any high school mathematics book. If you won't be using your computer for mathematics, don't get flustered by this material.

INT stands for INTeger, and makes a whole number out of a decimal fraction.

It is the most often used math function in BASIC. Look at this example:

```
10 A=10.258
20 PRINT INT(A)
```

INT simply chops off the fractional part of the number (.258) and PRINTs the number 10. Be cautious, though. INT cannot be used for rounding numbers. In other words, 10.568 will *not* become 11.

ABS means ABSolute and takes the minus sign off negative numbers. ABS is used like this:

```
10 A=-10
20 PRINT ABS(A)
```

SGN stands for SiGN. It determines whether a number is positive or negative. If the number is positive, SGN will be the number 1. If it is negative, it will be −1. Try this:

```
10 A=-20.258
20 PRINT SGN(A)
```

Or this:

```
10 A=-20.258
20 IF SGN(A)=1 THEN PRINT "POSITIVE NUMBER"
30 IF SGN(A)=-1 THEN PRINT "NEGATIVE NUMBER"
```

Change the number that A stands for to see how SGN works. (By the way, SGN(0)=0.)

SQR returns the square root of a number.

```
10 PRINT SQR(2)
```

SIN, COS and TAN return the SINe, COSine and TANgent of angles, which are always measured in radians.

ATN returns the ArcTaNgent of a number and is measured in radians. If you want to convert an angle in degrees to radians use the formula A(radians) = A(degrees) times pi divided by 180.

```
10 PRINT SIN(2)
20 PRINT COS(2)
30 PRINT TAN(2)
40 PRINT ATN(2)
```

DEF means DEFine and FN means FuNction. They are used to store an equation named by two variables, and to use that function in a program. The second variable is passed along to the equation. For example:

```
10 DEF FN B(D)=X+Y+D
20 X=5: Y=6
30 FOR D=1 TO 10
40 PRINT FN B(D)
50 NEXT D
```

In the above example, line 10 DEFines the FuNction named B(D) as X+Y+D. In line 20, X becomes 5 and Y becomes 6. Lines 30 to 50 PRINT ten results of the equation named B(D)—X+Y+D—or numbers from 12 to 22 as the value of D goes from 1 to 10.

## String-Handling Words

The computer can manipulate strings as well as numbers. You've already seen that strings can be added together or *concatenated.* (You cannot subtract one string from another, though.)

String-handling words are among the most powerful in Commodore BASIC. LEN stands for LENgth and determines the number of characters in a string. VAL means VALue and can turn a string containing numbers into real numbers the computer can work with. STR$ turns any number into a string. ASC is short for ASCII, the number code all characters are represented by. CHR$ is used to PRINT characters called by their ASCII number.

LEFT$, MID$ and RIGHT$ are words used to extract specific portions of strings.

## LEN, VAL and STR$

A string can be up to 255 characters long. Sometimes in a program, you may need to know the exact number of characters in a string. The most obvious way of counting the number of characters is to PRINT the string on the screen and count the number of places it takes up. This isn't always possible, since some strings are used to make pictures and others may have hidden spaces or cursor moves buried in them. Also, strings may vary in length each time a program is RUN. If a string is obtained using INPUT, for example, you have no control over the number of characters it will contain.

The only practical way is to use the BASIC word LEN, for LENgth. It is amazingly simple and can be used in a program or directly from the keyboard.

```
A$="ABCD1234"
PRINT LEN(A$)
```

or

```
10 A$="ABCD1234"
20 X=LEN(A$)
```

In either case, the answer to LEN(A$) will be 8. The use of LEN will become more apparent to you as you read on.

You know that strings can be any combination of characters—letters of the alphabet, symbols, cursor moves, editing commands, and even numbers. For example "1234" is a string and 1234 is a number. You cannot add strings to numbers, but you can turn a string *into* a number. To do so, just ask the computer for the VALue of the numbers inside the quotes.

```
10 A$="1234"
20 B=1234
30 A=VAL(A$)
40 PRINT A+B
```

One possible use for VAL is to help GET numbers from the keyboard. If you remember, GET was comparatively difficult to use in this manner. Try this example:

```
10 GET C$:IFC$="" THEN GOTO 10
20 C=VAL(C$)
30 PRINT C+100
```

The GET command is used to GET a *string* called C$. We can't do any arithmetic with C$, so we make C equal to the VALue of C$. If C$ is any other key—like a letter or a cursor key—C will be equal to 0. This works well, as you can see, for numbers between 0 and 9. But what if you need a number between 0 and 99? Here's one solution:

```
10 PRINT "ENTER A NUMBER BETWEEN 0 AND 99"
20 GET C$:IF C$=""THEN GOTO 20
30 PRINT C$;
40 GET D$:IF D$=""THEN GOTO 40
50 PRINT D$
60 E$=C$+D$
70 E=VAL(E$)
80 PRINT E+100
```

We've added a step here, if you notice. By PRINTing C$ and then D$ next to it, we can see which keys we've pressed. The two single-character strings, C$ and D$, are added together to make a two-digit number, and its VALue is taken. Beware of the nature of VAL, however. If you press 4 and a non-number key, like "M" for instance, the VALue of E$ will be 4, not 40. And, if you press a non-number key first, the VALue of E$ will be 0. When using this kind of routine, it might be a good idea to make a test to see that each key pressed is a number.

If, for some reason, you have a number that you want to turn into a string, you can reverse the above process by using STR$.

```
10 A=1234
20 A$=STR$(A)
```

Why would you want to turn a number into a string? One reason might be the difference in rules concerning the way numbers and strings PRINT on the screen. If you remember, an extra space is added when you PRINT a number next to a string or another number using a semicolon. By turning the number into a string, you can PRINT numbers next to one another without spaces.

When we say that VAL and STR$ turn strings into numbers and vice versa, we really don't do anything to the original variable, either string or numeric. If we made a new numeric variable named EE out of EE$, the original string variable (EE$) will still continue to exist. The same thing goes for using STR$.

## ASC and CHR$

ASC, as stated earlier, stands for ASCII, the name given to the number code for each character that the Commodore computers can use. ASC, with the character in parentheses and quotation marks, returns that character's unique number.

```
PRINT ASC("5")
```

The answer you will see on the video screen will *not* be 5, but 53. What's going on?

The number 53 is an ASCII code number that stands for the character numbered 53. ASCII is an acronym that stands for **A**merican **S**tandard **C**ode for **I**nformation **I**nterchange, and is pronounced ASK-EE. Almost all computers built today use ASCII to represent characters and to communicate with one another over telephone lines.

Commodore computers do not use *true* ASCII codes. They must use their own version of ASCII because the number of characters used by the computer— graphic symbols, lower case letters, cursor and editing symbols, color codes, etc.—is much greater than the original 128 characters defined as being true ASCII. Ever since the first PET computer, Commodore machines have used a variation nicknamed PET ASCII. How different is PET ASCII? Well, some characters are the same numbers as true ASCII, others are different; and since there are 256 PET ASCII character code numbers, there are 128 numbers that don't correlate to any of the original true ASCII numbers.

How much of a problem is this? Not a big problem, as long as you know that PET ASCII exists. Many programmers, especially novices, don't even worry about it. It does become an issue when you go outside of the machine to communicate with another computer or, perhaps, a printer.

For now, just be aware that the numbers that ASC gives you are PET ASCII numbers.

ASC will always return a character number, or the number of the very first character in a string. For example:

```
PRINT ASC("532 Elmwood Drive")
```

This example will also return the number 53, since 5 is the first character in the string.

When using ASC( ), null strings are not allowed. If you use ASC("") or ASC(A$) when A$ = "", the program will stop and you will see an ILLEGAL QUANTITY ERROR.

CHR$ can be thought of as the reverse of ASC. It takes a PET ASCII number and PRINTs its character.

```
PRINT CHR$(53)
```

There's that number 5 again. This method of PRINTing may seem a bit tedious. Why not just PRINT 5? Well, some characters are difficult, if not impossible to PRINT. Try PRINTing a quotation mark, for example.

```
10 A$= """
20 PRINT A$
```

No, that won't work at all. Now try this:

```
10 A$=CHR$(34)
20 PRINT A$
```

That PRINTs a quote mark because 34 is the code number for that character. You can't PRINT a carriage return (the same as pressing the RETURN key), either. But you *can* PRINT CHR$(13).

This is helpful when you PRINT# to a printer, for instance. Other codes like this are also recognized by printers and will perform certain special functions when sent to them.

Here's a list of the most interesting CHR$ codes inside your Commodore 64.

| *PRINT CHR$( )* | *FUNCTION* |
|---|---|
| 8 | Disables the SHIFT and COMMODORE key combination that switches between the graphic and typewriter mode. |
| 9 | Enables those keys after disabling them. |
| 13 | PRINTs a carriage return, same as pressing RETURN key; moves cursor to next line. |
| 14 | Switches from typewriter to graphic mode. |
| 34 | PRINTs a quote mark. |
| 142 | Switches from graphic to typewriter mode. |

Other CHR$ codes move the cursor around and change character colors, too. Look in the back of this book for a complete list of what these codes represent. Also check your printer manual for a summary of which CHR$ codes control its functions.

## LEFT$, MID$, RIGHT$

There is no easy way to understand these three very versatile commands except to sit down at the computer and try them. Each is used to pull apart strings and extract specific information from them. LEFT$ is used to read the leftmost characters in a string; RIGHT$ is used to read characters to the right. MID$ can pull out characters from the middle of the string.

Here's where LEN comes in, too.

```
10 A$="1234567890"
20 L=LEN(A$)
30 FOR I=1 TO L
40 PRINT LEFT$(A$,I)
50 NEXT I
```

If you RUN the above example, you should see this:

1
12
123
1234
12345
123456
1234567
12345678
123456789
1234567890

Why? LEFT$, will return everything left, beginning with the position indicated by the number inside the parentheses. We've used LEN to determine the last number in the FOR/NEXT loop so that we won't try PRINTing any more characters than there are in the string. Type the same program example, but use RIGHT$ instead of LEFT$, this time. Now RUN the program again. You'll see the reverse of what happened before.

0
90
890
7890
67890
567890
4567890
34567890
234567890
1234567890

That's because RIGHT$ returns everything right, beginning with the position indicated by the number inside the parentheses.

Using MID$ can get tricky and confusing if you don't keep track of what you're doing. You'll need two numbers inside the parentheses, not just one.

```
10 A$="1234567890 "
20 PRINT MID$(A$,5,2)
```

The first number tells the computer how many positions go into the string. The second number tells it how many characters, beginning with that position, to PRINT. The above example will PRINT 56 on the video screen.

For a more thorough demonstration, enter the following example:

```
10 A$="123456789"
20 L=LEN(A$)
30 FORI=1 TO L
40 FORK=1 TO L
50 PRINT MID$(A$,I,K)
60 NEXT K
70 NEXT I
```

To get a better look at what is going on, press the CTRL key to slow down the action while the program is RUNning. This may look like something of a puzzle, but it isn't. What you will see is completely logical and will reveal the strength behind MID$.

Let's use LEFT$, MID$, and RIGHT$ in a demonstration of the Commodore 64 real-time clock. Here's a short program that puts the clock in the upper left-hand corner of the screen. It takes apart TI$ and rearranges it so that it looks like the display of a digital clock. By changing the line numbers and using this as a subroutine, you can write programs that keep track of time while they are RUNning.

```
10 INPUT "HOURS";H$
20 INPUT "MINUTES";M$
30 TI$=H$+M$+"00"
40 PRINT "[press CLR]"
50 PRINT "[press HOME]";
60 PRINT "TIME";
70 PRINT LEFT$(TI$,2);":";MID$(TI$,2,2);":";
   RIGHT$(TI$,4)
80 GOTO 50
```

You must enter the hours, minutes, and seconds in two-digit form. So, if the time is 1:03, type 01 in response to HOURS, and 03 to MINUTES. The program assumes that the seconds will begin with 00. It takes the two strings, H$ and M$, and adds them to "00," then puts that string in place of TI$ to set the clock. In the main loop of the program, lines 50 to 80, here is what happens: The cursor is sent back to the HOME position (upper left-hand corner), stays on that line and begins PRINTing. It PRINTs, in this order, the word TIME, a space, the leftmost two characters of TI$ (the hours), a colon (":"), the middle two characters of TI$ (the minutes), another colon, and, finally, the rightmost two characters of TI$ (the seconds).

The whole process starts again when the program goes back to line 50 and PRINTs a new time over the last one. In operation, you see the seconds changing and the program looks like it is RUNing at a leisurely speed. Inside, however, the computer is going like crazy, PRINTing the line over and over, even if the time hasn't changed by a single second. If you want to incorporate this routine into one of your own programs, you may choose to use it as a subroutine, someplace out of the way from the main program.

(Take out the GOTO statement and insert RETURN; put the lines that set the clock at the beginning of your program. Each time you want to PRINT the clock on the screen, however, you will need to GOSUB to these lines. It might not be practical then to show the seconds.)

String handling and manipulation is an easy concept to learn, but it can remain confusing, even for experienced programmers. You will only master string handling with practice, patience, and a clear head.

# 8

# Word Processing: The Electronic Typewriter

"It's an interesting machine, but what do you actually *use* it for?"

That's one of the most frustrating questions asked of personal computer owners. It is also often the most difficult to answer. This section is about one of the most practical uses for your computer—word processing.

Even the simplest personal computers are extremely powerful. They can perform lightning fast calculations and keep track of information far better than a human being can. But not all of us need to make millions of calculations or keep so many records that we can't organize them some other way.

Every one of us, though, has written something at one time or another, from grocery lists to term papers, from letters to professional reports. As people, we aren't perfect. We make mistakes and, in our search for perfection, we change our minds. Consequently, we don't always say what we mean when we write.

Word processors let us express ourselves more clearly and accurately.

For the last few years, word processors have been known as machines that have taken the place of typewriters in offices. Inside these business machines are small computers, sometimes no more powerful than your Commodore 64. The difference is that these computers are dedicated to one single task—word processing.

You may have seen other word processors. Many, if not most, American newspapers no longer have typewriters in their city rooms and editorial offices. Instead, reporters write on things they call "VDT's," for **V**ideo (or **V**isual) **D**isplay **T**erminals. These are really just terminals that are connected to a giant computer with a souped-up word processing program. (In most of these systems, the computer also manages incoming wire service reports, and even controls a typesetter.)

One of the first word processing programs for large business computer systems was ATMS (for **A**utomated **T**ext **M**anagement **S**ystem), designed for IBM computers in the 1970s. A few years later, when the first personal computers began appearing, a landmark program called "Electric Pencil" introduced word processing to individual users. It started a revolution that has produced dozens of excellent word processors, including several for the Commodore 64 family.

## What is a Word Processor?

Essentially, the name says it all. A word processor is a program that processes words. This means working with words—rearranging and reorganizing them.

These are the important functions that make a word processor.

***Entering text*** This is the ability to write on the computer's keyboard and to store what you've written in memory. You should be able, of course, to read what you've written, as well.

***Editing text*** Editing is a vague term, at best. The most important editing features are the ability to insert and erase (or delete) words, sentences, and paragraphs. These are the functions most often used in any word processor. All the rest are frosting on the cake, but make the program more flexible and turn it into a professional-quality tool.

***Storage and retrieval*** This means that what you write can be stored on a disk (or perhaps cassette tape), then played back into the computer when you need to read or work on whatever you've written. There probably hasn't been a word processing program written that doesn't let you do this.

***Printing text*** The end result of any word processor is seeing what you have written on paper. With a good word processor program, you should also be able to change the shape (or format) of the printed text.

That, in a nutshell, is word processing. As you can see, this kind of program turns your computer into a powerful and sophisticated electronic typewriter.

Who can benefit most from word processors? Anyone who has a need to put his or her thoughts down on paper. Students often discover for the first time that they can write. Businessmen and other professionals find that they can improve their productivity by writing reports and correspondence faster and better. Professional writers, always plagued by deadlines, regard the word processor as a godsend. (This book was written on a Commodore computer using two different word processing programs.) If you're none of the above types, take heart. With a word processor you'll soon be writing the letters that you've been ignoring for months, dashing off notes to family and friends, and you may even tackle that idea for a novel that you've had for years. When writing duty does call, you'll find that having access to a word processor is the next best thing to having a secretary. Word processing is fun and impressive, too. Watching your ideas moving around on the screen can be endlessly fascinating, all by itself. (Just don't forget that this is a tool, though, not just a toy.)

## What You'll Need: Printers and Disks

Naturally, you're going to need a printer to begin word processing. It's what makes the system practical. You'll also need a program and some way to store what you've written—either a disk drive or cassette recorder.

***Printers*** A printer is a useful investment for reasons other than word processing. Though it is a necessity for word processing, a printer can also be used to LIST BASIC programs on paper, and with a data base manager, spreadsheet and other programs.

Two types of computer printers are commonly available: *Dot matrix* printers and *letter quality* printers.

Dot matrix printers produce characters by striking the paper (through a ribbon) with a group of electronically controlled wires. Each wire makes a dot on the page; each group of dots forms a letter, number, or other symbol. Because the character is made up of dots and is not solid, some dot matrix printers, particularly early ones, produce copy that can be comparatively difficult to read. Some of the new printers, on the other hand, space the dots closer together and their printing looks much closer to that of a typewriter. This improved dot matrix printing is called "correspondence quality."

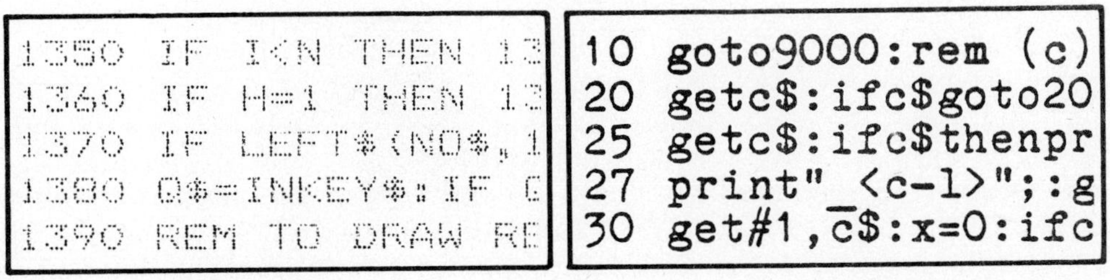


The speed of dot matrix printers ranges from about 80 to 160 characters per second. This kind of printer usually sells for about $300 to $1000 depending on features.

Some examples of dot matrix printers are the Epson MX-80, MX-100 and FX series, the C. Itoh Prowriters, the Star Micronics Gemini, and printers by Okidata and NEC. Commodore's own dot matrix printers are models 1515,

1525E, 4022, and 8023. (Not all of these will work directly with the Commodore 64 computers. More about this later.)

Letter quality printers are sometimes referred to as solid-font printers, because the characters they print are solid, like those produced by a typewriter. Some early letter quality printers used interchangeable IBM Selectric®-style "golfball" type elements. (A few of these are still around and for sale.) They were slow, printing about 12 to 14 characters per second.

Most modern letter quality printers use a type element called a "daisy wheel." This is a plastic, sometimes metal, wheel with flexible spokes (the "petals"). At the end of each spoke is a piece of type for one letter. As the wheel spins, an electronically controlled hammer hits the appropriate one, printing the character on paper. These daisy wheel printers produce copy that can't be distinguished from pages typed on an excellent typewriter, and, therefore, are preferred for word processing. Printing speeds for letter quality printers range from 15 to 55 characters per second.

Unfortunately, daisy wheel printers are complicated and are therefore more expensive than dot matrix machines. They begin at about $400 and although prices have dropped in the last few years, some still sell for over $2000. The least expensive daisy wheel printers (those sold by Smith-Corona® and Brother®, for example) are slow—under 20 characters per second. More expensive models—Qume®, Diablo®, and C.Itoh Starwriter®—are much faster, up to 55 characters per second, and offer many more features. (Related to daisy wheel printers are the NEC Spinwriters® which use a plastic "type thimble" instead of a wheel.) Commodore sells its own daisy wheel printer, the model 8300, which is a version of a Diablo machine.

The speeds of both dot matrix and letter quality printers look impressive. Even 10 characters per second is faster than a typist working at 90 words per minute. A double-spaced manuscript page, for example, is about 1500 characters and takes a little under a minute to print on a good letter quality printer. If you have a 100-page manuscript, that's about an hour and a half.

***Interfaces*** Most letter quality and dot matrix printers can't be used directly with the Commodore 64. They require what is known as an *interface*. Personal computers send information to printers in different ways. These are known as data standards. Printers sold by companies other than Commodore usually come equipped to work with one of the two most popular data standards, *parallel* or "Centronics parallel" (called that because Centronics, a printer manufacturer, promoted the standard), or *serial*. Serial printers take the form of data called RS-232, the same as most modems, or telephone links. Still another data standard is called *IEEE-488* (or "I-Triple E"). This is the standard originally used by the Commodore PET and CBM computers. Except for the model 1515 and 1525E printers, this is the standard that Commodore printers use.

The advantage of buying a printer other than Commodore's is that you will have a much wider variety to select from with different features and prices. The disadvantage is that you will need to purchase an interface at additional cost, and some software may occasionally not work *exactly* as planned. (This is rare, though.)

An interface is a small box that contains some electronic circuitry. It changes the organization of data from one standard to another. Think of the interface as a translator, listening to one language and simultaneously speaking another.

Commodore says that printers and disk drives designed for the Commodore 64 data standard shouldn't be used with equipment designed for Commodore's earlier computers. This means you can't use a standard 1541 disk drive (designed for the 64 family), with a printer originally intended to work with a PET or CBM computer. It also means that you can't use a 1525E printer (the 64's) with a 4040 or 8050 disk drive system (the PET's).

The earlier Commodore disk drives and printers are designed for the IEEE-488 data standard. To use these, you must use an IEEE-488 interface which usually plugs into the cartridge port. Commodore makes one such interface that is "officially" supported by the company. That is, Commodore has designed *its own* software to always work with it. Other manufacturers make IEEE-488 adapters, too.

You *can* mix a standard Commodore 1541 disk drive with a parallel-style printer via several different interfaces. Serial printers are another story. Although serial printers can accept RS-232 data with a connection to the user port (some additional hardware may be required), it is more difficult to use and few programs seem to be supporting this scheme.

The best bet for using a non-Commodore printer with the 64 family seems to be to choose a *parallel* printer—either dot matrix or letter quality—in conjunction with the proper interface. (Look at the section of this book called "Beyond BASIC" for details about these.) This will offer you the most flexibility. One added advantage in buying a parallel printer is that it will have resale value to users other than Commodore owners if you should decide to upgrade your system.

In any case, the most important thing to consider in assembling a word processing system is to shop carefully and ask questions. Make certain that the printer, interface, and word processor program you select are all compatible with each other. Ask friends who have put together a system, take up the problem at a user group meeting, or ask for a demonstration of the available programs at a computer store.

## Advanced Word Processing Functions

As you have learned, a word processor lets you write on the computer's keyboard, change what you've written, store the text on disk or tape, and get a copy on paper. Word processors differ in their capabilities, some of which are extremely powerful.

In addition to inserting and deleting words, sentences, and paragraphs, a good word processor will also be able to *move* these around the text. The way this usually works is by setting a *range* within the lines on the video screen. On command, you can move whatever is within that range—from a single word to several paragraphs—anywhere else in the text.

One reason for using a word processor is to send multiple, personalized letters using information from a name and address file. Since this information varies from letter to letter, it is organized as *variable blocks*. This function is also know as *mail merge* in some programs.

The opposite of variable text is information that occurs repeatedly from one manuscript to another. This kind of repeating information is called *boilerplate*. (The term comes from the legal profession, where it means to use any kind of standard clause in a contract or agreement, again and again.) The ability to easily add these repetitive pieces of prose into a manuscript is called *appending*.

Manuscript pages are best identified by having certain information at the top or bottom of each page. These lines, which could include the author's name, the title of the manuscript, and the page number, are called *headers* (if at the top) and *footers* (at the bottom).

For very long manuscripts, some word processors can make notes (on a floppy disk) to themselves. This note file is designed to be a *table of contents* or, with enough notes, an *index file*. This feature is a real help to anyone who has ever had the time-consuming job of preparing an index to a book or other long document.

Have you ever misspelled a word throughout what you are writing, only to go back and correct it each time? This task is trivial for a good word processor. It is called *search and replace*. You merely give the computer the incorrect and correct spelling and it goes to work, finding and fixing all of the mistakes.

Every word processing program is limited by the amount of memory it can use to store words. Since the Commodore 64 computers have 64K bytes of RAM memory, a good word processor can store many printed pages of text. Still, the length of a manuscript may be more than the capacity of the computer. For this reason, the full text will be broken down into *linked* disk or cassette tape files. These multiple files are also called *global* files.

One common criticism of the Commodore 64 family of computers is their 40 character-wide screen. A standard typewritten page is 60 characters wide, and doing any kind of writing where it is necessary to organize the page into columns can be a mess. So, some word processors allow the screen to actually be wider than the normal 40 characters. How is it done? The screen moves *horizontally*, left and right to read the longer lines. This *variable screen width* is a highly desirable feature. This does not mean, however, that a word processor that is limited to the standard 40-character screen is useless. On the contrary, some users (this author included) prefer this size screen over wider ones.

Going hand-in-hand with a wider screen is the ability to *manipulate columns* by duplicating and moving them. Some programs also have built-in *arithmetic functions* so that columns of numbers can be added or subtracted. Related is the capability to *sort* columns. With this, you can organize a column of names alphabetically, or an address file by ZIP code.

Before typing out a page on your printer, you should be able to see what it looks like. This function is often called *output to video*. Even though you may not be able to read all of the text on the screen (due to the 40-character width), you can get an idea of where pages begin and end. This is useful when writing letters, for making tables and charts, and for separating ideas within a manuscript.

Before printing out a copy of what you've written, you should be able to select *margins* (where the words begin and end on the line), *type size* (e.g., "pica" or 10-pitch type, and "elite" or 12-pitch), and *spacing* (single or double spaces between lines). The program should be capable of *justifying* (making each line length exactly the same), *centering* words and phrases, *underlining*, and typing words in *bold* print for emphasis.

From the sound of some of the above features, word processors are difficult to use. Well, yes and no. Depending on their degree of flexibility, there can be dozens of commands to learn before you can start using a word processing program. Most commands, however, are combinations of one or two keys and a good program gives you visual, on-screen clues to help you along.

Though word processors often resemble each other in their functions, each usually has its own unique command set. Switching, then, from one program to another means learning new commands, even though the basic functions of the programs are similar.

There's another problem, too, with switching between word processors. Most programs won't be able to read the disk or tape files written by other programs. Because of this, the program you choose will probably be the one that you will use for a long time.

## Four Commodore 64 Word Processors

At the time of this writing, several word processing programs had been introduced for the Commodore 64 family. Four of these have been selected as good examples. Each is a reasonably powerful program and is written, not in BASIC (which would make it too slow for practical use), but in *machine code*. All four programs are useful to various degrees, and each is slightly different in its approach to the essential functions of a word processor.

## Quick Brown Fox

QBF is best described as a "mini" word processor, and comes supplied as a cartridge that plugs into the back of the Commodore 64. Included with the package are a loose-leaf instruction manual and several pages of notes on the Commodore version of the program. (Other versions are designed to operate on the IBM-PC and CP/M style computers.) Everything is packaged like an expensive book in its own slipcase.

When the computer is turned on (always *with* the cartridge in place to prevent damage), the screen looks like this:

```
Quick Brown Fox
(C) 1982
```

A quick tap on the RETURN key and the "main menu" appears.

```
. . . Quick Brown Fox
Type
View
Print
```

```
B.View
G.Edit
L.Edit
Move
Delete
Zap Memory
Send
Receive
Clerk.?
```

Typing the first letter of any word listed on the screen makes the computer ready for that activity. **T**ype means to enter text into memory. (There are 37,886 bytes available to write in, or approximately 25 double-spaced manuscript pages.) Unlike most other word processors, QBF is what is known as a "line-oriented" editor. In the Type mode, you can only edit the line you are writing on. When you move to the next line, you must use another function of the program to edit what you've written.

One of QBF's good features is the fact that it does not break up words on the screen. Instead, it automatically moves the cursor to the next line. (Many word processors don't do this, and words are almost always broken at the end of a line, sometimes making them difficult to read on the screen.)

**L**.Edit (for line edit) is used to edit lines of text. The lines you have written appear at the bottom of the screen. Pressing the CRSR DOWN key brings the next line. Somewhat confusingly, pressing CRSR UP will display a new line—the previous one! So the screen looks like this:

```
over the lazy dog.
The quick brown fox jumped
```

This is the way QBF goes backwards and forwards in the text you're editing, always one new line being displayed at a time. The disadvantage of line-oriented editors is that there is no convenient way to simply move the cursor and begin working on an earlier line. The effect is unnerving, especially when you see complete sentences in reverse order. An additional inconvenience is that you are always working on the last few lines on the video screen, even while the rest of it is blank or unused.

This all sounds confusing, and it is, at first. You do adjust to this awkward scheme in very little time, however. The other Edit function in the program is **G**.Edit, the initial of which stands for "global" editing. **B**.View lets you read and change "boilerplate" text.

**D**elete and **M**ove are two more editing functions. They let you erase portions of the text and/or move them around. These work, but take a bit of practice to get accustomed to.

**Z**ap Memory is QBF's way of saying to erase all of, or clear, everything in memory. You must Zap before you load text from disk or tape, for example.

**S**end and **R**eceive are unique among the word processors reviewed for this book. Using a modem, you can send text written with QBF over the telephone lines to another computer using the same program. The accompanying manual offers some cautions, however. The book only says that "The quickest way to find out about Send/Receive is to try it."

**C**lerk takes care of making and reading disk or tape files of what you've written.

**V**iew and **P**rint are related; View lets you see what you will put on paper before it is printed using the Print command. The manual does a good job of describing *embedded commands*—special combinations of letters with the "#" sign that change spacing and margins, set tabs (like on a typewriter), center words and phrases, indent paragraphs, and print in heavy, bold face type. Some of these commands, says the manual, will work on only certain printers. It recommends that a specific interface, the Cardprint (see "Beyond BASIC"), be used with non-Commodore printers. Some printers can also be attached to the user port, according to the manual. It is probably a wise idea to have a dealer first demonstrate the program with the printer and interface you own or intend to buy.

QBF's manual, in an effort to be "user-friendly," makes the mistake of trying to be too cute, sometimes at the expense of the facts; and some information not common to versions for all computers is not always clear. But, since this is not a complicated program, learning to use it is still relatively simple. Lessons in the manual also help you along.

How useful is Quick Brown Fox? That depends on how often you will use it, how much writing you will be doing, and how well you adjust to its unusual editing style. Some people will probably pick up the "backwards" editing quickly. Others will struggle.

One note to those who do not own a disk drive: Since the program comes on a cartridge and can be used with a cassette recorder, this program may be your best bet to get into word processing. While far from perfect, it appears to do what it advertises.

(Quick Brown Fox—Quick Brown Fox, Inc., 548 Broadway, Suite 4F, New York, NY 10012.)

## WordPro 3 Plus/64

WordPro is the original word processing program for Commodore computers. It was designed by a bright Canadian programmer named Steve Punter who recognized its need several years ago and has since produced many upgraded versions. What's in a name? WordPro "3" means this is the third of those versions. (There's a "4" for the CBM 8032 professional computer.) The "Plus" means that it was upgraded after first being introduced for the original Commodore PET.

This version differs little from its PET counterpart, with a few exceptions. One is that the colors of the screen, border, and characters can be changed to suit your own tastes. Another is that the "Control" key—which puts the program in a kind of "command" mode—was the OFF RVS key on the PET. On the Commodore 64, you can use either the COMMODORE key, the CTRL key, or F1, a function key.

The program requires a disk drive and one of several different types of printers, specifically Commodore printers, the NEC Spinwriter, Diablo, Qume, and TEC (also known as the C. Itoh Starwriter). Other printers can be used, but some features (like underlining) may not operate correctly. Any interface can be used, as long as it does not in any way change the text sent to the printer. Both the Micro World Electronix and Cardprint interfaces have been tested with WordPro, and both work well. Because the Cardprint is a "smart" interface capable of operating in several different ways, it must be set up for WordPro by first typing in a few words of BASIC. This is a simple task and is thoroughly explained in the instructions that come with it.

WordPro is a good standard by which to judge other Commodore word processors. It is powerful, fast, and moderately easy to use. The WordPro manual, although wordy, is probably the best of any word processor manuals and includes good, thorough lessons on how to familiarize yourself with the program.

After LOADing WordPro from disk, the program asks a few questions to "customize" itself to your system. One that it asks is how many lines should be devoted to main memory? A maximum of 329 lines is allowed. This means that 13,160 bytes are available to write your text in, the equivalent of about 9 double-spaced manuscript pages. Another "extra"text area is available (you must take memory away from the main area to use it), and is usually used for variable blocks in printing personalized form letters. The extra text area can also be used to see a disk directory, if you choose.

The WordPro screen has 23 lines for entering text. At the top of it is a "status line" that looks like this:

```
WordPro 3 Plus     :X:I:S:C:N    C=1 L=1
```

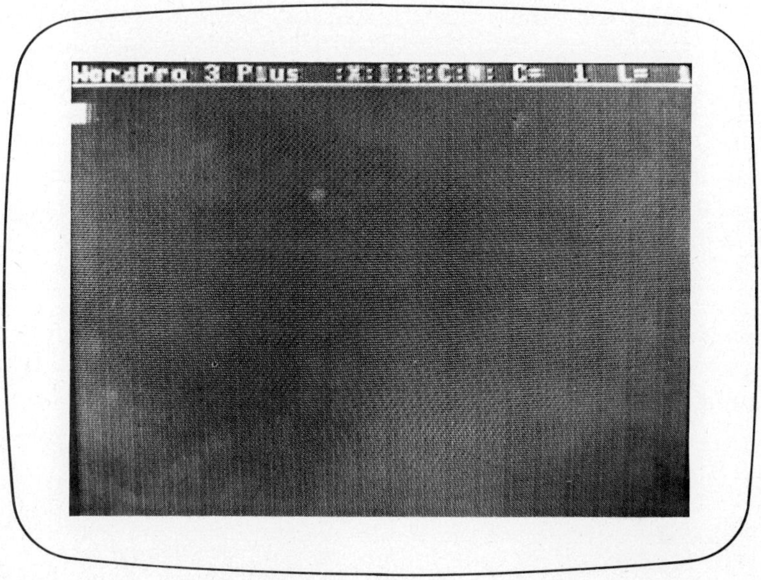

The letters grouped in the middle of the line remind you of what you are doing. **C** stands for "Control." You press one of the control keys to get to WordPro's functions. When you press it, the color of the **C** (in the ":X:I:S:C:N") is reversed. (Pressing the **C** a second time always cancels that order, except for a small "bug" in early versions of the program. More on that later.)

The other letters also show that you are in special WordPro modes. **I** stands for "Insert." In this mode, anything you type will be inserted into the text already on the screen. Everything after your new words moves to accommodate them. **X** means "extra text" and tells you when you are in the extra text memory, rather than the main area. **S** tells you that you are in a mode in which everything typed will be in capital letters. **N** stands for the "numeric" mode. This affects the way numbers appear on the screen.

**C**= and **L**= at the right of the line are always followed by numbers that tell you where the cursor is in relation to available memory. **C** means column number; **L** means line number.

WordPro's screen can be thought of as a "window" into memory. Whatever you do on it will also be done to the text in memory. When you type more than the screen will hold (23 lines), it will move up a line. Using the CRSR UP and DOWN keys, you can quickly "scroll" in either direction, forward or backward through the text, correcting or editing at any time. There are no separate Type and Edit functions to switch between. Using the INST/DEL key, you can erase words or spread them apart to insert other words. (If you have learned how to use the Commodore's editing keys, you've already got a jump on using WordPro.)

There are 46 different control key functions in WordPro, too many to summarize here. Major ones, however, include deleting words and sentences (control-D), setting a range of lines and transferring the text in range to another place (control-R and control-T), getting a disk directory (control-Ø), erasing the text (control-E) and printing out the text on paper (control-O).

In addition to the above control key functions, there are 23 different formatting commands that can be added to the text to determine its shape —margins, justification, centering, bold face printing, etc.—when printed on paper.

WordPro was the first word processor for the Commodore computers to offer the ability to do simple arithmetic. Numbers in the text can be added and subtracted very easily. More complicated math, though, must be done outside the program.

One disadvantage to WordPro is the lack of a way to preview what has been written as it will appear on paper. This "output to video" function is in versions of the program for the Commodore CBM 8032 computer (with an 80-character screen), but is missing on both the PET and 64 family versions.

WordPro's designers missed another opportunity on the 64 version. Like the PET and CBM versions, WordPro 3 Plus/64 takes up memory space usually devoted to BASIC programs. It does not, however, make use of the additional memory available in the 64. Using this would have dramatically increased the memory available to write into, cutting down on the number of linked or global files necessary for long manuscripts.

There is also a bug in some early versions of the program. Pressing the CTRL (or other control key), followed by E puts the program in the "erase" mode. Touching a control key again should cancel this order, but it doesn't. This is potentially disastrous. Professional Software, the company that sells the program in the U.S., says that users with these early versions should inquire about getting an upgraded, corrected copy.

Finally, the program uses a disk protection scheme that prevents making unauthorized copies. It is certainly the right of a software author or distributor to guard against piracy, but this also eliminates the possibility of making back-up copies of the program. If the original disk is damaged, it must be sent back to the distributor and a new disk can be purchased for a handling fee.

Though it is limited in some respects, WordPro 3 Plus/64 is a good writing tool that will even meet the demands of some professionals. Learning to use all of its functions can be time-consuming, but a couple hours of study is all it should take to start using it.

Note: Although WordPro 3 Plus/64 is an adaptation of a previous version of the program, a new one, specifically designed to use the features of the Commodore 64 family, is being prepared.

(WordPro 3 Plus/64—Professional Software, Inc., 51 Fremont Street, Needham, MA 02194.)

## Easy Script

Easy Script is Commodore's "official" word processor for the 64 family. At press time, the company indicated the possibility of including the program (and others) with the purchase of the portable version of the Commodore 64, so you may already have a copy.

Created for Commodore by Precision Software, a British company, Easy Script is very similar to WordPro in design, but very different in operation. Like WordPro, it is a character-oriented word processor in which the video screen acts as a window to the memory where text is stored. A disk drive (or cassette recorder) and printer are required, and, though early versions of the program appeared on disk, plans call for it to ultimately be distributed on a cartridge. This would mean that the program could be used without a disk drive.

Thankfully, Commodore hasn't gone so far as to restrict the program to work only with its own printers. While any Commodore printer can be used, it will also function with the Epson, NEC Spinwriter, Qume, Diablo, and other printers. In addition to printers connected the normal way (attached to the same connector as the disk drives), both parallel and serial (RS-232) printers can be connected to the 64's "user port" if you have the proper cables.

A preliminary manual and program used for this review indicate that 764 screen lines are available for writing text. That is 30,560 bytes, or about 20 double-spaced manuscript pages. Text space is expanded by using the additional memory in the 64 not usually available for BASIC programming. This comes as a welcome improvement to anyone who has run up against the limits of a computer's memory when writing. Manuscripts longer than 20 pages, of course, can be divided into linked, or global, files.

Unlike most other word processors, Easy Script makes use of the 64 family's function keys to simplify operation. Most often used are the F1 key, which acts like a control key to change operating modes, and F4, which puts the program in the "disk mode" to store and retrieve what you've written as well as to see disk directories.

Like WordPro, you can write and edit simultaneously, and a status line at the top of the screen reminds you of where you are in the text and which program mode you are in. Two other good features are variable screen width and the ability to preview what your printed manuscript will look like. Screen width can be set anywhere between 40 and an amazing *240 characters wide.* Though the screen still shows only 40 characters at a time, you can move left and right (in addition to up and down) for writing and reading long lines. Using the "output to video" command, you can actually see the entire page, exactly as it will be printed, again using the CRSR keys to move left and right. (A "quick scan" feature uses the F7 key to jump around for fast checking.)

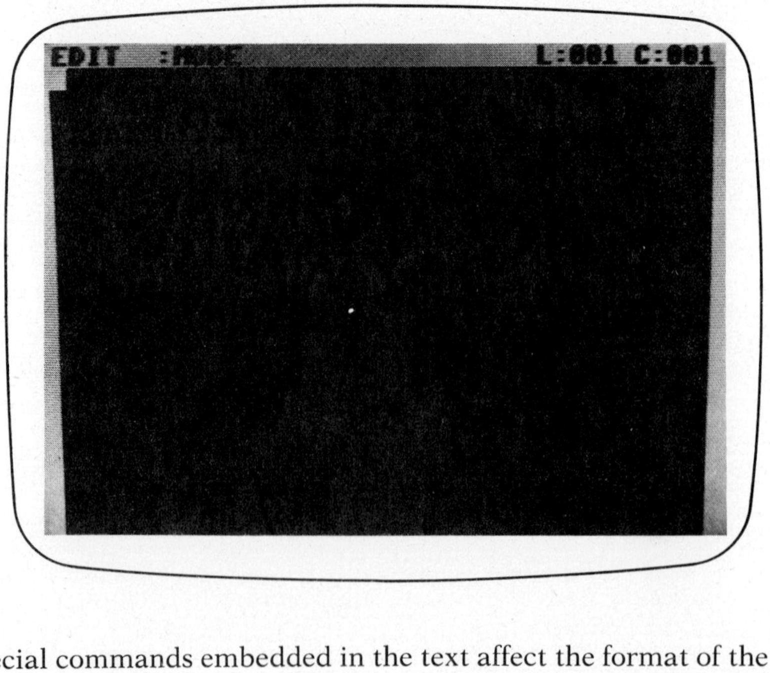


Special commands embedded in the text affect the format of the printed pages, and Easy Script's commands are almost exactly like WordPro's.

```
lm10:rm70:cn1
```

The above line (preceded by a check mark symbol in WordPro, a reversed asterisk in Easy Script) means the same thing to both programs: Set the left margin to 10 spaces, the right margin to 70 and center the line on the page. Other format codes, too, are the same, but Easy Script and WordPro will not accept each other's disk or tape files. And, while their basic functions are similar, most of Easy Script's commands are different, though just about as logical as WordPro's.

The fact that Commodore is sponsoring Easy Script means that it stands a good chance of becoming the standard word processor for the 64. As good as it is, it seems to lack a few functions. (There doesn't appear to be a numeric mode or arithmetic functions.) Still, it is a well-written program suitable for both amateur and professional users alike.

(Easy Script—Commodore Business Machines, 1200 Wilson Drive, West Chester, PA 19380.)

## PaperClip

PaperClip is kind of a "dream machine" word processor that hails from Batteries Included, a Canadian software company with a humorous name. (No batteries are included with the program, or are actually necessary.) Just about every feature you could think of in a word processing program is here. In fact, PaperClip is so powerful that it can take a long time to learn how to fully exploit its many, many features. There are nearly 150 different operation and format commands! Yet only a few of these are necessary to start working with it.

The program resembles both WordPro and Easy Script in its operation and commands. Though the manual fails to mention it, PaperClip will even accept disk files written by WordPro and, with some minor modifications, Easy Script. (Beware, though. WordPro won't accept PaperClip's files.) You can also store text on cassette tape files and probably LOAD the PaperClip program itself from tape. But since it is extremely long, using it without a disk drive is impractical.

Nearly any printer can be used with the program due to the novel way PaperClip has of customizing itself for use with your printer and interface. More than a dozen standard "printer files" are included on the same disk as the program. These are designed to work with the Commodore, Epson, NEC Spinwriter, TEC (C. Itoh), Diablo, and Olympia printers, and are entered with PaperClip itself. If none of the supplied files work with your printer, you can build one using a program that's also included. Instead of entering this file each time you want to print, yet another program will make a new version of PaperClip, with your printer information permanently in place.

Like Easy Script, you can write on a line longer than PaperClip's normal 40 characters—up to 126 characters. Again, you use the CRSR keys to move left and right, as well as backwards and forwards through text. You can also preview what you've written before it is printed on paper using an "output to video" command. Unlike Easy Script, however, PaperClip will not allow you to see the entire page—the right side is likely to be chopped off—due to the limitations of screen width. This is still useful for seeing where pages begin and end. You can also switch between video and printer output, so that only selected pages are printed. (This is great when you want to print only the last two pages of a very long manuscript.)

For jobs when columms of information (lists, etc.) are important, PaperClip will move these columns, perform simple arithmetic (addition and subtraction), and even *sort* numbers or words by values or alphabetically. This means you can set up a mailing list, put new entries at the bottom, then ask the program to insert them in their proper places on the list.

A table of contents, or index file, can also be generated automatically by the program. To use this feature, you type in special lines identifying the topics you're discussing. When you "output to video," PaperClip will take these comments and build a new disk file that indicates the page on which each topic appears.

Unlike the other word processors in this chapter, PaperClip comes furnished on an unprotected disk so you can easily make back-up copies to use if the original disk is damaged or destroyed. To protect the program against unauthorized copies, an electronic "key" is included. It plugs into the computer on control (joystick) port number 1, and PaperClip won't run without it. To hide from prying eyes, the electronic circuitry inside the key is embedded in rock-solid epoxy.

If there is one complaint about PaperClip, it is its instruction manual. This program is extremely powerful, yet the book does not go far enough in explaining the myriad of features. Particularly poor are the instructions on how to build printer files and make custom copies of the program. The printer files that are supplied on the master disk aren't identified well, either. To top it off, the book was written for the PET/CBM version of PaperClip and only one page is devoted to the differences between it and the 64 version. (Batteries Included promises to revise the book, and says that all owners of the program will be sent the new edition or update notes.)

Despite the poor manual, this is a terrific program that should satisfy virtually *anyone* who uses it. Its flexibility and compatibility with other programs makes it an invaluable addition to any Commodore 64 system.

(PaperClip 64—Batteries Included, 71 McCaul Street, Toronto, Ontario, Canada M5T-2X1)

## A Few Tips

Using a word processor will change the way that you write. In addition to the opportunities you have to correct errors, it can also improve the *quality* of your writing. For example, if you've used a word earlier that is more suitable in another place, don't hesitate to change it. Nor should you ever need to exclude ideas just because you thought of them late—go back and insert them where they belong.

Everyone establishes their own system for working, but here are a few tips to get you started:

- If possible, make a copy of the word processing program as the first file on each disk you use. That way, you'll cut down on shuffling disks back and forth out of the disk drive.
- Organize your disks, one for letters, one for school work, one for that pet project you've been working on, etc. That way, your work will always be easy to locate. Or, organize disks by time, labeling them by month or even week for easy reference.
- Try to put the title at the top of each text file as a non-printing comment. You'll never need to worry about storing it on disk by the wrong name.
- *Always* make back-up copies of your files if what you are working on is important. True misery is losing weeks of work. Update the back-up copies as you rewrite and edit so that they contain the same text as the masters. Save your work to disk or tape often, so that you won't lose all of it if you make an operating mistake.
- Make a copy of the command summary from your manual and keep it in front of you until you know the program backwards and forwards. If there is no such summary, make one for yourself.
- While proofreading from the video screen is tempting and saves paper, print out a checking copy. There's nothing like seeing words on paper to catch mistakes.
- Be sure to set up the place where you will work so that you will be comfortable—computer at the right height, plenty of room for working materials, no glare from back-lighting. Take frequent breaks so that you're not staring at the video screen for long periods of time.
- Don't be tempted to rewrite your work to death. Though word processors offer the chance to continually improve, too much rewriting can hurt what you created. Don't spend more time than it would take you to write on a typewriter. When the job is done, the work is over.

# 9

# Color, Graphics, Sound, and Games

Some personal computer owners never take advantage of the color, graphics, and sound features of their machines. To others these are among the most important aspects of any computer. There are those who would argue that these "frills" aren't important for "serious" computing—math, word processing, data base management, etc. They point a finger at video games.

Certainly advanced graphics and audio features make a machine perfect for games, but they offer even greater opportunities. Graphics are becoming more and more important and the computer is providing new ways of visualizing information. (Have you seen *USA Today*, the national newspaper? Many of its colorful "information graphics" are produced by computer.) Recent, advanced computers like the Xerox Star and Apple Lisa are also breaking new ground in the use of graphics.

Just because a computer can produce the bleeps and yelps of a video game doesn't mean that is *all* it can do. Computers can be musical, or reproduce human speech with startling accuracy.

The Commodore 64 family really shines when it comes to its graphic and sound capabilities. Unfortunately unlocking that power can be complex and time-consuming. That's because our only convenient link to the machine is the BASIC programming language. Making pictures and sounds with BASIC is a little like trying to describe a sunset or symphony with only a few words. There's little chance for poetry, but we can, with difficulty, get the idea across.

This chapter will introduce you to color, graphics, and sound on the Commodore 64 family. It isn't intended as a complete treatment of these topics, but only to whet your appetite for more. More is available, too, near the end of this book in two chapters entitled "Exploring Graphics" and "Exploring Sound." Those chapters will require you to come to them with a good understanding of other ideas in this book. Even they cannot teach you everything, though. Graphics and sound deserve a book all to themselves.

In this chapter, you will learn how to make your programs more attractive-looking, and how to start using a few graphic tricks. You'll learn how the computer can be taught to play simple songs. If you are interested in games, you may want to know about the computer's "random number generator"—it can toss a pair of dice or spin a wheel of fortune. Finally, you'll learn a little about the "control ports." That's where you plug in joysticks and game paddles.

## VICtor and SIDney

VIC and SID sound like a couple of guys who might inhabit a Las Vegas casino. In the case of the Commodore 64 computers, though, they are the names given to two incredibly capable microchips that control everything you see and hear on a television set or video monitor.

VIC stands for **V**ideo **I**nterface **C**ontroller, and SID is an acronym for the **S**ound **I**nterface **D**evice. Inside these two chips are more features than most computers can boast of.

VIC offers a variety of graphic modes. The first of these is the *character mode*. It is the one that the computer "comes alive" in and is the simplest to use. The PRINT command is used to put something on the screen. Though it is also the most limited, clever programmers are always finding new ways of making attactive video pictures in this mode.

One way of enhancing the appearance of a screen in the character mode is to *redefine* the computer's character set. The VIC chip can be instructed to change from its standard alphabet, numbers, and other symbols, to characters of your own design. Special symbols for math and science, other languages, even music can be programmed as new characters.

In the character mode, the video screen has 1,000 individual places (25 lines of 40 characters), and each is represented by 1 *byte* of memory. In total, 1,000 bytes are used for the screen. Since it can accommodate up to 16 different colors of characters on the screen at one time, additional memory stores this color information. For its color, each character requires only one-half byte, or four *bits*. (This may sound like a joke, but it isn't: These half-bytes are called "nybbles.") Another 500 bytes, then, are devoted to screen color.

Another graphic mode, called *high-resolution* graphics, is used to overcome the limitations of the character mode. With high-resolution graphics, the screen is made up completely of dots, called *pixels*, for picture elements.

(You cannot use the PRINT command, here.) Each dot represents a single bit in memory. The dimensions of a hi-res screen are 320 dots across by 200 down. This corresponds to 8,000 bytes of memory.

There can be two colors, one color for the background and another for the dots. One variation on this mode allows you to determine different *regions* on the screen, each region being an area of character-size blocks. You can set a different background and dot color within a region for colored hi-res screens, but only two colors can be used in each region.

You can double the number of colors used on the screen if you use another mode, called *multicolor.* Four different colors can be used simultaneously, but the screen's resolution is cut in half. A multicolor screen has only 160 dots across, but 200 down. (You can't use the PRINT command in multicolor mode, either.)

*Sprites* can be used in any graphic mode. These are small, high-resolution pictures stored in various places in memory. The VIC chip can recognize these pictures and put them on the video screen, where you can move them around using BASIC. A sprite is made up of as many as 540 dots—24 across by 21 down—or 63 bytes of memory. It can be in any one of the 64's sixteen colors, and can be doubled in width, height or both. These single-color sprites are the most impressive graphic device that inexperienced programmers can use. Another kind of sprite is a *multicolor sprite.* Like the multicolor hi-res screen, a multicolor sprite can be four colors, including the background color of the screen. Multicolor sprites are more difficult to use and program than single-color sprites.

Sprites, redefined characters and hi-res screens are explained in more detail in "Exploring Graphics." In this chapter, you'll learn about character graphics, and how to turn sprites on and off and move them on the screen.

VIC isn't the only chip to offer creative possibilities. What VIC does for your eyes, SID does for your ears.

Some computers can squeak and grunt. SID can croon, and, in the near future, may even talk. (Programmers are working on speech synthesizer programs for SID right now.) SID's three *voices* allow it to make three distinct sounds simultaneously. The chief difference between the audio capabilities of the 64 computer family and their predecessor, the VIC-20, is in the quality of sound produced. (The VIC-20 has no SID chip of its own.)

The components of a sound, as used by an electronic music synthesizer for instance, are *attack, decay, sustain* and *release* (ADSR). The differences in these are the primary reason why a piano sounds different than a banjo, or why a pipe organ doesn't sound like a Chinese gong. Attack, decay, sustain and release are measured in time—tiny fractions of a second. Each of SID's voices can have different ADSR settings.

Attack refers to the speed with which a note sounds. An example of a sharp, short attack is a banjo, or any other plucked instrument.

Decay comes after attack and is the falling action. In a piano, the original sound is loud, but gradually falls off to a "ringing" level.

The length of time that a note sounds is called its sustain value, and the time it needs to become completely silent again is called release.

These are simple concepts that are often very difficult to understand, and are covered in more detail in the chapter entitled "Exploring Sound." For right now, you'll learn how to get SID to make a sound, and how the computer can play musical notes and simple songs.

The shape that results from setting the ADSR is called an *envelope*. In addition to different ADSR settings, SID can give each voice a different basic sound, or *waveform*. Think of the waveform as the kind of cloth a shirt is cut from, and the style of the shirt itself as the envelope. The sound can then be further changed by the effects of various *filters*. If you're familiar with electronic music synthesizers, you'll also be interested to know that there is a *ring modulator* in the SID chip, and that you can actually mix "real" sound from a tape recorder, microphone, or musical instrument with the SID sound. (There's an input, pins numbered 5 and 2, on the Audio/Video plug at the back of the computer. Don't try connecting anything to these unless you know what you're doing.)

Finally, there are non-audio and non-video functions of SID and VIC. Inside VIC are memory locations used with a light pen. In the SID are memory locations used to read the position of game paddles.

As mentioned earlier, there are no words in BASIC that deal directly with VIC and SID. We can communicate with these chips, though, using POKE to put numbers into memory locations inside them. There are 24 memory locations in VIC, numbered 53248 to 53271. Inside SID are 25 locations that refer to sound making, numbered 53272 to 53296.

## RaNDom Notes

Before we go any further, let's take a look at a BASIC word you'll find in two of the programs in this chapter. That word is RND, for RaNDom. It produces random numbers in all the Commodore computers, from the VIC to the members of the 64 family.

Random numbers are an essential part of game playing. Every time you roll dice, spin a wheel, or shuffle cards, you get random numbers or a random sequence of numbers. They are produced by the computer with a mathematical formula called a *random number generator*. These numbers are actually not completely random, but the way the formula works is so clever that you won't see any pattern.

RND is used with a "seed" number, which determines how the random number is selected. You can use different seed numbers, and each is enclosed in parentheses following RND. Turn your computer off, then on again, and type this example:

```
10 FOR I=1 TO 5
20 PRINT RND(1)
30 NEXT I
```

You will see five numbers on the screen.

.185564016
.0468986348
.827743801
.554749226
.897233831

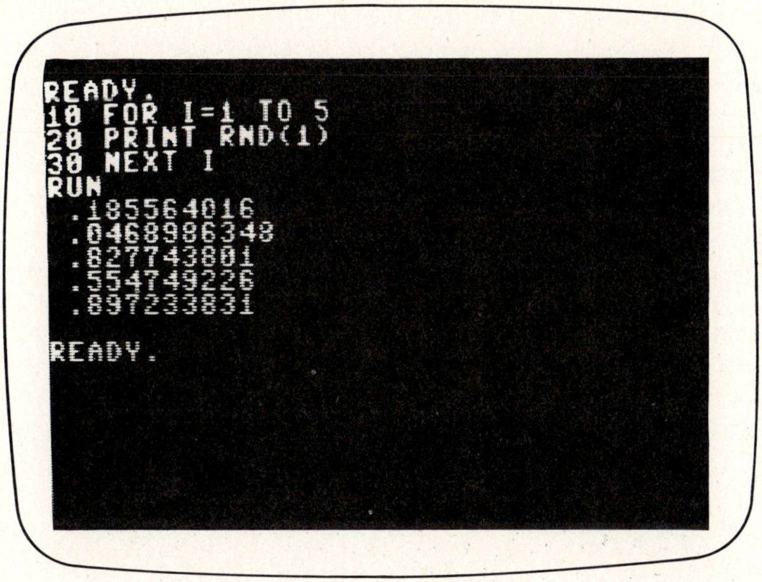


You may not see this *particular* sequence, but each time you turn the machine on and RUN this program, you will see the *same* sequence of numbers. You may ask why this sequence is the same if *random* numbers are supposed to be generated? Good question.

Here's how the random number generator works. When the computer is turned on, a "seed" number is automatically selected. This seed generates a list of numbers. Each time the RND function is used with *any* positive number in parentheses, the next number from the list is returned. Each time RND is used with a different negative number, a new list of numbers is selected. If RND is used with 0 (zero) a random number is generated, based on the TI clock. Here's an example:

```
10 X=RND(-1)
20 FOR I=1 TO 10
30 PRINT RND(1)
40 NEXT I
```

Each time you RUN this program, you will see the same sequence of numbers generated by RND(1). If you change the first *negative* seed, however, you will see a different list, but, again, the same one over and over. Try it. Change RND(−1) to RND(−2).

What is the best way to generate random numbers? One way is to first select a negative seed number at random, using the TI clock.

```
10 N=TI
20 X=RND(-N)
30 FOR I=1 TO 10
40 PRINT RND(1)
```

When RND is used this way, a different number (negative TI) is used as a seed. Each time the program is RUN, it generates a different list.

Or, you can use RND(0) which also generates random numbers based on a formula involving the TI clock. The advantage to either of these is that TI can be any number between 0 and 51,839,999, and you can never predict what it will be. Even if you could, it would be nearly impossible to wait for a specific seed number, since TI changes every 1/60 of a second.

You've probably already noticed that the numbers RND spits out aren't exactly the kind of numbers you'd want to use in a game. To get whole numbers instead of decimal point fractions, we will use a math function, INT, for INTeger. To set a range of numbers, we will multiply the RND number. Even if you're not good at arithmetic, you'll want to follow along. The example you'll see is the model for almost all uses of the random number generator.

Let's say that we want random numbers between 0 (zero) and 10. It's easy.

```
10 N=INT(10*RND(0))
20 PRINT N
30 GOTO 10
```

When you RUN this example, you'll see a steady stream of numbers between 0 and 10. The number that you multiply RND by always sets its range. INT tells the computer to take the whole number and eliminate any decimal fraction. In some cases, you may not want the number 0, only numbers between 1 and the last number in the range. All you need to do is add 1, like this:

```
10 N=INT(10*RND(0)+1)
20 PRINT N
30 GOTO 10
```

Using RND, be sure that you have typed the correct number of parentheses. If you have one too many or not enough, the computer will give you a SYNTAX ERROR message. Just remember that there should be an even number of parentheses and check for the directions they're facing.

Here's a quick example of how RND can work in a card game. We'll set up an array of the names of 52 cards in a deck. The program will let you "cut" the cards.

```
10 PRINT "[CLEAR]"
20 DIM CA$(52)
```

```
30 FOR I=1 TO 13:READ CA$(I):CA$(I)=CA$(I)+" OF
   HEARTS"
40 NEXT I
50 RESTORE
60 FOR I=14 TO 26:READ CA$(I):CA$(I)=CA$(I)+" OF
   SPADES"
70 NEXT I
80 RESTORE
90 FOR I=27 TO 39:READ CA$(I):CA$(I)=CA$(I)+" OF
   CLUBS"
100 NEXT I
110 RESTORE
120 FOR I=40 TO 52:READ CA$(I):CA$(I)=CA$(I)+" OF
    DIAMONDS"
130 NEXT I
150 PRINT "PRESS ANY KEY TO CUT THE CARDS"
160 CA=INT(52*RND(0)+1)
170 GET C$:IF C$=""THEN 170
180 PRINT CA$(CA)
190 GOTO 150
1000 DATA ACE,KING,QUEEN,JACK,10,9,8,7,6,5,4,3,2
```

This program doesn't shuffle the deck. In fact, the deck stays just as it looks when you break open a new pack, with all the cards in order. The RND statement picks a random number from 1 to 52, and displays the card for which it stands. You can see how RESTORE works, too. Only one line of DATA is all that is required; it is READ four different times. Each time, the suit—hearts, spades, clubs and diamonds—is added to the value of the card.

## Screen and Border Colors

Two memory locations in the VIC chip control the color of the video screen and its border. These are set by POKEing any of 16 numbers between 0 and 15 into these locations. POKE 53280 sets the color of the *border*, and POKE 53281 changes the color of the *screen*.

```
10 POKE 53280,11:POKE 53281,15
```

This line sets the screen to gray 3, the lightest gray (almost white), and the border to gray 1, the darkest gray. Each color in the Commodore 64 spectrum has its own number.

| *POKE 53280 53281* | *COLOR* |
|---|---|
| 0 | Black |
| 1 | White |
| 2 | Red |
| 3 | Cyan (powder blue) |
| 4 | Purple |
| 5 | Green |
| 6 | Blue |
| 7 | Yellow |
| 8 | Orange |
| 9 | Brown |
| 10 | Light Red (hot pink) |
| 11 | Gray 1 (dark gray) |
| 12 | Gray 2 (medium gray) |
| 13 | Light Green |
| 14 | Light Blue |
| 15 | Gray 3 (light gray) |

One way around the job of remembering each of these colors and memory locations is to define variables and use these instead of POKE numbers.

```
10 BORDER=53280: SCREEN=53281
20 REM COLORS FOLLOW
30 BL=0:WH=1:RE=2:CY=3:PU=4:GR=5:BU=6:YE=7
40 OG=8:BR=9:LR=10:G1=11:G2=12:LG=13:LB=14:
   G3=15
50 POKE SCREEN,RE: REM POKE SCREEN RED
60 POKE BORDER,GR: REM POKE BORDER GREEN
```

This is a good method of keeping track of memory locations inside VIC and SID. You must be careful, though, that your abbreviations don't duplicate one another (if you notice BL stands for black but BU means blue) and that they are not BASIC words or reserved variables (OG stands for orange, not OR).

## Character Colors

You know that pressing the CTRL (control) key and a number key (0 to 9), will change the color of the characters you type on the screen. You get another eight colors by pressing the COMMODORE key and a number key together. The names of the first set of eight colors are printed on the front of each number key, but the names of the second set are not.

Changing character colors is almost a necessity after you change the screen color, since some are practically unreadable against certain screen colors. But changing the color you are typing in does not change the color that a program will PRINT in.

Like the editing keys—CRSR up, down, left, right, INST/DEL and CLR/HOME—the color keys work with PRINT statements. Using PRINT and quotation marks and pressing a color key will not change the color you are typing in, but, instead, will leave a command mark that will change colors when the program is RUNning. The command mark is a symbol reversed against the background.

Try this: (Press the keys named inside the square brackets; don't type the words themselves.)

```
05 POKE 53281,11:POKE 53280,15
10 PRINT "[CTRL and BLK] BLACK     [CTRL and WHT] WHITE"
20 PRINT "[CTRL and RED] RED       [CTRL and CYN] CYN"
30 PRINT "[CTRL and PUR] PURPLE    [CTRL and GRN] GREEN"
40 PRINT "[CTRL and BLU] BLUE      [CTRL and YEL] YEL"
50 PRINT "[COMM and BLK] ORANGE    [COMM and WHT] BROWN"
60 PRINT "[COMM and RED] LT RED    [COMM and CYN] GRAY 1"
70 PRINT "[COMM and PUR] GRAY 2    [COMM and GRN] LT GREEN"
80 PRINT "[COMM and BLU] LT BLUE   [COMM and YEL] GRAY 3"
```

After you type the first quotation mark ("), any combination of CTRL or COMMODORE and a color key will leave its command mark. If you make a mistake and leave this "quote mode" (see "Some Essential Skills"), the color that you are typing in will change instead. To leave a color command mark, you must get back into the quote mode by correctly repositioning the cursor and typing a single quote mark.

When you RUN the above example, you will see each color name PRINTed in the correct color. One color, gray 3, will not be PRINTed because it is the same color as the background. Try changing the numbers with POKE 53281 to see which character colors work well with screen colors.

You will always continue to PRINT in the color selected until you indicate otherwise in your program. To highlight a particular word in text, you must change colors twice—once from the original color you have chosen, then once again to go back to that color. An example:

```
10 PRINT "[CTRL BLK]IN [CTRL RED] RED [CTRL BLK] AND BLACK"
```

## PRINTing Graphics

The graphic symbols you see on the fronts of almost all the keys are your clues to a simple system of PRINTing screen graphics. In combination, these symbols can be used to create borders, boxes, visual highlighting, and emphasis, and, with enough imagination, even pictures. The technique of making graphic displays with these symbols has various names, including "building-block graphics," and "mosaic graphics." We'll continue to call them character graphics.

Let's put a box on the video screen, using the graphic symbols. Remember to press the keys indicated within the square brackets.

```
10 PRINT "[CLR][CRSR DN]";
20 PRINT "[SPACE][SHIFT O][COMM Y][COMM Y][SHIFT P]"
```

```
30 PRINT "[SPACE][COMM H][SPACE][SPACE][SHIFT N]"
40 PRINT "[SPACE][SHIFT L][COMM P][COMM P][SHIFT @]"
```

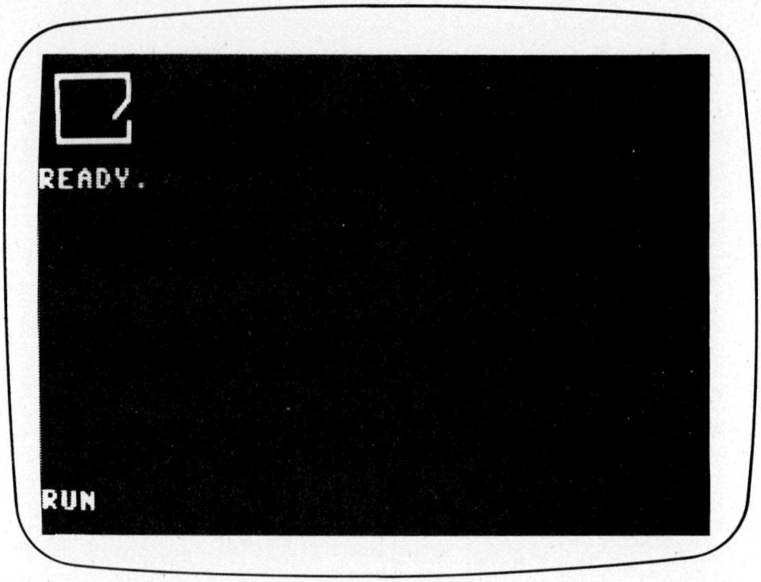


When you RUN the example, a square box should appear in the upper left-hand corner of the screen. If spaces were not PRINTed first in lines 20 to 40, or if the CRSR down (DN) in line 10 wasn't there, the edges of the box would merge with the background color. Use CRSR down to reposition the box on the screen. Change line 10 to:

```
10 PRINT "[CLR][5 CRSR DN]";
```

Instead of typing a single CRSR down, press the key five times. Now the box will be PRINTed lower on the screen. Try inserting spaces into lines 20 to 40, after the first quote mark. If you've inserted exactly the same number of spaces in each line, the box will move to the right.

As you can see, the box that will be PRINTed is clearly visible when you LIST the program lines. Be careful, however. If the line number jumps from 99 to 100, or from 100 to 1000, the difference in spacing may mislead you. Change line 40 to line 10000 and LIST again. Even though the box looks wrong in the LISTing, it will continue to PRINT correctly.

You can store some small screen graphics as strings, too. Each string can contain graphic symbols as well as CRSR moves that will put each symbol in its correct place.

SHIFT and the U, I, J and K keys will PRINT the graphic symbols used to make rounded corners. If we put all four of them together, we can make a ball. (It will be a little square-looking, though.) One way to put the ball on the screen is with two separate PRINT statements.

```
10 PRINT "[SHIFT U][SHIFT I]"
20 PRINT "[SHIFT J][SHIFT K]"
```

Since the cursor moves down and goes to the beginning of a new line after PRINTing the top half of the ball in line 10, the bottom half is positioned correctly by line 20. We can accomplish the same thing by PRINTing a string that represents the ball, complete with the correct CRSR moves. (CRSR LT is CRSR left.)

```
10 A$="[SHIFT U][SHIFT I][CRSR LT][CRSR LT][CRSR DN][SHIFT
   J][SHIFT K]"
20 PRINT "[CLR]";A$
```

Erasing screen graphics is done by PRINTing spaces. If we wanted to erase the ball in the above example, we could define another string as a block of four spaces and CRSR moves. Add these lines to the example:

```
30 FOR I=1 TO 1000:NEXT I
40 B$="[2 SPACES][2 CRSR LT][CRSR DN][2 SPACES]"
50 PRINT "[HOME]";B$
```

When the program gets to line 30, it will pause so that you can see the ball PRINTed. Line 40 defines B$ as a string that PRINTs a block of four spaces, the same size as the ball. When the cursor is positioned exactly as it was when the ball was PRINTed, B$ will erase it.

One advantage of defining a graphic as a string is that we can now PRINT it anywhere on the screen without worrying about the correct spacing. Change line 20 to this:

```
20 PRINT "[CLR][CRSR DN][CRSR RT]";A$
```

Experiment with the number of CRSR right and CRSR down keys pressed. Make sure you don't have more than the screen can handle, 25 CRSR downs or 40 CRSR rights.

The best rule to follow when creating graphics is to count the number of spaces and non-PRINTing characters (like CLR, CRSR moves and color command marks) to make sure you get what you want. Make a diagram on paper, following the movement of the cursor, if you need help. Another good idea is to always use HOME to put the cursor back at the upper left-hand corner before making any complicated moves. This becomes your reference point and never changes.

Be particularly careful about including semicolons where they belong. If you aren't clear what semicolons do, read about how they work with PRINT in Chapter 4. Semicolons are important in accurately positioning PRINTed character graphics.

Even veteran programmers make mistakes, however, and PRINTing a graphic display requires concentration. Programs with graphics in them seldom RUN correctly the first time. Write a graphic program in small chunks, testing each section as you write it.

## Digital Dice

We can use RND and character graphics in a program to simulate the roll of a pair of dice. The LISTing of this simple program follows. Enter it into the computer, pressing the keys indicated within the square brackets. If the square brackets contain a number and a key—like [8 CRSR DN]—then press that key the number of times you see, eight CRSR down keys in the case of this example. When you press the graphic keys (a key plus the SHIFT or COMMODORE key), you should see the graphic symbols that comprise the pictures of each die.

Line 10 of the program POKEs numbers into memory locations 53280 and 53281 to change the color of the screen to gray 3 (light gray) with a gray 1 (dark gray) border. A FOR/NEXT loop begins at line 30.

```
30 FOR I=1 TO 25
```

Here's what happens inside this loop: Two random numbers are generated, numeric variables D1 and D2, for die 1 and die 2. Each number has a range of from 1 to 6, since that is the number of possibilities for each die. One picture of each possible die is stored as a subroutine, beginning at line 1100.

The cursor is positioned in line 60 by placing it in the HOME position for reference, then moving it down 10 lines and over 15 spaces. ON is used in line 70 to PRINT the appropriate die. If D1 is 1, then the picture of a die with one spot is PRINTed. If D1 = 2 then the picture of a die with two spots is PRINTed, and so on. The cursor is repositioned in line 80, then the second die is PRINTed according to its value.

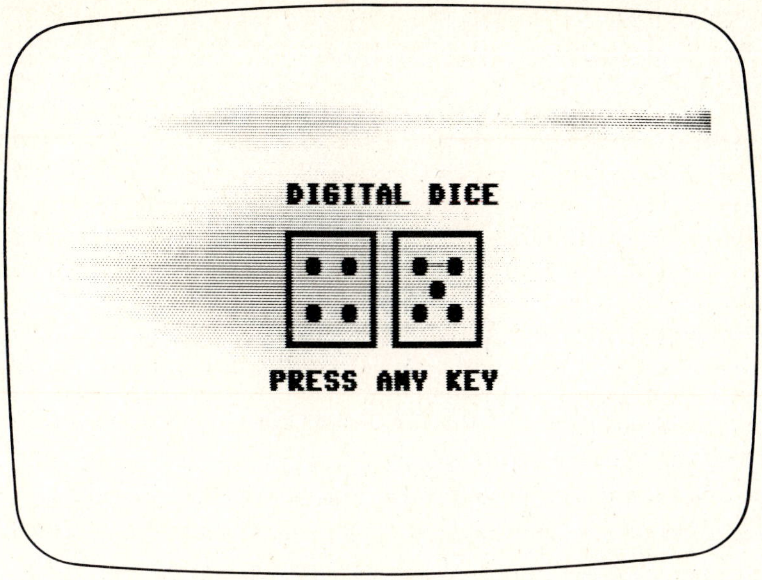


You might notice that each die is exactly alike, except for the pattern of its spots. When dice are PRINTed rapidly, one after another, the effect of a "roll" is simulated. This is the reason for the loop, FOR I=1 TO 25. The last set of random numbers, the 25th, is the pair of numbers the dice "land" on. In line 120, a GET statement waits for any key to be pressed, then "rolls" the dice again.

Entering this program is much simpler than it looks. To save time and effort, type the subroutine that PRINTs the picture of the die with the value of 1, from lines 1100 to 1170. Use the SHIFT key and the letter Q for making the spots. After you type the subroutine once, change the line numbers by typing over them and pressing RETURN. Then move the cursor to change the value of the die from 1 to 2, and press RETURN each time you make a change. Do this, changing the line numbers— 1100, 1200, 1300, 1400, 1500 and 1600—until subroutines for all six dice are created.

Be careful that the characters inside each square (the die) are spaces, not CRSR commands. The pictures will change correctly only if spaces erase one die value and PRINT the next.

```
"DIGITAL DICE"
10 POKE53280,11:POKE53281,15

20 PRINT"[CLR][BLK][8 CRSRS DN][15 CRSR RT]DIGITAL DICE";

30 FORI=1TO25

40 D1=INT(6*RND(0)+1)

50 D2=INT(6*RND(0)+1)

60 PRINT"[HOME][10 CRSR DN][15 CRSR RT]";

70 ON D1 GOSUB 1100,1200,1300,1400,1500,1600
```

```
80 PRINT"[HOME][10 CRSR DN][21 CRSR RT]";
90 ON D2 GOSUB 1100,1200,1300,1400,1500,1600
100 NEXTI
110 PRINT"[HOME][16 CRSR DN][14 CRSR RT]PRESS ANY KEY"
120 GET C$:IFC$=""THEN120
130 GOTO30
1100 PRINT"[SHIFT O][COMM Y][COMM Y][COMM Y][SHIFT P][CRSR LEFT][CRSR LEFT]
     [CRSR LEFT][CRSR LEFT][CRSR LEFT][CRSR DOWN]";
1110 PRINT"[COMM H][3 SPACES][COMM N][CRSR LEFT][CRSR LEFT][CRSR LEFT]
     [CRSR LEFT][CRSR LEFT][CRSR DOWN]";
1120 PRINT"[COMM H] [SHIFT Q] [COMM N][CRSR LEFT][CRSR LEFT][CRSR LEFT]
     [CRSR LEFT][CRSR LEFT][CRSR DOWN]";
1150 PRINT"[COMM H][3 SPACES][COMM N][CRSR LEFT][CRSR LEFT][CRSR LEFT]
     [CRSR LEFT][CRSR LEFT][CRSR DOWN]";
1160 PRINT"[SHIFT L][COMM P][COMM P][COMM P][COMM O]"
1170 RETURN
1200 PRINT"[SHIFT O][COMM Y][COMM Y][COMM Y][SHIFT P][CRSR LEFT][CRSR LEFT]
     [CRSR LEFT][CRSR LEFT][CRSR LEFT][CRSR DOWN]";
1210 PRINT"[COMM H][SHIFT Q][2 SPACES][COMM N][CRSR LEFT][CRSR LEFT][CRSR LEFT]
     [CRSR LEFT][CRSR LEFT][CRSR DOWN]";
1220 PRINT"[COMM H][3 SPACES][COMM N][CRSR LEFT][CRSR LEFT][CRSR LEFT]
     [CRSR LEFT][CRSR LEFT][CRSR DOWN]";
1250 PRINT"[COMM H][2 SPACES][SHIFT Q][COMM N][CRSR LEFT][CRSR LEFT][CRSR LEFT]
     [CRSR LEFT][CRSR LEFT][CRSR DOWN]";
1260 PRINT"[SHIFT L][COMM P][COMM P][COMM P][COMM O]"
1270 RETURN
1300 PRINT"[SHIFT O][COMM Y][COMM Y][COMM Y][SHIFT P][CRSR LEFT][CRSR LEFT]
     [CRSR LEFT][CRSR LEFT][CRSR LEFT][CRSR DOWN]";
1310 PRINT"[COMM H][SHIFT Q][2 SPACES][COMM N][CRSR LEFT][CRSR LEFT][CRSR LEFT]
     [CRSR LEFT][CRSR LEFT][CRSR DOWN]";
1320 PRINT"[COMM H][SPACE][SHIFT Q][SPACE][COMM N][CRSR LEFT][CRSR LEFT]
     [CRSR LEFT][CRSR LEFT][CRSR LEFT][CRSR DOWN]";
1350 PRINT"[COMM H][2 SPACES][SHIFT Q][COMM N][CRSR LEFT][CRSR LEFT][CRSR LEFT]
     [CRSR LEFT][CRSR LEFT][CRSR DOWN]";
1360 PRINT"[SHIFT L][COMM P][COMM P][COMM P][COMM O]"
1370 RETURN
1400 PRINT"[SHIFT O][COMM Y][COMM Y][COMM Y][SHIFT P][CRSR LEFT][CRSR LEFT]
     [CRSR LEFT][CRSR LEFT][CRSR LEFT][CRSR DOWN]";
```

```
1410 PRINT"[COMM H][SHIFT Q][SPACE][SHIFT Q][COMM N][CRSR LEFT][CRSR LEFT]
     [CRSR LEFT][CRSR LEFT][CRSR LEFT][CRSR DOWN]";
1420 PRINT"[COMM H][3 SPACES][COMM N][CRSR LEFT][CRSR LEFT][CRSR LEFT]
     [CRSR LEFT][CRSR LEFT][CRSR DOWN]";
1450 PRINT"[COMM H][SHIFT Q][SPACE][SHIFT Q][COMM N][CRSR LEFT][CRSR LEFT]
     [CRSR LEFT][CRSR LEFT][CRSR LEFT][CRSR DOWN]";
1460 PRINT"[SHIFT L][COMM P][COMM P][COMM P][COMM O]"
1470 RETURN
1500 PRINT"[SHIFT O][COMM Y][COMM Y][COMM Y][SHIFT P][CRSR LEFT][CRSR LEFT]
     [CRSR LEFT][CRSR LEFT][CRSR LEFT][CRSR DOWN]";
1510 PRINT"[COMM H][SHIFT Q][SPACE][SHIFT Q][COMM N][CRSR LEFT][CRSR LEFT]
     [CRSR LEFT][CRSR LEFT][CRSR LEFT][CRSR DOWN]";
1520 PRINT"[COMM H][SPACE][SHIFT Q][SPACE][COMM N][CRSR LEFT][CRSR LEFT]
     [CRSR LEFT][CRSR LEFT][CRSR LEFT][CRSR DOWN]";
1550 PRINT"[COMM H][SHIFT Q][SPACE][SHIFT Q][COMM N][CRSR LEFT][CRSR LEFT]
     [CRSR LEFT][CRSR LEFT][CRSR LEFT][CRSR DOWN]";
1560 PRINT"[SHIFT L][COMM P][COMM P][COMM P][COMM O]"
1570 RETURN
1600 PRINT"[SHIFT O][COMM Y][COMM Y][COMM Y][SHIFT P][CRSR LEFT][CRSR LEFT]
     [CRSR LEFT][CRSR LEFT][CRSR LEFT][CRSR DOWN]";
1610 PRINT"[COMM H][SHIFT Q][SHIFT Q][SHIFT Q][COMM N][CRSR LEFT][CRSR LEFT]
     [CRSR LEFT][CRSR LEFT][CRSR LEFT][CRSR DOWN]";
1620 PRINT"[COMM H][3 SPACES][COMM N][CRSR LEFT][CRSR LEFT][CRSR LEFT]
     [CRSR LEFT][CRSR LEFT][CRSR DOWN]";
1650 PRINT"[COMM H][SHIFT Q][SHIFT Q][SHIFT Q][COMM N][CRSR LEFT][CRSR LEFT]
     [CRSR LEFT][CRSR LEFT][CRSR LEFT][CRSR DOWN]";
1660 PRINT"[SHIFT L][COMM P][COMM P][COMM P][COMM O]"
1670 RETURN
```

## Sprite Graphics

Sprite graphics are more difficult to program in BASIC than character graphics. You do not use PRINT to put a sprite on the video screen. Instead, all sprite programming is done with POKE (and sometimes PEEK). You'll learn much more about sprite graphics in "Appendix 2: Exploring Graphics," but here is a quick description of how they work, along with a sprite demonstration program.

Sprites are objects described by POKEing values into blocks in the computer's memory. Each sprite requires 63 bytes of memory and is 24 dots across by 21 down. Each sprite block is numbered, from 0 to 255. The VIC chip can interpret these blocks of memory, color them, put them on the video screen, and move them around. The VIC can also expand the sprites horizontally, vertically, or in both directions, and make them appear to be in front of or behind characters PRINTed on the screen.

Each sprite is numbered from 0 to 7, and all eight sprites can be on the screen at once. Sprites pass over one another on the video screen, lending a three-dimensional effect when in motion. The level each sprite is on is determined by its number. In other words, sprite 0 always passes in *front* of sprite 1 on the screen. Sprite 5 can be seen *behind* sprite 4 if the two cross paths. More advanced sprite functions include ways to determine whether one sprite has collided with another, with a character, or the background screen. Another sprite graphics mode, called the multicolor sprite mode, lets you make sprites of up to four different colors, but cuts in half the number of dots across.

There are four distinct disadvantages to sprite graphics as designed for the Commodore 64 family.

First, the way that BASIC uses the computer's memory limits you to only three *different* sprites at one time. To solve the problem, you must change this BASIC memory use. (Not a problem, but tough for beginners to understand.) You can, however, use all eight sprites at once, as long as they are all identical.

Second, it is only convenient to move a sprite across *part* of the screen, the left two-thirds. Even though there are more than 300 screen positions on which to put sprites, any position on the right third means POKEing more than one memory location. This can be complicated in BASIC. As a result, you can expect to see many programs that limit sprites to the left side.

Third, sprites are difficult to design. You'll need some complicated and time-consuming math to determine the numbers that end up in the sprite memory blocks. The best way around the problem is to use a program called a sprite editor. You'll find a useful one near the end of this book.

Fourth, since there are no words *at all* in Commodore BASIC to handle sprites, it is almost impossible to *read* a BASIC program with sprites in it. This is remedied by using special programming tools. More about this later.

# The Old Shell Game

You can get some idea of how sprites look and are programmed by entering and studying the following demonstration. It is a version of the old shell game. A pea is hidden under one of three nutshells and the shells are shuffled. You must guess which shell is hiding it. Sprites, here, represent the nutshells and will always cover any characters PRINTed under them on the screen. That's how the shell sprites cover the "pea," a character that is actually a green SHIFTed Q.

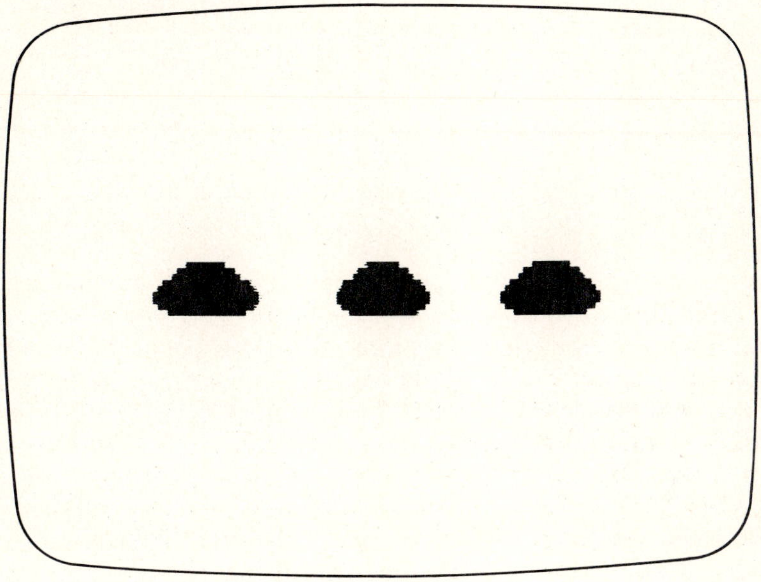

The program is worthy of the con men who made the old shell game (a classic ruse) famous. The pea doesn't move at all. Instead, a random number between 1 and 3 is generated and the pea is PRINTed under one of the three shells just before it is "lifted." This isn't really a game in that it RUNs continously, selecting random numbers and challenging you to pick the shell. With a little work however—an INPUT or GET statement could be inserted—you could change it to an interactive guessing game.

REMark statements are used quite heavily throughout the program to explain what is happening. A few comments are in order, however.

Line 30 "enables" the sprites. It tells the VIC chip which sprites and how many will be used. The program uses only three sprites, and each is identical. Their descriptions are POKEd into one sprite block, number 13. The memory locations 2040, 2041 and 2042 are not in the VIC chip. Instead, VIC looks at these numbers for the information about where the sprite pictures are described.

Lines 60, 70 and 80 position the sprites. Think of the screen as a window to the area in which sprites move. There are approximately 344 horizontal postions and 250 vertical positions where a sprite can be placed. (Variable X is used for horizonal, Y for vertical.) In some positions, the sprite will be invisible, hidden by the edges of the screen border. Position numbers are POKEd into the correct pairs of memory locations beginning at 53248 (horizontal position, sprite 0) and 53249 (vertical position, sprite 0). Remember, though, that numbers greater than 255 cannot be POKEd. (This is the problem of moving a sprite entirely across the screen.)

Animating the sprites—lifting, dropping, and "shuffling" the shells—is accomplished by POKEing one new value, horizontal or vertical, for each sprite. You can see how these work in the "reveal" subroutines at 13000, 13100, and 13200, and in the "shuffle" subroutine beginning at line 14000.

```
SHELL
10 PRINT"[CLR]";:POKE53280,12:POKE53281,15:REM COLOR SCREEN LIGHT GREY

20 V=53248:REM BASE OF VIDEO CHIP

30 POKEV+21,7:REM ENABLE SPRITES 0,1,2

35 FORI=0TO62:READD:POKE832+I,D:NEXT:REM READ DATA FOR SPRITE INTO
   BLOCK 13

40 POKE2040,13:POKE2041,13:POKE2042,13:REM ALL SPRITES DEFINED BY
   BLOCK 13

50 POKEV+39,9:POKEV+40,9:POKEV+41,9:REM COLOR ALL SPRITES BROWN

55 POKEV+23,7:POKEV+29,7:REM EXPAND ALL SPRITES IN X AND Y DIRECTIONS

60 POKEV+0,85:POKEV+1,120:REM PUT SPRITE 0 AT 85,120

70 POKEV+2,160:POKEV+3,120:REM PUT SPRITE 1 AT 160,120

80 POKEV+4,235:POKEV+5,120:REM PUT SPRITE 2 AT 235,120
```

```
90 PRINT"[BLU][HOME][15 CRSR DN][5 SPACES]WELCOME TO THE OLD SHELL
   GAME"
100 GOSUB30000:REM DELAY
110 GOSUB15000:REM CLEAR TEXT
120 PRINT"[BLU][HOME][15 CRSR DN][6 SPACES]THE OBJECT OF THE GAME
    IS TO "
130 PRINT"[BLU][HOME][15 CRSR DN][14 SPACES]FIND THE PEA"
135 GOSUB30000:REM DELAY
140 PRINT"[BLU][HOME][19 CRSR DN][13 SPACES]PEA > [GRN][SHIFT Q]
    [BLU] < PEA"
145 GOSUB30000
150 GOSUB15000:REM CLEAR SCREEN
165 GOSUB30000:REM DELAY
170 PRINT"[BLU][HOME][14 CRSR DN][16 SPACES]EXAMPLE:"
175 GOSUB30000:REM DELAY
190 GOSUB12000:REM PUT PEA UNDER CENTER
200 GOSUB13000:REM CENTER SHELL REVEAL
255 GOSUB30000:REM DELAY
270 GOSUB14000:REM SHUFFLE SHELLS
365 GOSUB30000:REM DELAY
370 PRINT"[BLU][HOME][15 CRSR DN][14 SPACES]WHERE IS IT?"
375 GOSUB30000:REM DELAY
380 A=INT(3*(RND(0))+1):
382 IFA=1THEN GOSUB 12000:GOSUB13200:GOSUB13100:GOSUB13000
384 IFA=2THEN GOSUB 12050:GOSUB13000:GOSUB13100:GOSUB13200
386 IFA=3THEN GOSUB 12100:GOSUB13200:GOSUB13000:GOSUB13100
410 GOSUB15000:REM CLEAR TEXT
420 GOSUB30000:GOSUB30000:GOSUB30000:REM TRIPLE DELAY
999 RUN
9999 REM SPRITE DATA FOLLOWS
10000 DATA 0,0,0,0,0,0,0,0,0
10010 DATA 0,0,0,0,0,0,0,0,0
```

```
10020 DATA 0,0,0,0,0,0,0,0,0
10030 DATA1,254,0,7,255,128,15,255,192
10040 DATA63,255,240,127,255,248,255,255,252
10050 DATA255,255,252,127,255,248,31,255,224
10060 DATA 0,0,0,0,0,0,0,0,0
12000 REM;PUT PEA UNDER CENTER SHELL
12010 PRINT"[HOME][12 CRSR DN][19 SPACES][GRN][SHIFT Q][BLU][11 SPACES]"
12020 RETURN
12050 REM: PUT PEA UNDER LEFT SHELL
12060 PRINT"[HOME][12 CRSR DN][10 CRSR RT][GRN][SHIFT Q][BLU][30 SPACES]"
12070 RETURN
12100 REM: PUT PEA UNDER RIGHT SHELL
12110 PRINT"[HOME][12 CRSR DN][29 SPACES][GRN][SHIFT Q][BLU]"
12120 RETURN
13000 REM: MIDDLE SHELL REVEAL
13010 FORI=120TO90STEP-1
13020 POKEV+2,160:POKEV+3,I
13030 NEXTI
13040 FORI=1TO500:NEXT I
13050 FORI=90TO120
13060 POKEV+2,160:POKEV+3,I
13070 NEXTI
13080 RETURN
13100 REM: RIGHT SHELL REVEAL
13110 FORI=120TO90STEP-1
13120 POKEV+0,235:POKEV+1,I
13130 NEXTI
13140 FORI=1TO500:NEXT I
13150 FORI=90TO120
13160 POKEV+0,235:POKEV+1,I
```

```
13170 NEXTI
13180 RETURN
13200 REM: LEFT SHELL REVEAL
13210 FORI=120TO90STEP-1
13220 POKEV+4,85:POKEV+5,I
13230 NEXTI
13240 FORI=1TO500:NEXT I
13250 FORI=90TO120
13260 POKEV+4,85:POKEV+5,I
13270 NEXTI
13280 RETURN
14000 REM: SHUFFLE THE SHELLS
14010 FORI=160TO85
14020 POKEV+2,I:POKEV+3,120
14030 NEXTI
14040 FORI=85TO235
14050 POKEV+0,I:POKEV+1,120
14060 NEXTI
14070 FORI=235TO85STEP-1
14080 POKEV+4,I:POKEV+5,120
14090 NEXTI
14100 RETURN
15000 REM: CLEAR TEXT FROM SCREEN
15010 PRINT"[BLU][HOME][14 CRSR DN][39 SPACES]"
15020 PRINT"[BLU][HOME][15 CRSR DN][39 SPACES]"
15030 PRINT"[BLU][HOME][16 CRSR DN][39 SPACES]"
15040 PRINT"[BLU][HOME][17 CRSR DN][39 SPACES]"
15050 PRINT"[BLU][HOME][18 CRSR DN][39 SPACES]"
15060 PRINT"[BLU][HOME][19 CRSR DN][39 SPACES]"
15070 RETURN
30000 REM:DELAY LOOP
30010 FORI=1TO1000:NEXT I
30020 RETURN
```

## SID Sound

Sound, like graphics, is a real challenge for any programmer. Like the VIC chip, there is no way to communicate with the SID chip other than POKEing numbers into its important memory locations. Even worse, you cannot use PEEK to see the numbers stored in these SID locations—PEEK will always return the number 0.

Here are a few facts about how SID makes its sounds. Don't worry about absorbing all of this now. It's offered only to give you a general understanding.

To produce any sound at all, the master volume control in the SID chip must be set. There are sixteen different volume levels, numbered from 0 (zero) to 15, with 0 as "off" and 15 as the loudest. This is set by POKEing a number into 54296.

Four values determine the kind of sound produced: Attack/decay, sustain/release, frequency and waveform.

Attack and decay are set by adding two numbers together and POKEing their sum into the correct memory location. The attack number you select should be either 128, 64, 32 or 16, or the sum of any of those numbers. Add the attack number to any decay number of 8, 4, 2 or 1, or the sum of any of those numbers. The larger the attack number is, the longer a note will take to "fade up." If the attack number is 0, the note will sound immediately. The larger the decay number is, the longer the decay will be. If the decay number is 16, the note will fade at a slower speed. Using zero, there will be no decay time.

To set the attack and decay for voice 1, POKE the sum of these numbers into memory location 54277. Voices 2 and 3 are set by POKEing a similar number into 54284 and 54291.

Sustain and release are set the same way as attack and decay. For voice 1, the sum of sustain and release numbers is POKEd into memory location 54278. The location for voice 2 is 54285, and for voice 3 is 54292.

The pitch, or frequency, of the sound produced is POKEd into two locations, a "high" location and a "low" location. Get the values for musical notes from the note/frequency table you will find at the end of this chapter. For voice 1, POKE 54272 with the "low" number, and 54273 with the "high" number. (Low and high don't refer to a number greater or less than the other. Low and high are two specific numbers you'll see on the note table.) For voice 2, this pair of locations is 54279 and 54280. For voice 3, the locations are 54286 and 54287.

You must select a waveform, or basic sound. Any of four different waveforms, each with a different tone, can be selected—triangle, sawtooth, pulse, and noise. The first three produce tones; noise is most often used for "percussive" sound effects, like a drum, a rifle shot, "hissing" sounds, or the roar of the surf.

The waveform memory location for voice 1 is 54276.

POKE 54276,33 for sawtooth waveform.
POKE 54276,17 for triangle waveform.

POKE 54276,65 for pulse waveform.
POKE 54276,129 for noise.

Voices 2 and 3 are set by POKEing the same numbers into memory locations 54283 (for voice 2) and 54290 (for voice 3).

When all this is done in a program, a note sounds continuously. To stop the sound, POKE all the locations for each voice with 0 (zero). When the proper information is POKEd into the necessary locations again, another note will sound.

Here's a little program that will make just one sound. Be sure that you have the sound on your television turned up, or, if you are using a video monitor, that the sound is connected.

```
10 VL=54296: REM VOLUME
20 LO=54272:HI=54273: REM PITCH LOW AND HI
30 WF=54276: REM WAVEFORM
40 AD=54277: REM ATTACK/DECAY
50 SR=54278: REM SUSTAIN/RELEASE
60 POKE VL,15
70 POKE AD,190:POKE SR,0
80 POKE WF,33
90 POKE LO,28:POKE HI,214
100 FOR I=1 TO 500:NEXT I: REM DURATION
110 POKE AD,0:POKE SSR,0:POKE WF,0:POKE VL,0
```

As you can see, making a single sound takes quite a bit of work. Experiment by changing the attack/decay, sustain/release and waveform numbers.

Playing even a simple song this way would require lots of programming. With a little ingenuity, we can write a program that plays one note after another. The LISTing for such a program can be found following a few words about how it works. It creates arrays of pitch numbers, notes in a song, and the duration each note should play. This musical information is stored as DATA statements.

The DATA statements that begin with line number 10000 contain information in groups of three. The first, C4, is the musical note—"C"—and the octave, the fourth of eight possible ones. The next two numbers are the high and low pitch numbers. Wherever you see "#" the note is a half-step, or sharp. Only two octaves are entered as DATA at present, but you can add the remaining notes by making new DATA statements following the given form and using numbers from the note/frequency table.

At the end of the DATA statement in line 10040 you'll see some unusual letters and numbers. "R,0,0" stands for a musical "rest" where no sound is produced. The READ statements in the program need the X as the last character in note DATA group to know that it is at the end of this information.

The DATA statements beginning on line 20000 are the song information in groups of two. The first contains the note, the second the duration. A duration of 16 represents a "whole note," 8 a "half note," 4 a "quarter note," and so on.

In the LISTing, the song table is really just two octaves of the eight-note musical scale. ("Do-re-mi," etc.) By changing the notes and their durations, you can enter simple, one-voice songs. Tempo is controlled by the value of "T" in line 300.

SONG

```
10 SID=54272:REM ADDRESS OF SID CHIP
20 DIM N$(94),NL(94),NH(94),S$(200),D(200),SH(200),SL(200)
30 X=1:REM X-1 WILL BECOME NUMBER OF NOTES IN MEMORY
40 READ N$(X):IF N$(X)="X"THEN 60:REM CHECK FOR END OF NOTE DATA
50 READ NH(X):READ NL(X):X=X+1:GOTO 40
60 N=1:REM N-1 WILL BECOME NUMBER OF NOTES IN SONG
70 READS$(N):IFS$(N)="X"THEN GOTO 90
80 READD(N):N=N+1:GOTO 70
90 FORI=1TON-1
100 FORK=1TOX-1:IFS$(I)=N$(K) THEN SL(I)=NL(K):SH(I)=NH(K):GOTO120
110 NEXTK
120 NEXTI
300 VL=54272:VH=54273:AD=54277:SR=54278:CR=54276:VO=54296:T=10:PRINT"[CLR]"
310 POKE VO,15:REM FULL VOLUME
320 FORI=1TON-1:REM BEGINNING OF PLAY LOOP
330 POKE VL,SL(I):POKE VH,SH(I)
340 PRINT"POKE SH,";SH(I);"POKE SL,";SL(I);"DURATION";D(I)
350 POKE AD,90:POKE SR,128:POKE CR,17
360 FORK=1TOT*D(I):REM DURATION LOOP
370 NEXT K
380 POKE AD,0:POKE SR,0:POKE CR,0:REM TURN OFF
390 NEXT I
400 POKEVO,0:REM VOLUME DOWN
9999 REM NOTE DATA C4 TO C6
10000 DATA C4,16,195,C#4,17,195,D4,18,209,D#4,19,239
10010 DATA E4,21,31,F4,22,96,F#4,23,181
10020 DATA G4,25,30,G#4,26,156,A4,28,49,A#4,29,233,B4,31,165,C5,33,135
```

```
10030 DATA C#5,35,134,D5,37,162,D#5,39,233,E5,42,62,F5,45,198,F#5,
      47,107
10040 DATA G5,50,60,G#5,51,197,A5,56,99,A#5,59,190,B5,64,188,C6,68,
      149,R,0,0,X
19999 REM SONG DATA, TWO OCTAVES
20000 DATA C4,16,D4,16,E4,16,F4,16,G4,16,A4,16,B4,16,R,16,R,16
20010 DATA C5,16,D5,16,E5,16,F5,16,G5,16,A5,16,B5,16,C6,16,X
```

***Musical Notes and Frequencies***

| MUSICAL NOTE | OSCILLATOR FREQUENCY | | |
|---|---|---|---|
| *OCTAVE* | *DECIMAL* | *HI* | *LOW* |
| C – 0 | 268 | 1 | 12 |
| C# – 0 | 284 | 1 | 28 |
| D – 0 | 301 | 1 | 45 |
| D# – 0 | 318 | 1 | 62 |
| E – 0 | 337 | 1 | 81 |
| F – 0 | 358 | 1 | 102 |
| F# – 0 | 379 | 1 | 123 |
| G – 0 | 401 | 1 | 145 |
| G# – 0 | 425 | 1 | 169 |
| A – 0 | 451 | 1 | 195 |
| A# – 0 | 477 | 1 | 221 |
| B – 0 | 506 | 1 | 250 |
| C – 1 | 536 | 2 | 24 |
| C# – 1 | 568 | 2 | 56 |
| D – 1 | 602 | 2 | 90 |
| D# – 1 | 637 | 2 | 125 |
| E – 1 | 675 | 2 | 163 |
| F – 1 | 716 | 2 | 204 |
| F# – 1 | 758 | 2 | 246 |
| G – 1 | 803 | 3 | 35 |
| G# – 1 | 851 | 3 | 83 |
| A – 1 | 902 | 3 | 134 |
| A# – 1 | 955 | 3 | 187 |
| B – 1 | 1012 | 3 | 244 |
| C – 2 | 1072 | 4 | 48 |
| C# – 2 | 1136 | 4 | 112 |
| D – 2 | 1204 | 4 | 180 |
| D# – 2 | 1275 | 4 | 251 |
| E – 2 | 1351 | 5 | 71 |
| F – 2 | 1432 | 5 | 152 |
| F# – 2 | 1517 | 5 | 237 |
| G – 2 | 1607 | 6 | 71 |
| G# – 2 | 1703 | 6 | 167 |
| A – 2 | 1804 | 7 | 12 |
| A# – 2 | 1911 | 7 | 119 |

| *OCTAVE* | *DECIMAL* | *HI* | *LOW* |
|---|---|---|---|
| B – 2 | 2025 | 7 | 233 |
| C – 3 | 2145 | 8 | 97 |
| C# – 3 | 2273 | 8 | 225 |
| D – 3 | 2408 | 9 | 104 |
| D# – 3 | 2551 | 9 | 247 |
| E – 3 | 2703 | 10 | 143 |
| F – 3 | 2864 | 11 | 48 |
| F# – 3 | 3034 | 11 | 218 |
| G – 3 | 3215 | 12 | 143 |
| G# – 3 | 3406 | 13 | 78 |
| A – 3 | 3608 | 14 | 24 |
| A# – 3 | 3823 | 14 | 239 |
| B – 3 | 4050 | 15 | 210 |
| C – 4 | 4291 | 16 | 195 |
| C# – 4 | 4547 | 17 | 195 |
| D – 4 | 4817 | 18 | 209 |
| D# – 4 | 5103 | 19 | 239 |
| E – 4 | 5407 | 21 | 31 |
| F – 4 | 5728 | 22 | 96 |
| F# – 4 | 6069 | 23 | 181 |
| G – 4 | 6430 | 25 | 30 |
| G# – 4 | 6812 | 26 | 156 |
| A – 4 | 7217 | 28 | 49 |
| A# – 4 | 7647 | 29 | 223 |
| B – 4 | 8101 | 31 | 165 |
| C – 5 | 8583 | 33 | 135 |
| C# – 5 | 9094 | 35 | 134 |
| D – 5 | 9634 | 37 | 162 |
| D# – 5 | 10207 | 39 | 223 |
| E – 5 | 10814 | 42 | 62 |
| F – 5 | 11457 | 44 | 193 |
| F# – 5 | 12139 | 47 | 107 |
| G – 5 | 12860 | 50 | 60 |
| G# – 5 | 13625 | 53 | 57 |
| A – 5 | 14435 | 56 | 99 |
| A# – 5 | 15294 | 59 | 190 |
| B – 5 | 16203 | 63 | 75 |
| C – 6 | 17167 | 67 | 15 |
| C# – 6 | 18188 | 71 | 12 |
| D – 6 | 19269 | 75 | 69 |
| D# – 6 | 20415 | 79 | 191 |
| E – 6 | 21629 | 84 | 125 |
| F – 6 | 22915 | 89 | 131 |
| F# – 6 | 24278 | 94 | 214 |
| G – 6 | 25721 | 100 | 121 |
| G# – 6 | 27251 | 106 | 115 |
| A – 6 | 28871 | 112 | 199 |
| A# – 6 | 30588 | 119 | 124 |
| B – 6 | 32407 | 126 | 151 |
| C – 7 | 34334 | 134 | 30 |
| C# – 7 | 36376 | 142 | 24 |
| D – 7 | 38539 | 150 | 139 |
| D# – 7 | 40830 | 159 | 126 |
| E – 7 | 43258 | 168 | 250 |
| F – 7 | 45830 | 179 | 6 |
| F# – 7 | 48556 | 189 | 172 |

| **MUSICAL NOTE** | **OSCILLATOR FREQUENCY** | | |
|---|---|---|---|
| *OCTAVE* | *DECIMAL* | *HI* | *LOW* |
| G – 7 | 51443 | 200 | 243 |
| G# – 7 | 54502 | 212 | 230 |
| A – 7 | 57743 | 225 | 143 |
| A# – 7 | 61176 | 238 | 248 |
| B – 7 | 64814 | 253 | 46 |

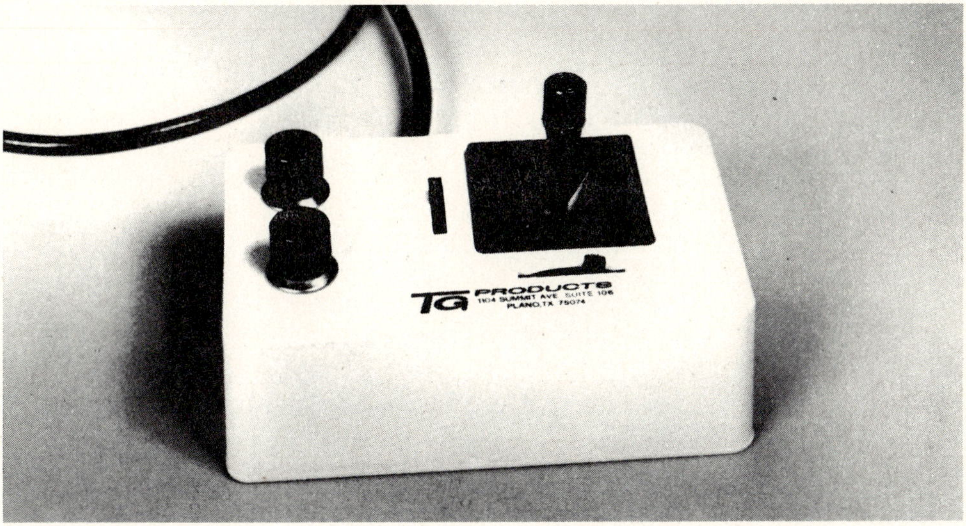


# The Joy of Joysticks

After you become comfortable with video graphics and sound, you will probably want to write your own games. The most popular game controller is the joystick. Using one with the Commodore 64 computers is very simple.

Joysticks are nothing new. As a controller, they originated in the days of the first aircraft and were adopted by Atari when the company introduced their video games in the mid-1970s. The Atari joystick quickly became a standard for video play and almost all of today's joysticks work just like Atari's.

The Atari-style joystick is a switch-type controller. (Another type is called an "analog" joystick, and is incompatible with switch-type sticks.) Inside are five switches, four for directions—north (up), south (down), east (right) and west (left)—and one for a "fire" button. Four other directions—northwest, northeast, southwest and southeast—come from two switches being closed at once.

If you have an Atari joystick (or one that works just like it), plug it into control port 2 on the right side of the computer. Why port 2? Control port 1 can be used, but programming it is slightly more complicated. So, for this lesson, we'll stay with port 2.

By PEEKing at a specific memory location, we can tell whether the joystick is being pushed in any direction.

```
10 PRINT PEEK(56320):GOTO 10
```

When you RUN this line, a steady stream of numbers should appear on the screen. The number should be 127. Now push the joystick up. What happens? Since you are closing a switch inside, the number changes. (A number from 0 to 255 is made up of eight bits. Five of these bits are represented by the switches inside the joystick.) We can use the numbers to interpret changes in direction.

```
10 A=PEEK(56320)
20 IF A=127 THEN PRINT "CENTER";
30 IF A=126 THEN PRINT "NORTH";
40 IF A=125 THEN PRINT "SOUTH";
50 IF A=123 THEN PRINT "WEST";
60 IF A=119 THEN PRINT "EAST";
70 IF A=122 THEN PRINT "NORTHWEST";
80 IF A=118 THEN PRINT "NORTHEAST";
90 IF A=117 THEN PRINT "SOUTHEAST";
100 IF A=121 THEN PRINT "SOUTHWEST";
110 B=PEEK(56320) AND 16
120 IF B=0 THEN PRINT "--FIRE":GOTO 10
130 PRINT "":GOTO 10
```

The results you get from the control port can be used in a program to make decisions and control what is PRINTed on the screen. Think of the joystick as a kind of mini-keyboard with only five keys. For example, instead of using GET and asking someone to PRESS ANY KEY, you could PEEK(56320) and look for the fire button to be pressed.

What about those cousins of the joysticks, the game paddles you have if you own a video game? Paddles do not have switches (they do have one, a fire button). Instead, they use *potentiometers,* like the volume control on your television or stereo. The computer can interpret these too, although it isn't as simple as using the joysticks. Paddles return numbers from 0 to 255. Turning a paddle all the way to the right makes the number 0; turning it completely to the left returns 255.

If you have game paddles, plug them into the other socket, control port 1. Now PEEK at memory location 54297.

```
10 PRINT PEEK(54298):GOTO 10
```

RUN this line and look at the screen. Turn one of the paddles. Try the other paddle if the numbers don't change from 0 to 255. (The paddle fire buttons are read by PEEKing another location, 56321.)

Now turn the paddle to the center and put it down. Chances are good that the number will still change slightly (up or down a number or two).

Because of this inaccuracy, you must do some arithmetic to get an average number. This is why paddles are more complicated to use than the joysticks. Commodore, in fact, suggests that the game paddles be read using a machine code, not a BASIC, subroutine.

## What's Left?

All that PEEKing and POKEing gets tedious, doesn't it? Much of this chapter may have left you asking what you've gotten yourself into. Fear not. Help is on the way.

The way around these preposterous PEEKs and POKEs is to use a programming tool designed for graphics and sound. Several program packages are scheduled for the Commodore 64 computers, and these are meant to solve some of the deficiencies in BASIC.

Commodore, itself, has developed a program called Easy Graphics (formerly VSP, the **V**ideo **S**upport **P**ackage). It is a cartridge program that plugs into the 64 machines and adds new words to BASIC. Among these are commands that change graphic modes, from character mode to hi-res screens, to multicolor mode, even a split screen that gives you both characters and high-resolution pictures together on the same screen.

With the built-in sprite editor in Easy Graphics you can design and save sprites and multicolor sprites. Other sprite commands move them across the screen (without the limitations of using the right side) and detect when a sprite collides with another sprite or a character. Joysticks and game paddles are easy to use and have their own commands.

Most important, perhaps, is a set of hi-res commands that draw circles, boxes and other shapes, each of which can be filled with colors using the PAINT command. For music fans, Easy Graphics includes a predefined set of nine musical voices, as well as designing your own "instruments," and commands for entering and playing multiple-voice music.

Commodore also has graphic and sound enhancements to BASIC in another cartridge program called Simons' BASIC. Developed in the United Kingdom by a young programmer, Simons' BASIC adds other useful features that bring the total of new BASIC commands to 114.

A music composer cartridge is marketed by Commodore in its line of video games. Though somewhat simple—it uses a character graphic display and stores songs on cassette tape—this cartridge might help you familiarize yourself with simple musical ideas.

You needn't wait for these tools, though. In "Appendix 2: Exploring Graphics," Paul F. Schatz' contribution to this book, you'll find graphics programs you can enter into your computer and use right now. In addition to some fascinating visual demonstrations, there's an easy-to-use sprite editor, and some routines that let you draw on high-resolution screens. If that's not enough, Dr. Frank Covitz offers his own very thorough explanation of music, sound, and the SID chip in "Appendix 3: Exploring Sound." In it, you'll find a program that plays three-voice music.

# 10

# Beyond BASIC

Your computer is part of a larger system. As time goes by, you may want to build on it, just as you would a stereo or video system. Each expansion will add new possibilities and new power. This computer isn't just a toy, and you might be amazed to see how much more capable it becomes as it grows. Your interest in the machine and, of course, your budget will dictate how and when you expand.

In which direction should you go? What new opportunities are there to seize? How much should you buy? Those are questions only you can answer. This last chapter is devoted to a glimpse of your system's future, from the practical to the exotic.

## Hardware and Enhancements

If you don't already have one, the first thing on your "wish list" should be Commodore's 1541 disk drive. Not only do programs LOAD and SAVE to and from disk much faster than from cassette, but the disk drive is practically a necessity for sophisticated programs like data base managers, spreadsheets, and word processors.

In going from the original PET and CBM to the Commodore 64, you may already have a model 2031, 4040, or 8050 dual disk drive. Since these are built around a different data standard, they cannot be directly connected to the 64. The solution is to use a disk interface. Several are available. One, called the "CIE" from Southwest Micro-Systems (2554 Southwell, Dallas, TX 75229), works well with the Commodore 64. It plugs into the cartridge port and connects to any of Commodore's PET and CBM disk drive systems. Using the CIE allows you to take advantage of the earlier disk drives' speed (they are much faster than the 1541) and reliability.

In addition to other manufacturers, Commodore has designed its own disk interface. When using *any* such interface, you do take a risk, however, that some software will not operate correctly. Commodore claims their "official" disk interface is the only one that is compatible . . . with their software. Still, if you have one of the earlier disk drives and a Commodore 64, there is no reason not to use the two together.

At the other end of the scale are cassette recorders. Some users buy a computer and disk drive, but never invest in a recorder. Having one, though, could open the door to more programs, and lets you trade programs with other users who might not have a disk drive. If you don't want to spend much money, you may be able to adapt a recorder you already own. That's what the "Cardette" claims to do. This little box from a company called Cardco (313 Matthewson, Wichita, KS, 67214) contains the circuitry necessary for using a portable cassette recorder with your computer.

Another kind of interface was already discussed in the chapter about word processing. A parallel printer interface will let you choose from the wide variety of printers on the market. Cardco's "Cardprint" box is quite good and offers amazing versatility because of its "smart" design. Just as with disk interfaces, you may find that some programs are especially designed to work only with Commodore's printers. This is a fairly rare occurrence and being able to choose from printers with many features justifies the purchase of an interface.

Another excellent addition to your system is a modem, an electronic device that lets your computer talk to other computers over the telephone. Commodore's modem is economical and does the job. (It attaches directly to the "user port.") With it, you can connect to information services such as Dow-Jones Information Retrieval Service, CompuServe, and The Source, which offer practical information, news, and recreational activities. If you are a businessman, you may be able to dial your company's computer directly with the modem. (Check with your data processing department about this.) Modems require software that turns the computer into a "terminal" to these other machines. Among Commodore's programs for this is a cartridge called "Easy Comm."

Modems from other manufacturers can also be used with the 64 family, but most require a special interface. Some, however, are worth the effort and expense, with advanced features for automatic telephone dialing and other "smart" functions.

If you use your computer in a school, laboratory, or office, there is another type of communications scheme you may be interested in. It is known as a Local Area Network (LAN) and links small computers together so that they may pass information and programs among each other and share common disk drives and printers.

One such LAN is specifically designed for linking as many as 32 Commodore 64 computers, disk drives, and printers. Called 64NET, it does not use wire, but rather hair-thin fiber optic strands. The information is converted to light and transmitted along the fiber optic, which can be as long as 1000 feet from the network's central hub, or "node," as it is called. (Prices vary with the size of the installation. Information available from American Photonics, Inc., Milltown Office Park, Route 22, Brewster, NY, 10509.)

You can add to your machine *inside* as well as out. Several enhancements to the Commodore 64 family are packaged as cartridge programs and add to the computer's versatility. Some add new commands to BASIC and others make programming simpler and more understandable.

Skyles Electric Works (231G South Whisman Road, Mountainview, CA, 94041) has been in the business of bettering Commodore computers for several years. One of their products is the "VicTree" (named so because it was originally designed for the VIC-20 and adapted to the Commodore 64.) This package boasts 42 additional BASIC commands, including words from Commodore's 4.0 BASIC (found on the CBM series) which make dealing with the disk drive easier. "VicTree" also offers programming aid words that automatically number and renumber program lines, delete lines, and search BASIC programs for words, numbers, and statements. Another Skyles product is aimed at cassette users. "Arrow" will cut LOAD and SAVE times to and from cassette to about a sixth of the ordinary time, and has its own set of programming aids, as well.

## Entertainment Programs

Because of the Commodore 64's advanced graphics capabilities, you're sure to see hundreds of very high-quality video games written for it. As a game machine, the '64 has few equals.

But mention should be made of a unique and challenging series of games. Actually, to call them games almost diminishes their creativity. These are the "Interlogic" prose adventures from Infocom (55 Wheeler Street, Cambridge, MA, 02138.) They are actually interactive stories in which you participate and affect the plot. Although the games use only text (read from the video screen), the creators of the series often refer to the use of "the world's most powerful graphics technology—your imagination."

Three of the games form the "Zork" trilogy, an underground adventure of mythological theme and proportion. Another, "Starcross," is a science-fiction adventure in the world of a mammoth alien spacecraft. In "Suspended," another SF opus, you are in cryogenic suspension in the master control complex of a planet whose mass transit, food production, and weather are your responsibility. You must learn how to control six robots, each with their own specialized senses, and solve the riddle of how the computerized complex actually operates.

"Deadline" is Infocom's homage to the detective thrillers of the 1930s and '40s. In it, you are the shamus, investigating the murder of a wealthy industrialist, questioning suspects, sending clues to the crime lab for analysis, and finally fingering the killer. But wait, the grand jury will indict only if there is enough evidence. Then there's a jury trial where the accused may still beat the rap.

Each of the Infocom games takes a long time to play. The company estimates 12 to 40 hours, depending on the game and level of your skill. You communicate with other characters in these stories in normal English sentences, and each game has a "vocabulary" of over 600 words. (Still, there are times when the computer won't understand you or will ask you to rephrase a question or command.)

The Infocom games are among the most sophisticated computer adventures yet created and are available for most other personal computers, as well as the Commodore 64. A cult has formed quickly around these, and there is even a "user group" that offers visual materials (maps, etc.) and hints.

## Spreadsheets and Advanced Software

All programs are not created equal, and a well-written program is a joy to behold and spectacular in operation.

There is a flood of software following the introduction of any popular computer, and the Commodore 64 family should prove no exception. Some programs, however, do not live up to their claims. Good programs, too, are likely to be expensive, reflecting the amount of time and effort necessary to write them. A good game is easy to spot—you either like it or you don't. But practical programs are more difficult to evaluate.

You've already read some tips about the features to look for in selecting a data base. Reviews of four word processing programs are in another chapter. So far, though, there has been only a passing mention of a very important type of program, the spreadsheet.

Spreadsheet programs, like word processors, can be given credit for helping to popularize personal computers. These are programs that help you do financial calculation and scheduling, budgeting, accounting, and any job where numbers are the main kind of information. In short, they allow you to enter tables of numbers which depend on one another and ask the question "what if?" When one number on the table is changed, other numbers that depend on it do, too. Tables are recalculated with stunning speed. In a good spreadsheet program, the table you build can be much, much larger than the video screen, which you use as a "window" moving around to see smaller sections at one time.

The first of these popular programs was "VisiCalc" which started the trend. Other "calcs" have followed—some better, some worse. (Among the least practical of these are the so-called "mini" spreadsheets which limit the size of the tables. Almost all of these are written in BASIC—far too slow for a good spreadsheet.)

One excellent spreadsheet for the Commodore 64 family is called "Calc Result." Written in Sweden, it takes full advantage of the computer's expanded memory and color capabilities. As many as 63 columns of 225 number "cells" comprise one "page" (or table), and up to 32 different pages can be used at once. Because of these multiple pages, "Calc Result" is called a "three-dimensional" spreadsheet. Numbers can actually be passed from page to page for calculation.

Number cells and the words that describe them can be colored. This, too, is probably the only multi-lingual spreadsheet. Its many "help" screens—instructions and reminders you can consult along the way—can be read in English, Spanish, German, French, Italian, Swedish (naturally), Dutch, and Finnish!

All of this means that "Calc Result" has several distinct advantages over the original "VisiCalc." But perhaps the best improvement is its ability to produce bar graphs in color on the video screen. (These same graphs can also be printed on Commodore's 1525E printer or in color on a new color plotter.) The book that comes with "Calc Result" and teaches you to use the program is quite good, though you should know what you're getting yourself into when you decide to buy any spreadsheet. "Calcs" are highly sophisticated programs with many features, and learning to use one to the fullest extent of its power can be as challenging as learning a programming language.

"Calc Result" is available from Computer Marketing Services (300 W. Marlton Pike, Cherry Hill, NJ, 08002). It comes packaged as a set of one disk and a cartridge program. (The disk can be duplicated to make back-up copies.) Though a disk drive is necessary for this "advanced" version of the program, another abridged version is available for use with cassette.

If your program needs run to numbers, but you don't need the flexibility of a spreadsheet, shop for software that accomplishes specific tasks. Business software varies greatly in quality however, and you should always ask for demonstrations when in the market for these. This is especially true of inventory, general ledger, and payroll programs. Some business programs are limited in their scope, but highly practical for certain applications. One good example is Commodore's "Easy Finance" package, which offers several different kinds of financial calculations, including buy/lease, loan, annuity, profit, and payback analysis.

## Other Languages

Human languages possess their own attributes. French, for example, is claimed to be very expressive. The classical languages—Greek and Latin—are regarded for their precision and strictness of form. Japanese and Chinese, we are told, are elegantly descriptive.

If a parallel can be drawn, then BASIC is to computers what English has become to the world. It is serviceable but complex, with almost as many exceptions as rules. And it has become a *de facto* standard, at least for personal computers.

Computer languages are large programs that interpret different styles of commands. Since the 64 family has the extra memory necessary to store

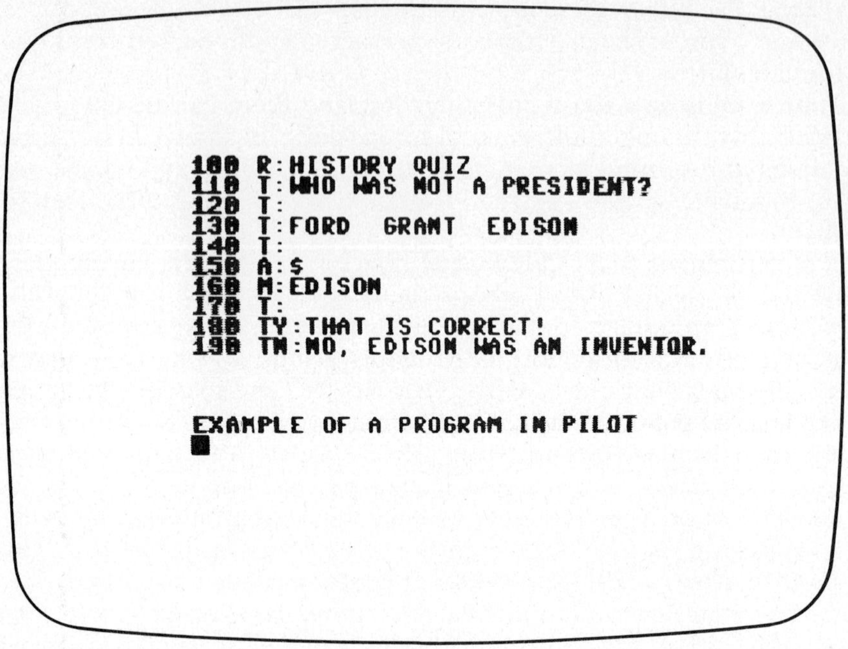


new languages, they are ideally suited to "learning" new languages. (The question is, are you?)

***Pilot*** One of these new languages is Pilot, which might best be described as tiny but powerful, limited in its application but, some say, perfectly suited for what it was designed for, education. It is becoming increasingly popular in classrooms, particularly elementary schools, and, with books and magazine columns devoted to it, a small but vocal cult of devotees has formed around it.

Pilot's disciples most often cite its deceptively simple commands (most of which are single letters instead of words) and its ability to understand the sometimes balky responses of very young children. Many educators tout the language's appeal to young programmers, some of whom can't yet read or write.

Pilot, like BASIC, has taken many different paths in its life. The most popular versions of microcomputer BASIC, for example, have been greatly enhanced since its original development at Dartmouth College. One enhancement to Pilot has been the addition of a graphic "turtle," a graphic device for drawing on the screen. Unfortunately, Commodore 64 Pilot has no such turtle (many will see this as a drawback), but it does take advantage of the 64's unique color graphic and sound capabilities.

Entering Commodore Pilot, you soon know that you are in a new kind of computer communication environment. It is LOADed from a floppy disk, and, because of the 64's unique architecture, takes the place of BASIC. In addition to an entirely new character set (with only passing resemblance to the 64's resident alphabet and numbers), you notice the first major difference. Pilot has four distinct modes, or ways of operation.

Pilot always begins in the *Command* mode. This is like a crossroads, where you decide where you'll go next. One choice you can take is to go to the *Immediate* mode, where you can test Pilot's single-letter commands, called "Op-codes" in "computerese." Once familiar with the commands, you can enter the *Edit* mode, where programs are composed. Finally, entering the *Run* mode puts your Pilot program into action.

Without delving into the details, the most obvious attraction of Pilot to educators is its suitability to creating classroom quizzes for computer-aided instruction. Its advantage seems to be the ability to decipher the correct answer by separating it from a long or jumbled response.

This is part of a Pilot program:

```
TS:What are the colors in the Canadian flag?
A:
M:red & white
```

The first line for instance, tells the screen to **T**ype (like PRINT in BASIC) the question "What are the colors in the Canadian flag?" (For the curious, the "S" in "TS:" means to clear the **S**creen.) The single letter "A," for **A**ccept, waits for the answer.

"M" means **M**atch any answer with "red" and "white" in it. By modifying the **M**atch command it will understand the answer of "white and red" (reverse order) or even misspelled words like "read" and "wite."

Equally interesting is Pilot's graphic capabilities. Although it will allow you to use the 64's high-resolution graphics, its use of "sprites"—those movable graphic objects on the video screen—is more straightforward.

Instead of using a "sprite generator" program, Pilot lets you simply draw a picture using several lines of a program. Each of the 21 lines of 24 dots in a program represents the appropriate data for the 64's video chip to interpret as a picture. Likewise, Pilot allows the memory locations for the 64's *SID* sound synthesizer chip to be filled by a single program line.

Pilot also includes op codes for logic and integer arithmetic, uses variables and has a few more graphic features. There are some drawbacks besides the missing turtle. The most obvious one is that you cannot see a disk directory while in the language.

***LOGO*** Some will find another new language, LOGO, more exciting. Developed at the Massachusetts Institute of Technolgy, LOGO is often called a "dialect" (or form of) LISP, a language used heavily by experimenters in artificial intelligence. The idea behind LOGO is unique. Its command words are called "procedures," and LOGO comes with a relatively small number of these.

Its power, though, comes from the fact that new procedures can be constructed out of the original ones, and these new procedures, too, can be used to create other new ones. Because of this, LOGO is often called "recursive." (For an example of something recursive, think of a drawing of an artist drawing a picture of himself drawing a picture of himself.) It is exactly this ability of "learning" new commands that makes LOGO so clever and fascinating.

Perhaps the most popular feature of LOGO is its turtle, the name given to a triangular cursor that draws on the computer's high-resolution screen. The cursor's name is not an attempt to be cute. The machine thinks of the turtle as an intelligent, moving thing with a pen in its belly. When the pen is down, it draws a line. Here's what a sequence that draws a square looks like:

```
TO SQUARE
PENDOWN
REPEAT 4 [FORWARD 50 RIGHT 90]
END
```

The process is simple. The turtle puts its pen down to draw and moves forward 50 units, each unit equal to a dot on the hi-res screen. Then the turtle turns right, 90 degrees. This is repeated four times to make the square. Once the computer knows how to make a square, you needn't repeat the sequence, only use the word SQUARE.

A virtual cult has formed around LOGO and its innovative concepts. LOGO buffs have embraced it for teaching computers to children, working with the handicapped, for music, graphic art, and the designing of "microworlds," visual simulations of everyday life. Commodore's LOGO was written by Terrapin, an aptly-named Cambridge, Massachusetts software house that specializes in LOGO. A preliminary copy used for this preview showed a version similar to Terrapin LOGO for the Apple II, with several enhancements. Newcomers and LOGO fans alike are sure to be pleased.

You won't be able to write a word processor or spreadsheet in LOGO, or do complex mathematics in Pilot. They aren't meant as replacements for BASIC and have personalities all of their own. Both these languages appeal to the imagination and the power of our minds.

***Fast BASIC*** The most common complaint about good old BASIC is that it is slow. (To computer professionals and those accustomed to working on larger machines, it is often intolerable.) From programming a video game to writing "number crunching" routines, it is seldom fast enough. Why is it so slow?

Most personal computers, your 64 included, store BASIC words as single characters in memory. The computer must interpet what the command means and look for the numbers that go along with it. Then it goes to routines in the BASIC ROMs, and does what it should. This all takes time, and is why Commodore BASIC is called an *interpreted* BASIC.

A *compiler*, however, turns the lines of a BASIC program into faster-running, more direct computer code. Though some commands do not benefit as much as others, the original program operates dozens of times faster.

One such compiler for the Commodore 64 family is Petspeed, a British program that originated on the PET and CBM, and has since been adapted. It is available in the United States from Small Systems Engineering (1056 Elwell Court, Palo Alto, CA, 94303).

Petspeed comes packaged on a disc and with an electronic security key that plugs into control port 2. (The program will not run without the key, which prevents piracy.) When operating, it LOADs the BASIC program to be compiled and begins taking it apart, piece by piece. Four separate "passes" eventually rewrite the program as a compiled, Petspeed version which can be LOADed, SAVEd and RUN normally. It cannot, however, be LISTed or edited. (The BASIC version remains intact on the same disk, though.)

In its design, Petspeed is something of a software engineering marvel. Tens of thousands of bytes of intermediate disk files are generated, and the whole operation takes place inside the computer and on a single disk. When Petspeed works, it works very well, indeed. Programs operate noticeably faster. The major problem with the compiler is that it is quirky. Some programs compile easily and smoothly, while others return puzzling error messages or simply "crash" the computer. (In testing it, Petspeed would even occasionally have trouble with a program that compiled correctly minutes before.)

Petspeed also had trouble with some programs containing character graphics, and many programs with sprites require some adjustment in the way they use memory space. Other oddities include a restriction on the number of characters in a program name (Petspeed allows names of only 10 letters) and the use of variables. (Using NEXT without a variable is legal in BASIC if the meaning is clear. Petspeed sometimes doesn't like this.) Most agonizing is that, while Commodore BASIC's INPUT statement was fixed in the VIC-20 and 64, Petspeed still compiles it as though it weren't. With INPUT, an answer of a null string ("") breaks the program.

Finally, despite the speed it adds to a program, compiling is a long and tedious process, due in part to the slow 1541 disk drive. A program the length of the data base demonstration in this book took over twenty minutes to compile with the disk drive spinning away, grinding from track to track. (It is a genuine endurance test for the little 1541.)

Petspeed would be a little less confounding if it were better documented. The entire instruction book for this powerful and complex program is only 3 pages long and offers only the barest details about how to use it and how it works. This is not a program for inexperienced programmers, even though those are the people who could probably benefit from it best. Petspeed, then, winds up being a paradox: There are too many problems to make it a reliable, everyday tool, yet its results can be very impressive.

***Simons' BASIC*** Commodore BASIC isn't a bad language. A version of Microsoft BASIC, it has very few peculiarities and no major "bugs." Its only real problem is that it didn't grow up with the company's computers. While it was serviceable for the original 8K PET, which had no color, sound, or high-resolution graphics, Commodore BASIC just isn't enough for the 64, which has all of those features. Programming even the most rudimentary graphics and sounds on the 64 is an endless job of PEEKing and POKEing.

Simons' BASIC doesn't only offer a solution to the problem, but almost makes the 64 into an entirely new computer. The 114 new commands are so comprehensive that they make Simons' BASIC more than a *good* language extension.

The origin of Simons' BASIC is interesting in itself. It was created by a sixteen-year-old British programmer named David Simons, whose parents gave him his first computer on his thirteenth birthday. According to the official company legend, Simons surveyed other BASICs and their extensions and picked from among their features.

Simons' BASIC comes packaged as a ROM cartridge and its new commands are grouped into several categories: Programming aids ("toolkit" commands and other conveniences); new BASIC words for inputting information; arithmetic and math extensions; disk functions; high-resolution graphics; screen manipulation; sprite graphics words; error trapping schemes; music notation, and commands that read controllers (light pens, joysticks, paddles, etc.). Finally, another set of new words are used for structured programming, and can make this BASIC very FORTRAN-like, if you choose to use them.

Space prohibits going into detail about Simons' BASIC. (It deserves a book all its own.) But this is one of the best, most comprehensive pieces of software available for the Commodore 64 and, in fact, for computers in general. If you have picked up the basics of BASIC, you should have no trouble understanding the new commands. At press time, no prices were set by Commodore, who will sell the Simons' BASIC cartridge. Still, short of an exorbitant price tag, Simons' BASIC is a must for Commodore 64 owners.

***Assembly Language*** True program speed comes upon entering the final realm of programming—machine code. It is programmed in "assembly language," with the use of a program called an "assembler." (Logically, the equivalent of LISTing a program in assembly code is called "disassembling" it.) There are fewer commands in assembly language than in BASIC, and each one is called a *mnemonic* because it is a three-letter abbreviation for the command. However, programming is more difficult for several reasons. Conventional, decimal numbers are not used. It requires hexadecimal numbers—a number system with a base of 16 numbers instead of 10. This makes arithmetic, especially decimal point arithmetic, tough.

Assembly language also deals with the machine on its own terms, so you must completely understand where everything inside the computer is located and where programs can and cannot be stored. Nor are there any ERROR messages when writing programs this way. When an assembly language program has a flaw in it, the computer often "crashes" without giving a clue as to why. Programming in BASIC is like driving on an expressway. Assembly language is like taking the back roads and stopping in every little town along the way. It is the way to learn the countryside, but it takes longer and demands more attention to detail.

There's no reason to be scared away from the challenge, though. Many novice programmers have mastered assembly language, and those who have prefer it to BASIC for many things. The jobs that are easier in BASIC can still be done that way, with fast machine code portions being called with the SYS command.

To write assembly code, you'll need an assembler and other associated programming tools. The version sold by Commodore is very good and is used by the company's own software development team. Another good assembler is MAE (from Eastern House Software, 3239 Linda Drive, Winston-Salem, NC, 27106). Its designers boast that a version was used on NASA's Space Shuttle project.

## Human-to-Machine Interfacing

That's computer jargon for ways to communicate with the machine. The most often used way of talking to any computer is through the keyboard, of course. But it's not the only way. You already know that you can use joysticks and game paddles. Have you ever heard of a light pen?

A light pen is not a pen that writes in light. It is a pen-shaped sensor that is used to point out objects on the screen. The computer can detect the position of the light pen and this information is then passed along to the program to use in making decisions. Inside the light pen is a light-sensitive transistor connected to control port 1 via some electronic circuitry.

Light pens are especially good for programs where choices are always made from a menu. Pointing at your choice keeps the program moving along. Light pens can also be good for games or educational programs where children can't be expected to type on the keyboard. Few commercial programs are written for a light pen, but you can expect to see some come along. So, you'll need to modify programs or write them yourself, but rewriting should be minimal. Simple PEEK statements read where the pen is pointing on the screen. This is easy on the Commodore 64 computers since special light pen memory locations are built into the VIC chip.

Not all light pens are the same. Differences in the size and brightness of video screens make some work better than others. One very good light pen previewed for this book is manufactured and sold by Madison Computer (1825 Monroe Street, Madison, WI, 53711). The pen tested was sturdy, reliable, and looked like a desk set, with a wooden base for it when not in use. It comes with several demonstration programs, "Othello," a novel "Hangman" game, and an excellent routine to copy programs and files from one disk to another on a single 1541 disk drive.

Light also plays a part in communicating with your computer on a *touch-sensitive* video screen, maybe the ultimate in computer communication. No need for a light pen here. You just touch an object on the screen and the computer knows what you're doing. How does it work?

The most popular scheme for touch-sensitivity is to frame the video screen with light sources and light detectors. Most use *infrared* light, which is invisible, and infrared detectors opposite the light sources. They are arranged in such a way that when you touch the screen, you break two beams of light—one for the horizontal position and one for the vertical. The computer interprets this information and makes its decision.

The most visible touch-sensitive video screens in the world are located in EPCOT Center at Walt Disney World in Orlando, Florida, where they are used for computer demonstrations and games, and as part of the exposition's World Key information system. Dozens of other touch screens are behind-the-scenes, controlling EPCOT's ride and show mechanisms.

EPCOT's touch screens were engineered by Carroll Touch Technology (2902 Farber Drive, Champaign, IL, 61821), a pioneer in the technique. Carroll sells a kit that you can experiment with using your Commodore 64 or most any personal computer. It is a frame that can be mounted on the screen of a 12-inch video monitor. The frame uses infrared light to send position information back to the computer via an RS-232 data connection. Being a pioneer has its price, however. The cost of Carroll's experimenter and evaluation system is over $1000.

In the beginning of this book you were told that there was a world inside the computer you have before you, and that the possibilities were practically limitless. Perhaps you believe that more now. It is fun to think of these possibilities in a world that is filled with limitations, and fun to be part of the ground-breaking movement that personal computing and technology is today.

We should be proud, though, not of our machines, but what *we* can make them do. Take delight not in what you have, but in what *you* can do. The real buried treasures you may discover are your own abilities.

# Appendix 1

# Exploring the Commodore 64

*Jim Butterfield*

Inside the Commodore 64 there's a whole world to explore. You can look at the inner workings of the computer, and even try changing things around to see what happens.

You don't need to open up the computer to do this. You may peek inside the computer's workings "logically"—in fact, you'll use a function called PEEK to look around. Similarly, you won't need to fiddle with wires in order to poke around the innards and change the way things work—you have a POKE command to make the changes for you.

We'll go on a quick tour of the inner workings of the Commodore 64, looking at a few points of interest on our way. After our familiarization tour, you'll be able to explore on your own.

## Why Tinker?

Why would you want to rummage around a computer's insides? There are several reasons.

First, you sometimes need—in fact, you're sometimes instructed—to do this. The Commodore 64 user guide, for example, instructs you to change the screen border color with a POKE 53280,X where X is a color code number from 0 to 15. You are being told to change something within the computer's innards. As you gain more experience, you'll develop a roster of addresses that are useful for various jobs.

Secondly, it's a useful way to gain insight into the workings of the machine. You may examine the data that is stored within the computer. You can try tampering with it to see what happens.

A word about tampering with the computer's memory: you can't hurt anything. The worst that can happen is that the computer might stop working. If that happens, all you need to do is to turn the power off and on again . . . and the machine will be back in operation.

## The Computer's Memory

The computer uses its memory for just about everything it does. Almost all its important activities are related to memory, which contains such things as computer instructions, data, your programs, and a copy of the screen. There are lots of things in there.

Memory consists of cells in which information can be stored; each cell has an "address." There are 65536 cells which may be reached in the Commodore 64; the addresses start at 0 and go up to 65535. Each cell may contain any value from 0 to 255. Various areas of memory have been assigned for specific jobs; you'll get to know certain addresses quite well after a while.

There are three kinds of memory devices used in a computer; one kind isn't really memory at all. Let's talk about them and where they are located.

## Kinds of Memory

RAM is memory we can write (POKE) and read (PEEK). It's like a storage area: we can put information there; later, we can go back and look at the information we have stored. When you type a program into the Commodore 64, it is stored in RAM. When your program calculates values, these will be stored into (and recalled from) RAM. RAM, by the way, stands for Random Access Memory; that's not a very meaningful name.

The Commodore 64 in its usual configuration has RAM available from address 2 to address 40959, and from address 49152 to 59151. The lower block is used for BASIC programs and working values; the upper block isn't used at all by BASIC. As we'll discuss later, you have more RAM than this available which you can put to work in your 64 if desired.

ROM is fixed memory; you can read it (PEEK it), but you can't store into it. The values in ROM have been set at the factory, and can't be changed. ROM stands for Read Only Memory, which is a fair description. It may seem limiting to have ROM which cannot be changed, but if you don't like what's in a ROM, you can swap it out and put RAM in its place. ROM holds the main logic of the computer: how to calculate a square root, for example, or how to write information to a cassette tape. Most of the "built-in" features of any computer are usually built into ROM.

The Commodore 64 usually has ROM available from address 40960 to 49151 and from 57644 to 65535. The first block tells the computer how to recognize and implement the BASIC language; the second, how to do input/output activities such as keyboard, screen, disk, or tape. There's a third ROM tucked away inside the 64 where we can't usually PEEK it . . . this is the character generator, which shows how to draw each character on the screen. And if you plug in a video game, chances are you're plugging in an extra ROM, containing instructions on how to play the game.

The third type of memory device is called an Interface. These are not really memory, since we can't be sure that information stored here will be available for us to recall at a later time. Their main job is to perform interfacing to things outside the central computer. There's a Video Interface Chip which creates the image we see on the screen. There's a Sound Interface Device which makes the sounds that we hear. And there are two Complex Interface Adaptors which make connections to the keyboard, to and from disk, from the joysticks . . . and perform other functions as well, such as timing.

The Video Interface Chip is located at addresses 53262 to 53286 in the Commodore 64. The Sound Interface Device is located at addresses 54272 to 54300. And the two Complex Interface Adaptors are located at 56230 to 56335 and 56576 to 56591. Locations 0 and 1 have special interface functions of their own: their most important job is to control the way the other chips appear in memory.

## Memory Maps

You'll find some lengthy "memory maps" at the end of this appendix. Their purpose is to give you a hint as to how the various locations are used.

RAM is the most fun, since we can try changing things to see what happens. We'll browse a little more in RAM in just a moment.

We can't change ROM, so its structure is of interest mostly for study purposes. If we want to analyze in detail how the machine works, we can peruse ROM. To do so, we'll need to understand a new type of language: 6502 machine language.

The 6502 is a very close relative of the 6510 microprocessor used in the Commodore 64. The instructions in ROM are 6502-type instructions . . . it's a whole specialized field of study to learn how to read them.

The Interface chips are very practical to use; indeed, many of the interface locations are mentioned in the 64 User's Guide . . . you'll need to know some of them in order to make sounds, or to change some of the screen characteristics.

You may note that the interface chips are drawn as charts. That's because many interface locations control more than one activity. The memory cell is composed of individual control elements, called "bits," which are coded using the following numbers:

128 64 32 16 8 4 2 1

For example, if you see that a given location contains a value of 20, a little arithmetic will reveal that the bit marked 16 and the bit marked 4 are "on" and all the others are off. No other combination of bits gives a total of 20.

When you reference the Interface chip charts, you'll see the individual bits and see how to combine them to make a composite control value.

## RAMbling

RAM memory is so much fun that it's worth talking about a little more. We'll look through the addresses, and pick out a few interesting ones.

Addresses 2 to 1023 is a work area for the computer; it's very rich with important locations. The area from 2 to 255 is called "zero page" and it's jammed with the computer's working values. If you command PRINT PEEK(203), for example, you'll discover whether a key is being held down at the moment or not: a value of 64 means that no key is being pressed. This isn't much use as a direct statement: you'd need to be very fast to take your hand from the RETURN key before the answer is printed. But within a program, PEEK(203) can tell you that someone is holding a key. Which key? The GET statement will tell you.

*Locations 256 to 511* are fairly quiet. This is used for an inner computer work area called the "stack" . . . you won't get much useful action in this area.

*Locations 512 to 677* are quite busy. One of my favorites here is location 650, which controls how the keyboard keys repeat. You may have noticed that cursor keys and the space bar repeat; try POKEing 650 with values such as 255, 127, and 0 and see what happens.

*Locations 768 to 819* are specialized. They contain a number of "link" addresses which allow machine language programmers to change the behavior of the computer. They do this by changing the addresses stored within the links to new addresses of their own. This way, they can make the computer do marvelous new things. If you don't have machine language skills, all you'll do by changing these locations is cause the machine to behave erratically . . . or not at all.

*From 828 to 1019*, we have a cassette buffer area. If you use cassette tape to store or recall information, this memory area will change as the tape data is handled. If you don't happen to be using the cassette, this area is free and available . . . it's often popular as an area for "sprites" to enliven screen graphics.

*Locations 1024 to 2047* are used for "screen memory." Here's a fun area: POKEing to this area will cause a character to appear on the screen—try any value from 0 to 255; each will create a different screen character. It works both ways: if a program PEEKs one of these addresses, it will "see" what's on the screen in the corresponding location. Many games POKE and PEEK the screen area to create lively animation.

*From 2048 to 40959* we have the memory where the computer keeps the BASIC program that we type in. When the program runs, its variables and arrays are also stored in the same area. This area is a bit hard to use, since BASIC uses it, but you might like to explore the way a program is stored . . . it's more complex than you might think.

*2048 to 40969* is a large area, and you might not need it all to hold your BASIC program. You can trim it down so as to release space for sprites or machine language programs . . . we can't go into the details here, but it involves fiddling with the addresses stored in 43 and 44 (start-of-BASIC) or in 55 and 56 (limit of BASIC). How do you read an address stored in two bytes? Well, you PEEK the first byte, and add it to 256 times the PEEK of the second byte. This gets tricky . . . a BASIC program can't change its own start and end addresses while it is running, of course. As we said, we can't go into the details here.

There's extra RAM up at *addresses 49152 to 53247* and normally nobody uses it. It's a great place for experiments . . . especially trying out machine language programs to see if they work.

## The Great Memory Shuffle

It seems that we have clearly identified the pieces and places. But wait—the Commodore 64 has a secret. Hint: it's in the name.

The Commodore 64 has RAM everywhere . . . 64K of it, in fact, which amounts to 65536 locations. Even at addresses where we have ROM, there's RAM lurking behind it . . . waiting to be used.

For example, if we PRINT PEEK(45000), we'll get the contents of ROM memory . . . it's part of the BASIC instructions. But if we POKE 45000,100 the computer knows that we can't store into ROM . . . so it stores the value, 100, into the RAM behind the ROM. Can you read the RAM? Not with the ROM in the way: another PEEK to 45000 will just show us the ROM contents. But we can flip the ROM away by using the controls in address 1.

Wait just a moment. If we flip the ROM away, we'll lose BASIC. That's bad, because we need it in order to give commands . . . even POKE is a BASIC command. Is there any way we can move out the ROM and still keep BASIC?

It's easy, once you think of it. Just copy the ROM into the RAM beneath, and when we electronically make the ROM disappear, BASIC will still be there in the RAM. This gives us something new: a way to change BASIC.

Let's copy BASIC from the ROM into the RAM beneath. Type the following line:

```
FOR J=40960 TO 49151:POKE J,PEEK(J):NEXT J
```

At first glance this seems like nonsense. We are POKEing into each location the same information that we have just found there. But once we understand that it's coming from ROM and going into RAM, the whole thing makes sense. It will take a little while for the computer to copy all eight thousand odd bytes. When it's finished, type:

```
POKE 1,54
```

And BASIC is now operating out of RAM. Try this:

```
POKE 41848,66
```

Your machine should now reply BEADY instead of READY. You've changed BASIC . . . in a minor way, but it's still a genuine change.

You may restore the BASIC ROM by typing POKE 1,55. BEADY will once again become READY.

## Summary

I can only hint at the treasures that you can uncover if you like rambling through the insides of your machine. You don't need to, of course: the 64 can be used as the sensible, straightforward machine you always knew it was. But isn't it fun to tinker sometimes?

***Commodore 64 Memory Map, Compiled by Jim Butterfield***

| *Hex* | *Decimal* | *Description* |
|---|---|---|
| 0000 | 0 | Chip directional register |
| 0001 | 1 | Chip I/O; memory & tape control |
| 0003-0004 | 3-4 | Float-Fixed vector |
| 0005-0006 | 5-6 | Fixed-Float vector |
| 0007 | 7 | Search character |
| 0008 | 8 | Scan-quotes flag |
| 0009 | 9 | TAB column save |
| 000A | 10 | 0 = LOAD, 1 = VERIFY |
| 000B | 11 | Input buffer pointer/# subscrpt |
| 000C | 12 | Default DIM flag |
| 000D | 13 | Type: FF = string, 00 = numeric |
| 000E | 14 | Type: 80 = integer, 00 = floating point |
| 000F | 15 | DATA scan/LIST quote/memry flag |
| 0010 | 16 | Subscript/FNx flag |
| 0011 | 17 | 0 = INPUT;$40 = GET;$98 = READ |
| 0012 | 18 | ATN sign/Comparison eval flag |
| 0013 | 19 | Current I/O prompt flag |
| 0014-0015 | 20-21 | Integer value |
| 0016 | 22 | Pointer: temporary strg stack |
| 0017-0018 | 23-24 | Last temp string vector |
| 0019-0021 | 25-33 | Stack for temporary strings |
| 0022-0025 | 34-37 | Utility pointer area |
| 0026-002A | 38-42 | Product area for multiplication |
| 002B-002C | 43-44 | Pointer: Start-of-BASIC |
| 002D-002E | 45-46 | Pointer: Start-of-Variables |

***Commodore 64 Memory Map continued***

| *Hex* | *Decimal* | *Description* |
|---|---|---|
| 002F-0030 | 47-48 | Pointer: Start-of-Arrays |
| 0031-0032 | 49-50 | Pointer: End-of-Arrays |
| 0033-0034 | 51-52 | Pointer: String-storage (moving down) |
| 0035-0036 | 53-54 | Utility string pointer |
| 0037-0038 | 55-56 | Pointer: Limit-of-memory |
| 0039-003A | 57-58 | Current BASIC line number |
| 003B-003C | 59-60 | Previous BASIC line number |
| 003D-003E | 61-62 | Pointer: BASIC statement for CONT |
| 003F-0040 | 63-64 | Current DATA line number |
| 0041-0042 | 65-66 | Current DATA address |
| 0043-0044 | 67-68 | Input vector |
| 0045-0046 | 69-70 | Current variable name |
| 0047-0048 | 71-72 | Current variable address |
| 0049-004A | 73-74 | Variable pointer for FOR/NEXT |
| 004B-004C | 75-76 | Y-save; op-save; BASIC pointer save |
| 004D | 77 | Comparison symbol accumulator |
| 004E-0053 | 78-83 | Misc work area, pointers, etc |
| 0054-0056 | 84-86 | Jump vector for functions |
| 0057-0060 | 87-96 | Misc numeric work area |
| 0061 | 97 | Accum#1: Exponent |
| 0062-0065 | 98-101 | Accum#1: Mantissa |
| 0066 | 102 | Accum#1: Sign |
| 0067 | 103 | Series evaluation constant pointer |
| 0068 | 104 | Accum#1 hi-order (overflow) |
| 0069-006E | 105-110 | Accum#2: Exponent, etc. |
| 006F | 111 | Sign comparison, Acc#1 vs #2 |
| 0070 | 112 | Accum#1 lo-order (rounding) |
| 0071-0072 | 113-114 | Cassette buff len/Series pointer |
| 0073-008A | 115-138 | CHRGET subroutine; get BASIC char |
| 007A-007B | 122-123 | BASIC pointer (within subrtn) |
| 008B-008F | 139-143 | RND seed value |
| 0090 | 144 | Status word ST |
| 0091 | 145 | Keyswitch PIA: STOP and RVS flags |
| 0092 | 146 | Timing constant for tape |
| 0093 | 147 | Load=0, Verify=1 |
| 0094 | 148 | Serial output: deferred char flag |
| 0095 | 149 | Serial deferred character |
| 0096 | 150 | Tape EOT received |
| 0097 | 151 | Register save |
| 0098 | 152 | How many open files |
| 0099 | 153 | Input device, normally 0 |
| 009A | 154 | Output CMD device, normally 3 |
| 009B | 155 | Tape character parity |
| 009C | 156 | Byte-received flag |
| 009D | 157 | Direct=$80/RUN=0 output control |
| 009E | 158 | Tp Pass 1 error log/char buffer |
| 009F | 159 | Tp Pass 2 err log corrected |
| 00A0-00A2 | 160-162 | Jiffy Clock HML |
| 00A3 | 163 | Serial bit count/EOI flag |
| 00A4 | 164 | Cycle count |
| 00A5 | 165 | Countdown,tape write/bit count |
| 00A6 | 166 | Tape buffer pointer |
| 00A7 | 167 | Tp Wrt ldr count/Rd pass/inbit |

***Commodore 64 Memory Map continued***

| *Hex* | *Decimal* | *Description* |
|---|---|---|
| 00A8 | 168 | Tp Wrt new byte/Rd error/inbit cnt |
| 00A9 | 169 | Wrt start bit/Rd bit err/stbit |
| 00AA | 170 | Tp Scan;Cnt;Ld;End/byte assy |
| 00AB | 171 | Wr lead length/Rd checksum/parity |
| 00AC-00AD | 172-173 | Pointer: tape bufr, scrolling |
| 00AE-00AF | 174-175 | Tape end adds/End of program |
| 00B0-00B1 | 176-177 | Tape timing constants |
| 00B2-00B3 | 178-179 | Pntr: start of tape buffer |
| 00B4 | 180 | 1=Tp timer enabled; bit count |
| 00B5 | 181 | Tp EOT/RS232 next bit to send |
| 00B6 | 182 | Read character error/outbyte buf |
| 00B7 | 183 | # characters in file name |
| 00B8 | 184 | Current logical file |
| 00B9 | 185 | Current secndy address |
| 00BA | 186 | Current device |
| 00BB-00BC | 187-188 | Pointer to file name |
| 00BD | 189 | Wr shift word/Rd input char |
| 00BE | 190 | # blocks remaining to Wr/Rd |
| 00BF | 191 | Serial word buffer |
| 00C0 | 192 | Tape motor interlock |
| 00C1-00C2 | 193-194 | I/O start address |
| 00C3-00C4 | 195-196 | Kernel setup pointer |
| 00C5 | 197 | Last key pressed |
| 00C6 | 198 | # chars in keybd buffer |
| 00C7 | 199 | Screen reverse flag |
| 00C8 | 200 | End-of-line for input pointer |
| 00C9-00CA | 201-202 | Input cursor log (row, column) |
| 00CB | 203 | Which key: 64 if no key |
| 00CC | 204 | 0=flash cursor |
| 00CD | 205 | Cursor timing countdown |
| 00CE | 206 | Character under cursor |
| 00CF | 207 | Cursor in blink phase |
| 00D0 | 208 | Input from screen/from keyboard |
| 00D1-00D2 | 209-210 | Pointer to screen line |
| 00D3 | 211 | Position of cursor on above line |
| 00D4 | 212 | 0=direct cursor, else programmed |
| 00D5 | 213 | Current screen line length |
| 00D6 | 214 | Row where cursor lives |
| 00D7 | 215 | Last inkey/checksum/buffer |
| 00D8 | 216 | # of INSERTs outstanding |
| 00D9-00F2 | 217-242 | Screen line link table |
| 00F3-00F4 | 243-244 | Screen color pointer |
| 00F5-00F6 | 245-246 | Keyboard pointer |
| 00F7-00F8 | 247-248 | RS-232 Rcv pntr |
| 00F9-00FA | 249-250 | RS-232 Tx pntr |
| 00FF-010A | 256-266 | Floating to ASCII work area |
| 0100-103E | 256-318 | Tape error log |
| 0100-01FF | 256-511 | Processor stack area |
| 0200-0258 | 512-600 | BASIC input buffer |
| 0259-0262 | 601-610 | Logical file table |
| 0263-026C | 611-620 | Device # table |
| 026D-0276 | 621-630 | Sec Adds table |
| 0277-0280 | 631-640 | Keybd buffer |

***Commodore 64 Memory Map continued***

| *Hex* | *Decimal* | *Description* | |
|---|---|---|---|
| 0281-0282 | 641-642 | Start of BASIC Memory | |
| 0283-0284 | 643-644 | Top of BASIC Memory | |
| 0285 | 645 | Serial bus timeout flag | |
| 0286 | 646 | Current color code | |
| 0287 | 647 | Color under cursor | |
| 0288 | 648 | Screen memory page | |
| 0289 | 649 | Max size of keybd buffer | |
| 028A | 650 | Repeat all keys | |
| 028B | 651 | Repeat speed counter | |
| 028C | 652 | Repeat delay counter | |
| 028D | 653 | Keyboard Shift/Control flag | |
| 028E | 654 | Last shift pattern | |
| 028F-0290 | 655-656 | Keyboard table setup pointer | |
| 0291 | 657 | Keyboard shift mode | |
| 0292 | 658 | 0 = scroll enable | |
| 0293 | 659 | RS-232 control reg | |
| 0294 | 660 | RS-232 command reg | |
| 0295-0296 | 661-662 | Bit timing | |
| 0297 | 663 | RS-232 status | |
| 0298 | 664 | # bits to send | |
| 0299-029A | 665 | RS-232 speed/code | |
| 029B | 667 | RS-232 receive pointer | |
| 029C | 668 | RS-232 input pointer | |
| 029D | 669 | RS-232 transmit pointer | |
| 029E | 670 | RS-232 output pointer | |
| 029F-02A0 | 671-672 | IRQ save during tape I/O | |
| 02A1 | 673 | CIA 2 (NMI) Interrupt Control | |
| 02A2 | 674 | CIA 1 Timer A control log | |
| 02A3 | 675 | CIA 1 Interrupt Log | |
| 02A4 | 676 | CIA 1 Timer A enabled flag | |
| 02A5 | 677 | Screen row marker | |
| 02C0-02FE | 704-766 | (Sprite 11) | |
| 0300-0301 | 768-769 | Error message link | |
| 0302-0303 | 770-771 | BASIC warm start link | |
| 0304-0305 | 772-773 | Crunch BASIC tokens link | |
| 0306-0307 | 774-775 | Print tokens link | |
| 0308-0309 | 776-777 | Start new BASIC code link | |
| 030A-030B | 778-779 | Get arithmetic element link | |
| 030C | 780 | SYS A-reg save | |
| 030D | 781 | SYS X-reg save | |
| 030E | 782 | SYS Y-reg save | |
| 030F | 783 | SYS status reg save | |
| 0310-0312 | 784-785 | USR function jump | (B248) |
| 0314-0315 | 788-789 | Hardware interrupt vector | (EA31) |
| 0316-0317 | 790-791 | Break interrupt vector | (FE66) |
| 0318-0319 | 792-793 | NMI interrupt vector | (FE47) |
| 031A-031B | 794-795 | OPEN vector | (F34A) |
| 031C-031D | 796-797 | CLOSE vector | (F291) |
| 031E-031F | 798-799 | Set-input vector | (F20E) |
| 0320-0321 | 800-801 | Set-output vector | (F250) |
| 0322-0323 | 802-803 | Restore I/O vector | (F333) |
| 0324-0325 | 804-805 | INPUT vector | (F157) |
| 0326-0327 | 806-807 | Output vector | (F1CA) |

***Commodore 64 Memory Map continued***

| *Hex* | *Decimal* | *Description* | |
|---|---|---|---|
| 0328-0329 | 808-809 | Test-STOP vector | (F6ED) |
| 032A-032B | 810-811 | GET vector | (F13E) |
| 032C-032D | 812-813 | Abort I/O vector | (F32F) |
| 032E-032F | 814-815 | Warm start vector | (FE66) |
| 0330-0331 | 816-817 | LOAD link | (F4A5) |
| 0332-0333 | 818-819 | SAVE link | (F5ED) |
| 033C-03FB | 828-1019 | Cassette buffer | |
| 0340-037E | 832-894 | (Sprite 13) | |
| 0380-03BE | 896-958 | (Sprite 14) | |
| 03C0-03FE | 960-1022 | (Sprite 15) | |
| 0400-07FF | 1024-2047 | Screen memory | |
| 0800-9FFF | 2048-40959 | BASIC RAM memory | |
| 8000-9FFF | 32768-40959 | Alternate: ROM plug-in area | |
| A000-BFFF | 40960-49151 | ROM: BASIC | |
| A000-BFFF | 40960-59151 | Alternate: RAM | |
| C000-CFFF | 49152-53247 | RAM memory, including alternate | |
| D000-D02E | 53248-53294 | Video Chip (6566) | |
| D400-D41C | 54272-54300 | Sound Chip (6581 SID) | |
| D800-DBFF | 55296-56319 | Color nybble memory | |
| DC00-DC0F | 56320-56335 | Interface chip 1, IRQ (6526 CIA) | |
| DD00-DD0F | 56576-56591 | Interface chip 2, NMI (6526 CIA) | |
| D000-DFFF | 53248-53294 | Alternate: Character set | |
| E000-FFFF | 57344-65535 | ROM: Operating System | |
| E000-FFFF | 57344-65535 | Alternate: RAM | |
| FF81-FFF5 | 65409-65525 | Jump Table, Including: | |

FFC6 - Set Input channel
FFC9 - Set Output channel
FFCC - Restore default I/O channels
FFCF - INPUT
FFD2 - PRINT
FFE1 - Test Stop key
FFE4 - GET

## Processor I/O Port (6510)

| | | | | | | | | | |
|---|---|---|---|---|---|---|---|---|---|
| $0000 | IN | IN | OUT | IN | OUT | OUT | OUT | OUT | DDR 0 |
| $0001 | | | Tape Motor | Tape Sense | Tape Write | D-ROM Switch | EF RAM Switch | AB RAM Switch | PR 1 |

## SID (6581)

| Voice 1 | Voice 2 | Voice 3 | Register | Voice 1 | Voice 2 | Voice 3 |
|---|---|---|---|---|---|---|
| $D400 | $D407 | $D40E | Frequency L | 54272 | 54279 | 54286 |
| $D401 | $D408 | $D40F | Frequency H | 54273 | 54280 | 54287 |
| $D402 | $D409 | $D410 | Pulse Width L | 54274 | 54281 | 54288 |
| $D403 | $D40A | $D411 | 0 0 0 0 / Pulse Width H | 54275 | 54282 | 54289 |
| $D404 | $D40B | $D412 | Voice Type: NSE, PUL, SAW, TRI; Key | 54276 | 54283 | 54290 |
| $D405 | $D40C | $D413 | Attack Time 2ms - 8ms; Decay Time 6ms - 24 sec | 54277 | 54284 | 54291 |
| $D406 | $D40D | $D414 | Sustain Level; Release Time 6ms 24 sec | 54278 | 54285 | 54292 |

Voices (write only)

| | | |
|---|---|---|
| $D415 | 0 0 0 0 0 / Filter Frequency L | 54293 |
| $D416 | Filter Frequency H | 54294 |
| $D417 | Resonance; Filter Voices: Ext, V3, V2, V1 | 54295 |
| $D418 | Passband: V3 off, HI, BP, LO; Master Volume | 54296 |

Filter & Volume (write only)

| |
|---|
| Paddle X (A/D #1) |
| Paddle Y (A/D #2) |
| Noise 3 (random) |
| Envelope 3 |

Sense (read only)

Note: Special Voice Features
(TEST, RING MOD, SYNC)
are omitted from the above diagram.

## CIA (IRQ) (6526)

| | | | | | | | | | | |
|---|---|---|---|---|---|---|---|---|---|---|
| $DC00 | Paddle Sell A | Paddle Sell B | | Joystick 0 Fire | Right | Left | Down | Up | PRA | 56320 |
| | Keyboard Row Select (inverted) | | | | | | | | | |
| $DC01 | | | | Joystick 1 Fire | Right | Left | Down | Up | PRB | 56321 |
| | Keyboard Column Read | | | | | | | | | |
| $DC02 | $FF-All Output | | | | | | | | DDRA | 56322 |
| $DC03 | $00-All Input | | | | | | | | DDRB | 65323 |
| $DC04 | Timer A | | | | | | | | TAL | 56324 |
| $DC05 | | | | | | | | | TAH | 56325 |
| $DC06 | Timer B | | | | | | | | TBL | 56326 |
| $DC07 | | | | | | | | | TBH | 56327 |
| ~ | | | | | | | | | | |
| $DC0D | | | | Tape Input | | | Timer Interrupt B | A | ICR | 56333 |
| $DC0E | | | | | One Shot | Out Mode | Time PB6 Out | Timer A Start | CRA | 56334 |
| $DC0F | | | | | One Shot | Out Mode | Time PB7 Out | Timer B Start | CRB | 56335 |

## CIA 2 (NMI) (6526)

| | | | | | | | | | | |
|---|---|---|---|---|---|---|---|---|---|---|
| $DD00 | Serial IN | Clock IN | Serial OUT | Clock OUT | ATN OUT | RS-232 OUT | VIC II addr 15 | VIC II addr 14 | PRA | 56576 |
| $DD01 | DSR IN | CTS IN | | DCD* IN | RI* IN | DTR OUT | RTS OUT | RS-232 IN | PRB | 56577 |
| $DD02 | $3F-Serial | | | | | | | | DDRA | 56578 |
| $DD03 | $00-P.U.P. All Input or $06-RS-232 | | | | | | | | DDRB | 56579 |
| $DD04 | Timer A | | | | | | | | TAL | 56580 |
| $DD05 | | | | | | | | | TAH | 56581 |
| $DD06 | Timer B | | | | | | | | TBL | 56582 |
| $DD07 | | | | | | | | | TBH | 56583 |
| ~ | | | | | | | | | | |
| $DD0D | | | | RS-232 IN | | | Timer Interrupt B | A | ICR | 56589 |
| $DD0E | | | | | | | | Timer A Start | CRA | 56590 |
| $DD0F | | | | | | | | Timer B Start | CRB | 56591 |

## VIDEO (6566)

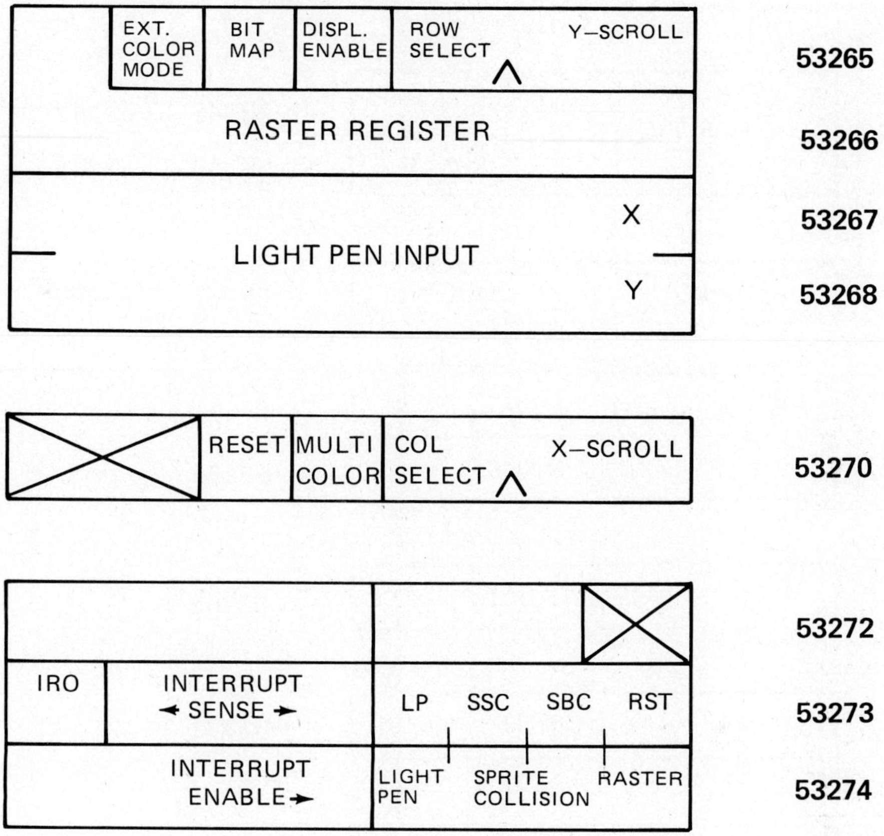


## COLOR REGISTERS

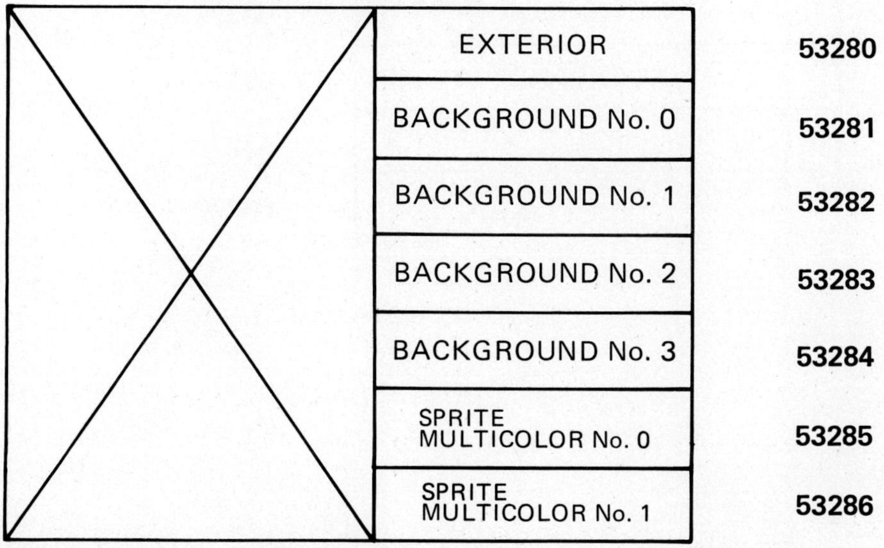

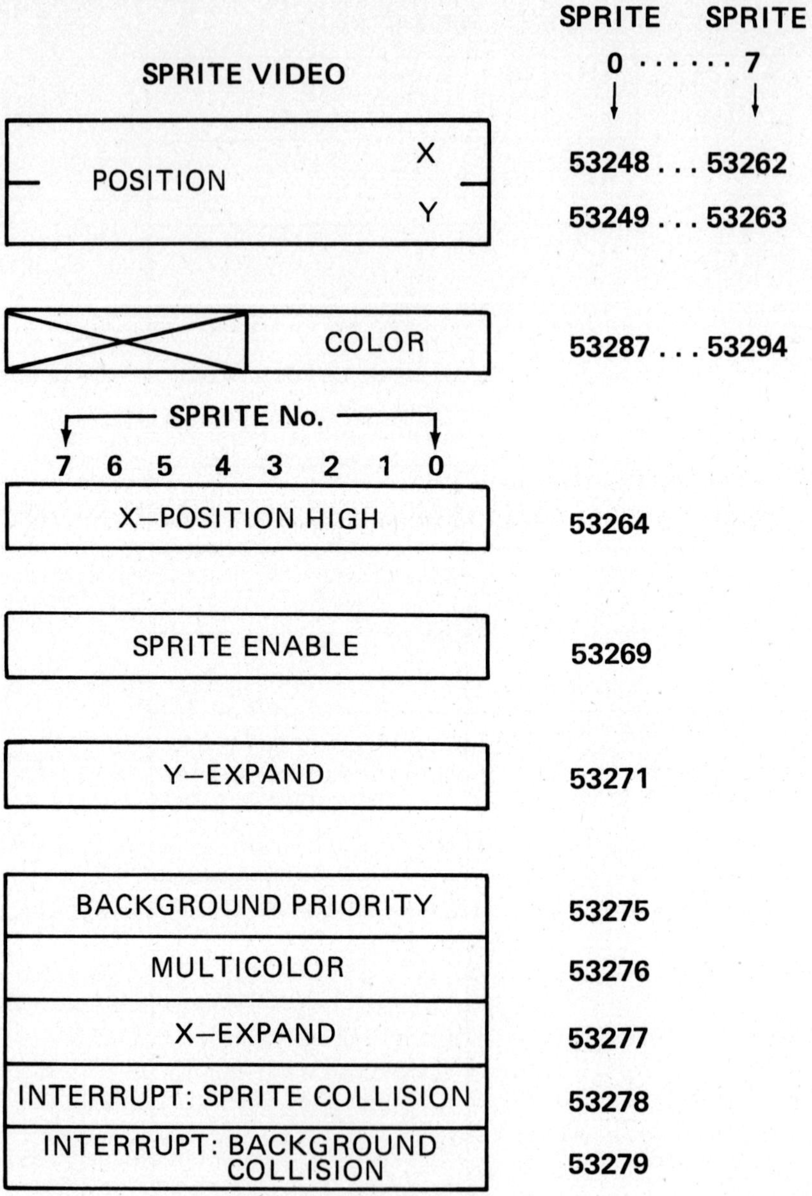
SPRITE VIDEO
SPRITE 0 ······ SPRITE 7
POSITION X
POSITION Y
53248 . . . 53262
53249 . . . 53263
COLOR
53287 . . . 53294
SPRITE No.
7 6 5 4 3 2 1 0
X–POSITION HIGH
53264
SPRITE ENABLE
53269
Y–EXPAND
53271
BACKGROUND PRIORITY
53275
MULTICOLOR
53276
X–EXPAND
53277
INTERRUPT: SPRITE COLLISION
53278
INTERRUPT: BACKGROUND COLLISION
53279

# Appendix 2

# Exploring Graphics on the Commodore 64

*Paul F. Schatz*

The Commodore 64 has some very powerful graphics capabilities including high-resolution ("bit map") graphics, several color display modes, characters that you can redefine, and moving colored objects called sprites. Designing and programming computer graphics can be a complex process, and the Commodore 64's features can be combined in so many ways that the task of explaining all the options quickly becomes overwhelming. Making it even more difficult is the fact that the Commodore 64 comes out of its box without any graphics commands in its BASIC.

Using the graphics on the Commodore 64 requires a more fundamental understanding of just how the computer works. This chapter will explain in simple language how numbers stored in the computer's memory are translated into a picture on the video screen. You will learn something about three special graphics features—sprites, programmable characters, and bit map graphing. Each will be explained and demonstrated with some simple programs. With a working knowledge of these features, you will be able to program some impressive pictures.

## Is It All Done With Mirrors?

The key to understanding the graphics is understanding how numbers in the computer's memory are used to define a picture. You will have to understand what is meant by the term *byte*. When you first turn on your computer, one line of the message which appears on the screen reads:

```
64K RAM SYSTEM 38911 BYTES FREE
```

The BYTES FREE refers to the number of memory locations, also called registers, the computer has for storing characters which make up a BASIC program. Earlier in this book, bytes were equated with characters. Any one of 256 different characters can be placed into a memory location. These characters are represented by the numbers 0 to 255. Why only 256 characters? Why not more? Or less? The answer to this question lies in how the computer stores numbers. Each memory location can be considered a set of eight switches, numbered 0 to 7, which can be turned on or off. If each switch is assigned a number, as shown in Figure 1, any number from 0 to 255 can be represented by adding the numbers of the "on" switches.

| | | | | | | | | |
|---|---|---|---|---|---|---|---|---|
| SWITCH | 7 | 6 | 5 | 4 | 3 | 2 | 1 | 0 |
| NUMBER | 128 | 64 | 32 | 16 | 8 | 4 | 2 | 1 |

**Figure 1.**

The condition of the switches can be represented by 1's and 0's, with 1 representing "on" and 0 being "off." The series of 1's and 0's is called a binary number. It can stand for a more conventional decimal number. (The numbers we use every day are called decimals because they use ten different digits, 0 through 9.) In computer jargon, these switches are called *bits*, and a *byte* is eight of these bits. For example, the number 16 is represented by switch four turned on (1) and all the other switches turned off (0).

| | | | | | | | | |
|---|---|---|---|---|---|---|---|---|
| SWITCH | 7 | 6 | 5 | 4 | 3 | 2 | 1 | 0 |
| ON/OFF | 0 | 0 | 0 | 1 | 0 | 0 | 0 | 0 |
| NUMBER | 128 | 64 | 32 | 16 | 8 | 4 | 2 | 1 |

The number 129 is represented with switches zero and seven "on," and switches six, five, four, three, two, and one "off."

| | | | | | | | | |
|---|---|---|---|---|---|---|---|---|
| SWITCH | 7 | 6 | 5 | 4 | 3 | 2 | 1 | 0 |
| ON/OFF | 1 | 0 | 0 | 0 | 0 | 0 | 0 | 1 |
| NUMBER | 128 | 64 | 32 | 16 | 8 | 4 | 2 | 1 |

The largest decimal number that can be represented by a byte is 255—all eight bits are one, or "on ." Table 1 gives the eight-bit binary numbers for decimal numbers from 0 to 255. This will be a handy reference when programming graphics.

In computer graphics a byte is used to define a row of dots, or picture elements on the video display. These picture elements are called *pixels*. The

***TABLE 1: Binary–Decimal Conversion***

Bits 0-3 are at the tops of the columns. Bits 4-7 are at the start of the rows.
Example: The binary representation of 18 is 0001 0010 (second row - third column).

| | 0000 | 0001 | 0010 | 0011 | 0100 | 0101 | 0110 | 0111 | 1000 | 1001 | 1010 | 1011 | 1100 | 1101 | 1110 | 1111 |
|---|---|---|---|---|---|---|---|---|---|---|---|---|---|---|---|---|
| 0000 | 0 | 1 | 2 | 3 | 4 | 5 | 6 | 7 | 8 | 9 | 10 | 11 | 12 | 13 | 14 | 15 |
| 0001 | 16 | 17 | 18 | 19 | 20 | 21 | 22 | 23 | 24 | 25 | 26 | 27 | 28 | 29 | 30 | 31 |
| 0010 | 32 | 33 | 34 | 35 | 36 | 37 | 38 | 39 | 40 | 41 | 42 | 43 | 44 | 45 | 46 | 47 |
| 0011 | 48 | 49 | 50 | 51 | 52 | 53 | 54 | 55 | 56 | 57 | 58 | 59 | 60 | 61 | 62 | 63 |
| 0100 | 64 | 65 | 66 | 67 | 68 | 69 | 70 | 71 | 72 | 73 | 74 | 75 | 76 | 77 | 78 | 79 |
| 0101 | 80 | 81 | 82 | 83 | 84 | 85 | 86 | 87 | 88 | 89 | 90 | 91 | 92 | 93 | 94 | 95 |
| 0110 | 96 | 97 | 98 | 99 | 100 | 101 | 102 | 103 | 104 | 105 | 106 | 107 | 108 | 109 | 110 | 111 |
| 0111 | 112 | 113 | 114 | 115 | 116 | 117 | 118 | 119 | 120 | 121 | 122 | 123 | 124 | 125 | 126 | 127 |
| 1000 | 128 | 129 | 130 | 131 | 132 | 133 | 134 | 135 | 136 | 137 | 138 | 139 | 140 | 141 | 142 | 143 |
| 1001 | 144 | 145 | 146 | 147 | 148 | 149 | 150 | 151 | 152 | 153 | 154 | 155 | 156 | 157 | 158 | 159 |
| 1010 | 160 | 161 | 162 | 163 | 164 | 165 | 166 | 167 | 168 | 169 | 170 | 171 | 172 | 173 | 174 | 175 |
| 1011 | 176 | 177 | 178 | 179 | 180 | 181 | 182 | 183 | 184 | 185 | 186 | 187 | 188 | 189 | 190 | 191 |
| 1100 | 192 | 193 | 194 | 195 | 196 | 197 | 198 | 199 | 200 | 201 | 202 | 203 | 204 | 205 | 206 | 207 |
| 1101 | 208 | 209 | 210 | 211 | 212 | 213 | 214 | 215 | 216 | 217 | 218 | 219 | 220 | 221 | 222 | 223 |
| 1110 | 224 | 225 | 226 | 227 | 228 | 229 | 230 | 231 | 232 | 233 | 234 | 235 | 236 | 237 | 238 | 239 |
| 1111 | 240 | 241 | 242 | 243 | 244 | 245 | 246 | 247 | 248 | 249 | 250 | 251 | 252 | 253 | 254 | 255 |

leftmost pixel of a set of eight pixels is the same as bit number 7 of a byte. Wherever a switch in the byte is on, the pixel is on. Wherever a switch is off, the pixel is off. One way of looking at the byte is as if the switches were controlling a row of eight light bulbs. By placing several rows of light bulbs next to one another, a picture can be created, just like the large electric billboards in ballparks.

Sprites, programmable characters, and bit map graphics are all similar in that the images are made from rows of eight pixels defined by the contents of memory locations. The graphics features differ in the number of memory locations used for displaying the image and in how the computer arranges the rows of pixels, end to end and/or side by side.

## Who's Pulling the Strings?

The memory locations are used for creating an image, and how the information is displayed on the screen is determined by the **V**ideo **I**nterface **C**ontroller chip—the VIC chip. This is the sophisticated microchip inside the Commodore 64 that generates the video signals. The VIC chip increases the efficiency of the computer in terms of memory utilization and program execution time. Many of the tasks performed by the VIC—sprites for instance—can be done on computers with complicated programs. But a program that does what the VIC does with sprites will need memory space and run slower than making and controlling sprites with a chip.

To answer the question that might arise, this chip named VIC is *not* the same one that is inside Commodore's wildly successful computer, the VIC-20. It is related, but in name only. This VIC is much, much more powerful than its little cousin.

How the VIC chip makes its pictures is determined by what's inside the 47 memory locations inside of it, numbered 53248 to 53294. Dramatic changes on the screen can be made by changing the values in any of these locations.

Some of the locations are groups of on/off switches. For example, location 53269 can be considered eight switches which turn on and off individual sprites. There are also switches for changing graphics modes, such as character, bit map, and extended background color modes. Still other locations tell the VIC chip where video information is stored in the computer's memory.

Before continuing, you must know that the VIC chip has some limitations. The most important one is that it can only look at 16,384 (16K) memory locations. Any video information must be within this 16K block of memory. When the Commodore 64 is turned on, the VIC chip is set so that the 16K block of memory it looks at extends from location 0 to location 16383. This will place some contraints on where the video display information is stored since certain areas of this memory are used by the computer for other tasks. Most notable are locations 0 to 827 which are used by BASIC and the operating system for storing pointers and other numbers. Another potential conflict is the section of memory where a BASIC program is stored. The computer starts storing a BASIC program at location 2048 and continues on up. Many programs are short enough so that there is room left at the end of the first 16K block for storing video display information. However, a long program can consume all of the memory from location 2048 to 16383. In this case, it is possible to tell the VIC chip to get its video information from a different 16K block of memory. Since this introduction is going to try to keep things simple, the topic of switching the video information to locations other than 0 to 16383 is going to be avoided.

## How Do I Talk to VIC?

The BASIC words needed for altering the contents of the Video Interface Controller chip are PEEK, POKE, AND, OR, and NOT. Unless you have been programming for a while, these may be unfamiliar to you.

PEEK is used for looking at the contents of a specific memory location. Try this:

```
PRINT PEEK(53272)
```

The computer responds by PRINTing the number 21. The contents of memory location 53272 control where the character set is located. Switch to the other built-in character set by pressing the COMMODORE key while holding the SHIFT key down. PEEK at location 53272 again. There's a different number in there now. The computer is getting the characters from a different section of memory.

POKE is used for putting numbers into specific memory locations. Another way of changing the character set is with the POKE command.

```
POKE 53272, 21
```

Which character set is the computer using? Change the character set again with

```
POKE 53272, 23
```

Only whole numbers between 0 and 255 can be POKEd into memory locations. Any other will produce an ILLEGAL QUANTITY ERROR message.

Unfortunately, the explanation of the words AND, OR, and NOT is not as straightforward as that for PEEK and POKE. These words are called *logical* operators which, in graphics, are used for turning on and off specific switches, or bits, without changing any of the other bits. Let's look at how they are used.

OR is used for setting bits. For example, to turn on bit 1 of location 53272 without affecting any of the other bits, we use this command:

```
POKE 53272, PEEK(53272) OR 2
```

PEEK gets the character stored at location 53272. The number following OR determines which bits are set. OR 2 sets bit 1 in the binary number to one. POKE puts the new number back into location 53272.

| | | | | | | | | |
|---|---|---|---|---|---|---|---|---|
| SWITCH | 7 | 6 | 5 | 4 | 3 | 2 | 1 | 0 |
| ON/OFF | 0 | 0 | 0 | 0 | 0 | 0 | 1 | 0 |
| NUMBER | 128 | 64 | 32 | 16 | 8 | 4 | 2 | 1 |

That's the number 2, above. Since the only "on" switch is number 2, it sets that bit in any number it is used with. More than one bit can be set at a time. For example, OR 129 will set both bit 7 and bit 0 of a byte to 1's.

| | | | | | | | | |
|---|---|---|---|---|---|---|---|---|
| SWITCH | 7 | 6 | 5 | 4 | 3 | 2 | 1 | 0 |
| ON/OFF | 1 | 0 | 0 | 0 | 0 | 0 | 0 | 1 |
| NUMBER | 128 | 64 | 32 | 16 | 8 | 4 | 2 | 1 |

Table 1 can be used for determining the decimal number that follows OR sets specific bits.

Bits are cleared using a combination of the AND and NOT commands. For example, to clear bit 1 of location 53272, enter the command

```
POKE 53272, PEEK(53272) AND NOT 2
```

The PEEK command gets the character. Bit 1 is cleared with the AND NOT 2 command, and the new character is put back into location 53272.

## Sprites

One of the most exciting features of the Commodore 64 is its sprite graphics. Sprites are pictures you create which the computer treats separately from the rest of its graphics. These little pictures are defined in 63 bytes of memory and can be moved around the video screen with BASIC programming commands. By placing numbers into specific memory locations in the VIC chip, up to eight objects can be made to appear and disappear, change color and size, and change shape and location. This makes it possible to get smooth and impressive animation in a BASIC program.

A sprite picture is defined by the contents of a block of 63 memory locations. The first row of the sprite is defined by the contents of the first three memory locations, the second row by the contents of the next three memory locations, and so on. A sprite has 21 rows. Since each memory location controls eight pixels, and a sprite row contains 24 pixels, the resolution of a sprite is 24 dots across by 21 dots deep. Figure 2 shows the arrangement of characters, or bytes, in the memory locations.

| | | |
|---|---|---|
| BYTE 1 | BYTE 2 | BYTE 3 |
| BYTE 4 | BYTE 5 | BYTE 6 |
| BYTE 7 | BYTE 8 | BYTE 9 |
| • | • | • |
| • | • | • |
| • | • | • |
| BYTE 55 | BYTE 56 | BYTE 57 |
| BYTE 58 | BYTE 59 | BYTE 60 |
| BYTE 61 | BYTE 62 | BYTE 63 |

**Figure 2. Memory Map of Sprite.**

The way that sprites are used in a program can be broken down into several steps.

1. Design a sprite picture.
2. Convert the sprite picture into numbers.
3. Store the numbers in the computer's memory.
4. Tell the computer where the sprite picture numbers are stored.
5. Define the color of the sprite.
6. Tell the computer where the sprite should be on the screen.
7. Turn on the sprite.

How do you go about determining which numbers are required to produce a desired sprite image? First, you need the proper tools: a sheet of graph paper, a pencil, and an eraser—a BIG eraser. Graph paper with eight to ten squares per inch is a good size because there is enough room to write numbers between the lines. Next, outline an area 24 squares horizontally and 21 squares vertically on the graph paper. The 504 squares within the outlined area represent the 504 pixels (63 bytes) that make up the sprite image.

Create the sprite picture by filling in the squares. Usually there will be lots of redrawing, so mark lightly at first. After you are satisfied with the image, you are ready to figure out the numbers the computer will need to display the sprite. The grid is divided into three vertical columns of eight squares each. The columns correspond to the columns of bytes in Figure 2. The binary numbers of each set of eight pixels are found by substituting 1's for filled squares and 0's for empty squares. You can look up the decimal numbers in Table 1.

A specific example of creating a sprite from numbers is illustrated with the horse-shaped sprite in Figure 3. An asterisk represents an "on" pixel and a period represents an "off" pixel.

```
 0,   0,   0        ........   ........   ........
 0,   0,   0        ........   ........   ........
 0,   0,  12        ........   ........   ....**..
 0,   0,  62        ........   ........   ..*****.
 0,   0, 126        ........   ........   .******.
 0,   0, 255        ........   ........   ********
 0,   1, 251        ........   .......*   *****.**
 0, 127, 241        ........   .*******   ****...*
 3, 255, 240        ......**   ********   ****....
 3, 255, 240        ......**   ********   ****....
 4, 255, 240        .....*..   ********   ****....
 0, 255, 240        ........   ********   ****....
 0, 224,  60        ........   ***.....   ..****..
 1,  96,  20        .......*   .**.....   ...*.*..
 2, 192,  10        ......*.   **......   ....*.*.
 2, 128,  10        ......*.   *.......   ....*.*.
 2, 128,   4        ......*.   *.......   .....*..
12, 128,   2        ....**..   *.......   ......*.
 0, 128,   0        ........   *.......   ........
 0, 192,   0        ........   **......   ........
 0,  64,   0        ........   .*......   ........
```

**Figure 3. Horse Sprite.**

If you look closely and study the example, you'll see that the numbers in the horse sprite do indeed describe the picture. For example, the last memory location in the third row shows that bit 2 and bit 3 are on and the rest of the bits are off. This corresponds to decimal numbers eight and four which add up to twelve.

Now we've got to find 63 memory locations in the computer's memory where the sprite data can be stored. The VIC chip divides the 16K graphics memory block into 256 sprite memory blocks. The blocks actually contain 64 locations because it is easier for the computer to think of them that way. The last memory location in a sprite data block is never used. These sprite blocks are numbered 0 to 255. You must be careful that none of the blocks overlap other graphics data that you'll learn about, like screens, character sets, and bit maps.

The number of the first memory location in any sprite block is always a multiple of the number 64. (Locations 64, 128, 192, etc.) If you are not using more than three sprites, a convenient place to store sprite pictures is in an area used by the cassette recorder, called the cassette buffer. It is located in memory locations 828 to 1023. The sprite blocks in this buffer are called number 13 (locations 832 to 895), number 14 (locations 896 to 959), and number 15 (locations 960 to 1023).

This limitation of three sprite data blocks does not mean that the number of sprites is limited to three. There can still be up to eight sprites, but only three different sprite shapes. If more than three different sprite shapes are used in a program, it is necessary to move special pointers and reserve RAM space at the end of the graphics block, or move the place where BASIC programs are stored. We'll leave that for now, and take it up again later, when we talk about programmable characters and bit maps.

The next step after designing the sprite and deciding where to place it in memory is to write a few program lines that READ and store the DATA in the selected locations. These lines will store the numbers for the horse sprite from the DATA statements into sprite block 13.

```
100 READ SB: IF SB<0 THEN 1000
110 SS = SB*64
120 FOR I = 0 TO 62: READ SD
130 POKE SS + I, SD: NEXT I
140 GOTO 100
150 DATA 13
160 DATA 0, 0, 0, 0, 0, 0, 0, 0, 12
170 DATA 0, 0, 62, 0, 0, 126, 0, 0, 255
180 DATA 0, 1, 251, 1, 127, 241, 3, 255, 240
190 DATA 3, 255, 240, 4, 255, 255, 0, 255, 240
200 DATA 0, 224, 60, 1, 96, 20, 2, 192, 10
210 DATA 2, 128, 10, 2, 128, 4, 12, 128, 2
220 DATA 0, 128, 0, 0, 192, 0, 0, 64, 0
•
•
•
```

```
999 DATA -1
1000 REM: START PROGRAM
```

Line 100 READs the first DATA statement. This is the sprite block number and is used to calculate the number of its first memory location (line 110). Lines 120 and 130 READ the next 63 numbers from the DATA statements and store them in 63 consecutive memory locations, starting at the location calculated in statement 110, location 832.

After 63 numbers are READ, the computer is told by line 140 to go back to line 100 where it READs the number in the DATA statement following the sprite data. If this is another sprite block number, the program calculates a starting location for another sprite data block. It then READs and stores the next 63 numbers in that data block. If the number statement 100 READs is a negative number, the program branches to the next part of the program. The negative number is a way to tell the program there is no more sprite data to READ.

The VIC chip has to know which data block to use for drawing a sprite. The Commodore 64 uses the last eight memory locations of screen RAM memory as pointers to the sprite blocks. The sprite block pointers for sprites 0 to 7 are locations 2040 to 2047, respectively. Continuing with the horse sprite program, sprites 0–3 can be told to appear as horses with the statements

```
1010 FOR I = 0 TO 3
1020 POKE 2040 + I, 13: NEXT I
```

If you notice, we can have more than one sprite, even though only one sprite picture is stored in memory.

The colors of the horses are defined by POKEing in numbers into locations 53287 to 53294. These control the colors of the eight sprites numbered 0 to 7.

```
1030 POKE 53287, 0: REM SPRITE 0 - BLACK
1040 POKE 53288, 1: REM SPRITE 1 - WHITE
1050 POKE 53289, 9: REM SPRITE 2 - BROWN
1060 POKE 53290, 12: REM SPRITE 3 - MED GRAY
```

Eight sprites numbered 0 to 7 are turned on or off by setting (1's) or clearing (0's) the corresponding bits in location 53269. Bit 0 turns on sprite 0, bit 1 turns on sprite 1, etc. For example, to turn on sprite 1, the number 2 (00000010) is placed in location 53269. Table 1 is again useful for determining the decimal number to be POKEd in location 53269. Up to eight sprites can be turned on at the same time. Here's what you'd do to turn on four sprites:

```
1070 POKE 53269, 15: REM TURN ON SPRITES 0 - 3
```

The most complicated aspect of using the sprites is placing them at specific locations on the screen. Each sprite uses two memory locations plus part of a third memory location to define its position on the display. Complicating things even more, the video "map" on which the sprites are displayed is *larger* than the screen! (This way, sprites can be smoothly moved onto the screen from the edges, behind the screen border.)

The upper left corner of a visual sprite block is used for its position on the screen. To have a full sprite appear on the screen, the vertical position must be 50 or greater but not greater than 229. The horizontal position number must be 24 or greater but not greater than 320. The VIC registers which define the positions are given in Table 2.

**TABLE 2: Sprite Position Registers**

| *Sprite* | *Vertical Position* | *Horizontal Position* |
|---|---|---|
| 0 | 53249 | 53248 + bit 0 of 53264 |
| 1 | 53251 | 53250 + bit 1 of 53264 |
| 2 | 53253 | 53252 + bit 2 of 53264 |
| 3 | 53255 | 53254 + bit 3 of 53264 |
| 4 | 53257 | 53256 + bit 4 of 53264 |
| 5 | 53259 | 53258 + bit 5 of 53264 |
| 6 | 53261 | 53260 + bit 6 of 53264 |
| 7 | 53263 | 53262 + bit 7 of 53264 |

Since the vertical position is never greater than 255 only one register per sprite is needed for this. However, the horizontal position does exceed 255 and a second memory location is needed to represent numbers greater than 255. The extra number is never going to be more than 1, so bits in memory location 53264 are used to indicate that 256 needs to be added to the number in a sprite's horizontal position memory location. This gets tricky. By using the extra bit, numbers for the horizontal position can be as large as 511. (You won't see the sprite if the horizontal position number is more than 344, though.) To remove some of the confusion, the horizontal positions of the sprites in our first example will not be greater than 255. Add the following commands to the program to position the horses around the screen.

```
1080 POKE 53248, 15: POKE 53249, 60: REM SPRITE 0
     POSITION
1090 POKE 53250, 160: POKE 53251, 150: REM SPRITE 1
     POSITION
1100 POKE 53252, 255: POKE 53253, 229: REM SPRITE 2
     POSITION
1110 POKE 53254, 100: POKE 53255, 235: REM SPRITE 3
     POSITION
1120 POKE 53281, 13: REM LIGHT GREEN SCREEN
1130 PRINT "[CLR]"
```

The program is now ready to run. Part of a black horse will appear at the left edge of the screen near the top, a white horse will be near the center of the screen, a brown horse will be near the bottom right, and part of a gray horse will be on the bottom edge. Try modifying the program by changing the colors and positions of the sprites. Since the program is using only one register for the horizontal position, none of the sprites is on the right third of the screen. Placing sprites in this area will be discussed and demonstrated later.

An interesting experiment is to position the sprites so that they overlap one another by various amounts. Notice that if sprite 0, the black horse, overlaps any of the other sprites, it is sprite 0 which is seen in its entirety. Similarly, sprite 1, the white horse, has priority over sprites 2 - 7. This ranking continues until sprite 7 which appears behind all the other sprites.

Try listing the program while the sprites are still on the screen. Notice that the characters appear behind the sprites. The priority of the sprites relative to the characters (or foreground on a bit map) is determined by the contents of location 53275. This is another of those registers where each bit selects the mode of the corresponding sprite. If a bit is set to 1, the corresponding sprite will appear behind characters. A clear bit assigns the sprite priority over characters. Enter POKE 53275, 15. Now all the sprites appear in back of the characters of the listing. If the value POKEd is 3, sprites 0 and 1 appear behind the characters and sprites 2 and 3 appear in front of the characters.

If there is a conflict of priorities, the sprite over sprite priority takes precedence. For example, if sprite 1 is defined as having priority over characters and sprite 0 is defined to appear behind characters, an overlap of all three will result in the characters appearing in front of sprite 0. If sprite 0 is moved away, the characters will disappear, leaving sprite 1. If sprite 1 is now moved away, the characters will reappear.

The dimensions of the sprites can be expanded both horizontally and vertically. A bit set to 1 in location 53271 expands the corresponding sprite vertically. A bit set to 1 in location 53277 expands the corresponding sprite horizontally. Try the following experiment. Modify statements 1080, 1090, 1100, 1110 in the horse sprite program.

```
1080 POKE 53248, 30: POKE 53249, 70: REM SPRITE 0
     POSITION
1090 POKE 53250, 200: POKE 53251, 70: REM SPRITE 1
     POSITION
1100 POKE 53252, 30: POKE 53253, 170: REM SPRITE 2
     POSITION
1110 POKE 53254, 200: POKE 53255, 170: REM SPRITE 3
     POSITION
```

RUN the program and the four horses appear on the screen. In the direct mode enter POKE 53271, 10: POKE 53277, 12. The sprites will change in appearance. Sprite 0 is unchanged from before, sprite 1 is doubled in height, sprite 2 is doubled in width, and sprite 3 is doubled in both width and height.

So far we have kept things simple by not using a horizontal position greater than 255. However, after you start to use sprites you will not want to be limited to this range. The following program demonstrates how to move a sprite beyond the 255 limit. It also demonstrates how animation can be achieved by changing the shape of a sprite as it moves across the screen. The program defines eight sprite shapes, an ordered set of views of a galloping horse. Each time the sprite is moved, sprite 0 data block pointer, memory location 2040, is changed. The program tests to see if the last data block is being used. If it is, sprite 0 data block pointer is initialized to the first block of the set.

To move a sprite beyond the 255th horizontal position on the screen requires the use of memory location 53264. This location keeps track of which sprites are displayed on the right-hand portion of the screen. If the bit corresponding to a displayed sprite is one, then the computer adds 256 to the number in the sprite's horizontal position memory location and uses the resulting number to position the sprite on the screen. If the entire horizontal range is going to be used, a program will have to make sure the bit in location 53264 is zero if the horizontal position is less than 256, and one if the horizontal position is 256 or greater. Statements 1090 to 1100 are used for positioning sprite 0.

Let us examine in detail how sprite 0 is positioned on the screen. The vertical position (memory location 53249) is kept constant. The variable X corresponds to the horizontal position. In statement 1090, the horizontal position is ANDed with 255 and placed in location 53248. The AND 255 adjusts the horizontal position value so that the number placed in location is between 0 and 255. Attempting to place a number outside this range in a memory location causes the computer to respond with an error message. If the horizontal position is less than 256, the result of X AND 255 is equal to X. If the horizontal position is greater than 256, the result of X AND 255 is equal to 256-X. The program checks to see if the horizontal position is greater than 255. If it is, bit 0 is set to one in location 53264 and the program skips to the next program statement. The next statement (statement 1100) is carried out if the horizontal position of the sprite is less than 256. This statement clears bit 0 of location 53264 to zero.

"GALLOP"

```
10 POKE 52,62:POKE56,62:CLR: REM MOVE TOP OF BASIC
20 READ SB: IF SB<0 THEN 1000: REM READ SPRITE DATA LOCATION
30 SS=SB*64
40 FOR I = 0 TO 62: READ SD
50 POKE SS+I, SD
60 NEXT I
70 GOTO 20
100 DATA 248,0, 0, 0, 0, 0, 0, 0, 0, 0, 0, 0, 0, 0, 0, 12, 0, 0
110 DATA 30, 0, 0, 62, 0,124,255, 1,255,243, 3,255,240, 6,255,240, 12
120 DATA255,224, 0,239,224, 1,231,192, 1,193,192, 2,129, 64, 2,130, 64
130 DATA 4,140, 64, 0, 0, 64, 0, 0, 64, 0, 0, 32,249, 0, 0, 0, 0
140 DATA 0, 0, 0, 0, 96, 0, 0,240, 0, 1,240, 0, 1,248, 0,255,200
150 DATA 3,255,192, 2,255,128, 4,255,128, 12,255,128, 8,127, 0, 0, 55
160 DATA128, 0, 51, 64, 0, 51, 32, 0, 49, 64, 0, 31,192, 0, 12, 0, 0
171 DATA 8, 0, 0, 4, 0, 0, 0, 0,250, 0, 0, 0, 0, 0, 0, 0
180 DATA 96, 0, 0,240, 0, 1,240, 0, 1,248, 0,199,200, 1,255,128, 7
190 DATA255,128, 15,255,128, 25,255,128, 49,255,128, 1,223,192, 0,194, 64
200 DATA 0,193, 64, 0,229, 64, 0,147, 64, 0,136, 64, 0, 68, 0, 0, 64
210 DATA 0, 0, 32, 0,251, 0, 0, 0, 0, 0, 0, 0, 0, 0, 0, 0, 30
220 DATA 0, 0, 62, 0, 0,127, 0, 0,251, 0, 63,249, 1,255,240, 3,255
230 DATA240, 7,127,240, 4,127,240, 0,115,248, 0,240, 8, 0,176, 8, 1
240 DATA160, 12, 1, 32, 10, 1, 32, 1, 1, 16, 0, 1, 16, 0, 0,136, 0
250 DATA252, 0, 0, 0, 0, 0, 0, 0, 0, 12, 0, 0, 62, 0, 0,126, 0
260 DATA 0,254, 0, 1,251, 0,127,241, 3,255,240, 3,255,240, 4,255,240
270 DATA 0,255,240, 0,224, 60, 1, 96, 20, 2,192, 18, 2,128, 10, 2,128
280 DATA 10, 12,128, 4, 0,128, 2, 0,192, 0, 0, 64, 0,253, 0, 0, 0
290 DATA 0, 0, 0, 0, 0, 0, 0, 0, 0, 0, 0, 28, 0, 0,126, 0, 0
300 DATA254, 0,115,251, 3,255,243, 6,255,240, 12,255,240, 0,255,224, 1
310 DATA255,224, 3,193,240, 7,128, 72, 31, 0, 68, 2, 0, 66, 2, 0, 33
```

```
320 DATA 2, 0, 32, 2, 0, 32, 2, 0, 16,254, 0, 0, 0, 0, 0, 0, 0
330 DATA 0, 0, 0, 0, 0, 0, 0, 28, 0, 0, 62, 0, 0,126, 0,255,251
340 DATA 3,255,241, 6,255,240, 12,255,240, 0,255,224, 1,199,224, 3,193
350 DATA240, 3, 0,144, 14, 0,136, 2, 0,132, 4, 0,130, 12, 1, 1, 0
360 DATA 1, 0, 0, 0,128,255, 0, 0, 0, 0, 0, 0, 0, 0, 0, 0, 0
370 DATA 12, 0, 0, 28, 0, 0, 62, 0,120,254, 3,255,247, 6,255,241, 12
380 DATA255,224, 0,255,224, 1,255,224, 1,195,224, 3, 1, 96, 2, 1, 32
390 DATA 4, 2, 32, 8, 2, 16, 0, 4, 16, 0, 4, 16, 0, 4, 8, 0, 4
400 DATA 8,-1
1000 PRINT"[CLR]"
1010 POKE 53287, 9: REM SPRITE0 - BROWN
1020 POKE 53269, 1: REM ENABLE SPRITE0
1030 POKE 53249, 150: REM SPRITE0 - Y POSITION
1040 POKE 53277, 1: REM DOUBLE WIDTH SPRITE
1050 POKE 53281, 13: REM LIGHT GREEN SCREEN
1060 SD=248: POKE 2040, SD: REM SELECT BLOCK
1070 FOR X= 0 TO 345 STEP 6: REM MOVE ACROSS SCREEN
1080 FOR T = 0 TO 50: NEXT T: REM DELAY LOOP
1090 POKE 53248, X AND 255: IF X>255 THEN POKE 53264, 1: GOTO 1110
1100 POKE 53264, 0
1110 SD = SD+1: IF SD=256 THEN SD=248: REM CHANGE SHAPE
1120 POKE 2040, SD
1130 NEXT X
1140 GOTO 1070
```

## Summary of Sprite Registers

The sprite registers can be divided into two types. The first type is the register which stores information for only one sprite (one sprite/register). These are listed in Table 3.

***TABLE 3: Eight-Bit Sprite Registers***

| *Sprite* | *Horizontal Position (Bits 0–7)* | *Vertical Position* | *Color* |
|---|---|---|---|
| 0 | 53248 | 53249 | 53287 |
| 1 | 53250 | 53251 | 53288 |
| 2 | 53252 | 53253 | 53289 |
| 3 | 53254 | 53255 | 53290 |
| 4 | 53256 | 53257 | 53291 |
| 5 | 53258 | 53259 | 53292 |
| 6 | 53260 | 53261 | 53293 |
| 7 | 53262 | 53263 | 53294 |

The second type uses one register to store information for all eight sprites (one sprite/bit). Each bit controls the mode of the corresponding sprite. These registers are listed in Table 4.

***TABLE 4: One-Bit Sprite Registers***

| *Register* | *Function* |
|---|---|
| 53264 | Horizontal position greater than 255 |
| 53269 | Turn on and off sprites |
| 53271 | Vertical doubling |
| 53275 | Priority over characters |
| 53277 | Horizontal doubling |

A selected bit is set to 1 by ORing the existing value in a register with the appropriate number. A bit is cleared to 0 by ANDing the existing value with the complement of the number used to set the bit. The general form of the statement to set a bit is

```
POKE [location] OR B2
```

The general form to clear a bit is

```
POKE [location], PEEK([location]) AND NOT B2
```

In these statements, [location] refers to the one bit sprite register and B2 depends on the sprite number (see Figure 1).

Designing and entering sprites can become quite laborious. A sprite editor program can eliminate much of the drudgery while giving the user direct visual feedback as the sprite is being created. The following program is a sprite editor that allows you to create a sprite, see how it looks on the screen, and then list the commands for creating the sprite in a program. The program divides the video display into three areas. The large 24 by 21 character grid is for editing the sprite. As the sprite is created, it will appear in an outlined area in the upper right of the screen. Expanded sprites are displayed in an outlined area in the lower right. The cursor mode is indicated by a letter. In the drawing mode, D, pixels are turned on wherever the cursor moves. In the erase mode, E, pixels are turned off wherever the cursor moves. In the normal mode, N, cursor movement has no effect on the pixels. After a sprite has been created, the commands and DATA statements that would create the sprite in a program can be listed to the screen or to a printer. The sprite editor commands are listed in Table 5.

**TABLE 5: Sprite Editor Commands**

| *Key* | *Function* |
|---|---|
| * | Turn on pixel at cursor |
| space | Turn off pixel at cursor |
| cursor left | Move cursor left |
| cursor right | Move cursor right |
| cursor up | Move cursor up |
| cursor down | Move cursor down |
| return | Move cursor to left edge |
| home | Move cursor to upper left corner |
| clear | Clear screen and home cursor |
| X | Expand sprite horizontally |
| Y | Expand sprite vertically |
| B | Expand sprite both ways |
| L | List commands |
| F1 | Select background color |
| F3 | Select sprite color |
| F7 | Select cursor mode |
| Q | Quit program |

```
"SPRITE"
5 CS=2:BG=1:PL=0:REM WHITE BACKGROUND, RED SPRITE

7 PM(0)=14:PM(1)=4:PM(2)=5

10 POKE 53280,6:POKE53281,1:REM BLUE BORDER, WHITE SCREEN

20 SC=1024:SP=832:CR=55296:REM SCREEN AND COLOR RAM

30 REM COLOR RAM TO GIVE CYAN POKED CHARACTERS

40 PRINT"[CLR]":FOR I=0TO999:POKECR+I,3:NEXT I

50 PRINT"[HOME][BLU][RVS ON]    SPRITE EDITOR BY PAUL SCHATZ  [RVS OFF]"

60 REM OUTLINE WORKING AREA

70 POKE SC+81,112:POKE SC+106,110:POKE SC+961,109:POKE SC+986,125

80 FOR I=0TO23:POKE SC+82+I,114:POKESC+962+I,113:NEXT I

90 FOR I=0TO20:POKE SC+121+(40*I),107:POKE SC+146+(40*I),115:NEXT I

100 REM COLOR WORKING AREA RED

110 FOR I=0TO20:FOR J=0TO23:POKE CR+122+(40*I)+J,2:NEXT J,I

115 GOSUB1700:REM COLOR SPRITE AREAS

120 REM OUTLINE FOR SPRITE
130 POKE SC+110,112:POKE SC+115,110:POKE SC+270,109:POKE SC+275,125

140 FOR I=0TO3:POKE SC+111+I,64:POKE SC+271+I,64 :NEXTI

150 FORI=0TO2: POKE SC+150+(40*I),93:POKE SC+155+(40*I),93:NEXT I
```

```
160 FORI=0TO2:FORJ=0TO3:POKESC+151+(40*I)+J,160:NEXTJ,I
170 PRINT"[HOME][CRSR DOWN][CRSR DOWN][28 CRSR RT]S[CRSR DOWN]
    [CRSR LEFT]P [CRSR DOWN][CRSR LEFT]R[CRSR DOWN][CRSR LEFT]I
    [CRSR DOWN][CRSR LEFT]T[CRSR DOWN][CRSR LEFT]E"
200 REM OUTLINE FOR EXPANSIONS
210 POKE SC+710,112:POKE SC+718,110:POKE SC+990,109:POKE SC+998,125
220 FOR I=0TO6:POKE SC+711+I,64:POKE SC+991+I,64:NEXTI
230 FOR I=0TO5:POKE SC+750+(40*I),93:POKE SC+758+(40*I),93:NEXT I
240 FORI=0TO5:FORJ=0TO6:POKESC+751+(40*I)+J,160:NEXTJ,I
250 PRINT"[HOME][16 CRSR DN][28 CRSR RT]";
260 PRINT"[CRSR DOWN]E[CRSR DOWN][CRSR LEFT]X[CRSR DOWN][CRSR LEFT]P
    [CRSR DOWN][CRSR LEFT]A[CRSR DOWN][CRSR LEFT]N[CRSR DOWN][CRSR LEFT]D
    [CRSR DOWN][CRSR LEFT]E[CRSR DOWN][CRSR LEFT]D[HOME]"
300 REM COMMAND TABLE
305 PRINT"[HOME][7 CRSR DN][30 CRSR RT]CURSOR:":PRINT
310 PRINT"[28 CRSR RT]COMMANDS:"
320 PRINT"[29 CRSR RT][LT RED]L[BLU]IST"
330 PRINT"[29 CRSR RT][LT RED]Q[BLU]UIT"
340 PRINT"[29 CRSR RT]EXPAND [LT RED]X[BLU]"
350 PRINT"[29 CRSR RT]EXPAND [LT RED]Y[BLU]"
360 PRINT"[29 CRSR RT]EXPAND [LT RED]B[BLU]OTH"
370 PRINT"[CRSR UP][29 CRSR RT][LT RED]F1  F3  F7[BLU]"
380 POKESC+318,PM(PL):POKECR+318,10
400 REM MOVE SPRITE DATA TO SCREEN
410 GOSUB1000
420 REM PUT SPRITE IN BOX
430 GOSUB1200
440 REM HOME AND TURN ON CURSOR
450 PRINT"[RED][HOME][CRSR DOWN][CRSR DOWN]":POKE211,2:POKE204,0
500 REM GET COMMAND
510 GETA$:IFA$=""THEN510
520 IF A$="Q"THENPOKE53269,0:PRINT"[CLR]":END
530 IFA$="L"THEN GOSUB2000:GOTO40
540 IFA$="X"THEN GOSUB1400
550 IFA$="Y"THEN GOSUB1500
560 IFA$="B"THEN GOSUB1600
570 IFA$="[HOME]"THEN GOSUB1300:GOTO450
580 IFA$="[CLR]"THEN GOSUB1100:GOSUB900:GOTO450
590 IFA$="[CRSR UP]"THEN GOSUB3000
600 IFA$="[CRSR DOWN]"THEN GOSUB3100
```

```
610 IFA$="[CRSR LEFT]"THEN GOSUB3200
620 IFA$="[C-R]"THEN GOSUB3300
630 IFA$=CHR$(13)THEN GOSUB3400
640 IFA$=" "THEN GOSUB3500:GOSUB3300
650 IFA$="*"THEN GOSUB3600:GOSUB3300
660 IFA$="[F1]"THENBG=BG+1:GOSUB1700
670 IFA$="[F3]"THENCS=CS+1:GOSUB1800
680 IFA$="[F7]"THENPL=PL+1:IFPL>2THENPL=0
690 POKESC+318,PM(PL)
700 GOTO510
900 REM CLEAR SCREEN
905 POKE 204,1:REM TURN OFF CURSOR
910 FOR I=0TO20:FOR J=0TO23:POKE SC+122+(40*I)+J,32:NEXT J,I
920 RETURN
1000 REM SUBROUTINE - MOVE SPRITE TO SCREEN
1005 POKE 204,1:REM TURN OFF CURSOR
1010 FOR I=0TO20:FORJ=0TO2:FORK=7TO0STEP-1
1020 CH=32:IF(PEEK(SP+(3*I)+J)AND(2[UP ARROW]K))THEN CH=204
1030 POKE(SC+122+(40*I)+(8*J)+(7-K)),CH
1040 NEXT K,J,I:RETURN
1100 REM SUBROUTINE - CLEAR SPRITE
1110 FOR I=0TO62:POKE832+I,0:NEXTI:RETURN
1200 REM SUBROUTINE - SPRITE TO SCREEN
1210 POKE 2040,13:REM SPRITE DATA IN LOCATIONS 832-894 (64*13=832)
1220 POKE 53248,20:POKE53264,1:REM X COORDINATE OF SPRITE 0
1230 POKE53249,75:REM Y COORDINATE OF SPRITE 0
1240 POKE 53287,CS:REM COLOR OF SPRITE 0
1250 POKE 53269,1:REM ENABLE SPRITE 0
1260 RETURN
1300 REM MOVE CURSOR REPLACE CHARACTER
1310 LO=SC+(40*PEEK(214))+PEEK(211):REM GET POSITION
1320 CH=32:POKE204,1:REM TURN OFF CURSOR
1330 IF(PEEK(LO)AND127)<>32THENCH=204
1340 POKELO,CH:RETURN
1400 REM EXPAND X
1410 POKE2041,13: REM SPRITE DATA 832-894
1420 POKE53277,2:REM EXPAND X ON SPRITE 1
1430 POKE53271,0:REM NO Y EXPANSION
```

```
1440 POKE53250,20:POKE53264,PEEK(53264)OR2:REM X COORDINATE OF SPRITE 1
1450 POKE53251,197:REM Y COORDINATE OF SPRITE 1
1460 POKE53288,CS:REM COLOR OF SPRITE 1
1470 POKE53269,3:REM ENABLE SPRITE 0 AND SPRITE 1 (2+1=3)
1480 RETURN
1500 REM EXPAND Y
1510 POKE2041,13: REM SPRITE DATA 832-894
1520 POKE53277,0:REM NO X EXPANSION
1530 POKE53271,2:REM EXPAND Y ON SPRITE 1
1540 POKE53250,20:POKE53264,PEEK(53264)OR2:REM X COORDINATE OF SPRITE 1
1550 POKE53251,197:REM Y COORDINATE OF SPRITE 1
1560 POKE53288,CS:REM COLOR OF SPRITE 1
1570 POKE53269,3:REM ENABLE SPRITE 0 AND SPRITE 1 (2+1=3)
1580 RETURN
1600 REM EXPAND X AND Y
1610 POKE2041,13: REM SPRITE DATA 832-894
1620 POKE53277,2:REM EXPAND X ON SPRITE 1
1630 POKE53271,2:REM EXPAND Y ON SPRITE 1
1640 POKE53250,20:POKE53264,PEEK(53264)OR2:REM X COORDINATE OF SPRITE 1
1650 POKE53251,197:REM Y COORDINATE OF SPRITE 1
1660 POKE53288,CS:REM COLOR OF SPRITE 1
1670 POKE53269,3:REM ENABLE SPRITE 0 AND SPRITE 1 (2+1=3)
1680 RETURN
1700 REM COLOR BACKGROUND FOR SPRITE AREAS
1710 IFBG>15THENBG=0
1720 FORI=0TO2:FORJ=0TO3:POKECR+151+(40*I)+J,BG:NEXTJ,I
1730 FORI=0TO5:FORJ=0TO6:POKECR+751+(40*I)+J,BG:NEXTJ,I:RETURN
1800 REM COLOR SPRITES
1810 IFCS>15THENCS=0
1820 POKE53287,CS:POKE53288,CS:RETURN
2000 REM LIST ROUTINE
2010 POKE204,1:POKE53269,0:REM DISABLE SPRITE
2020 INPUT"[CLR][CRSR DOWN][BLU]WHICH SPRITE";S:IFS>7ORS<0THEN2020
2030 INPUT"WHICH DATA BLOCK";B
2040 INPUT"TO [RVS ON]P[RVS OFF]RINTER OR [RVS ON]S[RVS OFF]CREEN";
     B$:PRINT"[CLR]"
2050 OD=3:IF B$="P"THENOD=4
2060 OPEN1,OD:IFOD=4THENGOSUB2500
2070 VC=53248:BP=2040
```

```
2080 PRINT#1," 1000 POKE53269 , PEEK(53269) OR";2[UP ARROW]S;
2085 PRINT#1,":REM ENABLE SPRITE";S;CHR$(13);
2090 PRINT#1," 1010 POKE";BP+S;",";B;
2095 PRINT#1,":REM SPRITE";S;"DATA AT";B*64;"TO";B*64+62;CHR$(13);
2100 PRINT#1," 1020 FOR I= 0TO62: READ DT: POKE";B*64;"+I,Q: NEXT I";
     CHR$(13);
2105 PRINT#1," 1030 IF ABS(X/256)THEN POKE 53264, PEEK(53264) OR";
2107 PRINT#1,2[UP ARROW]S;":X=X-256";CHR$(13);
2110 PRINT#1," 1040 POKE";VC+2*S;", X :REM X COORDINATE OF SPRITE";S;
     CHR$(13);
2120 PRINT#1," 1050 POKE";VC+1+2*S;
2125 PRINT#1,", Y :REM Y COORDINATE OF SPRITE";S;CHR$(13);
2130 PRINT#1," 1060 POKE";53287+S;",";CS;":REM COLOR OF SPRITE";S;CHR$(13);
2140 PRINT#1," 1070 POKE 53277 , PEEK(53277) OR";2[UP ARROW]S;
2145 PRINT#1,":REM EXPAND X OF SPRITE";S;CHR$(13);
2150 PRINT#1," 1080 POKE 53271 , PEEK(53271) OR";2[UP ARROW]S;
2155 PRINT#1,":REM EXPAND Y OF SPRITE";S;CHR$(13);
2160 IFOD=3THENPRINT#1,CHR$(13);"[RVS ON]PRESS ANY KEY TO CONTINUE[RVS OFF]":
     GOSUB2300
2170 FORI=0TO6
2180 PRINT#1,1090+I*10;"DATA";
2190 FORJ=0TO7:PRINT#1,PEEK(SP+I*9+J);",";:NEXTJ
2200 PRINT#1,PEEK(SP+I*9+8);CHR$(13);:NEXTI
2210 PRINT#1:CLOSE1:PRINT:PRINT"[RVS ON]PRESS ANY KEY TO RETURN TO EDITOR
     [RVS OFF]"
2300 GETC$:IFC$=""THEN2300
2310 RETURN
2500 REM SUBROUTINE - PRINT SPRITE IMAGE
2505 OPEN4,4,4
2510 PRINT#4,"SPRITE IMAGE";CHR$(13);CHR$(13);
2520 PRINT#4,"..........................";CHR$(13);
2530 FOR I = 0TO20:LN$=""
2540 FOR J=0TO2:FORK=7TO0STEP-1
2550 CA$=" ":IF(PEEK(SP+(3*I)+J)AND(2[UP ARROW]K))THENCA$="*"
2560 LN$=LN$+CA$:NEXTK,J
2570 PRINT#4,".";LN$;".";CHR$(13);:NEXT I
2580 PRINT#4,"..........................";CHR$(13);
2585 PRINT#4,CHR$(13);CHR$(13);
2590 RETURN
3000 REM MOVE UP
```

```
3010 IF PEEK(214)<4THEN RETURN
3012 IFPL=2THENGOSUB3500
3014 IFPL=1THENGOSUB3600
3020 GOSUB 1300:CM=PEEK(211):RO=PEEK(209)-40
3025 IF RO<0THEN RO=256+RO:POKE210,PEEK(210)-1
3030 POKE209,RO:POKE211,CM:POKE204,0:REM MOVE CURSOR AND TURN ON FLASH
3040 POKE214,PEEK(214)-1:POKE201,PEEK(201)-1:RETURN
3100 REM MOVE DOWN
3110 IF PEEK(214)>22THEN RETURN
3112 IFPL=2THENGOSUB3500
3114 IFPL=1THENGOSUB3600
3120 GOSUB 1300:CM=PEEK(211):RO=PEEK(209)+40
3125 IF RO>255THEN RO=RO-256:POKE210,PEEK(210)+1
3130 POKE209,RO:POKE211,CM:POKE204,0:REM MOVE CURSOR AND TURN ON FLASH
3140 POKE214,PEEK(214)+1:POKE201,PEEK(201)+1:RETURN
3200 REM MOVE LEFT
3210 IF PEEK(211)<3THEN RETURN
3212 IFPL=2THENGOSUB3500
3214 IFPL=1THENGOSUB3600
3220 GOSUB 1300
3230 POKE211,PEEK(211)-1:POKE204,0:REM MOVE CURSOR AND TURN ON FLASH
3240 RETURN
3300 REM MOVE RIGHT
3310 IF PEEK(211)>24THEN RETURN
3312 IFPL=2THENGOSUB3500
3314 IFPL=1THENGOSUB3600
3320 GOSUB 1300
3330 POKE211,PEEK(211)+1:POKE204,0:REM MOVE CURSOR AND TURN ON FLASH
3340 RETURN
3400 REM RETURN
3410 GOSUB1300
3420 POKE211,2:POKE204,0
3430 RETURN
3500 REM CLEAR BIT
3510 LO=SC+(40*PEEK(214))+PEEK(211)
3520 POKELO,32
3530 J=INT((PEEK(211)-2)/8):K=9-PEEK(211)+(J*8)
```

```
3540 I=PEEK(214)-3
3550 POKE(SP+(3*I)+J),PEEK(SP+(3*I)+J)AND(255-(2[UP ARROW]K))
3570 RETURN
3600 REM SET BIT
3610 LO=SC+(40*PEEK(214))+PEEK(211)
3620 POKELO,204
3630 J=INT((PEEK(211)-2)/8):K=9-PEEK(211)+(J*8)
3640 I=PEEK(214)-3
3650 POKE(SP+(3*I)+J),PEEK(SP+(3*I)+J)OR(2[UP ARROW]K)
3670 RETURN
```

## Characters

The Commodore 64 has two built-in sets of characters, each containing 256 characters. It is possible to alternate between the character sets by pressing the shift key and the Commodore key simultaneously. When the Commodore 64 is turned on, the upper case/graphics character set is used. The alternate character set has lower and upper case letters. The character set which is displayed is determined by the contents of bits 1–3 of register 53272. Try this experiment. Turn on the computer and enter

```
PRINT PEEK(53272)
```

The value returned will be 21. Now press the shift and Commodore keys to change to the other character set. PEEK location 53272 again. The value returned will be 23.

To see what characters are included in each set, enter the following program.

```
10 POKE 53281,0: REM WHITE SCREEN
20 SC=1024: CR=55286: REM SCREEN AND COLOR RAM
   LOCATIONS
30 PRINT"[CLR][BLK]": REM CLEAR SCREEN
40 FOR I = 0 TO 255
50 POKE SC + 80 + 2*I,I: POKE CR + 80 + 2*I, 0: NEXT I
60 POKE 53272, 21: REM TURN ON GRAPHICS CHARACTER SET
70 PRINT"[HOME]GRAPHICS CHARACTER SET"
80 GET A$: IF A$ = "" THEN 80
90 POKE 53272, 23: REM TURN ON U/L CASE CHARACTER SET
100 PRINT"[HOME]U/L CASE CHARACTER SET"
110 GET A$: IF A$ = "" THEN 110
120 GOTO 60
```

All 256 characters are displayed on the screen. Pressing any key toggles between the two sets.

Besides using either of these character sets, you can define a completely new character set. Thus, a personalized set of characters can be created for foreign languages, animation, drafting, etc. The character descriptions of the customized characters are stored in RAM. The amount of RAM required for 256 characters is 2048 locations. The contents of bits 1-3 of register 53272 point to the start of a 2K RAM block containing the character set. Bits 4-7 of 53272 point to the start of screen RAM, therefore it is important to change bits 1-3 without altering the higher bits. This is accomplished with the statement

```
POKE 53272, (PEEK(53272) AND 240) OR CS
```

The values for CS are given in Table 6. Values that result in conflicts with BASIC or the operating system are not in the table.

***TABLE 6: Character Set Pointer***

| *Start of character set* | | *CS* |
|---|---|---|
| 4096 | (Graphics characters) | 4 |
| 6144 | (Upper/lower case) | 6 |
| 8192 | | 8 |
| 10240 | | 10 |
| 12288 | | 12 |
| 14336 | | 14 |

Notice that the descriptions of the built-in character sets are at locations 4096 and 6144. Because of the manner in which the Commodore 64 accesses the character descriptions, these locations cannot be used for user defined character storage. These RAM locations do not actually have the character descriptions. Just before the computer is ready to display a character on the screen, the computer switches on a ROM which the video chip thinks is addressed at 4096. The ROM which contains the character descriptions is actually located from 53248 to 57343.

To learn how to define a character set, it is useful to first examine how a character is created. Each character in the Commodore 64 is a dot pattern built on an 8 x 8 matrix. For example, character 0, the @, is a pattern of pixels as shown in Figure 4.

```
60  • • * * * * • •
102 • * * • • * * •
110 • * * • * * * •
110 • * * • * * * •
96  • * * • • • • •
98  • * * • • • * •
60  • • * * * * • •
0   • • • • • • • •
```

**Figure 4. Pixel pattern of CHR$(0) ("@").**

The * represents an on pixel and the • represents an off pixel. The computer stores this picture in eight consecutive memory locations. Each number is a description of the dot pattern for a row, and the numbers are ordered from the top row down. The numbers used to describe a row are derived from the 8 bit binary representation of that number. The eight numbers to describe @ are 60, 102, 110, 110, 96, 98, 60, and 0. These numbers are stored in eight sequential memory locations. The description of character 1, the letter A, is stored in the next eight memory locations. When the computer is commanded to display character zero, the video display chip takes the eight numbers from the memory locations assigned to character zero and reconstructs the @ on the screen. When commanded to display the letter A, the second group of eight numbers is used.

The first step in defining a new character is to construct a dot picture of it on an 8 x 8 matrix. Get out some graph paper and outline an area eight squares by eight squares. Create a character by filling in the squares. Each of the rows is translated into a binary number by substituting ones for filled squares and zeroes for empty squares. The decimal number equivalents are found in Table 1.

Once you are satisfied with the set of characters you have designed, you are ready to begin programming. First, you must reserve the memory space for the character set to protect it from being clobbered by the BASIC system. This is accomplished by moving the end of memory and the beginning of string pointers. Enter the statement

```
10 POKE52,56:POKE56,56:CLR
```

The above statement will not allow BASIC to use the locations above 14336. The character set, located in RAM locations 14336 to 16383, will not be disturbed.

It is a good idea to move the characters from the character generator ROM into the reserved space. This ensures that there will be a character description for every character number. It is easiest to move down 256 contiguous characters. To allow the computer to access the memory locations in the character ROM for anything other than displaying characters, it is necessary to turn off the keyboard and switch on the character ROM. The following code moves the entire graphics character set into a new location.

```
10 POKE52,56:POKE56,56:CLR
20 POKE 56334, PEEK(56334) AND 254
30 POKE 1, PEEK(1) AND 251
40 FORI=0 TO 2047
50 POKE I + 14336, PEEK(53248 + I)
60 NEXTI
70 POKE 1, PEEK(1) OR 4
80 POKE 56334, PEEK(56334) OR 1
```

Statements 20 and 30 allow access to the character ROM locations. Statements 70 and 80 restore the computer to its original state. The value of the PEEK determines which characters are transferred. Table 7 shows which groups of character descriptions start at different locations.

It is possible to selectively move in groups of characters or individual characters. For example, the following code would build a character set such that screen characters 0 to 127 are the upper/lower case characters, screen characters 128 to 191 are the graphics characters, and screen characters 192 to 255 are the reverse field graphics characters.

```
10 POKE 52, 56: POKE 56, 56: CLR
20 POKE 56334, PEEK(56334) AND 254
30 POKE 1, PEEK(1) AND 251
40 FORI=0 TO 1023: POKE I + 14336, PEEK(55296 + I):
   NEXT I
50 FORI=0 TO 511: POKE I + 15360, PEEK(53760 + I):
   NEXT I
60 FORI=0 TO 511: POKE I + 15872, PEEK(54784 + I):
   NEXT I
70 POKE 1, PEEK(1) OR 4
80 POKE 56334, PEEK(56334) OR 1
```

***TABLE 7: Character ROM Locations***

| *PEEK* | *Character Set Transferred* | *Screen Display Code* |
|---|---|---|
| 53248 + I | Upper case letters | 0– 63 |
| 53760 + I | Graphic characters | 64–127 |
| 54272 + I | Reverse field upper case | 128–191 |
| 54784 + I | Reverse field graphics | 192–255 |
| 55296 + I | Lower case letters | 0– 63 |
| 55808 + I | Upper case letters | 64–127 |
| 56320 + I | Reverse field lower case | 128–191 |
| 56832 + I | Reverse field upper case | 192–255 |

A convenient method for placing the description of custom characters into the reserved RAM is to use a FOR/NEXT loop to READ DATA and to POKE the values into the appropriate memory locations. The following BASIC code accomplishes this.

```
90 READ CN:IF CN<0 THEN 1000
100 FOR I=0TO7: READ CD
110 POKE 14336 + 8*CN + I, CD: NEXT I
120 GOTO 90
130 DATA 0, 40, 16, 146, 214, 254, 238, 198, 0
140 DATA etc.
•
•
999 DATA -1
1000 POKE 53272, (PEEK(53272) AND 240) OR 14:REM START
     OF PROGRAM
```

Statement 90 READs the first number of the DATA statements. This is the character number of the character to be defined. It also serves as a flag to signal when there is no more DATA to be read. The last DATA statement contains a character number which is negative and the program branches to a part of the program which utilizes the new characters. Statement 100 READs the next eight values in a DATA statement. In statement 110 the character number, CN, and the row index, I, are used to calculate the memory location where the row descriptor will be placed. Statement 120 sends the program back to statement 90 where a new character number is read. Statement 1000 is the start of the program which uses the new character set. The character set pointer in location 53272 is reset at the start of the program.

There is an alternate method for defining characters that may be easier to use because the input is closely related to the visual image. It is slower and consumes more memory than the first method. It is most useful when only a few characters are going to be redefined.

```
90 READ CN: IF CN<0 THEN 1000
100 FOR I= 0 TO 7: READ CD$
110 BY = 14336 + 8*CN + I: POKE BY,0
120 FOR J= 0 TO 7
130 IF MID$(CD$, J+1, 1)= "" GOTO 150
140 POKE BY, PEEK(BY) OR 2 (7-J)
150 NEXT J: NEXT I
160 GOTO 90
170 DATA 0
171 DATA "  * *   "
172 DATA "   *    "
173 DATA "*  *  * "
174 DATA "** * ** "
175 DATA "******* "
176 DATA "*** *** "
177 DATA "**   ** "
178 DATA "        "
•
•
•
•
999 DATA -1
1000 POKE 53272, (PEEK(53272) AND 240) OR 14
```

There are some limitations inherent in the previous methods of incorporating new characters. The most serious limitation is the amount of memory consumed with the character defining program and the associated DATA statements. If only a few characters are redefined and the rest of the program is fairly short, the amount of memory left may not be a constraint. However, if a lot of characters are redefined or if the program using the character set is sizeable, another method for READing in the character set will have to be used. Even with a better method, any program with redefined characters gobbles up 2048 bytes of the RAM area to store the characters.

The most straightforward solution to a memory squeeze is to divide the program into two parts. The first program allocates space and sets up a new character set. The second program, which uses the redefined character set, is then loaded in to the computer.

The following program loads in a character set which replaces the letters A to Z of the graphics character set with the corresponding Gothic style letters. Notice that besides replacing characters 1 through 26, the characters 129 through 154 are replaced. These are the reverse field characters for A to Z.

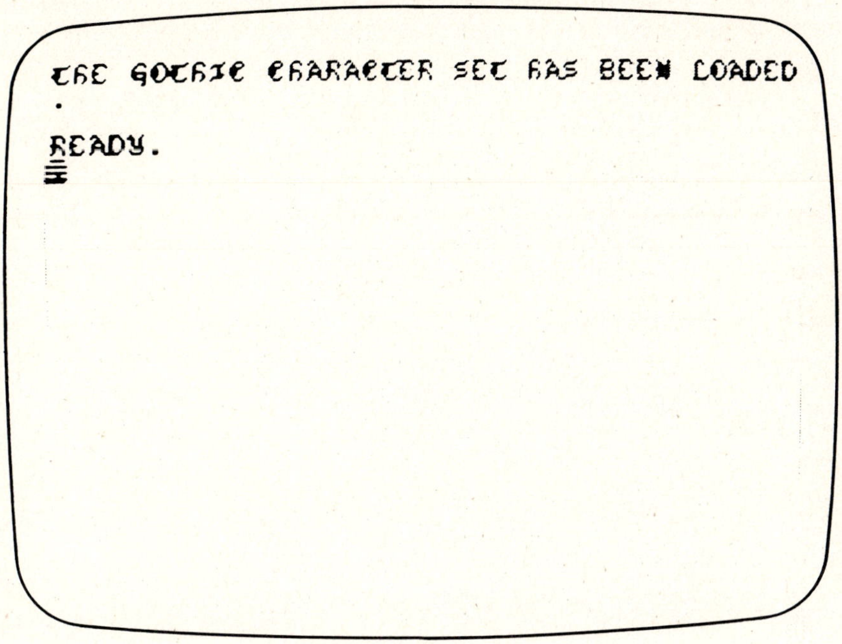


"GOTHIC CHAR"

```
10 POKE52, 56: POKE56, 56:CLR: REM MOVE TOP OF BASIC

20 POKE 56334, PEEK(56334) AND 254

30 POKE 1, PEEK(1) AND 251

40 FOR I = 0 TO 511

50 POKE I + 14336, PEEK(53248 +I)

60 NEXT I: REM TRANSFER CHARACTER SET

70 POKE 1, PEEK(1) OR 4

80 POKE 56334, PEEK(56334) OR 1

90 READ CN: IF CN<0 THEN 1000

100 FOR I= 0 TO 7: READ CD

110 POKE 14336 + 8 * CN + I, CD

120 POKE 14336 + 8 * (128 + CN) + I, 255-CD: NEXT I

130 GOTO 90: REM DEFINE NEW CHARACTERS
```

```
140 POKE 56334, PEEK(56334) OR 1
150 READ CN: IF CN<0 THEN 1000
160 FOR I= 0 TO 7: READ CD
170 POKE 14336 + 8 * CN + I, CD: POKE 14336 +8*NEXT I
180 GOTO 150: REM DEFINE NEW CHARACTERS
200 DATA 1, 48, 72, 20, 34, 62, 34, 65, 0
202 DATA 2, 92, 34, 66, 124, 66, 34, 92, 0
204 DATA 3, 28, 34, 84, 80, 80, 34, 28, 0
206 DATA 4, 88, 100, 66, 66, 66, 100, 88, 0
208 DATA 5, 92, 34, 64, 112, 64, 34, 92, 0
210 DATA 6, 92, 34, 32, 120, 32, 32, 64, 0
212 DATA 7, 28, 34, 64, 94, 98, 62, 2, 6
214 DATA 8, 28, 34, 32, 60, 34, 34, 36, 0
216 DATA 9, 2, 60, 72, 8, 10, 60, 64, 0
218 DATA 10, 1, 2, 2, 2, 34, 68, 56, 0
220 DATA 11, 66, 36, 40, 112, 40, 36, 66, 0
222 DATA 12, 24, 36, 32, 32, 32, 33, 94, 0
224 DATA 13, 84, 42, 42, 106, 42, 42, 64, 0
226 DATA 14, 66, 50, 42, 106, 42, 42, 68, 0
228 DATA 15, 28, 34, 81, 81, 81, 34, 28, 0
230 DATA 16, 92, 34, 34, 124, 32, 32, 64, 0
232 DATA 17, 56, 84, 34, 2, 12, 26, 124, 0
234 DATA 18, 92, 34, 34, 120, 36, 34, 66, 0
236 DATA 19, 2, 60, 64, 60, 2, 60, 64, 0
238 DATA 20, 1, 126, 48, 80, 80, 33, 30, 0
240 DATA 21, 33, 82, 18, 18, 18, 18, 12, 0
242 DATA 22, 76, 178, 34, 34, 34, 20, 8, 0
244 DATA 23, 128, 92, 82, 82, 82, 84, 40, 0
246 DATA 24, 34, 84, 12, 8, 24, 37, 66, 0
248 DATA 25, 66, 164, 36, 36, 26, 66, 60, 0
250 DATA 26, 126, 2, 4, 8, 16, 32, 64, 126
990 DATA -1
```

```
1000 POKE 53272, (PEEK(53272)AND 240) OR 14
1010 POKE 53281,1: PRINT"[CLR]"
1020 PRINT"[BLK]THE GOTHIC CHARACTER SET HAS BEEN LOADED."
1030 NEW
```

By periodically changing the characters displayed on the screen, an illusion of motion can be created. The following short programs will demonstrate this. In the first example, the normal character set is used. Enter and run the following program.

```
1010 S$="[white]..........A.....................
     ........"
1020 PRINT"[clear]";S$;"[home]";
1030 FOR I = 0 TO 38
1040 PRINT "O[cursor left]";
1050 FOR T = 0 TO 100: NEXT T
1060 PRINT " C[cursor left]";
1070 FOR T = 0 TO 100: NEXT T
1080 NEXT I
```

This program can be enhanced with custom characters. Add the following statements to the beginning of the program.

```
10 POKE52,56:POKE56,56:CLR
20 POKE 56334, PEEK(56334) AND 254
```

```
30 POKE 1, PEEK(1) AND 251
40 FORI=0 to 2047
50 POKE I + 14336, PEEK(53248 + I)
60 NEXTI
70 POKE 1, PEEK(1) OR 4
80 POKE 56334, PEEK(56334) OR 1
90 READ CN: IF CN<0 THEN 1000
100 FOR I= 0 TO 7: READ CD$
110 BY = 14336 + 8*CN + I: POKE BY,0
120 FOR J= 0 TO 7
130 IF MID$(CD$, J+1, 1)= "" GOTO 150
140 POKE BY, PEEK(BY) OR 2↑(7-J)
150 NEXT J: NEXT I
160 GOTO 90
170 DATA 1: REM REDEFINE A
171 DATA "  *****   "
172 DATA "*******  "
173 DATA "*   *   *  "
174 DATA "*   *   *  "
175 DATA "*******  "
176 DATA "*******  "
177 DATA "* * * *  "
178 DATA "         "
180 DATA 3: REM REDEFINE C
181 DATA "   ***    "
182 DATA "  *****   "
183 DATA "****      "
184 DATA "**        "
185 DATA "****      "
186 DATA "  *****   "
187 DATA "   ***    "
188 DATA "          "
190 DATA 15: REM REDEFINE O
191 DATA "   ***    "
192 DATA "  *****   "
193 DATA "*******  "
194 DATA "*******  "
195 DATA "*******  "
196 DATA "  *****   "
197 DATA "   ***    "
198 DATA "          "
200 DATA 46: REM REDEFINE PERIOD
201 DATA "          "
202 DATA "          "
203 DATA "          "
204 DATA "    **    "
205 DATA "    **    "
```

```
206 DATA "              "
207 DATA "              "
208 DATA "              "
1000 POKE 53272,30
1010 S$="[white]..........A......................
     ........."
1020 PRINT"[clear]";S$;"[home]";
1030 FOR I = 0 TO 38
1040 PRINT "O[cursor left]";
1050 FOR T = 0 to 100: NEXT T
1060 PRINT " C[cursor left]";
1070 FOR T = 0 TO 100: NEXT T
1080 NEXT I
```

Now RUN the program. Notice the difference the new characters make in the program's visual appeal. To get back to the normal character set, enter

```
POKE 53272, 21
```

## Bit Map Graphics

The Commodore 64 is capable of displaying 64,000 dots on the screen. It is a simple matter to confirm this by a calculation. As was mentioned in the section on programmable characters, each character on the screen is made up of dots in an 8 by 8 matrix. Since a row is 40 characters long and there are 25 rows, the computer is displaying 320 dots in the horizontal direction and 200 dots in the vertical direction. The state (off or on) of each dot on the screen corresponds to the status of a bit (0 or 1) in the computer's memory. In the bit map mode, each dot on the screen can be individually turned on and off. The display on the screen is an image of a section of the computer's RAM. Since there are 64,000 dots on the screen and there are 8 bits in a byte, the bit map requires a block of 8,000 memory locations.

The memory locations are mapped on the screen in a manner similar to the way the bytes which make up a character are mapped on the screen, in sets of eight bytes arranged vertically. Figure 5 explains the arrangement much better than is possible with words.

| *Character Column* | *0* | *1* | *2* | ...... | *38* | *39* | *Vertical Position* |
|---|---|---|---|---|---|---|---|
| Row | 0 | 8 | 16 | ...... | 304 | 312 | 0 |
| | 1 | 9 | 17 | ...... | 305 | 313 | 1 |
| | 2 | 10 | 18 | ...... | 306 | 314 | 2 |
| 0 | 3 | 11 | 19 | ...... | 307 | 315 | 3 |
| | 4 | 12 | 20 | ...... | 308 | 316 | 4 |
| | 5 | 13 | 21 | ...... | 309 | 317 | 5 |
| | 6 | 14 | 22 | ...... | 310 | 318 | 6 |
| | 7 | 15 | 23 | ...... | 311 | 319 | 7 |
| | 320 | 328 | 336 | ...... | 624 | 632 | 8 |
| | 321 | 329 | 337 | ...... | 625 | 633 | 9 |
| | 322 | 330 | 338 | ...... | 626 | 634 | 10 |
| 1 | 323 | 331 | 339 | ...... | 627 | 635 | 11 |
| | 324 | 332 | 340 | ...... | 628 | 636 | 12 |
| | 325 | 333 | 341 | ...... | 629 | 637 | 13 |
| | 326 | 334 | 342 | ...... | 630 | 638 | 14 |
| | 327 | 335 | 343 | ...... | 631 | 639 | 15 |
| Character rows 2–23 | | | | | | | |
| | 7680 | 7688 | 7696 | ...... | 7984 | 7992 | 192 |
| | 7681 | 7689 | 7697 | ...... | 7985 | 7993 | 193 |
| | 7682 | 7690 | 7698 | ...... | 7986 | 7994 | 194 |
| 24 | 7683 | 7691 | 7699 | ...... | 7987 | 7995 | 195 |
| | 7684 | 7692 | 7700 | ...... | 7988 | 7996 | 196 |
| | 7685 | 7693 | 7701 | ...... | 7989 | 7997 | 197 |
| | 7686 | 7694 | 7702 | ...... | 7990 | 7998 | 198 |
| | 7687 | 7695 | 7703 | ...... | 7991 | 7999 | 199 |
| Horizon. | 0–7 | 7–15 | 16–23 | | 304–311 | 312–319 | |

**Figure 5: Arrangement of Bit Map.**

If the horizontal and vertical positions of a pixel on the bit map are designated as PX and PY, respectively, an equation to calculate the specific memory location, ML, which contains the corresponding bit, can be derived. The character row, RW, and character column, CL, of the memory location are obtained by dividing the horizontal and vertical coordinates. The quotients are the character row and character column.

```
CL = INT(PX/8)
RW = INT(PY/8)
```

The first memory location in the character block of a specific row and column, FML, is defined by the following relationship.

```
FML = 8*CL + 320*RW
FML = 8*(CL + 40*RW)
```

An offset into the character block has to be added to the first memory location of the character block to obtain the location which contains the designated pixel. The offset, OY, is the remainder when 8 is divided into PY. The following relationship determines OY.

```
OY = PY - 8*INT(PY/8)
OY = PY - 8*RW
```

The memory location which contains the pixel at (PX, PY) is equal to the first memory location of the character block plus the offset. Substituting for OY and collecting similar terms, we get

```
ML = 8*(CL + 40*RW) + OY
ML = 8*(CL + 40*RW) + PY -8*RW
ML = 8*(CL + 39*RW) + PY
```

Substituting for CL and RW, the relationship becomes

```
ML = 8*INT(PX/8) + 39*(INT(PY/8)) + PY
```

This assumes a bit map starting at address 0. The location of the bit map can vary depending on how it is set up. The address of the byte in the bit map is determined by adding an offset equal to the starting address of the bit map.

```
ML = SA + 8*INT(PX/8) + 39*(INT(PY/8)) + PY
```

The location of the bit in the byte which controls the pixel is the remainder when PX is divided by 8. The remainder is the offset to the right.

```
offset to right= PX - 8*INT(PX/8)
```

For example, if PX = 19, the remainder after dividing by eight is three. The bit to be set is three bits to the right of the leftmost bit. The bit arrangement on the screen has the highest bit of a memory location, bit 7, in the leftmost position. In the example, the third bit to the right is bit 4. The number of the bit to be set or cleared for a specific PX is described by the relationship

```
BT = 7 - (PX - 8*INT(PX/8))
```

A pixel is turned on by ORing the existing contents of a location with 2 to the bit power. A pixel is turned off by ANDing the existing contents of a location with the complement of 2 to the bit power. The procedure for plotting or erasing a point on the bit map can be summarized as follows:

1. Find the memory location and bit referred to by the pixel coordinates, PX and PY.

```
ML = SA + 8*(INT(PX/8) + 39*INT(PY/8)) + PY
BT = 7 - (PX - 8*INT(PX/8))
```

2. Plot a point,

```
POKE ML, PEEK(ML) OR (2↑BT)
```

or erase a point,

```
POKE ML, PEEK(ML) AND NOT (2↑BT)
```

The colors of the foreground (pixel on) and background (pixel off) displayed on the bit map are determined by a color map. This color map is not to be confused with the color RAM used in the character mode. The map is a 1K area of RAM. The contents of each byte in the color map define the foreground and background colors of an 8 by 8 region on the screen. The position of each region corresponds to the position a character would occupy on a text screen. The color byte is divided into two parts. Bits 0–3 define the screen color and bits 4–7 define the foreground color. All 16 colors available to the Commodore 64 can be used in any combination. The only limitation is that no more than two colors can be within any 8 by 8 color region. Table 8 lists the values for all the color combinations.

The bit map mode is selected by the condition of bit 5 of location 53265. The command to turn on the bit map is

```
POKE 53265, PEEK(53265) OR 32
```

The bit map is turned off with

```
POKE 53265, PEEK(53265) AND NOT 32
```

The following program demonstrates the bit map graphics mode. First, the area to be used for the bit map must be protected from BASIC. This is accomplished by changing the end of BASIC and the start of string pointers.

```
10 POKE 52, 32: POKE56, 32: CLR
```

The bit map and color map locations are selected. The bit map is located from 8192 to 16383 and the color map is located from 1024 to 2023. The bit map is then turned on.

```
20 SA = 8192: SC = 1024
30 POKE 53272, 24: REM BIT MAP AND COLOR MAP LOCATIONS
40 POKE 53265, PEEK(53265) OR 32: REM TURN ON BIT MAP
```

Next, the color map is filled with ones. This gives a white screen and black dots. The bit map is cleared by filling the bit map locations with zeroes. These sections of the program are written as subroutines.

```
50 GOSUB 230: REM COLOR SCREEN
60 GOSUB 250: REM CLEAR SCREEN
```

**TABLE 8: Color Bytes for BITMAP Mode**
**Foreground colors are the columns. Background colors are the rows.**

| | *Blk* | *Wht* | *Red* | *Cyan* | *Prpl* | *Grn* | *Blue* | *Yel* | *Orng* | *Brwn* | *Lt Red* | *Dark Gray* | *Med Gray* | *Lt Grn* | *Lt Blue* | *Lt Gray* |
|---|---|---|---|---|---|---|---|---|---|---|---|---|---|---|---|---|
| Black | 0 | 1 | 2 | 3 | 4 | 5 | 6 | 7 | 8 | 9 | 10 | 11 | 12 | 13 | 14 | 15 |
| White | 16 | 17 | 18 | 19 | 20 | 21 | 22 | 23 | 24 | 25 | 26 | 27 | 28 | 29 | 30 | 31 |
| Red | 32 | 33 | 34 | 35 | 36 | 37 | 38 | 39 | 40 | 41 | 42 | 43 | 44 | 45 | 46 | 47 |
| Cyan | 48 | 49 | 50 | 51 | 52 | 53 | 54 | 55 | 56 | 57 | 58 | 59 | 60 | 61 | 62 | 63 |
| Purple | 64 | 65 | 66 | 67 | 68 | 69 | 70 | 71 | 72 | 73 | 74 | 75 | 76 | 77 | 78 | 79 |
| Green | 80 | 81 | 82 | 83 | 84 | 85 | 86 | 87 | 88 | 89 | 90 | 91 | 92 | 93 | 94 | 95 |
| Blue | 96 | 97 | 98 | 99 | 100 | 101 | 102 | 103 | 104 | 105 | 106 | 107 | 108 | 109 | 110 | 111 |
| Yellow | 112 | 113 | 114 | 115 | 116 | 117 | 118 | 119 | 120 | 121 | 122 | 123 | 124 | 125 | 126 | 127 |
| Orange | 128 | 129 | 130 | 131 | 132 | 133 | 134 | 135 | 136 | 137 | 138 | 139 | 140 | 141 | 142 | 143 |
| Brown | 144 | 145 | 146 | 147 | 148 | 149 | 150 | 151 | 152 | 153 | 154 | 155 | 156 | 157 | 158 | 159 |
| Light Red | 160 | 161 | 162 | 163 | 164 | 165 | 166 | 167 | 168 | 169 | 170 | 171 | 172 | 173 | 174 | 175 |
| Dark Gray | 176 | 177 | 178 | 179 | 180 | 181 | 182 | 183 | 184 | 185 | 186 | 137 | 188 | 189 | 190 | 191 |
| Medium Gray | 192 | 193 | 194 | 195 | 196 | 197 | 198 | 199 | 200 | 201 | 202 | 203 | 204 | 205 | 206 | 207 |
| Light Green | 208 | 209 | 210 | 211 | 212 | 213 | 214 | 215 | 216 | 217 | 218 | 219 | 220 | 221 | 222 | 223 |
| Light Blue | 224 | 225 | 226 | 227 | 228 | 229 | 230 | 231 | 232 | 233 | 234 | 235 | 236 | 237 | 238 | 239 |
| Light Gray | 240 | 241 | 242 | 243 | 244 | 245 | 246 | 247 | 248 | 249 | 250 | 251 | 252 | 253 | 254 | 255 |

```
230 FOR I = SC TO SC+999: POKE I, 1: NEXT I
240 RETURN
250 FOR I = SA TO SA+7999: POKE I, 0:NEXT I
260 RETURN
```

The first point is plotted in the middle of the bit map. The point plotting is written as a subroutine.

```
70 PX = 159: PY = 99: GOSUB 270 :REM PLOT POINT

270 ML = SA + 8*(INT(PX/8) + 39*INT(PY/8)) + PY
280 BT = 7 - (PX - 8*INT(PX/8))
290 POKE ML, PEEK(ML) OR (2↑BT)
300 RETURN
```

After plotting the first point on the bit map, the program reads joystick port two. This is the port towards the back of the computer. If there is any input from the joystick, the program plots a new point and then goes back to read the joystick port.

```
80 GOSUB 110: IF J = 15 THEN 80: REM READ JOYSTICK
90 GOSUB 270: REM PLOT NEW POINT
100 GOTO 80
110 J = PEEK(56320) AND 15
120 IF (J AND 8)=0 THEN PX = PX+1: REM RIGHT
130 IF (J AND 4)=0 THEN PX = PX-1: REM LEFT
140 IF (J AND 2)=0 THEN PY = PY+1: REM DOWN
150 IF (J AND 1)=0 THEN PY = PY-1: REM UP
160 IF PY>199 THEN PY = 199
170 IF PY<0 THEN PY = 0
180 IF PX>319 THEN PX = 319
190 IF PX<0 THEN PX = 0
200 GET A$: IF A$ = "[CLR]" THEN GOSUB 250: GOSUB 270:
    REM CLEAR SCREEN
210 IF A$= "[F7]" THEN 310: REM EXIT ON F7
220 RETURN
```

If the CLR/HOME key is pressed while the shift key is held down, the bit map is cleared. Pressing the F7 key turns off the bit map and ends the program.

```
310 POKE 53272, 21: REM NORMAL SCREEN AND CHARACTERS
320 POKE 53265, PEEK(53265) ANDNOT32: REM TURN OFF
    BIT MAP
330 END
```

This program turns your Commodore 64 into a joystick-controlled sketch pad.

The description of the high-resolution graphics up to this point has been very limited in scope. For one thing, any BASIC program is limited to 6K in size by the memory and graphics configuration. Furthermore, the commands used to enable the bit map and plot points on it are cumbersome. These shortcomings can be remedied using the following program, MINIGRAPH. The program loads a set of machine language routines into memory locations 36883 to 37681. Enabling the bit map and plotting on it are reduced to single commands. The bit map is located outside the BASIC program RAM locations leaving 33K of RAM for writing programs. And as an added bonus, the routines are executed very rapidly since they are written in machine code. When entering the numbers in the DATA statements, it is extremely important to be accurate. An incorrect number can send the computer into never-never land. If that happens, the only way to regain control is to turn the computer off. This results in the loss of the program in the memory at the time.

Enter the program and save it on tape or disk. This is a utility program that will be loaded into the computer and run before any other program that uses the routines is loaded. The routines are called with a SYS command. A SYS command sends the computer to the designated location in the memory and executes the machine code there. After executing the routine, the computer returns control to the BASIC program. The bit map is enabled with the command

```
SYS 50195
```

The bit map is disabled with

```
SYS 50198
```

The bit map is cleared, i.e., all the bits are zero, with

```
SYS 50207
```

The colors displayed on the bit map are set with

```
SYS 50210, F, B
```

F and B are numbers or variables with a value from 0 to 15. The first number, F, sets the foreground color and B sets the background color. A point is plotted on the bit map with the command

```
SYS 50201, X, Y, M
```

X and Y are the horizontal and vertical positions of the point. The horizontal position can be from 0 to 319 and the vertical position can be from 0 to 199. The upper left corner is 0, 0. The last variable, M, sets the plotting mode. If the value of M is one, a point is plotted in the foreground color. If M is two, a point is plotted in the background color. If M is zero, the color of the point is flipped. If the point at that location is in the foreground color, it is changed to the background color, and vice versa. A line is drawn with the command

```
SYS 50204, X, Y, M
```

X and Y are the horizontal and vertical positions of the end point of the line. The starting point of the line is defined by either the point plotting command or by the end point of the last line drawn. The drawing mode is the same as in the point plotting routine. Values outside the allowed ranges for X, Y, M, F, and B will cause an ILLEGAL QUANTITY ERROR.

NOTE: This line drawing command must *always* be either the last instruction in a BASIC program line, or must be alone on its *own* line. If not, you will see an ERROR message. If SYNTAX and ILLEGAL ERRORs begin appearing in any program that uses MINIGRAPH, check for this unique problem.

The program following MINIGRAPH demonstrates how to use the routines to draw several geometric shapes on the bit map screen. To exit the program, hold down any key.

```
MINIGRAPH.DAT                               COMMODORE 64

10 PRINT"[CLR]MINIGRAPH LOADER BY PAUL SCHATZ"
20 PRINT"PLEASE WAIT..."
30 A = 0: FOR I = 50195 TO 50975: READ BY
40 POKE I, BY: A = A + BY: NEXT I
50 IF A<>95619 THEN PRINT"ERROR IN DATA STATEMENTS": STOP
60 PRINT"[CLR]MINIGRAPH INSTRUCTIONS"
70 PRINT"[CRSR DOWN]TURN ON BITMAP        -SYS 50195"
80 PRINT"TURN OFF BITMAP        -SYS 50198"
90 PRINT"CLEAR BITMAP           -SYS 50207"
100 PRINT"COLOR BITMAP          -SYS 50210,F,B"
110 PRINT"PLOT POINT @ X,Y      -SYS 50201,X,Y,M"
```

```
120 PRINT"DRAW LINE TO X,Y        -SYS 50204,X,Y,M"
130 PRINT"[CRSR DOWN]F = FOREGROUND          B = BACKGROUND"
140 PRINT"X = 0 TO 319            Y = 0 TO 199"
150 PRINT"M = 0, 1, OR 2 (FLIP, DRAW, OR ERASE)
160 NEW
200 DATA 76,244,198, 76, 7,199, 76, 37,196, 76,114,197, 76, 30,197, 76, 66
210 DATA197,169, 0,141, 4,196, 32,253,174, 32,235,183,224,200,144, 3, 76
220 DATA 26,199,142, 3,196,166, 20,165, 21,240, 8,201, 1,208,240,224, 64
230 DATA176,236,141, 2,196,142, 1,196, 32,253,174, 32,158,183,224, 3,176
240 DATA220,142, 0,196,173, 0,196,240, 27, 74,144, 12, 32,174,196, 32,135
250 DATA196, 29,158,196,145,251, 96, 32,174,196, 32,135,196, 61,166,196,145
260 DATA251, 96, 32,174,196, 32,135,196, 93,158,196,145,251, 96,173, 1,196
270 DATA 41, 7,170,120,160, 52,132, 1,160, 0,177,251,160, 55,132, 1, 88
280 DATA160, 0, 96,128, 64, 32, 16, 8, 4, 2, 1,127,191,223,239,247,251
290 DATA253,254,169, 0,133,251,169,224,133,252,173, 1,196, 41,248, 24,101
300 DATA251,133,251,173, 2,196,101,252,133,252,173, 3,196, 72, 41, 7, 24
310 DATA101,251,133,251,144, 2,230,252,104, 74, 74, 74, 10,170,189,236,196
320 DATA 24,101,251,133,251,189,237,196,101,252,133,252, 96, 0, 0, 64, 1
330 DATA128, 2,192, 3, 0, 5, 64, 6,128, 7,192, 8, 0, 10, 64, 11,128
340 DATA 12,192, 13, 0, 15, 64, 16,128, 17,192, 18, 0, 20, 64, 21,128, 22
350 DATA192, 23, 0, 25, 64, 26,128, 27,192, 28, 0, 30,162, 32,169,224,133
360 DATA252,169, 0,133,251,168,145,251,200,208,251,230,252,202,208,246, 96
370 DATA 32,253,174, 32,158,183,224, 16,144, 3, 76, 26,199, 96,169,192,133
380 DATA252,169, 0,133,251, 32, 52,197,138, 10, 10, 10, 10,141, 9,196, 32
390 DATA 52,197,138, 13, 9,196,162, 2,160, 0,145,251,200,208,251,230,252
400 DATA202, 16,246,145,251,200,192,232,144,249, 96,169, 0,141, 8,196,141
410 DATA 10,196, 32,253,174, 32,235,183,224,200,144, 3, 76, 26,199,142, 7
420 DATA196,166, 20,165, 21,240, 8,201, 1,208,240,224, 64,176,236,141, 6
430 DATA196,142, 5,196, 32,253,174, 32,158,183,201, 3,176,220,142, 0,196
440 DATA173, 5,196, 56,237, 1,196,141, 12,196,173, 6,196,237, 2,196,141
450 DATA 13,196, 16, 20,206, 10,196, 56,169, 0,237, 12,196,141, 12,196,169
460 DATA 0,237, 13,196,141, 13,196,169, 0,141, 11,196,173, 7,196, 56,237
470 DATA 3,196,141, 14,196,173, 8,196,237, 4,196,141, 15,196, 16, 20,206
```

```
480 DATA 11,196, 56,169, 0,237, 14,196,141, 14,196,169, 0,237, 15,196,141
490 DATA 15,196,169, 0,141, 18,196,173, 14,196, 56,237, 12,196,173, 15,196
500 DATA237, 13,196,144, 27,174, 14,196,173, 12,196,141, 14,196,142, 12,19
510 DATA174, 15,196,173, 13,196,141, 15,196,142, 13,196,206, 18,196,173, 1
520 DATA196,141, 16,196,173, 13,196,141, 17,196, 32, 91,196,173, 18,196,20
530 DATA 18,173, 1,196,205, 5,196,208, 27,173, 2,196,205, 6,196,208, 19
540 DATA240, 16,173, 3,196,205, 7,196,208, 9,173, 4,196,205, 8,196,208
550 DATA 1, 96,173, 18,196,208, 6, 32,192,198, 76,118,198, 32,218,198, 32
560 DATA152,198, 32,152,198, 16, 20,173, 18,196,208, 6, 32,218,198, 76,140
570 DATA198, 32,192,198, 32,172,198, 32,172,198, 32, 91,196, 76, 64,198,17
580 DATA 16,196, 56,237, 14,196,141, 16,196,173, 17,196,237, 15,196,141, 1
590 DATA196, 96,173, 16,196, 24,109, 12,196,141, 16,196,173, 17,196,109, 1
600 DATA196,141, 17,196, 96,173, 10,196,208, 9,238, 1,196,208, 3,238, 2
610 DATA196, 96,173, 1,196,208, 3,206, 2,196,206, 1,196, 96,173, 11,196
620 DATA208, 9,238, 3,196,208, 3,238, 4,196, 96,173, 3,196,208, 3,206
630 DATA 4,196,206, 3,196, 96,173, 0,221, 41,252,141, 0,221,169, 59,141
640 DATA 17,208,169, 8,141, 24,208, 96,173, 0,221, 9, 3,141, 0,221,169
650 DATA 27,141, 17,208,169, 21,141, 24,208, 96, 32, 7,199, 76, 72,178
```

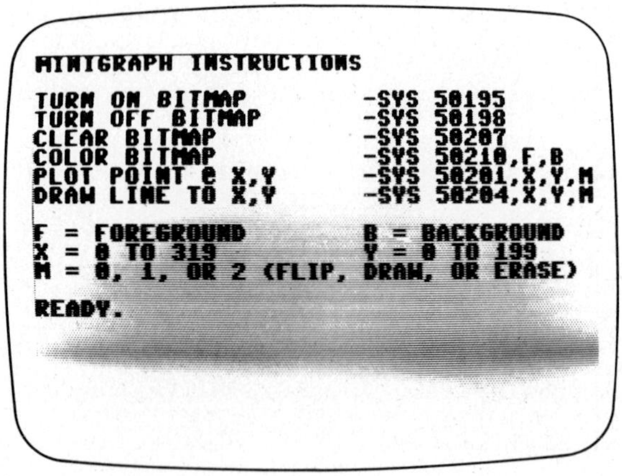


MINIGRAPH.DEMO COMMODORE 64

```
10 PRINT"[CLR]MINIGRAPH DEMO"
20 PRINT"BY PAUL SCHATZ"
30 GOSUB 1000: REM PAUSE
40 SYS50207: REM CLEAR BITMAP
```

```
50 SYS50210,1,2: REM COLOR BITMAP
60 SYS50195: REM TURN ON BITMAP
70 N1=30: N2=33: REM DRAW SQUARES
80 FORI=0 TO 12:X1=N1-2*I:X2=N2+I[UP ARROW]2
90 SYS50201,X1,X1,1: REM PLOT POINT
100 SYS50204,X2,X1,1
110 SYS50204,X2,X2,1
120 SYS50204,X1,X2,1
130 SYS50204,X1,X1,1
140 NEXT I
150 GOSUB 1000
160 SYS 50210, 5, 1
170 SYS 50207
180 FP=1:A1 =77: B1 =23: DL =9: C =0
190 FOR I =0 TO 40: C =C+DL: A = A1*C*/180: B =B1*C*/180
200 X =INT(100*SIN(A)+160.5)
210 Y = INT(80*COS(B)+100.5)
220 IF FP=1 THEN FP =0: SYS50201,X,Y,0:GOTO 240
230 SYS 50204, X, Y, 0
240 NEXT I
250 GOSUB 1000
260 SYS 50210, 7, 2
270 SYS 50207
280 X1 = 0: X2 = 319
290 FOR I = 0 TO 199
300 Y1 = I: Y2 = 199-I
310 SYS 50201, X1, Y1, 0
320 SYS 50204, X2, Y2, 0
330 NEXT I
340 Y1 = 199: Y2 =0
350 FOR I=0 TO 319
360 X1=I: X2=319-I
370 SYS 50201, X1, Y1, 0
```

```
380 SYS 50204, X2, Y2, 0
390 NEXT I
400 GOSUB 1000
410 SYS 50210, 0, 10
420 SYS 50207
430 FP=1:A1 =13: B1 =26: DL =6: C =0
440 FOR I =0 TO 80: C =C+DL: A = A1*C*/180: B =B1*C*/180
450 X =INT(100*COS(A)+160.5)
460 Y = INT(80*SIN(B)+100.5)
470 IF FP=1 THEN FP =0: SYS50201,X,Y,1:GOTO 240
480 SYS 50204, X, Y, 1
490 NEXT I
500 GOSUB 1000
510 SYS 50210, 15, 12
520 SYS 50207
530 FOR X = 0 TO 319
540 Y=INT(100+70*SIN(X/10))
550 SYS50201,160,10,1
560 SYS50204, X, Y, 1
570 NEXT X
900 GET A$: IFA$=""THEN 30
910 SYS50198
920 END
1000 FOR I=0TO2000:NEXTI:RETURN
```

## A Few Concluding Remarks

This chapter is a very brief and basic introduction to the Commodore 64 graphics. Hopefully it will give you a starting point for incorporating the graphics features into your own programs. Table 9 lists all 47 memory locations which control the VIC chip. The last column indicates the graphics feature each location affects, S for sprites, B for bit map mode, and C for character mode. This table will be a handy reference when you are ready to experiment with further graphic features.

***TABLE 9: Video Interface Controller Memory Locations***

| *Location* | | *Video Operation* | |
|---|---|---|---|
| 53248 | | Sprite0 horizontal position (low byte) | S |
| 53249 | | Sprite0 vertical position | S |
| 53250 | | Sprite1 horizontal position (low byte) | S |
| 53251 | | Sprite1 vertical position | S |
| 53252 | | Sprite2 horizontal position (low byte) | S |
| 53253 | | Sprite2 vertical position | S |
| 53254 | | Sprite3 horizontal position (low byte) | S |
| 53255 | | Sprite3 vertical position | S |
| 53256 | | Sprite4 horizontal position (low byte) | S |
| 53257 | | Sprite4 vertical position | S |
| 53258 | | Sprite5 horizontal position (low byte) | S |
| 53259 | | Sprite5 vertical position | S |
| 53260 | | Sprite6 horizontal position (low byte) | S |
| 53261 | | Sprite6 vertical position | S |
| 53262 | | Sprite7 horizontal position (low byte) | S |
| 53263 | | Sprite7 vertical position | S |
| 53264 | Bits 0-7 | High order bit of horizontal position sprites 0-7 | S |
| 53265 | Bits 0-2 | Vertical position for scrolling | BC |
| | Bit 3 | Select number of rows (24 or 25) | BC |
| | Bit 4 | Blank screen | |
| | Bit 5 | Select bitmap mode | B |
| | Bit 6 | Select extended background color mode | C |
| | Bit 7 | High order bit of raster position | |
| 53266 | | Raster position | |
| 53267 | | Horizontal position light pen | |
| 53268 | | Vertical position light pen | |
| 53269 | Bits 0-7 | Turn on and off sprites 0-7 | S |
| 53270 | Bits 0-2 | Horizontal position for scrolling | BC |
| | Bit 3 | Select number of columns (38 or 40) | BC |
| | Bit 4 | Select multicolor mode | BC |
| 53271 | Bits 0-7 | Double height—sprites 0-7 | S |
| 53272 | Bits 1-3 | Character set pointer | C |
| | Bit 3 | Bitmap pointer | B |
| | Bits 4-7 | Character screen or colormap pointer | BC |
| 53273 | | Interrupt register | |
| 53274 | | Interrupt register | |
| 53275 | Bits 0-7 | Priority register for sprites 0-7 | S |
| 53276 | Bits 0-7 | Select multicolor sprites 0-7 | S |
| 53277 | Bits 0-7 | Double width sprites 0-7 | S |
| 53278 | Bits 0-7 | Sprite with sprite collisions | S |
| 53279 | Bits 0-7 | Sprite with character collision | S |
| 53280 | Bits 0-3 | Border color | BC |
| 53281 | Bits 0-3 | Screen color | C |
| 53282 | Bits 0-3 | Character multicolor 1 | C |
| 53283 | Bits 0-3 | Character multicolor 2 | C |
| 53284 | Bits 0-3 | Sprite multicolor 1 | S |
| 53285 | Bits 0-3 | Sprite multicolor 2 | S |
| 53286 | Bits 0-3 | Sprite0 color | S |
| 53287 | Bits 0-3 | Sprite1 color | S |
| 53288 | Bits 0-3 | Sprite2 color | S |
| 53289 | Bits 0-3 | Sprite3 color | S |
| 53290 | Bits 0-3 | Sprite4 color | S |
| 53291 | Bits 0-3 | Sprite5 color | S |
| 53292 | Bits 0-3 | Sprite6 color | S |
| 53293 | Bits 0-3 | Sprite7 color | S |

# Appendix 3

# Exploring Sound and Music

*Dr. Frank H. Covitz*

Of the 5 human senses, sound is probably second only to sight in importance. ("A picture is worth 1000 words.") Certainly the amount of information received by the ear and processed by the brain is prodigious. Think about it for a minute: All speech, including the identity of the speaker in all possible spoken languages. All the content of past, present, and future music, including subtleties such as orchestration, playing styles, and various musical instruments. The almost infinitely varied natural sounds from the rush of surf to the song of a canary.

Just as it can take many written words to describe a picture, you can expect some difficulty in using words to describe sounds, particularly if our goal is to understand them well enough to be creative. The SID (Sound Interface Device) chip in the Commodore 64 is capable of producing a wide variety of sounds with high-fidelity quality. To use this resource to any extent approaching its full capability, let's first agree on some principles we will need to understand descriptions of sound.

It should be very clear that we are talking about vibrations. In normal hearing, vibrations in the air are picked up by the mechanisms in the ear and converted to nerve signals for the brain to interpret. If the vibrations are very low in frequency, we can actually feel them as well as hear them—put your hand in front of a reasonably large loudspeaker playing throbbing rock music! We need to understand the details of vibrations if we are to understand what makes up a sound and create the sounds we want.

Vibrations can be represented in forms other than actual pressure fluctuations in the air. We will use those forms which are the most convenient. For example, though the information recorded on audio magnetic tapes (magnetic fluctuations) or phonograph records (surface fluctuations) is not sound in itself, it can be easily converted into sound by amplifiers and speakers. For our specific purposes, the information needed to construct a sound will be in the form of numbers stored in our computer's memory. What these numbers mean, where they go, and how they become sound will be discussed later.

The questions are two: 1) What are the fundamental characteristics of the vibrations which make up sound? 2) How can we use these characteristics to "create" a particular sound?

## The Fundamentals of Tones

Let's first consider the case of the relatively simple sounds we call tones. For our purpose, a tone is a steady sound with a definite pitch. By steady, I mean that it doesn't change in quality with time (except of course that it has a beginning and an end). The term pitch is somewhat subjective, but it can mean that the sound has a dominant frequency with which, for example, we could whistle along "in tune."

*Frequency* is a number which specifies the rate of change of a vibration. The units of frequency were once called *cycles-per-second*, but, in honor of the pioneering contributions of Heinreich Rudolph Hertz in the fundamentals of electromagnetic waves and related phenomena, the name *Hertz* (abbreviated as Hz) has been universally adopted.

Since it is so important to have a good understanding of the meaning of frequency, let's use a couple of examples. Think about the motion of the pendulum in a grandfather clock. The frequency of that motion should be very close to exactly 1/2 Hz (each half-swing takes one second). In this case, you can actually see and count the vibrations; for sound, the frequencies are much too high to see the individual cycles, except with the aid of something like an oscilloscope. Let's go another step higher and take the case of an ordinary flat knife resting half on and half off the edge of a table. By holding the flat edge firmly against the table and "plucking" the overhanging part, you will set it into vibration with a frequency of about 10 Hz.

For audible sounds, the frequency limits of human hearing are usually 20 Hz to 20,000 Hz, although the average person will not be able to hear much above 15,000 Hz or below 30 Hz. (You can still "feel" these low frequencies, however.) Wait just a minute!! If we can only hear down to about 20 Hz, how come we can easily hear the table knife vibration, which I just said had a frequency about 10 Hz? What you are really hearing is the sound of the blade hitting the table edge at a rate of about 10 hits per second, and you can hear each hit.

The details of this vibration are actually quite a bit more complex than the pendulum's motion, and take us into the lowest level of what we are going to discuss, namely, the "pure" tone.

The pendulum's motion is pure in that there is no point in its travel where either the speed or direction changes abruptly. The sound of a tuning fork is close to a pure tone. Although pure tones are very rare in nature, we need to understand them, since any tone can be constructed by mixing pure tones of the right frequencies and amplitudes. Since pure tones are easy to generate by electronics, they form the basis for artificially synthesizing and analyzing sounds.

To understand this point clearly, let's take the case of that slow-moving pendulum again, but with some differences. Instead of a disc supported by a stiff rod, as in the grandfather clock, imagine that our pendulum consists of a bucket of sand suspended by a flexible string. The sand will be allowed to trickle out of a small hole in the bottom of the bucket. If we were to set this pendulum in motion, while pulling a long sheet of paper underneath, we would see the sand forming a pattern; something like that shown in the following figure:

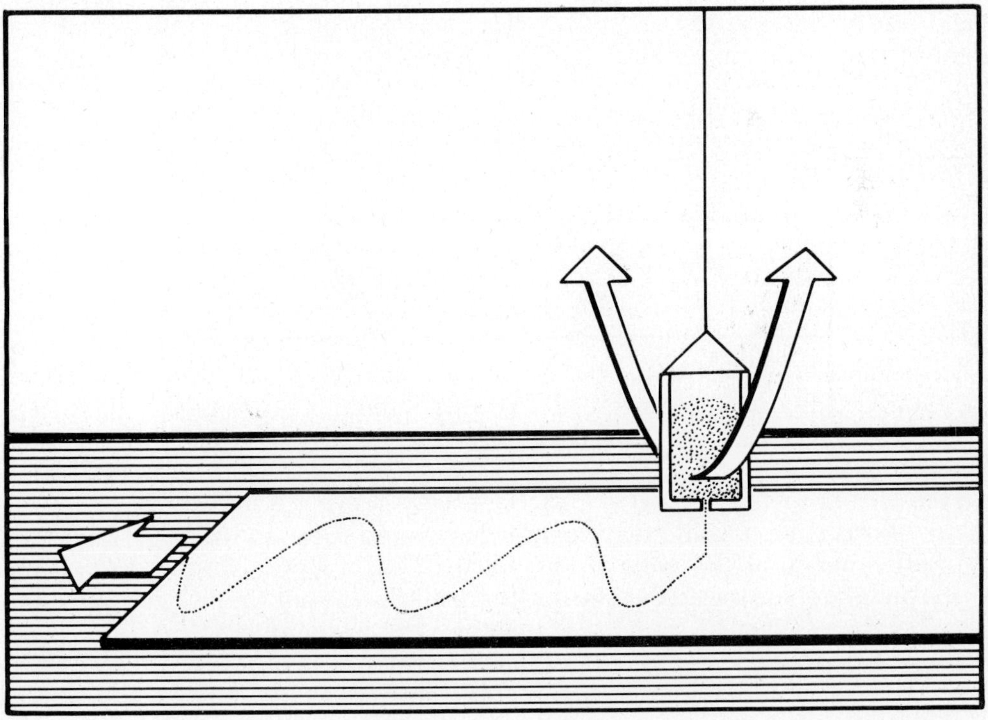

**Figure 1. Sand pendulum**

In a more idealized visual form, we have:

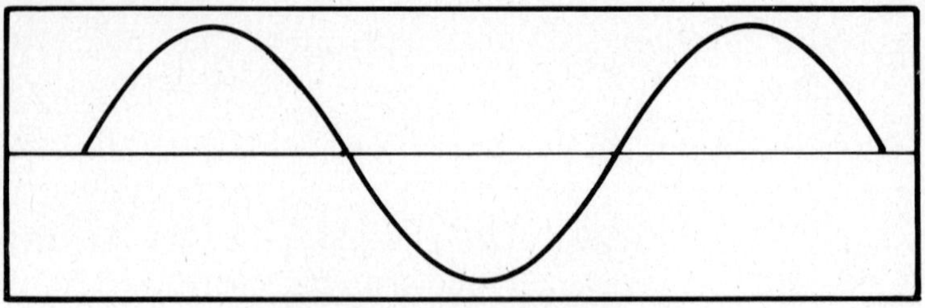

**Figure 2. Sine waveform**

Theoretically, the motion of the sand pendulum will continue for quite a while, so that over a fairly large number of swings, we only need two numbers to represent its motion quite well—the *amplitude* (how far away from the center it reaches) and the *frequency* (the number of swings per second). The shape of the curve representing this idealized motion is called a sine *waveform*. If we could see the motion of a tuning fork, it would look quite similar. For the tuning fork, though, the amplitude will be related to the loudness of the sound it produces, and its frequency related to the perceived pitch of the sound.

Now think of the pendulum with the sand trickling out, tracing its motion on the paper, and imagine what would happen if during its smooth back and forth motion you were to strike the string above the bucket with a sharp blow, sort of like a mini-karate chop. Now, in addition to the slow swinging, an additional vibration of much higher frequency would set in, and our sand picture of the resulting motion would look something like this:

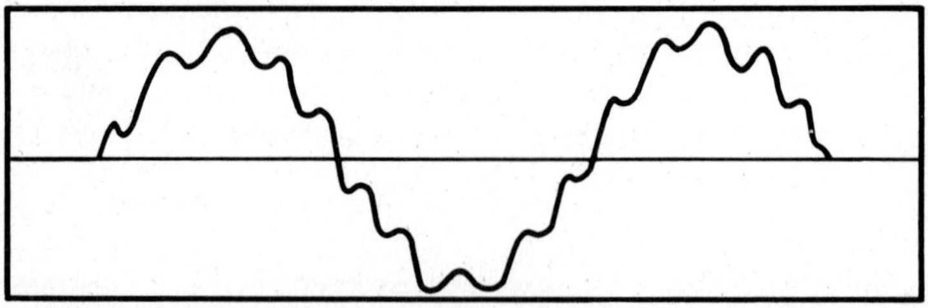

**Figure 3. Sine waveform with high frequency component**

If this were a sound waveform, what would it sound like? The sensation of pitch would be the same as that for the tone of a pure sine waveform, but the quality of the tone would be noticeably different—it would have a "brighter" or more "lively" sound. The technical term for this property is *timbre* (pronounced "tamber" as in tambourine, not "timber" as in lumberjack).

The waveforms of most real sounds would be quite a bit more complex than the example just given, and it is difficult if not impossible to predict exactly what most complex waveforms would sound like from only their visual representation. However, no matter how complex its shape, any repetitive waveform can be broken down (by a rather complicated mathematical procedure known as "Fourier analysis") into components, called *harmonics*. Each of these components would have the sine waveform shape (each with its own amplitude), and each would have a frequency which is an integer multiple of the lowest frequency component.

This lowest frequency component, for the most part, is what gives the tone its pitch, and the relative amounts of the higher ones, called *harmonics*, give it its timbre. Specifically, it is easier (but still very difficult) to understand, predict, and modify sounds based on knowledge of the harmonic content, compared to examining its waveform.

Had enough of this technical jargon? Let's just look at the following table to make sure we are talking the same language before going on to putting the amazing SID chip to work and creating some tones.

| *Technical Term* | *Audible Equivalent* |
|---|---|
| Frequency | Pitch |
| Amplitude | Loudness |
| Harmonic content | Timbre |

## Addressing SID

Think of the SID chip as a house with rooms and floors, and our exploration of it as an adventure game. To get into a particular room, we need to know the address of the house as well as the name of the room. At this stage, we are only going to explore the rooms having to do with frequency and amplitude (or pitch and loudness). As far as the computer's microprocessor is concerned, the SID is accessed just like any other piece of memory, so we are going to use POKEs to get data into SID. The SID chip has 29 registers (a register to the SID is the same as a memory location) located at addresses starting at location 54272. Rather than constantly keying in or remembering that formidable number, let's use the computer to do much of the remembering by entering this program line:

```
10 SID = 54272
```

(Remember that the Commodore BASIC looks only at the first two characters of a variable name, so we shouldn't use any other variable name starting with SI). SID can handle three separate sounds, which we will call voices. (For addressing purposes, think of them as three separate floors of the house). Each voice needs a frequency, so we need to know where to put the pitch information:

```
20 F1 = SID : F2 = SID + 7 : F3 = SID + 14
```

For starters, let's only deal with one voice, so we will silence voices two and three by putting zeroes in their frequency registers:

```
30 FOR I = 0 TO 1 : POKE F2+I,0 : POKE F3+I,0 : NEXT I
```

It takes two POKEs per voice to get the frequency data into the registers. This is because the number representing the frequency has a range 0 to 65535, which is greater than can be POKEd into any single memory location. SID solves this by using two adjacent memory locations, the first representing the low part of the number (think of it as a fraction), and the second representing the high part (think of it as a whole number).

Suppose we have a number, F, in the range 0 to 65535 that we want to put into SID. We use these formulas: FH = INT(F/256) and FL = F−256*FH. FH and FL mean Frequency High and Frequency Low. A quirk of the 64's microprocessor requires these double numbers to be stored into registers with the low part first and the high part second. So, for example, we would put this number into frequency register 1 via: POKE F1,FL : POKE F1+1,FH (remember that F1 and F1+1 are the addresses of the registers, and FL and FH are the numbers that go into the registers.)

Is the number we just put into the frequency registers the frequency we will get when we start the sound going? No. The frequency, in Hz, is related to the number in the register, F, by the following equation:

F = HZ*16.40439

Let's give voice 1 a frequency of 1000 Hz. In BASIC we should enter:

```
40 HZ = 1000 : C = 16.40439
50 F = HZ*C
60 FH = INT(F/256)
70 FL = F-256*FH
80 POKE F1,FL : POKE F1+1,FH
```

If you actually entered this example, you wouldn't get any sound. That's because the SID still doesn't know enough about what you want. SID needs to know at least 3 more things before it can make a sound—the overall volume (loudness of all 3 voices), the amplitude envelope (2 registers for each voice) and the waveform type (1 register for each voice). These will be explained in detail later, but for now let's just list the addresses of these registers:

```
90 W1 = F1+4 : W2 = F2+4 : W3 = F3+4 : REM FOR WAVEFORM
   TYPE
100 A1 = F1+5 :A2 = F2+5 : A3 = F3+5 : REM FOR ATTACK/
    DECAY
110 S1 = F1+6 :S2 = F2+6 : S3 = F3+6 : REM FOR SUSTAIN/
    RELEASE
120 VOL = SID+24 : REM TOTAL VOLUME
```

Without worrying about the numbers that go into these registers (that will come later), just add the following program lines:

```
130 POKE VOL,15
140 POKE A1,85 : POKE S1,85
150 WV=64 : POKE W1,WV+1
160 FOR I=0 TO 1000 : NEXT I
170 POKE W1,WV
```

If you have entered these new lines into the computer and RUN them, you should finally (whew!) have produced a sound from SID. Now will be a good point to SAVE the program from lines 10-120 since we will be using them again. After SAVEing, feel free to experiment with numbers that go into A1 and S1 (line 140), the value for WV in line 150 (use 128, 64, 32, or 16 for now), and the loop end value in line 160. You may get some feeling for what's happening at this point, but if not, take heart, the next section will clarify any mysteries of A1, S1, and W1, and more.

A review of the addresses we have used up to now and their meaning is in order:

| *Name* | *Address* | *Meaning* |
|---|---|---|
| Voice #1: | | |
| SID | 54272 | Base address for SID |
| F1 | SID | Frequency, low part |
| | F1+1 | Frequency, high part |
| W1 | F1+4 | Waveform/control register |
| A1 | F1+5 | Attack/decay register |
| S1 | F1+6 | Sustain/release register |
| Voice #2: | | |
| F2 | SID+7 | Frequency, low part |
| | F2+1 | Frequency, high part |
| W2 | F2+4 | Waveform/control register |
| A2 | F2+5 | Attack/decay register |
| S2 | F2+6 | Sustain/release register |
| Voice #3: | | |
| F3 | SID+14 | Frequency, low part |
| | F3+1 | Frequency, high part |
| W3 | F3+4 | Waveform/control register |
| A3 | F3+5 | Attack/decay register |
| S3 | F3+6 | Sustain/release register |
| All Voices: | | |
| VOL | SID+24 | Volume 0-15 register |

```
BASIC PROGRAM TO SET UP SID ADDRESSES
10 SID = 54272 : REM BASE ADDRESS
20 C = 16.40439 : REM FOR CONVERTING HZ TO REGISTER
   VALUE
30 F1=SID : F2 = SID+7 : F3 = SID+14 : REM
   FREQUENCY REGISTERS
40 W1 = F1+4 : W2 = F2+4 : W3 = F3+4 : REM WAVEFORM/
   CONTROL REGISTERS
50 A1 = F1+5 : A2 = F2+5 : A3 = F3+5 : REM ATTACK/DECAY
   REGISTERS
60 S1 = F1+6 : S2 = F2+6 : S3 = F3+6 : REM SUSTAIN/
   RELEASE REGISTERS
70 VOL = SID+24 : REM OVERALL VOLUME FROM 0 TO 15
```

I *strongly* urge you to enter this program piece if you haven't already done so, and SAVE it, since it will always be used as an opening procedure for setting up for SID programs.

## Moving on to Dynamics

At this point, you should have some understanding about the nature of sound, the general meaning of frequency, pitch, and timbre, as well as the specific SID registers dealing with frequency. Now, we will go over the SID registers having to do with *waveform type* and control, the registers dealing with *attack, decay, sustain, release,* and the registers associated with *volume* and *filtering*.

***Waveform/Control Register*** The registers we have been calling W1, W2, and W3, have a dual purpose, as have several other SID registers. Any memory location in your computer can only hold a number between 0 and 255. This number is made up of eight individual bits—each of which can be set to one or zero, "on" or "off." Bits are numbered from zero (the bit farthest to the right) to seven (leftmost). The individual bits of the waveform/control register have the specific meanings as follows:

| *Bit #* | *Weight* | *Meaning* |
|---|---|---|
| 7 | 128 | Select noise waveform |
| 6 | 64 | Select pulse waveform |
| 5 | 32 | Select sawtooth waveform |
| 4 | 16 | Select triangle waveform |
| 3 | 8 | Reset voice output |
| 2 | 4 | Ring modulation on |
| 1 | 2 | Synchronization on |
| 0 | 1 | Start ASDR |

The "weight" numbers are added together for each bit you "set" to get a number from 0 to 255. This gives us the technique for controlling the individual bits. For example, let's use the variable WC to represent the contents of the waveform control register for voice #1 (this was labeled WV in our previous section). If we start off with WC = whatever, and want to turn on only one bit, say bit 7, we would do:

```
WC = WC OR 128:POKE W1,WC
```

The reason for using WC is that PEEK won't work with the SID registers. WC is a variable that stands for the contents of memory location W1. We can call the SID registers "write only," since once we POKE in a number, we can't read it.

To turn off only bit 7, we would do:

```
WC = WC AND 254:POKE W1,WC
```

If you find this confusing, you should re-read the section in Appendix 2 about AND and OR. Several of the SID registers are bit-oriented, so you will need to know how to control individual bits if you are going to fully understand SID programming.

Each SID voice must be assigned a waveform type consisting of either *triangle, sawtooth, pulse,* or *noise* (see figure below) as controlled by the correct bits.

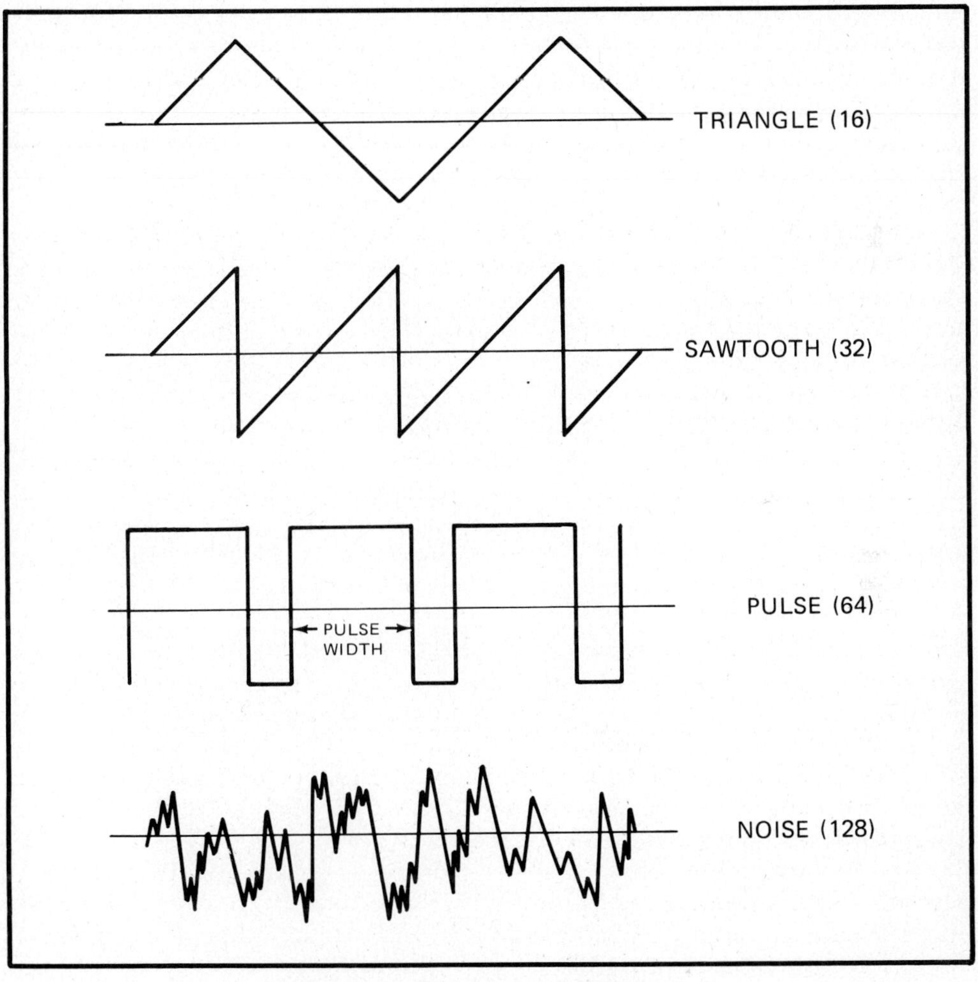


**Figure 4. The SID waveforms**

Let's briefly discuss the quality, or timbre, of these waveforms. The simplest and purest is the *triangle* waveform (bit #4), one cycle of which consists of a smooth straight line of increasing value up to its maximum, followed by a straight line of the opposite slope going down to its minimum value, as the name suggests. Although the slope changes abruptly at the top and bottom, the actual values along the waveform have no such abrupt change.

The next waveform the SID can produce is the *sawtooth* waveform (bit #5), which, as the name suggests, consists of a straight line slope from its minimum value to its maximum, and at the start of its next cycle the amplitude drops abruptly back to the minimum. This abrupt change in amplitude results in a much richer sound than the triangle and a more "brilliant" timbre.

The last periodic waveform the SID can produce is the *pulse* waveform (bit #6), which consists of a partial cycle during which the amplitude has a constant negative value, and then a constant positive amplitude for the remainder of its cycle. Another number is needed to describe the pulse waveform—a *duty cycle*.

Changes in the duty cycle affect the harmonics of the sound and its overall characteristics. By changing the duty cycle, you can produce a *square waveform*, which is less rich than the sawtooth, but much richer than the triangle waveform, and has a characteristic "metallic" or "reedy" sound. As you move the duty cycle to a value of zero, the pulse waveform sounds very harsh and "buzzy." The SID chip allows you to change this duty cycle while a sound is in progress, achieving a striking *dynamic* timbre—we will experiment with this effect later.

The noise waveform (bit #7) is also available for each of the three SID voices. Noise is the presence of many frequencies, and the noise waveform creates sound without pitch. Nevertheless, noise can have a variety of timbres, depending primarily on the distribution of frequencies. Emphasizing the high frequencies gives it a "hissy" character, while emphasizing the lows gives it a "rumbling" character. The timbre of the noise waveform in the SID can be varied by changing the frequency values in the appropriate registers while the sound is in progress.

Let's review: Before a SID voice can be played, it must be assigned a waveform type—noise, pulse, sawtooth, or triangle depending on the setting of bits #7,6,5, and 4 of the waveform/control register. Each has its characteristic timbre, and the timbres of the pulse and noise waveforms can be controlled *dynamically*. Before moving on, remember one more important point. Only one of the waveform types should be selected at a time. Each voice, however, can have its own waveform.

Of the other bits in the waveform/control registers (W1,W2, and W3), bits #3,2, and 1 won't concern us yet; bit 0 is literally the "key" to setting the SID chip into action. When this bit is "on" the sound begins. When this bit is "off," the sound starts to die out. So, assuming you have set WC to a valid waveform type (128,64,32, or 16), you would activate voice #1 with POKE W1,WC+1 and release voice #1 with POKE W1,WC. You can also silence a voice at any time by setting its frequency register to 0 with POKE F1,0:POKE F1+1,0 for voice #1, etc.

***ADSR*** We are now ready to delve into something called ADSR. **A**ttack, **D**ecay, **S**ustain and **R**elease comprise the particular way that the amplitude, or loudness, of a sound changes with time. Many sounds, particularly musical ones, can be simulated by an amplitude "envelope" consisting of the 4 *phases* just mentioned. With the SID chip, you can control the rate, or length of time, attack, decay, and release take. The value of sustain is amplitude, or loudness, not rate or time. Each one of these ADSR phases can have 1 of 16 values, a number from 0 to 15 represented with 4 bits. Each SID chip is eight bits, so ADSR phases are paired as attack/decay and sustain/release. Each four bits is called a *nybble*.

The attack and decay nybbles go into registers A1, A2, and A3 (each voice can have its own ADSR), and the sustain, amplitude, and release nybbles go into registers S1, S2, and S3. The beginning of a sound can be likened to opening a gate, so it is referred to as "gating on" the sound. Here is the sequence of events that takes place when a voice is "gated on" by setting bit 0 of the waveform/control register (see above):

The amplitude, or loudness, of the sound rises from zero to a maximum at a rate governed by the attack nybble. It then decays, or begins to fade out, at a rate governed by the decay nybble until the loudness reaches the value specified by the sustain nybble. The voice remains at the sustain amplitude until it is "gated off" by turning off bit 0 of the waveform/control register. Then the loudness fades to zero at a rate given by the release nybble.

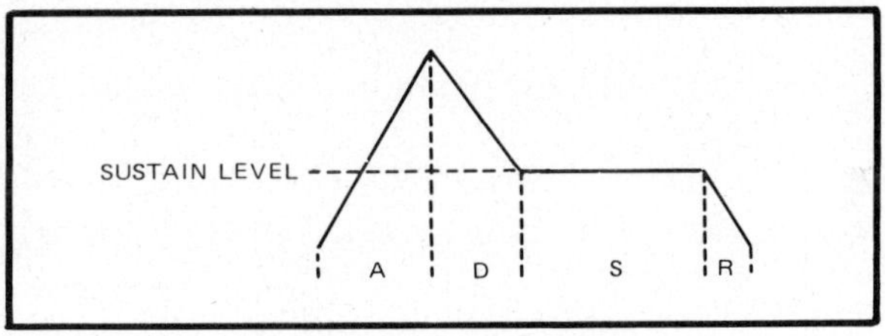


**Figure 5. ADSR envelope**

Here is a table that gives you the rates for the 16 different nybbles (ms = milliseconds, s = seconds):

| *Nybble* | *Attack* | *Decay/Release* |
|---|---|---|
| 0 | 2 ms | 6 ms |
| 1 | 8 ms | 24 ms |
| 2 | 16 ms | 48 ms |
| 3 | 24 ms | 72 ms |
| 4 | 38 ms | 114 ms |
| 5 | 56 ms | 168 ms |
| 6 | 68 ms | 204 ms |
| 7 | 80 ms | 240 ms |
| 8 | 100 ms | 300 ms |
| 9 | 250 ms | 750 ms |
| 10 | 500 ms | 1.5 s |
| 11 | 800 ms | 2.4 s |
| 12 | 1 s | 3 s |
| 13 | 3 s | 9 s |
| 14 | 5 s | 15 s |
| 15 | 8 s | 24 s |

Attack and decay rates go into registers A1, A2, and A3 (each voice can have its own ADSR), and the sustain amplitude and release rate go into registers S1, S2, and S3. These have only to be set once, and not each time a sound is to be played. Let's give a concrete example to make sure we understand what is necessary to get a particular ADSR. A "blown" sound, for example as in a trumpet note, has a fast attack and decay rate, a relatively loud sustain, and a fairly rapid release rate. Let's use a 16 ms attack rate, a 72 ms decay rate, a sustain amplitude of 12, and a release rate of 114 ms. With the help of the table above, we have:

AD = (attack/decay) = 16*2 + 3
SR = (sustain/release) = 16*12 + 4

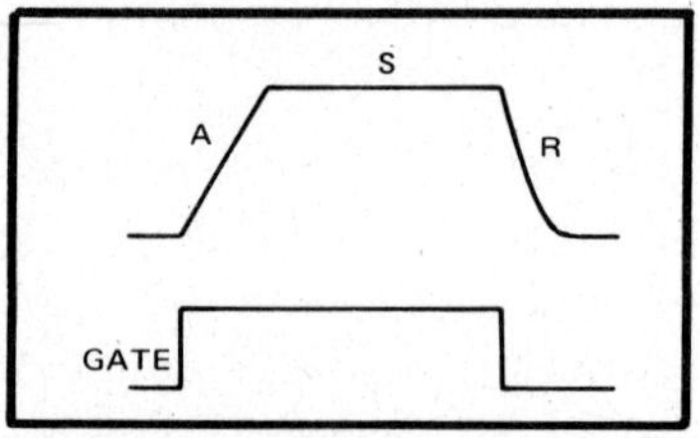


**Figure 6. Blown sound**

For voice 1, we do POKE A1,35: POKE S1,196. No sound, right? Remember, we also have to specify waveform type and frequency, and then gate the voice on. Also, keep in mind that the release doesn't happen until you gate the voice off. Here are a few sets of ADSRs to give you a better feel for what's needed. Experiment with the waveform type to get the timbre you want. First numbers are attack/decay, second are sustain/release

Percussion—9,8 = very fast attack (16*0), moderate decay (9), zero sustain amplitude (16*0), and medium release (8). (Try noise waveform.)

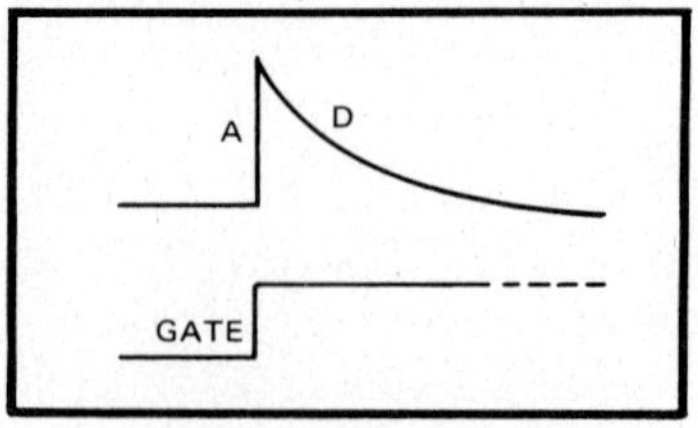


**Figure 7. Percussion**

Piano—10,48 = very fast attack (16*0), medium release (10), low sustain amplitude (16*4), and very fast release (0). (Try sawtooth waveform.)

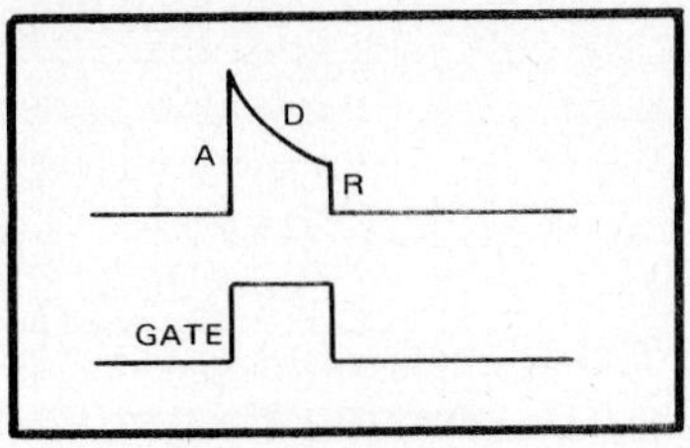


**Figure 8. Piano**

Organ—0,240 = very fast attack (16*0), no decay (0), high sustain amplitude (15*16), and very fast release (0). (Try pulse waveform.)

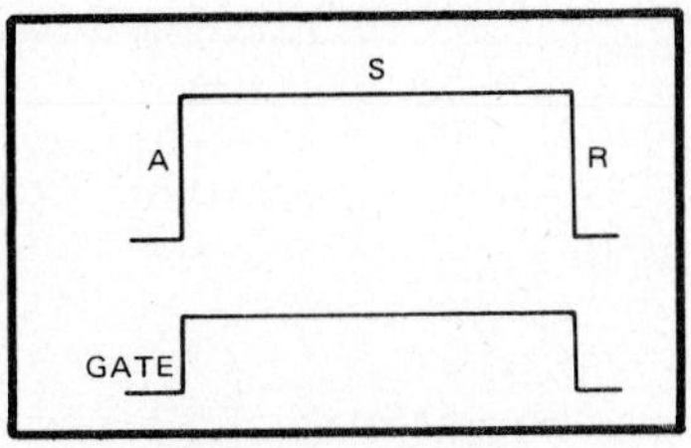


**Figure 9. Organ**

Violin—133,165 = moderately slow attack (8*16), medium decay (5), medium sustain amplitude (10*16), and medium release (5). (Try pulse waveform.)

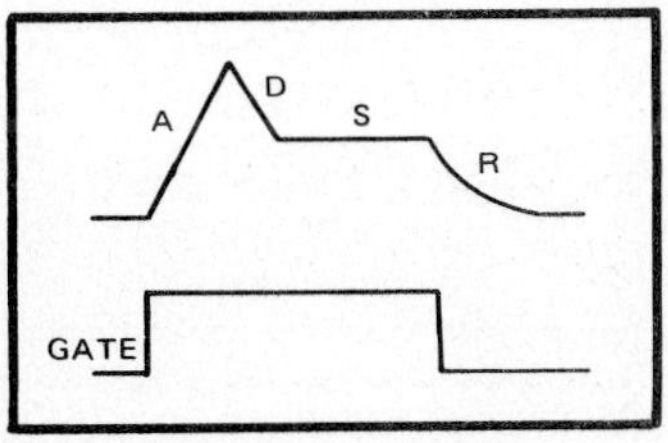


**Figure 10. Violin**

Keep in mind that the SID chip's main versatility is in creating sounds not easily made by real instruments. For example, one could easily reverse the normal type ADSR's to create a pretty strange sound.

As we've seen, the SID has many registers and functions, and it will be helpful, if not essential, to keep these organized if we are to use it to its full capability. The SID functions can be conveniently grouped into two categories: The ones that affect individual voices, and the ones that affect all of the voices at once. Starting at the base address for SID, the first three groups of seven are for individual voices. The next four control the filter and overall volume of the chip, and the remaining four are special. (We haven't gotten to these yet.) Let's list the registers and their contents:

| *Register* | *Meaning* |
|---|---|
| 0,7,14 | Frequency (low byte) |
| 1,8,15 | Frequency (high byte) |
| 2,9,16 | Pulse width (low byte) |
| 3,10,17 | Pulse width (bits 0–3 are high nybble) |
| 4,11,18 | Control register |
| | Bit 0–gate (1 = start, 0 = release) |
| | Bit 1—sync bit |
| | Bit 2—ring modulation bit |
| | Bit 3—test bit |
| | Bit 4—triangle waveform |
| | Bit 5—sawtooth waveform |
| | Bit 6—pulse waveform |
| | Bit 7—noise waveform |
| 5,12,19 | Attack/Decay register |
| 6,13,20 | Sustain/Release register |
| 21 | Filter frequency (bits 0,1,2 form low part) |
| 22 | Filter frequency (high byte) |
| 23 | Resonance/Filter Register |
| | Bit 0—connect voice 1 through filter |
| | Bit 1—connect voice 2 through filter |
| | Bit 2—connect voice 3 through filter |
| | Bit 3—connect external signal through filter |
| | Bits 4–7—filter resonance |
| 24 | Mode/Volume |
| | Bits 0–3—overall volume |
| | Bit 4—select low-pass filter |
| | Bit 5—select band-pass filter |
| | Bit 6—select high-pass filter |
| | Bit 7—disconnect voice 3 from audio output |
| The following are read-only: | |
| 25 | POTX |
| 26 | POTY |
| 27 | Output of oscillator 3 |
| 28 | Envelope of voice 3 |

For relatively simple sounds (like the ones used for music, as opposed to the ones used for sound effects), the important registers we've discussed—at SID+0 to 20—set up the frequency, waveform type, (and pulse width, if we've selected pulse waveform), envelope, and whether to start a voice going (gate bit = 1) or to release it (gate bit = 0). The low nybble of register 24 controls the overall volume. For musical sounds there is a sane way to handle all these pieces of information, and that is just what we will discuss in the next section.

## The Well-Tempered Computer

Up to now, we've not heard too much from SID; we've mainly discussed theory of sound and SID organization. We'll just take a moment to consider what kinds of frequencies to use, and we will be ready to play some music with SID. If we stick to Western music (the music of Western civilization, that is, not the "wild west"), this is fairly straightforward. A musical "scale" consists of 12 pitches (do, re, mi, fa, sol, la, ti, and the 5 sharps or flats in between) per octave. In each octave, the frequencies come from the preceding one. In the so-called equal-tempered scale (the one most commonly used), each of the steps is a fixed multiple of the preceding one. The fixed ratio of the equal-tempered scale is actually a compromise that allows many tuned instruments to play in harmony with each other.

This fixed multiple is (and has to be) the 12th root of two (which is equal to 1.0594630943593. . . .where did he get all those numbers!?). This number, when multiplied by itself twelve times, results in 2; in other words it gets us to the next octave, and everything can start over again, only doubled in pitch. In principle, then, we only have to agree on the exact frequency for one particular note, and we can derive ALL of the other ones by successive multiples (to go higher in pitch) and divides (to go lower in pitch).

Musicians have internationally agreed that the note A4 (the "la" in the 4th octave) will have a frequency of exactly 440 Hz. From this piece of information, and the conversion factor given in the section on the frequency register, we could calculate the appropriate double-byte number for each note in the equal-tempered scale that we wanted to play. Would we put you and your computer through all that work every time we want to play a note? No. Instead, we'll take advantage of the octave relationship to shorten this considerably, by calculating a table of only 12 frequency values (the 13th value starts the next higher octave), and we can quickly get the correct values for the notes of other octaves by dividing by 2 the appropriate number of times.

Here is a BASIC program to calculate (once and for all) the frequency values for the "top" octave (attach this to our fundamental address program, given earlier.)

```
100 DIM F(12) : REM F(1) IS SID FREQ FOR A6, F(12) IS
    SID FREQ FOR G#7
110 A7=8*440 : REM FREQUENCY IN Hz FOR HIGHEST A-NOTE
    IN 7TH OCTAVE
120 K=2*(1/12) : REM THE EQUAL TEMPERAMENT INTERVAL
130 FRQ=A7*C : REM CONVERT TO SID VALUE, C=16.40439
    FROM PREVIOUS PROGRAM
140 FOR I=12 TO 1 STEP -1
150 FRQ=FRQ/K : REM GET NEXT LOWER HALF- STEP
160 F(I)=FRQ
170 NEXT I
```

At this point, let's clear out the SID registers to prevent any "hang-overs" from any previous program from interfering, and set up a few other initial conditions:

```
200 FOR I = 0 TO 28: POKE SID+I,0:NEXT I
210 POKE VOL, 15 : REM SET OVERALL VOLUME TO MAXIMUM
220 TI$="000000" : REM SET TIMER TO 0
```

```
230 DIM N(12) : REM TO HOLD PARAMETERS
240 FOR I = 1 TO 9 : READ N(I) : REM READ SOUND
    PARAMETERS FOR EACH VOICE
250 NEXT I
260 REM FOLLOWING DATA ARE EXAMPLES ONLY, FEEL FREE
    TO USE YOUR OWN
270 DATA 16,16,16 : REM WAVEFORM TYPE FOR EACH
    VOICE
280 DATA 55,55,55 : REM ATTACK/DECAY FOR EACH VOICE
290 DATA 55,55,55 : REM SUSTAIN/RELEASE FOR EACH
    VOICE
300 POKE W1,N(1) : POKE W2,N(2) : POKE W3, N(3) : REM
    INSTALL ADSR
310 POKE A1,N(4) : POKE A2,N(5) : POKE A3,N(6)
320 POKE S1,N(7) : POKE S2,N(8) : POKE S3,N(9)
330 FOR I=1 TO 3 : REM TAKE CARE OF PULSE
340 READ W : N(I+9)=W*4096
360 NEXT I
370 DATA .5,.5,.5 : REM MUST BE A FRACTION BETWEEN 0
    AND .5
380 POKE F1+3,INT(N(10)/256):POKE F1+2,
    N(10)-256*INT(N(10)/256)
390 POKE F2+3,INT(N(11)/256):POKE F2+2,
    N(11)-256*INT(N(11)/256)
400 POKE F3+3,INT(N(12)/256):POKE F3+2,
    N(12)-256*INT(N(12)/256)
```

(Remember, the pulse width will affect the sound only if you have selected the pulse waveform with 64 as the waveform type.)

If you intend to try your hand at music programming, SAVE the whole program for later use: lines 10-70 (sets up SID addresses), lines 100-160 (calculates the top octave of the equal-temperament scale), and lines 200 onward. (We may change this last section later.) The SID chip is now set to play music if we give it some data. Let's start off simply by using only one voice, but feel free to change the waveform type and ADSR data.

```
490 S = 1 : REM TEMPO CONSTANT

500 READ TM : REM READ NOTE DURATION
510 IF TM=0 THEN 9999 : REM DONE IF TM=0
520 IF TM<0 THEN 9999 : REM DONE IF TM<0
530 T=TI+S*TM : REM THIS TELLS US WHEN TO STOP
    PLAYING A NOTE
540 READ N,O : REM READ NOTE AND OCTAVE #
550 FR=F(N)/(2*O) : REM CALCULATE FREQUENCY FOR SID
560 FH=INT(FR/256) : FL=FR-256*FH
570 POKE F1,FL : POKE F1+1,FH : REM INSTALL FREQUENCY
```

```
580 POKE W1,N(1)+1 : REM ATTACK BEGINS
590 IF TI<T THEN 590 : REM WAIT FOR NOTE TO END
600 POKE W1,N(1) : REM RELEASE BEGINS
610 GOTO 500 : REM GET MORE DATA

700 DATA 40,4,2
710 DATA 40,6,2
720 DATA 40,8,2
730 DATA 40,9,2
740 DATA 40,11,2
750 DATA 40,1,1
760 DATA 40,3,1
770 DATA 40,4,1
780 DATA 0

9999 FOR I=0 TO 28 : POKE SID+I,0 : NEXT I : END : REM
     SILENCE SID, AND END
```

Now RUN the program—pretty neat, right? This is a good point to experiment a bit with waveform types and ASDRs for our 1 voice piece. Try the pulse waveform (put a 64 as the 1st number in line 270), and use different pulse widths (first number in line 370). Now for a bit more explanation. The variable TI used in line 590 is special. It is the computer's internal timer, just like TI$, except it is a number (not a string like TI$), and it is measured in units of 1/60th of a second. So the 40's in the DATA statements beginning on line 700 mean 40/60ths of a second, or about .67 second.

Line 590 is the key to accurate timing, since it doesn't depend on the time it takes BASIC to execute a statement like the FOR/NEXT loop we previously used to get a delay. If you study the program, you'll see that the reason for testing the variable TM for both zero and negative numbers (lines 510 and 520) is to look for two conditions. After playing for a while, you may want to change the waveform or ADSR, for example, by READing in more DATA and POKEing into the right place. If TM equals zero, the program will "branch" to let you do that. A negative value for TM means you are completely finished. In our example, both cases took us to line 9999, the end of the program.

There are several ways we could have encoded our notes—for example using string values like A2,C#3,Bb1. . . or actually using frequency values like 880, 2113, 987.2. . . . or do,re,mi. . . .or perhaps even graphically as in a musical score. We obviously could have done something similar with durations. However, the way I have outlined is a good compromise between readability and speed of decoding. It is certainly not sacred, so if you later feel more comfortable with other notations, go to it and try your hand at programming them. For now, stick with it and use the following table and figure to help you translate:

| *Note #* | *Music symbol* |
|---|---|
| 1 | la or A |
| 2 | (le) or A# or Bb |
| 3 | ti or B |
| 4 | do or C |
| 5 | (di) or C# or Db |
| 6 | re or D |
| 7 | (ra) or D# or Eb |
| 8 | mi or E |
| 9 | fa or F |
| 10 | (fi) or F# or Gb |
| 11 | sol or G |
| 12 | (si) or G# or Ab |

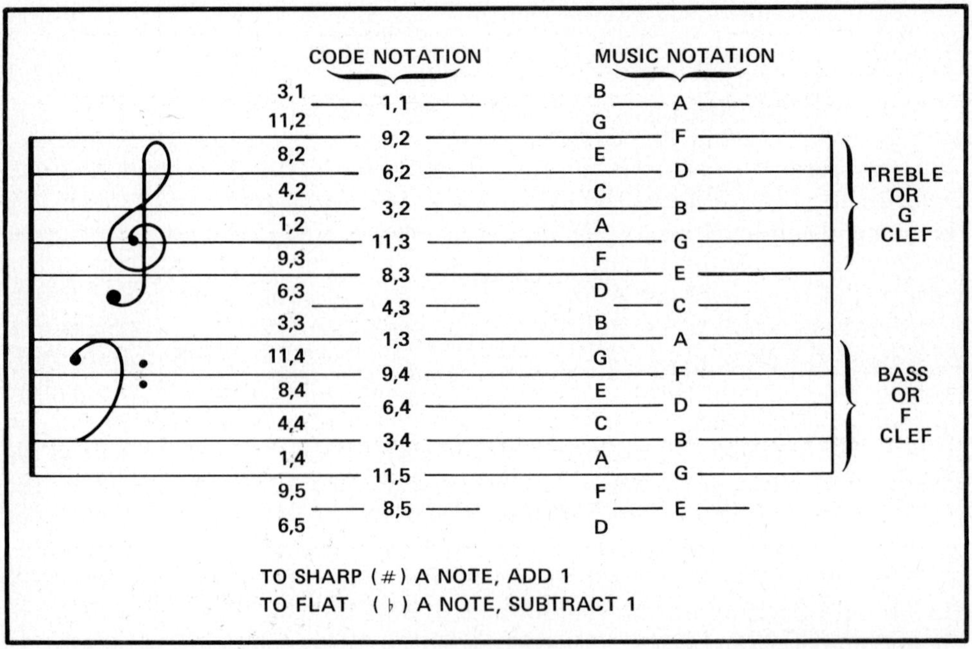


So now you know why we used the sequence 4,6,8,9,11,1,3,4 for our note codes to play a C-scale, and why we switched from two octaves down to one octave between 11 and 1. In conventional music notation, durations are indicated either directly as fractions of a whole note, such as ¼ note, ½ note, etc., or by means of graphic symbols. If we arbitrarily call 160 60th of a second the duration value for a whole note, then a whole note is encoded with a 160, a ½ note will have the value 80, a ¼ note gets the value 40, etc. This technique allows you to have "oddball" durations such as a ⅓ note = 53 (160/3), or a dotted quarter note = 60 (40 + one half of 40). Of course, you don't have to follow this convention, and you could have any reasonable timing constant you like. In any case, here is a table that will take you from conventional notation to what we're using as duration values.

| NAME | SYMBOL | VALUE | NAME | SYMBOL | VALUE |
|---|---|---|---|---|---|
| DOTTED WHOLE |  | 240 | DOTTED EIGHTH |  | 30 |
| WHOLE |  | 160 | QUARTER TRIPLET |  | 27 |
| DOTTED HALF |  | 120 | EIGHTH |  | 20 |
| HALF |  | 80 | EIGHTH TRIPLET |  | 13 |
| DOTTED QUARTER |  | 60 | SIXTEENTH |  | 10 |
| QUARTER |  | 40 | THIRTY-SECOND |  | 5 |

As in real life everything is relative, so the value for S (in line 490) is a scale factor which multiplies the time value, and is our way of permitting tempo (overall speed of the music) control with a single number. If S were 2, then the tempo would be 2 times slower; if it were ½, the tempo would be 2 times faster. Try setting S=2 and S=.5 to verify that it works the way you expect. At this point, you should definitely try your hand with the note DATA statements to get different tunes encoded, which will give you practice in getting the durations and note values correct.

OK, assuming you've experimented with single voice tunes, we'll go on to something even more fun, multiple-voice music. I think you can see how we will proceed. Our DATA statements will now consist of three sets of information instead of one. We could do three sets of POKEs to get the SID chip activated. This would be fine if all 3 notes always started and finished at the same time, but this is not usually the case in most music.

In much music, the notes frequently don't "line up." This gives it its multiple-voice sound. Two general techniques are prevalent in encoding music for computers. One is called "horizontal," which simply has the timing and frequency values for each voice in a separate table (as you would read each voice in a score by scanning it horizontally). This would be relatively easy to use if we had a separate timer for each voice.

The other technique is called "vertical," which means that data for all three voices are grouped together, as if they were musical chords. (This is closer to how people read and play multi-part music.) The complication in vertical coding arises when, say, one voice needs to be changed, while the other two need to continue sounding. Although both methods could be implemented, it will be easier to program for vertical encoding.

What this means is that data must be made available to the program each time something "new" is about to happen, that is every time one or more voices needs to be set into an attack or a release. For example, suppose we had three notes that started together, but one of them was a quarter note, while the others were half notes. We would split this vertically into two separate "events." Each event, for our purpose, means a new DATA statement. In the first event, we would start all notes into their attack phase. The duration for our timer would get the value for a quarter note. The next event would pick up another quarter note duration, and release (or pick up a new attack) for the original quarter note, while the other two would be left sounding. It is critical that you understand why the sum of the two events must add up to the half note, and why the first event must be a quarter note in duration. If you see this clearly, you are in excellent shape for what follows; if not, try to follow along and perhaps it will become clearer as we give you some more examples.

Here is our three-voice program, starting with the first simple example in the data of lines 800-880. We assume you have our opening program already present (up to line 400):

```
410 BYTE=256 : Z=0 : W=1 : M=-1 : REM CONSTANTS
420 DIM FH(12,6),FL(12,6),O(6) : REM FOR FREQUEN-
    CIES AND OCTAVE DIVIDER
430 FOR J=0 TO 6 : O(J)=2*J : NEXT J
440 FOR I=1 TO 12 : FOR J=0 TO 6
450 FR=F(I)/O(J) : FH(I,J)=INT(FR/BY) : FL(I,J)=FR-
    BY*FH(I,J)
460 NEXT J,I
490 S = 1 : REM TEMPO CONSTANT


500 READ TM : T=TI+S*TM : REM READ EVENT DURATION, AND
    SET TIME VALUE
510 IF TM=Z THEN 9999 : REM DONE IF TM=0
520 IF TM<Z THEN 9999 : REM DONE IF TM<0
530 :
540 READ N1,O1,N2,O2,N3,O3 : REM NOTE AND OCTAVE #'S
550 REM RELEASE BEGINS HERE
560 IF N1 THEN POKE W1,N(1)
570 IF N2 THEN POKE W2,N(2)
580 IF N3 THEN POKE W3,N(3)
590 REM ATTACK BEGINS HERE
600 IF N1 >Z THEN POKE F1,FL(N1,O1):POKE F1+W,
    FH(N1,O1) : POKE W1,N(1)+W
610 IF N2 >Z THEN POKE F2,FL(N2,O2):POKE F2+W,
    FH(N2,O2) : POKE W2,N(2)+W
620 IF N3 >Z THEN POKE F3,FL(N3,O3) : POKE F3+W,
    FH(N3,O3) : POKE W3,N(3)+W
630 :
```

```
640 IF TI>T THEN 500 : REM GET MORE DATA
650 GOTO 640 : REM WAIT FOR TIMER
```

This is slightly different in style from our previous music program. We gave variable names to our most heavily used constants—256, 1,0, and −1—in order to gain speed, since BASIC doesn't have to repeatedly make conversions. We also *pre*calculated the octave divisors into array O(I), and the entire frequency table in FH(I,J) and FL(I,J). (You should delete the REMarks and extra spaces from your working version.) Speed is more critical now since 3 sets of parameters have to be installed into SID instead of one, and of course the ear is very sensitive to timing differences when three sounds are supposed to sound simultaneously. As before, you should definitely SAVE this piece of the program (call it SIDMUSIC3 if you want to) before proceeding.

Now enter this set of DATA statements:

```
800 DATA 40,04,2,04,1,00,0
810 DATA 40,06,2,03,1,00,0
820 DATA 40,08,2,01,2,00,0
830 DATA 40,09,2,11,2,00,0
840 DATA 40,11,2,09,2,00,0
850 DATA 40,01,1,08,2,00,0
860 DATA 40,03,1,06,2,00,0
870 DATA 40,04,1,04,2,00,0
880 DATA 0

9999 FOR I=0 TO 28 : POKE SID+I,0 : NEXT I : END:REM
     SILENCE SID, WE'RE DONE
```

After you RUN this, you will see that the "events" here are very simple, since each of the two voices were synchronized, one playing a C-scale up, and the other playing it down. Now let's get just a little more complex, and you will see why we need the extra condition (IF N1>Z in the program).

```
800 DATA 40,04,2,04,1,00,0
810 DATA 40,06,2,00,0,00,0
820 DATA 40,08,2,01,2,00,0
830 DATA 40,09,2,00,0,00,0
840 DATA 40,11,2,09,2,00,0
850 DATA 40,01,1,00,0,00,0
860 DATA 40,03,1,06,2,00,0
870 DATA 40,04,1,00,0,00,0
```

The 0's for the note ID in the second voice means "don't do anything"; i.e., keep sustaining. So, we now have a series of ¼ notes in voice 1, playing against a series of ½ notes in voice 2. Do you see that playing a single ½ note is not the same as playing two ¼ notes? Remember, each time we "play" a note it goes into an attack mode. Try adding the following lines to make sure you understand the significance. (Delete line 880, first.)

```
900 DATA 40,04,2,04,1,00,0
910 DATA 40,06,2,04,1,00,0
920 DATA 40,08,2,01,2,00,0
930 DATA 40,09,2,01,2,00,0
940 DATA 40,11,2,09,2,00,0
950 DATA 40,01,1,09,2,00,0
960 DATA 40,03,1,06,2,00,0
970 DATA 40,04,1,06,2,00,0
980 DATA 0
```

Makes a difference, right? Now, suppose instead of wanting to play ¼ notes against ½ notes, we want to make the second voice to also play ¼ notes but with a ¼ "rest" in between? In our 1 voice program there was no provision for rests, in case you didn't already notice it. In music, rests are quite important even though, or better yet, because they force silence. To take care of this case, we are going to use −1 in our note code to indicate that we want that voice to release without immediately attacking. And that's why we needed the extra conditionals. So try the following to hear the effect.

```
900 DATA 40,04,2,04,1,00,0
910 DATA 40,06,2,-1,0,00,0
920 DATA 40,08,2,01,2,00,0
930 DATA 40,09,2,-1,0,00,0
940 DATA 40,11,2,09,2,00,0
950 DATA 40,01,1,-1,0,00,0
960 DATA 40,03,1,06,2,00,0
970 DATA 40,04,1,-1,0,00,0
980 DATA 0
```

Makes a difference, right? Now let's put it all together with some real music. What could be better suited to the 3-voice SID than a Bach 3-part Sinfonia? The first few measures of the Sinfonia #10 are reproduced below, so you can follow along with the encoding.

**Figure 13. Sample musical score**

Here's the program code for the first measure:

```
795 REM MEASURE 1
800 DATA 20,00,0,00,0,11,5
802 DATA 20,11,3,00,0,00,0
804 DATA 10,00,0,00,0,03,4
806 DATA 10,10,3,00,0,00,0
808 DATA 10,11,3,00,0,00,0
810 DATA 10,01,2,00,0,00,0
812 DATA 10,03,2,00,0,11,5
814 DATA 10,04,2,00,0,00,0
816 DATA 10,06,2,00,0,00,0
818 DATA 10,03,2,00,0,00,0
9997 DATA 0
```

Try RUNning this little bit before you continue the programming. I suggest you RUN and listen after entering each measure.

```
819 REM MEASURE 2
820 DATA 20,08,2,00,0,04,4
822 DATA 20,06,2,00,0,00,0
824 DATA 20,04,2,00,0,00,0
826 DATA 20,03,2,00,0,00,0
828 DATA 20,01,2,00,0,06,4
830 DATA 20,11,3,00,0,00,0
832 DATA 20,10,3,00,0,00,0
834 DATA 20,08,3,00,0,00,0
836 DATA 20,06,3,00,0,06,5
838 DATA 20,04,2,00,0,00,0
840 DATA 20,03,2,00,0,00,0
842 DATA 20,01,2,00,0,00,0
```

Voice 2 still hasn't made its appearance yet, but will in the following measure; event structure like measure 1:

```
844 REM MEASURE 3
846 DATA 40,03,2,00,0,11,5
848 DATA 40,00,0,06,3,00,0
850 DATA 20,00,0,00,0,11,4
852 DATA 20,01,2,05,3,00,0
854 DATA 20,03,2,06,3,00,0
856 DATA 20,05,2,08,3,00,0
858 DATA 20,06,2,10,3,10,4
860 DATA 20,00,0,11,3,00,0
862 DATA 20,00,0,01,2,00,0
864 DATA 20,00,0,10,3,00,0
866 REM MEASURE 4
868 DATA 10,00,0,03,2,11,4
870 DATA 10,00,0,01,2,00,0
872 DATA 10,00,0,11,3,00,0
```

```
874 DATA 10,00,0,10,3,00,0
876 DATA 10,00,0,08,3,01,3
878 DATA 10,00,0,06,3,00,0
880 DATA 10,00,0,05,3,00,0
882 DATA 10,00,0,03,3,00,0
884 DATA 10,05,2,01,3,01,4
886 DATA 10,00,0,11,3,00,0
888 DATA 10,00,0,10,3,00,0
890 DATA 10,00,0,08,3,00,0
```

Notice the forced rest (−1,0) for voice 3 in the 5th event of the following measure

```
892 REM MEASURE 5
894 DATA 10,06,2,10,3,06,4
896 DATA 10,00,0,01,3,00,0
898 DATA 10,00,0,03,3,00,0
900 DATA 10,00,0,05,3,00,0
902 DATA 10,00,0,06,3,-1,0
904 DATA 10,05,2,08,3,00,0
906 DATA 10,06,2,10,3,00,0
908 DATA 10,08,2,11,3,00,0
910 DATA 10,10,2,01,2,00,0
912 DATA 10,11,2,03,2,00,0
914 DATA 10,01,1,04,2,00,0
916 DATA 10,10,2,01,2,00,0
918 REM MEASURE 6
920 DATA 10,03,1,06,2,00,0
922 DATA 10,01,1,00,0,00,0
924 DATA 10,11,2,03,2,00,0
926 DATA 10,10,2,00,0,00,0
928 DATA 10,08,2,11,3,00,0
930 DATA 10,06,2,00,0,00,0
932 DATA 10,04,2,08,3,00,0
934 DATA 10,03,2,00,0,00,0
936 DATA 10,04,2,01,2,00,0
938 DATA 10,11,2,00,0,00,0
940 DATA 10,10,2,00,0,00,0
942 DATA 10,08,2,00,0,00,0
```

Voice 3 comes back again in the following measure, and picks up the theme.

```
944 REM MEASURE 7
946 DATA 10,06,2,00,0,00,0
948 DATA 10,00,0,04,2,00,0
950 DATA 10,00,0,03,2,11,4
952 DATA 10,00,0,01,2,00,0
954 DATA 10,00,0,03,2,00,0
```

```
956 DATA 10,06,2,00,0,10,4
958 DATA 10,08,2,00,0,11,4
960 DATA 10,09,2,00,0,01,3
962 DATA 10,11,2,00,0,03,3
964 DATA 10,00,0,01,2,04,3
966 DATA 10,00,0,03,2,06,3
968 DATA 10,00,0,11,3,03,3
```

Makes you feel like continuing, doesn't it? I hope you've got the hang of it. Try changing the nature of the voices, and adjust the tempo until it suits you. A few suggestions—in "live" music the durations cannot be precise (nor should they be, else you will get an "organ grinder" effect). You can get a more "human" sound if you vary the duration values by slowly increasing, then decreasing the duration values. That's one of the reasons we chose this particular way of coding—it doesn't restrict you to exact ⅛, ¼, etc., durations—even though we didn't do it in our example. (Some composers will give you specific instructions on tempo changes; *rit.* for retard; *acc.* for accelerate; *a tempo for* "go back to original tempo;" and others.) You should also try your hand at programming more convenient ways of encoding the music and ways of SAVEing just the DATA. (Hint—you can READ the data, then PRINT # to tape or disk and INPUT # when you want it back.) Another suggestion for advanced programmers and/or musicians: Try experimenting with different temperaments, or other than 12-tone scales.

## Sounds from Hyperspace

This section is fun. You can't go wrong with sound effects, since *you* decide what the "rules" are. One of the most versatile sound effect features of SID is the noise waveform, which hasn't been used yet. Although it is true that noise does not have a definite pitch, it does have "coloration" which can be controlled. SID creates noise by outputting random numbers as its "waveform," but the rate at which it does this depends on what has been stored in the frequency register. At low rates, the noise will sound "staticky," at high rates "hissy." The quality can be 250 : further controlled by the filter (which we haven't used yet), and of course, a voice used with noise still has controllable ADSR. So let's put some of these into effect. LOAD in the opening program (lines 100-190) to define some of the SID addresses.

```
100 POKE VOL,15 : REM SET VOLUME TO MAXIMUM
110 WV=128 : REM NOISE WAVEFORM
120 AT=1 : REM ATTACK RATE
130 DE=8 : REM DECAY RATE
140 SU=8 : REM SUSTAIN AMPLITUDE
150 RE=10 : REM RELEASE RATE
160 FRQ=1000 : REM FREQUENCY IN HZ
170 TM=6 : REM TIME IN SECONDS
180 :
```

```
190 FR=FR*C : FH=INT(FR/256) : FL=FR-256*FH : REM GET
    HIGH AND LOW BYTE
200 TI$="000000" : TM=TM*60 : REM TIME IN JIFFIES
210 :
220 POKE A1,16*AT+DE : REM INSTALL ATTACK/DECAY RATES
230 POKE S1,16*SU+RE : REM INSTALL SUSTAIN AMPLITUDE
    AND RELEASE RATE
240 POKE F1,FL : POKE F1+1,FH : REM INSTALL FREQUENCY
250 :
260 T=TI+TM : POKE W1,WV+1 : REM START THE SOUND
270 IF TI<T THEN 270 : REM KEEP NOTE GOING
280 POKE W1,WV : REM RELEASE
```

RUN this repeatedly, first trying out different values for FRQ (cannot be higher than 3900 Hz), then with different numbers for AT, DE, SU, and RE. (Note that if TM is too small, the release happens before the sustain is reached, which can give you the effect of controlling the volume.) Try both very low frequencies (around 20 Hz) as well as very high frequencies (around 3000 Hz). With fast attack (AT=0), and no sustain (SU=0) you can get gunshots, door slams, footsteps, and various "impulse" type sounds. With medium attack and decay, medium sustain amplitudes, and long releases, you can get wind, surf, distant explosions, thunder and other types of "rushing sounds."

There are also filters inside the SID which let you "color" the sounds produced by the chip. The use of the filters can be complicated, especially programming SID from BASIC. You can, however, study the following sound effect examples and change the numbers POKEd into the registers for the filter that we haven't discussed. As the names suggest, the high pass filter allows only frequencies higher than the resonance frequency to pass through; the low pass filter allows only frequencies lower than the resonance frequency to pass through; and the band pass filter allows only frequencies somewhat above and below the resonance frequency to pass through.

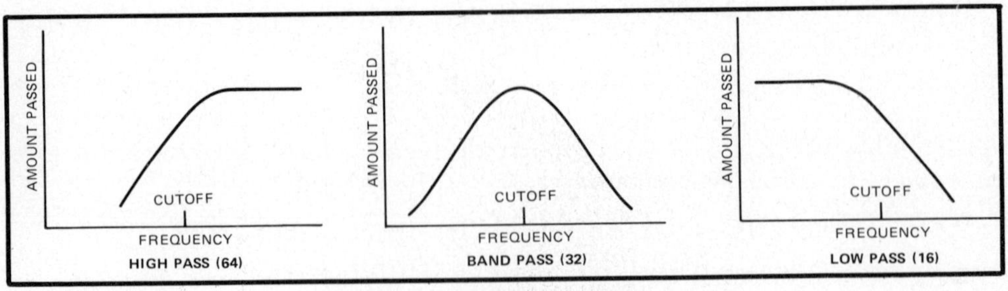


**Figure 14. Filter modes**

To play with the filter, add the following lines to the sound effect above:

```
172 MODE = 32 : REM FILTER MODE
174 RS =15 : REM FULL RESONANCE
176 RFRQ=10000 : REM FILTER FREQUENCY
```

```
178 RF =(RFRQ-30)/5.8:RH = INT(RF/8):RL=RF-8*RH :
    REM RESONANCE FREQUENCY

242 POKE SID+23,16*RS+1 : REM INSTALL RESONANCE,
    CONNECT VOICE 1 TO FILTER
244 POKE SID+21,RH : POKE SID+22,RL : REM INSTALL
    FILTER FREQUENCY
246 POKE VOL,MO + 15 : REM INSTALL FILTER MODE,
    VOLUME TO MAXIMUM
```

RUN this, experimenting with MODE (line 172), values 64 (high pass), 32 (band-pass), and 16 (low pass). Also, check out the effects of changing FRQ (line 160) and RFRQ (line 176). You will find that, in general, the overall volume is diminished, since the filter in many cases removes a lot of the "energy" in the sound. Also experiment, of course, with the attack/decay and sustain/release values.

The full effect of the filter can better be heard by changing its resonance frequency while the sound is sustaining. You can do this simply by changing/adding the following lines:

```
270 ML=1.1 : REM FACTOR WHICH CHANGES RESONANCE
    FREQUENCY
280 E=8:W=1:HI=2000:LO=500 : REM CONSTANTS TO
    SPEED COMPUTATIONS
290 IF TI>TM THEN 360 : STOP WHEN TIMER EXCEEDS TM
300 RF=RF*ML
310 IF RF>HI AND ML>W THEN ML=W/ML : RF = RF*ML : REM
    MAKES RF REVERSE
320 IF RF<LO AND ML<W THEN ML=W/ML : RF = RF*ML
330 RH = INT(RF/E) : RL = RF - E*RH : REM CALCULATE
    LOW, HIGH PARTS
340 POKE SID+21,RL : POKE SID+22 RH : REM INSTALL
    RESONANCE FREQUENCY
350 GOTO 300
360 POKE W1,WV : REM GO INTO RELEASE PHASE
```

Now you have some filter dynamics to play with. Try changing ML (line 270) which controls the rate of the filter frequency sweep. SAVE this program, called SIDNOISE.

You probably already guessed that not only can noise be "tailored" by the filter, but so can the other waveform types. You will find that the sawtooth and pulse waveforms are the best ones to use since they are rich in harmonics, and are therefore most affected by filtering. So try the effect of WV=64 and WV=32 in our previous program.

Finally, here is a set of sound effects that illustrate many of the principles we have been discussing. As usual, I assume you have our opening program (lines 10-90) already LOADed in. The title and REMs should be sufficient for you to figure out what is going on, and you can experiment liberally.

GUNSHOT

```
100 POKE F1,200 : POKE F1+1,40 : REM FREQUENCY, VOICE 1
110 POKE A1,0+15 : REM FAST ATTACK, SLOW DECAY
120 POKE S1,0 : REM NO SUSTAIN, FAST RELEASE
130 FOR I = 15 TO 0 STEP -1 : REM 15 STEPS
140 POKE W1,128+1 : REM NOISE WAVEFORM  FOR VOICE 1, START ATTACK
150 POKE VOL,I : REM DYNAMIC VOLUME IS OK FOR NOISE WAVEFORM
160 NEXT I
170 POKE W1,0 : REM RELEASE VOICE 1
```

DOLL CRYING

```
100 POKE VOL,15 : REM VOLUME TO MAXIMUM
110 POKE A1,15 : REM FAST ATTACK, SLOW DECAY
120 POKE S1,0 : REM NO SUSTAIN, FAST RELEASE
130 POKE F1+1,40 REM FREQ. HIGH FOR VOICE 1 DOESN'T CHANGE
140 POKE W1,32+1 : REM SAWTOOTH WAVEFORM FOR VOICE 1, START ATTACK
150 FOR I = 200 TO 5 STEP -2 : REM FREQUENCY SWEEP DOWN
160 POKE F1,I : REM SWEEP FREQUENCY LOW
170 NEXT I
180 FOR I = 150 TO 5 STEP -2 : REM SECOND FREQUENCY SWEEP
190 POKE F1,I
200 NEXT I
210 POKE W1,0 : RELEASE VOICE 1
```

VIBRATO

```
100 POKE SID+3,4 : REM 25% PULSE WIDTH
110 POKE A1,2*16+9 : POKE S1,5*16+9 : REM SET ADSR FOR VOICE 1
```

```
120 POKE F3,120 : REM FREQ. FOR VOICE 3 IS 7.5 HZ
130 POKE W3,16 : REM TRIANGLE WAVEFORM FOR VOIC 3
140 POKE VOL,128+15 : REM VOICE 3 DISCONNECTED, MAXIMUM VOLUME
150 READ FR,DR : REM READ FREQUENCY, DURATION
160 IF FR=0 THEN END
170 POKE W1,64+1 : REM VOICE 1 ATTACK
180 FOR T = 1 TO DR*3 : REM # OF CYCLES
190 FQ = FR+PEEK(SID+27)/2 : REM READ VOICE 3 OUTPUT, ADJUST
    FREQUENCY
200 FH = INT(FQ/256) : FL = FQ AND 255 : REM FREQUENCY HIGH, LOW
210 POKE F1,FL : POKE F1+1,FH
220 NEXT T
230 POKE W1,64 : REM RELEASE VOICE 1
240 GOTO 150 : REM GO FOR MORE DATA
250 :
260 DATA 4817,2,5103,2,5407,2
270 DATA 8583,4,5407,2,8583,4
280 DATA 5407,4,8583,12,9634,2
290 DATA 10207,2,10814,2,8583,2
300 DATA 9634,4,10814,2,8583,2
310 DATA 9634,4,8583,12
320 DATA 0,0
```

SIREN

```
100 R3 = SID+27 : REM V3 READ
110 BYTE=256 : K = 3.5 : REM CONSTANTS
```

```
111 POKE F3,5 : REM V3 FREQUENCY 1/3 HZ
112 POKE W3,16 : REM V3 IS TRIANGLE
120 POKE F1+3,2 : REM 12% V1 DUTY CYCLE
130 POKE VOL,128+15 : REM V3 OFF, VOLUME SET TO MAXIMUM
140 POKE S1,15*16+0 : REM V1 MAXIMUM SUSTAAIN, FAST RELEASE
150 POKE A1,0 : REM V1 FAST ATTACK, FAST DECAY
160 POKE W1,64+1 : REM V1 ATTACK WITH PULSE WAVEFORM
170 FR = 7000 : REM V1 FREQ = 440 HZ
180 FOR T = 1 TO 400 : REM FREQ. SWEEP
190 FQ = FR + K* PEEK(R3) : ADJUST FREQUENCY
200 FH = INT(FQ/BY) : FL = FQ-BY*FH
210 POKE F1,FL : POKE F1+1,FH : REM INSTALL NEW FREQUENCY
220 NEXT T
230 POKE W1,0 : RELEASE VOICE 1
```

HAMMERING

```
100 RF = SID+23 : REM RESONANCE/FILTER
110 FC = SID+21 : REM FILTER CUT-OFF
120 POKE F1+1,30 : REM V1 FREQ = 480 HZ
130 POKE A1,0+6 : REM V1 FAST ATTACK, MEDIUM DECAY
140 POKE S1,0 : REM V1 NO SUSTAIN, FAST RELEASE
150 POKE FC+1,150 : REM FILTER FREQ.
160 POKE RF,0+1 : REM NO RESONANCE, V1 CONNECTED TO FILTER
170 POKE VOL,64+15 : REM HIGH-PASS MODE, MAXIMUM VOLUME
180 FOR I = 1 TO 15 : REM # OF CLAPS
190 POKE W1,128+1 : REM ATTACK WITH V1 NOISE
200 FOR J = 1 TO 200 : NEXT J : REM DELAY
210 POKE W1,128 : REM RELEASE V1
```

```
220 FOR J = 1 TO 100 : NEXT J : REM DELAY
230 NEXT I
240 END
```

MOSQUITO

```
100 POKE F1+1,100 : REM V1 FREQ. 1600 HZ
110 POKE A1,13*16+13 : REM V1 SLOW ATTACK, SLOW DECAY
120 POKE S1,0 : REM V1 NO SUSTAIN, FAST RELEASE
130 POKE F3+1,28 : REM V3 FREQ. 450 HZ
140 POKE VOL,15 : REM MAXIMUM VOLUME
150 POKE W1,16+2+1 : REM V1 IS TRIANGLE, SYNC WITH V3, ATTACK
160 FOR I = 1 TO 5000 : NEXT I : REM DELAY
170 POKE W1,16+2 : REM RELEASE VOICE 1
180 FOR I = 1 TO 1000 : NEXT I : REM DELAY
190 POKE W1,0 :REM RELEASE V1
200 END
```

CLOCK CHIME

```
100 POKE F1+1,130 : REM V1 FREQ = 2000 HZ
110 POKE A1,0+9 : REM V1 FAST ATTACK/MEDIUM DECAY
120 POKE F3+1,30 : REM V3 FREQ = 480 HZ
130 POKE VOL,15 : REM MAXIMUM VOLUME
140 FOR I = 1 TO 12 : REM 12 CHIMES
150 POKE W1,16+4+1 : REM V1 IS TRIANGLE, RING MODULATE WITH
    V3, ATTACK
160 FOR J = 1 TO 500 : NEXT J : REM DELAY
170 POKE W1,16+4 : REM RELEASE V1
```

```
180 FOR J = 1 TO 100 : NEXT J : REM DELAY
190 NEXT I : REM NEXT CHIME
200 POKE W1,0 : REM RELEASE V1
210 END
```

# Appendix 4

# Error Messages

*****************************************************************

ERROR ERROR ERROR ERROR ERROR ERROR ERROR ERROR ERROR

**BAD SUBSCRIPT ERROR**

A bad subscript is just what its name implies—a subscript number too big for the size of the array DIMensioned. If a DIMension line reads DIM A$(100), for instance, there can be no variable named A$(101). This ERROR also happens when no DIM statement is used at all and variables with subscript numbers larger than 11 are used. Check variables used as subscripts for the problem.

*****************************************************************

*****************************************************************

ERROR ERROR ERROR ERROR ERROR ERROR ERROR ERROR ERROR

**CAN'T CONTINUE ERROR**

CONT can be used to continue a program after the RUN/STOP key was pressed or the word STOP was used. If you change any line in the program during a break, however, the above ERROR will appear. It will also be seen when the program has not been RUN at all. In either case, RUN the program (again).

*****************************************************************

****************************************************************
ERROR ERROR ERROR ERROR ERROR ERROR ERROR ERROR ERROR

**EXTRA IGNORED**

This is really an ERROR that you cannot correct, and happens when your answer to an INPUT statement contains a comma where one does not belong. Commas are used by the Commodore computers as special characters. The only time that they are allowed within an answer to INPUT is when the program is looking for several answers at once. Like this:

```
10 INPUT A$,B$,C$
```

Commas in strings will also cause problems when they are stored and recalled to and from disk information files.

****************************************************************

****************************************************************
ERROR ERROR ERROR ERROR ERROR ERROR ERROR ERROR ERROR

**FILE NOT FOUND**

This message will appear if you try to LOAD a program or file from disk that does not exist. If you are sure that you have the program, check the disk directory to see if it is on that particular disk, or check your spelling. The disk drive expects absolute accuracy when asking for a program by name. Avoid this ERROR by using an asterisk for pattern matching purposes.

****************************************************************

****************************************************************
ERROR ERROR ERROR ERROR ERROR ERROR ERROR ERROR ERROR

**FILE NOT OPEN ERROR**
**FILE OPEN ERROR**

When using data-handling words PRINT#, INPUT# and GET#, you must first OPEN a file, otherwise a FILE NOT OPEN ERROR will occur. This also happens with CMD, a word used to transfer information meant to be PRINTed on the video screen to a printer or disk drive, is used without OPENing the correct file, and with the word CLOSE, as well. FILE OPEN ERRORs will be seen when you try to OPEN a file that has been OPENed but not CLOSEd. Always check the file sequence to make sure the file is CLOSEd after use.

****************************************************************

************************************************************
ERROR ERROR ERROR ERROR ERROR ERROR ERROR ERROR ERROR

**ILLEGAL DIRECT**

While many BASIC words can be typed directly from the keyboard and used outside a program, INPUT cannot. This is logical, considering its use.

************************************************************

************************************************************
ERROR ERROR ERROR ERROR ERROR ERROR ERROR ERROR ERROR

**ILLEGAL QUANTITY ERROR**

When this ERROR occurs in a program line with a POKE statement, check to see that no number greater than 255 or less than 0 (zero) is being put into a location in memory. If variables are used, check the numbers they stand for to see if they were calculated to greater than 255 or less than 0.

************************************************************

************************************************************
ERROR ERROR ERROR ERROR ERROR ERROR ERROR ERROR ERROR

**ILLEGAL QUANTITY ERROR**

Integer variables are recognized by the percent sign ('%'). If this ERROR occurs in a line with an integer variable, check to see that the variable does not stand for a number greater than 32767 or less than −32768. If the ERROR is not in a line with an integer variable, check for problems with POKE.

************************************************************

************************************************************
ERROR ERROR ERROR ERROR ERROR ERROR ERROR ERROR ERROR

**NEXT WITHOUT FOR ERROR**

Using the word NEXT without opening a loop with FOR produces this message. This will also happen if NEXT is used with the wrong variable.

```
10 FOR I=1 TO 10
20 NEXT K
```

No ERROR message will be given if the reverse happens—FOR is used without NEXT. Instead, the loop will simply not continue as it should.

************************************************************

*************************************************************

ERROR ERROR ERROR ERROR ERROR ERROR ERROR ERROR ERROR

**NOT INPUT FILE ERROR**
**NOT OUTPUT FILE ERROR**

Cassette tape files are OPENed as either INPUT or OUTPUT files, depending on their secondary address. An address of 1 means that the tape file is OPENed for recording information to it. You cannot use INPUT# or GET#, or the first ERROR will be seen. If no secondary address number is used with the cassette recorder, the computer assumes that information will be recalled from it. Using PRINT# will produce the second ERROR message.

*************************************************************

*************************************************************

ERROR ERROR ERROR ERROR ERROR ERROR ERROR ERROR ERROR

**OUT OF DATA**

Count the number of pieces of information in DATA statements, then check to see how many times the program uses READ. (One way is to look for FOR/NEXT loops with READ in them.) Check the DATA statements in the program LISTing you are entering from, or compare the information used to prepare the DATA statements.

*************************************************************

*************************************************************

ERROR ERROR ERROR ERROR ERROR ERROR ERROR ERROR ERROR

**OVERFLOW ERROR**

This ERROR occurs when you attempt to work with the largest number that the computer can use, 1.70141884E+38, or the number multipled by 1 followed by 38 zeroes. The solution (not always possible) is to break up your calculations so that this number is never achieved.

*************************************************************

*************************************************************

ERROR ERROR ERROR ERROR ERROR ERROR ERROR ERROR ERROR

**REDIM'D ARRAY ERROR**

DIM can be used only once to create an array of a variable. Once that array is created, it cannot be DIMensioned again, or reDIMensioned. This will occur primarily when editing programs or trying to link two programs with DIM statements in them together.

*************************************************************

**************************************************************
ERROR ERROR ERROR ERROR ERROR ERROR ERROR ERROR ERROR

## REDO FROM START

This message appears whenever you answer an INPUT statement with a string, when it expects a number. Correct the situation by answering with a number.

**************************************************************

**************************************************************
ERROR ERROR ERROR ERROR ERROR ERROR ERROR ERROR ERROR

## RETURN WITHOUT GOSUB

GOSUB and RETURN work together. This message will appear if a program encounters RETURN without being told to GOSUB. It is most often seen when a program line is called with GOTO instead.

**************************************************************

**************************************************************
ERROR ERROR ERROR ERROR ERROR ERROR ERROR ERROR ERROR

## STRING TOO LONG ERROR

Strings can only be 255 characters long. String ERRORs are likely to occur when you concatenate, or add, one string to another. Check the length of each string when looking for the source of this ERROR.

**************************************************************

**************************************************************
ERROR ERROR ERROR ERROR ERROR ERROR ERROR ERROR ERROR

## SYNTAX ERROR

Syntax ERRORs can be caused by dozens of problems, but all are associated with BASIC "grammar." The most common problems are misspellings and missing punctuation marks, paricularly colons (':') and commas (','). Also look for use of semicolons (';') in place of colons, and make certain parentheses are closed. Check the rules for use of problem words.

**************************************************************

*****************************************************************
ERROR ERROR ERROR ERROR ERROR ERROR ERROR ERROR ERROR

**TYPE MISMATCH ERROR**

This kind of ERROR is always caused by trying to put a character into a numeric variable or an actual number into a string variable. Strings and numbers don't mix. Trouble statements look like this:

```
10 A$=9 (or) A$=A
```

or

```
10 A="EXAMPLE" (or) A=A$
```

*****************************************************************

*****************************************************************
ERROR ERROR ERROR ERROR ERROR ERROR ERROR ERROR ERROR

**UNDEFINED STATEMENT ERROR**

You must use GOSUB and GOTO with line numbers that are actually used in the program. This ERROR often happens when you edit programs or change line numbers and forget to change the GOTO and GOSUB statements that refer to them. Check line numbers in which the ERROR occurs, then try to LIST that line. Since RUN can also be used with line numbers, UNDEFINED STATEMENT ERRORs can occur this way, too.

*****************************************************************

# Appendix 5

# ASCII/CHR$ Codes & Base Conversion Table

| PRINTS | CHR$ | PRINTS | CHR$ | PRINTS | CHR$ | PRINTS | CHR$ |
|---|---|---|---|---|---|---|---|
| | 0 | CRSR ↓ | 17 | " | 34 | 3 | 51 |
| | 1 | RVS ON | 18 | # | 35 | 4 | 52 |
| | 2 | CLR HOME | 19 | $ | 36 | 5 | 53 |
| | 3 | INST DEL | 20 | % | 37 | 6 | 54 |
| | 4 | | 21 | & | 38 | 7 | 55 |
| WHT | 5 | | 22 | • | 39 | 8 | 56 |
| | 6 | | 23 | ( | 40 | 9 | 57 |
| | 7 | | 24 | ) | 41 | : | 58 |
| DISABLES SHIFT C= | 8 | | 25 | * | 42 | ; | 59 |
| ENABLES SHIFT C= | 9 | | 26 | + | 43 | < | 60 |
| | 10 | | 27 | , | 44 | = | 61 |
| | 11 | RED | 28 | – | 45 | > | 62 |
| | 12 | CRSR → | 29 | . | 46 | ? | 63 |
| RETURN | 13 | GRN | 30 | / | 47 | @ | 64 |
| SWITCH TO LOWER CASE | 14 | BLU | 31 | 0 | 48 | A | 65 |
| | 15 | SPACE | 32 | 1 | 49 | B | 66 |
| | 16 | ! | 33 | 2 | 50 | C | 67 |

| PRINTS | CHR$ | PRINTS | CHR$ | PRINTS | CHR$ | PRINTS | CHR$ |
|---|---|---|---|---|---|---|---|
| D | 68 | | 99 | | 130 | | 161 |
| E | 69 | | 100 | | 131 | | 162 |
| F | 70 | | 101 | | 132 | | 163 |
| G | 71 | | 102 | f1 | 133 | | 164 |
| H | 72 | | 103 | f3 | 134 | | 165 |
| I | 73 | | 104 | f5 | 135 | | 166 |
| J | 74 | | 105 | f7 | 136 | | 167 |
| K | 75 | | 106 | f2 | 137 | | 168 |
| L | 76 | | 107 | f4 | 138 | | 169 |
| M | 77 | | 108 | f6 | 139 | | 170 |
| N | 78 | | 109 | f8 | 140 | | 171 |
| O | 79 | | 110 | SHIFT RETURN | 141 | | 172 |
| P | 80 | | 111 | SWITCH TO UPPER CASE | 142 | | 173 |
| Q | 81 | | 112 | | 143 | | 174 |
| R | 82 | ● | 113 | BLK | 144 | | 175 |
| S | 83 | | 114 | CRSR | 145 | | 176 |
| T | 84 | ♥ | 115 | RVS OFF | 146 | | 177 |
| U | 85 | | 116 | CLR HOME | 147 | | 178 |
| V | 86 | | 117 | INST DEL | 148 | | 179 |
| W | 87 | | 118 | Brown | 149 | | 180 |
| X | 88 | | 119 | Lt. Red | 150 | | 181 |
| Y | 89 | ♣ | 120 | Grey 1 | 151 | | 182 |
| Z | 90 | | 121 | Grey 2 | 152 | | 183 |
| [ | 91 | ♦ | 122 | Lt. Green | 153 | | 184 |
| £ | 92 | | 123 | Lt. Blue | 154 | | 185 |
| ] | 93 | | 124 | Grey 3 | 155 | | 186 |
| ↑ | 94 | | 125 | PUR | 156 | | 187 |
| ← | 95 | | 126 | CRSR | 157 | | 188 |
| | 96 | | 127 | YEL | 158 | | 189 |
| ♠ | 97 | | 128 | CYN | 159 | | 190 |
| | 98 | Orange | 129 | SPACE | 160 | | 191 |

192 to 223 = 96 to 127
224 to 254 = 160 to 190
255 = 126

## *BASE CONVERSION TABLE*

| *BIN* | *DEC* | *HEX* | *BIN* | *DEC* | *HEX* |
|---|---|---|---|---|---|
| 0 | 0 | 00 | 110101 | 53 | 35 |
| 1 | 1 | 01 | 110110 | 54 | 36 |
| 10 | 2 | 02 | 110111 | 55 | 37 |
| 11 | 3 | 03 | 111000 | 56 | 38 |
| 100 | 4 | 04 | 111001 | 57 | 39 |
| 101 | 5 | 05 | 111010 | 58 | 3A |
| 110 | 6 | 06 | 111011 | 59 | 3B |
| 111 | 7 | 07 | 111100 | 60 | 3C |
| 1000 | 8 | 08 | 111101 | 61 | 3D |
| 1001 | 9 | 09 | 111110 | 62 | 3E |
| 1010 | 10 | 0A | 111111 | 63 | 3F |
| 1011 | 11 | 0B | 1000000 | 64 | 40 |
| 1100 | 12 | 0C | 1000001 | 65 | 41 |
| 1101 | 13 | 0D | 1000010 | 66 | 42 |
| 1110 | 14 | 0E | 1000011 | 67 | 43 |
| 1111 | 15 | 0F | 1000100 | 68 | 44 |
| 10000 | 16 | 10 | 1000101 | 69 | 45 |
| 10001 | 17 | 11 | 1000110 | 70 | 46 |
| 10010 | 18 | 12 | 1000111 | 71 | 47 |
| 10011 | 19 | 13 | 1001000 | 72 | 48 |
| 10100 | 20 | 14 | 1001001 | 73 | 49 |
| 10101 | 21 | 15 | 1001010 | 74 | 4A |
| 10110 | 22 | 16 | 1001011 | 75 | 4B |
| 10111 | 23 | 17 | 1001100 | 76 | 4C |
| 11000 | 24 | 18 | 1001101 | 77 | 4D |
| 11001 | 25 | 19 | 1001110 | 78 | 4E |
| 11010 | 26 | 1A | 1001111 | 79 | 4F |
| 11011 | 27 | 1B | 1010000 | 80 | 50 |
| 11100 | 28 | 1C | 1010001 | 81 | 51 |
| 11101 | 29 | 1D | 1010010 | 82 | 52 |
| 11110 | 30 | 1E | 1010011 | 83 | 53 |
| 11111 | 31 | 1F | 1010100 | 84 | 54 |
| 100000 | 32 | 20 | 1010101 | 85 | 55 |
| 100001 | 33 | 21 | 1010110 | 86 | 56 |
| 100010 | 34 | 22 | 1010111 | 87 | 57 |
| 100011 | 35 | 23 | 1011000 | 88 | 58 |
| 100100 | 36 | 24 | 1011001 | 89 | 59 |
| 100101 | 37 | 25 | 1011010 | 90 | 5A |
| 100110 | 38 | 26 | 1011011 | 91 | 5B |
| 100111 | 39 | 27 | 1011100 | 92 | 5C |
| 101000 | 40 | 28 | 1011101 | 93 | 5D |
| 101001 | 41 | 29 | 1011110 | 94 | 5E |
| 101010 | 42 | 2A | 1011111 | 95 | 5F |
| 101011 | 43 | 2B | 1100000 | 96 | 60 |
| 101100 | 44 | 2C | 1100001 | 97 | 61 |
| 101101 | 45 | 2D | 1100010 | 98 | 62 |
| 101110 | 46 | 2E | 1100011 | 99 | 63 |
| 101111 | 47 | 2F | 1100100 | 100 | 64 |
| 110000 | 48 | 30 | 1100101 | 101 | 65 |
| 110001 | 49 | 31 | 1100110 | 102 | 66 |
| 110010 | 50 | 32 | 1100111 | 103 | 67 |
| 110011 | 51 | 33 | 1101000 | 104 | 68 |
| 110100 | 52 | 34 | 1101001 | 105 | 69 |

**BASE CONVERSION TABLE (Continued)**

| *BIN* | *DEC* | *HEX* | *BIN* | *DEC* | *HEX* |
|---|---|---|---|---|---|
| 1101010 | 106 | 6A | 10011111 | 159 | 9F |
| 1101011 | 107 | 6B | 10100000 | 160 | A0 |
| 1101100 | 108 | 6C | 10100001 | 161 | A1 |
| 1101101 | 109 | 6D | 10100010 | 162 | A2 |
| 1101110 | 110 | 6E | 10100011 | 163 | A3 |
| 1101111 | 111 | 6F | 10100100 | 164 | A4 |
| 1110000 | 112 | 70 | 10100101 | 165 | A5 |
| 1110001 | 113 | 71 | 10100110 | 166 | A6 |
| 1110010 | 114 | 72 | 10100111 | 167 | A7 |
| 1110011 | 115 | 73 | 10101000 | 168 | A8 |
| 1110100 | 116 | 74 | 10101001 | 169 | A9 |
| 1110101 | 117 | 75 | 10101010 | 170 | AA |
| 1110110 | 118 | 76 | 10101011 | 171 | AB |
| 1110111 | 119 | 77 | 10101100 | 172 | AC |
| 1111000 | 120 | 78 | 10101101 | 173 | AD |
| 1111001 | 121 | 79 | 10101110 | 174 | AE |
| 1111010 | 122 | 7A | 10101111 | 175 | AF |
| 1111011 | 123 | 7B | 10110000 | 176 | B0 |
| 1111100 | 124 | 7C | 10110001 | 177 | B1 |
| 1111101 | 125 | 7D | 10110010 | 178 | B2 |
| 1111110 | 126 | 7E | 10110011 | 179 | B3 |
| 1111111 | 127 | 7F | 10110100 | 180 | B4 |
| 10000000 | 128 | 80 | 10110101 | 181 | B5 |
| 10000001 | 129 | 81 | 10110110 | 182 | B6 |
| 10000010 | 130 | 82 | 10110111 | 183 | B7 |
| 10000011 | 131 | 83 | 10111000 | 184 | B8 |
| 10000100 | 132 | 84 | 10111001 | 185 | B9 |
| 10000101 | 133 | 85 | 10111010 | 186 | BA |
| 10000110 | 134 | 86 | 10111011 | 187 | BB |
| 10000111 | 135 | 87 | 10111100 | 188 | BC |
| 10001000 | 136 | 88 | 10111101 | 189 | BD |
| 10001001 | 137 | 89 | 10111110 | 190 | BE |
| 10001010 | 138 | 8A | 10111111 | 191 | BF |
| 10001011 | 139 | 8B | 11000000 | 192 | C0 |
| 10001100 | 140 | 8C | 11000001 | 193 | C1 |
| 10001101 | 141 | 8D | 11000010 | 194 | C2 |
| 10001110 | 142 | 8E | 11000011 | 195 | C3 |
| 10001111 | 143 | 8F | 11000100 | 196 | C4 |
| 10010000 | 144 | 90 | 11000101 | 197 | C5 |
| 10010001 | 145 | 91 | 11000110 | 198 | C6 |
| 10010010 | 146 | 92 | 11000111 | 199 | C7 |
| 10010011 | 147 | 93 | 11001000 | 200 | C8 |
| 10010100 | 148 | 94 | 11001001 | 201 | C9 |
| 10010101 | 149 | 95 | 11001010 | 202 | CA |
| 10010110 | 150 | 96 | 11001011 | 203 | CB |
| 10010111 | 151 | 97 | 11001100 | 204 | CC |
| 10011000 | 152 | 98 | 11001101 | 205 | CD |
| 10011001 | 153 | 99 | 11001110 | 206 | CE |
| 10011010 | 154 | 9A | 11001111 | 207 | CF |
| 10011011 | 155 | 9B | 11010000 | 208 | D0 |
| 10011100 | 156 | 9C | 11010001 | 209 | D1 |
| 10011101 | 157 | 9D | 11010010 | 210 | D2 |
| 10011110 | 158 | 9E | 11010011 | 211 | D3 |

**BASE CONVERSION TABLE (Continued)**

| *BIN* | *DEC* | *HEX* | *BIN* | *DEC* | *HEX* |
|---|---|---|---|---|---|
| 11010100 | 212 | D4 | 11101010 | 234 | EA |
| 11010101 | 213 | D5 | 11101011 | 235 | EB |
| 11010110 | 214 | D6 | 11101100 | 236 | EC |
| 11010111 | 215 | D7 | 11101101 | 237 | ED |
| 11011000 | 216 | D8 | 11101110 | 238 | EE |
| 11011001 | 217 | D9 | 11101111 | 239 | EF |
| 11011010 | 218 | DA | 11110000 | 240 | F0 |
| 11011011 | 219 | DB | 11110001 | 241 | F1 |
| 11011100 | 220 | DC | 11110010 | 242 | F2 |
| 11011101 | 221 | DD | 11110011 | 243 | F3 |
| 11011110 | 222 | DE | 11110100 | 244 | F4 |
| 11011111 | 223 | DF | 11110101 | 245 | F5 |
| 11100000 | 224 | E0 | 11110110 | 246 | F6 |
| 11100001 | 225 | E1 | 11110111 | 247 | F7 |
| 11100010 | 226 | E2 | 11111000 | 248 | F8 |
| 11100011 | 227 | E3 | 11111001 | 249 | F9 |
| 11100100 | 228 | E4 | 11111010 | 250 | FA |
| 11100101 | 229 | E5 | 11111011 | 251 | FB |
| 11100110 | 230 | E6 | 11111100 | 252 | FC |
| 11100111 | 231 | E7 | 11111101 | 253 | FD |
| 11101000 | 232 | E8 | 11111110 | 254 | FE |
| 11101001 | 233 | E9 | 11111111 | 255 | FF |

# GLOSSARY

**Array**—A grouping of information stored by the computer in its memory, usually organized as subscripted variables.

**ASCII**—A code of 128 numbers where each stands for a character, letter, number, symbol or signal. Commodore computers use a variation called PET ASCII, with 255 code numbers. **A**merican **S**tandard **C**ode for **I**nformation **I**nterchange.

**BASIC**—**B**eginners **A**ll-purpose **S**ymbolic **I**nstruction **C**ode. A programming language that has become the standard for personal computers.

**Bit**—The simplest division of memory, which can contain only a 1 or 0; likened to a switch that is either on or off. Eight of these bits comprise a byte.

**Branching**—When a computer program goes from one part of itself to another, out of sequence.

**Byte**—The standard division of memory. Can contain numbers from 0 to 255. Eight bits.

**Cassette Buffer**—That area in memory used for temporary storage and transferring information from the cassette player to the computer's main memory.

**Cold Start**—A complete resetting of the machine in which memory is cleared and programs are destroyed.

**Compiled BASIC**—The program that translates BASIC into intermediate code or machine code that runs many times faster than interpreted BASIC.

**Concatenate**—To add one thing to another, usually strings when used in computing.

**Copy Protect**—A scheme to prevent unauthorized copies of a program.

**Crash**—When a computer quits operating, apparently inexplicably.

**Cursor**—The mark on the screen that indicates a typing location. From the French word.

**Data**—Any information.

**Data Base**—An organized collection of information accessed by a program called a Data Base Manager.

**Decrement**—Decrease a number by one or some other regular step.

**DOS**—A **D**isk **O**perating **S**ystem, the program that controls a disk storage device.

**Exponent**—A number that tells how many times a number is multiplied by itself.

**Floppy Disk**—A flexible plastic disk on which information is recorded magnetically.

**Garbage Collection**—A function of Commodore BASIC in which the computer halts to reorganize the memory used for storing variables, especially strings.

**Global**—Refers to several different tape or disk files that are all part of a larger file. A word processing file, for instance, can be much longer than the computer can contain at one time, and is broken down into smaller, linked parts called global files.

**Graphic Mode**—When the computer displays upper case letters and graphic symbols.

**Hacker**—A computer enthusiast identified by his or her tireless devotion to programming and learning about the machine.

**Increment**—Increase a number by one or some other regular step.

**Integer**—A whole number, or a number minus its decimal fraction.

**Interface**—An electronic circuit that connects one device to another. Usually used to connect computers to printers and disk drives designed for a different data standard.

**Interpreted BASIC**—Method of storing BASIC as individual commands that are interpreted by the computer one by one. The actual operating code is contained in a larger program, called BASIC.

**Jiffy**—A 60th of a second as used by the computer's clock. (TI)

**K**—From "kilo," for one thousand. One "K" of memory is actually 1,024 bytes.

**Language**—A set of instructions, rules, and words for communicating with the computer.

**Loop**—A number of program lines that form a repetitive pattern, usually with GOTO or FOR/NEXT.

**Machine Code**—The most elemental code or language the computer's microprocessor understands. Also called machine language and, occasionally, assembly language.

**Memory Map**—A key to the locations in the computer's memory; describes the function of various portions of the memory.

**Menu**—A screen list of choices offered by a program.

**Microchip**—An electronic integrated circuit (IC), miniaturized to microscopic proportions and manufactured of the metal, silicon.

**Microprocessor**—An electronic integrated circuit with its own set of instructions that can be programmed for various activities and functions.

**Modem**—A device that converts digital information to audio signals so they can be sent over the telephone lines.

**Nesting**—When one loop is inside another.

**Null String**—An empty string, indicated by quotation marks that enclose no characters—"".

**Number Crunching**—Slang for any complicated, repetitive mathematical activity.

**Nybble**—Four bits; half a byte.

**Operating System**—The master program that oversees the functions of a computer. (OS)

**Parallel**—The data standard in which eight bits of information are sent at once, over eight different wires. A printer standard also called "Centronics Parallel."

**Pattern Matching**—A technique used by the Commodore computers to identify tape and disk programs or files.

**Pixel**—A picture element, or one of many dots that comprise an image on a high-resolution screen.

**Program**—A list of instructions written in a computer language that breaks down a problem into smaller, easier-to-solve pieces.

**RAM**—**R**andom **A**ccess **M**emory; memory that can store information and be erased. Usually loses that information when power is interrupted.

**Random Number**—Any number selected at random. A number generated by a formula used to simulate randomness is strictly speaking "pseudo random."

**Real Time**—Time measured in hours, minutes, and seconds. Can be 24-hour notation instead of am and pm.

**ROM**—**R**ead **O**nly **M**emory; memory in which information is permanently stored and not destroyed when power to the machine is turned off.

**Screen Memory**—The portion of memory that contains text or pictures displayed on the video screen.

**Sequential File**—A tape or disk file containing information, not a program.

**Serial**—The data standard in which bits are sent sequentially over a pair of wires. Sometimes called "RS-232 serial," although serial data need not conform to this one specific standard.

**Smart**—From "intelligent" machine; shorthand description of any electronic device controlled by its own internal microprocessor and program. The Commodore disk drives are, for example, smart devices.

**Sort**—A program or routine that reorganizes information, usually by number or alphabetically.

**Sprite**—Also called a movable object block (MOB), it is a small, high-resolution picture defined independently in memory that can be placed anywhere on the video screen.

**String**—A single character or group of characters, letters, symbols, numbers, or editing commands. If a string contains numbers, the computer regards them as characters without numeric value.

**Structured Programming**—A technique in which GOTO commands are seldom used, this kind of program usually consists of many distinct subroutines designed to make the program easier to read.

**Subroutine**—A program within a program called with GOSUB.

**Syntax**—The correct usage of any word or command, either in a spoken or computer language.

**Typewriter Mode**—When the computer displays upper- and lower-case letters of the alphabet.

**Warm Start**—A way to reset the machine that does not disturb the contents of memory. Programs are left intact.

**Word Processing**—Electronic text preparation; typing and editing on the computer's video screen.

**Write Protect**—Usually refers to the notch on a floppy disk which determines whether or not the disk can be recorded on.

**Zero Page**—The area of memory containing locations 0 to 255.

# Index

# Acknowledgments

Few books are written without the help of many people, and this one is no exception. I would like to thank those who took an interest in my work and helped with information, tips, and hints.

Many thanks to Mr. Steve Murri, Mr. Bob Fairbairn, and Ms. Diane LeBold of Commodore Business Machines. Their cooperation was vital.

I greatly appreciate the time spent by those who reviewed the content of the book, particularly Mr. Gene Streitmatter, whose insightful comments were both valuable and encouraging.

Thanks, too, to Mr. Michael Richter, whose program was used in preparing the listings in the book, and to Mr. William Seiler for his friendship, enormous technical knowledge, and historical perspective.

My contributors Dr. Frank Covitz, Mr. Jim Butterfield and, in particular, Mr. Paul Schatz, each added to the scope of this book. They are good company.

Thank you to the personnel at the Robert J. Brady division of Prentice-Hall: Messrs. Harry Gaines, David Culverwell and Terry Anderson, and to Ms. Laura Dysart Marcy who brought this book to the company's attention.

As always, thank you to my family, especially my father, who had the foresight to understand the impact of computers many years before others did.

Finally, the personal and professional contributions of Ms. Beth Abrohams were the most important to me. Thanks, Beth.